THEORY OF COMPUTER SCIENCE
(Automata, Languages and Computation)

Second Edition

K.L.P. MISHRA

Formerly Professor
Department of Electrical and Electronics Engineering
and Principal, Regional Engineering College
Tiruchirapalli

and

N. CHANDRASEKARAN

Professor
Department of Mathematics
St. Joseph's College
Tiruchirapalli

Prentice-Hall of India Private Limited
New Delhi - 110 001
2001

Rs. 150.00

THEORY OF COMPUTER SCIENCE (Automata, Languages and Computation), 2nd Ed.
by K.L.P. Mishra and N. Chandrasekaran

ISBN-81-203-1271-6

The export rights of this book are vested solely with the publisher.

Tenth Printing (Second Edition)   ...   ...   November, 2001

Published by Asoke K. Ghosh, Prentice-Hall of India Private Limited, M-97, Connaught Circus, New Delhi-110001 and Printed by Bhuvnesh Seth at Book Kraft, Narela Industrial Park, Delhi-110040.

Contents

Preface

This edition is the result of the feedback received from the students and teachers who had welcomed the first edition. In response to the desire of many of them, we have added detailed solutions to most of the problems given in the Exercises (only a very brief hint to the problems was given in the first edition).

The solutions to Exercises added to this edition are completely new and elaborate. We have also added a detailed section on Parsing. This forms an additional section in Chapter 6 at the end of the chapter. Also, a very brief introduction to NP-Completeness is added at the end of Chapter 7. There is no other change in the text except for a few corrections in the text.

Constructive criticism and suggestions for further improvement will be warmly welcomed.

K.L.P. Mishra
N. Chandrasekaran

Preface to the First Edition

The theory of formal languages arose in the 50's when computer scientists were trying to use computers to translate one language into another. Although not much was achieved at that time in translation of natural languages, it paved the way for describing computer languages (such as ALGOL 60) later. In the mid-thirties, Turing machine was introduced to develop the theory of computability. It turned out that Turing machines were the most general devices for accepting formal languages. Partial recursive functions and primitive recursive functions arose as functions which can be computed by a mechanical device (such as computers). Now the theories of formal languages, automata and computation, which have emerged respectively as mathematical models of programming languages, computers and capability of a computer, have wide range of applications in compiling techniques, robotics, artificial intelligence (AI), and knowledge engineering.

Although there are several books available today, which cover the three theories—automata, languages and computation—separately, very few books combine the three theories and give adequate examples. This book is an attempt to fill this gap. It is intended for undergraduate and postgraduate students of science and engineering offering courses in computer science, and MCA students.

The text is self-contained as mathematical preliminaries are included in Chapter 1 along with several examples. Graphical illustrations are provided wherever possible to improve the readability.

The book begins with an overview of mathematical preliminaries and goes on to discuss the general theory of automata, properties of regular sets and regular expressions, and the basics of formal languages. Besides, sufficient attention is devoted to such topics as push-down automata and its relation with context-free languages, Turing machines and linear bounded automata, the basic concepts of computability such as primitive recursive functions and partial recursive functions. The text also gives an indepth analysis of context-free languages covering normal forms, pumping lemma and decision algorithms, and predicate calculus which has wide applications in artificial intelligence (AI) and knowledge engineering.

Numerous examples have been provided to illustrate the basic concepts. While dealing with theorems and algorithms, emphasis is laid on constructions. (In most of the constructions, recursion has been used.) Each construction is immediately followed by an example and only then the formal proof is given so that the reader can master the techniques involved in the construction before taking up the formal proof. Exercises are included at the end of each chapter and hints/solutions for selected exercises are given at the end of the book.

The book is designed for a one-year course, but by a judicious choice of topics, it can be used as a one-semester text, depending on the requirement of the student.

We would like to thank our colleagues and students who have been of enormous help to us in the preparation of the manuscript. Our sincere thanks are due to Uma Parvathi Chandrasekaran who helped us considerably in the preparation of the manuscript and offered valuable suggestions. We are particularly grateful to the reviewer whose constructive comments have greatly enriched the text. We wish to thank the publishers, Prentice-Hall of India, for the meticulous care they took in processing the manuscript, both at the editorial and production stages. Besides, we wish to thank K. Nadimuthu of Regional Engineering College, Tiruchirapalli for his excellent typing of the manuscript. Finally, the encouragement and inspiration provided by the authorities of the Regional Engineering College, Tiruchirapalli and St. Joseph's College, Tiruchirapalli are gratefully acknowledged.

Any suggestions for improving the contents of the text would be gratefully received.

K.L.P. Mishra
N. Chandrasekaran

Notations

Symbol	Meaning	Section in which the symbol appears first and is explained
$a \in A$	a belongs to the set A	1.1.1
$A \subseteq B$	A is a subset of B	1.1.1
$\varnothing$	The null set	1.1.1
$A \cup B$	The union of the sets A and B	1.1.1
$A \cap B$	The intersection of the sets A and B	1.1.1
$A - B$	The complement of B in A	1.1.1
A^c	The complement of A	1.1.1
2^A	The power set of A	1.1.1
$A \times B$	The cartesian product of A and B	1.1.1
$\bigcup\limits_{i=1}^{n} A_i$	The union of the sets $A_1, A_2, ..., A_n$	1.1.1
$*, \bigcirc$	binary operations	1.1.2, 1.1.3
xRy	x is related to y under the relation R	1.1.1
$xR'y$	x is not related to y under the relation R	1.1.4
$i \equiv j$	i is congruent to j modulo n	1.1.4
C_a	The equivalence class containing a	1.1.4
R^+	The transitive closure of R	1.1.5
R^*	The reflexive-transitive closure of R	1.1.5
$R_1 \bigcirc R_2$	The composite of the relations R_1 and R_2	1.1.5
$f\colon X \to Y$	function from X to Y	1.1.6
$f(x)$	The image of x under f	1.1.6
$\lceil x \rceil$	The smallest integer $\geq x$	1.2.2
Σ^*	The set of all srings over alphabet set Σ	1.3
$\wedge$	The empty string	1.3
Σ^+	The set of all nonempty strings over Σ	1.3
$\lvert x \rvert$	The length of the string x	1.3

Symbol	Meaning	Section in which the symbol appears first and is explained
$(Q, \Sigma, \delta, q_0, F)$	a finite automaton	2.2
$\mathcal{C}$	left end marker in input tape	2.2
$\mathcal{S}$	right end marker in input tape	2.2
$(Q, \Sigma, \delta, Q_0, F)$	a transition system	2.3
$(Q, \Sigma, \Delta, \delta, \lambda, q_0)$	A Mealy/Moore machine	2.8
π	partition corresponding to equivalent of states	2.9
π_k	partition corresponding to k-equivalence of states	2.9
(V_N, Σ, P, S)	a grammar	3.1.1
$\alpha \underset{G}{\Rightarrow} \beta$	α directly derives β in grammar G	3.1.2
$\alpha \underset{G}{\overset{*}{\Rightarrow}} \beta$	α derives β in grammar G	3.1.2
$\alpha \underset{G}{\overset{n}{\Rightarrow}} \beta$	α derives β in n steps in grammar G	3.1.2
$L(G)$	The language generated by G	3.1.2
$\mathscr{L}_0$	The family of type 0 languages	3.3
$\mathscr{L}_{\text{csl}}$	The family of context sensitive languages	3.3
$\mathscr{L}_{\text{cfl}}$	The family of context free languages	3.3
$\mathscr{L}_{\text{rl}}$	The family of regular languages	3.3
$\mathbf{R}_1 + \mathbf{R}_2$	The union of regular expressions $\mathbf{R}_1$ and $\mathbf{R}_2$	4.1
$\mathbf{R}_1\mathbf{R}_2$	The concatenation of regular expressions $\mathbf{R}_1$ and $\mathbf{R}_2$	4.1
$\mathbf{R}^*$	The iteration (closure) of $\mathbf{R}$	4.1
$\mathbf{a}$	The regular expression corresponding to $\{a\}$	4.1
$|V_N|$	The number of elements in V_N	5.3
$(Q, \Sigma, \Gamma, \delta, q_0, Z_0, F)$	a pushdown automaton	6.1
ID	an instantaneous description of a pda	6.1
$\overset{*}{\underset{A}{\vdash}}$	move relation in a pda A	6.1
$(Q, \Sigma, \Gamma, \delta, q_0, b, F)$	a Turing machine	7.1

Symbol	Meaning	Section in which the symbol appears first and is explained
P and NP	classes	7.10
$Z(x)$	image of x under zero function	9.2
$S(x)$	image of x under successor function	9.2
U_i^n	projection function	9.2
nil (x)	The image of x under nil function	9.2
cons $a(x)$	concatenation of a and x	9.2
cons $b(x)$	concatenation of b and x	9.2
$p(x)$	image of x under predecessor function	9.2
—	proper subtraction function	9.2
$|x|$	absolute value of x	9.2
id	identity function	9.2
μ_y	minimisation function	9.3
χ_A	characteristic function of the set A	9. Ex.
T	truth value	10.1
F	false value	10.1
$\neg$	The logical connective NOT	10.1
$\wedge$	The logical connective AND	10.1
$\vee$	The logical connective OR	10.1
$\Rightarrow$	The logical connective IF ... THEN ...	10.1
T	any tautology	10.1
F	any contradiction	10.1
$\forall$	for every	10.4
$\exists$	There exists	10.4
$\equiv$	equivalence of predicate formulas	10.4

1

Mathematical Preliminaries

In this chapter we introduce concepts of set theory and graph theory. Also we define strings and discuss properties of strings and operations on strings. In the final section we deal with the principle of induction, which will be used for proving many theorems throughout the book.

1.1 SETS, RELATIONS AND FUNCTIONS

1.1.1 SETS AND SUBSETS

A set is a well-defined collection of objects, e.g. the set of all students in a college. The collection of all books in a college library is also a set. (The individual objects are called *members* or *elements* of the set.)

We use capital letters A, B, C, ... for denoting sets. The small letters a, b, c, ... are used to denote elements of any set. When a is an element of the set A, we write a $\in$ A. When a is not an element of A we write a $\notin$ A.

Various Ways of Describing a Set

(i) *By listing its elements.* We write all the elements of the set (without repetition) and enclose them within braces. We can write the elements in any order. For example, the set of all positive integers divisible by 15 and less than 100 can be written as {15, 30, 45, 60, 75, 90}.

(ii) *By describing the properties of the elements of the set.* For example, the set {15, 30, 45, 60, 75, 90} can be described as: $\{n \mid n$ is a positive integer divisible by 15 and less than 100$\}$. (The description of the property is called predicate. In this case the set is said to be implicitly specified.)

(iii) *By recursion.* We define the elements of the set by a computational rule for calculating the elements. For example, the set of all natural numbers leaving a remainder 1 when divided by 3 can be described as

$$\{a_n \mid a_o = 1, a_{n+1} = a_n + 3\}$$

When the computational rule is clear from the context, we simply specify the set by some initial elements. The previous set can be written as {1, 4, 7, 10, ...}. The four elements given suggest the computational rule $a_{n+1} = a_n + 3$.

Subsets and Operations on Sets

A set A is said to be a subset of B (written as $A \subseteq B$) if every element of A is also an element of B.

Two sets A and B are equal (we write $A = B$) if their members are the same. In practice, to prove that $A = B$, we prove $A \subseteq B$ and $B \subseteq A$.

A set with no element is called an empty set, also called a null set or a void set, and is denoted by $\emptyset$.

We define some operations on sets.

$A \cup B = \{x | x \in A \text{ or } x \in B\}$, called union of A and B.

$A \cap B = \{x | x \in A \text{ and } x \in B\}$, called the intersection of A and B.

$A - B = \{x | x \in A \text{ and } x \notin B\}$, called the complement of B in A.

A^c denotes $U - A$, where U is the universal set, the set of all elements under consideration.

The set of all subsets of a set A is called the power set of A. It is denoted by 2^A.

Let A and B be two sets. Then $A \times B$ is defined as $\{(a, b) | a \in A \text{ and } b \in B\}$. ($(a, b)$ is called an ordered pair and is different from (b, a).)

Definition 1.1 Let S be a set. A collection $\{A_1, A_2, ..., A_n\}$ of subsets of S is called a partition if $A_i \cap A_j = \emptyset$ $(i \neq j)$ and $S = \overset{n}{\underset{i=1}{\cup}} A_i$ (i.e., $A_1 \cup A_2 \cup ... \cup A_n$).

For example, if $S = \{1, 2, 3, ..., 10\}$, then $\{\{1, 3, 5, 7, 9\}, \{2, 4, 6, 8, 10\}\}$ is a partition of S.

1.1.2   SETS WITH ONE BINARY OPERATION

A binary operation $*$ on a set S is a rule which assigns, to every ordered pair (a, b) of elements from S, a unique element denoted by $a * b$.

Addition, for example, is a binary operation on the set Z of all integers. (Throughout this book Z denotes the set of all integers.)

Union is a binary operation on 2^A, where A is any nonempty set.

We give below five postulates on binary operations.

Postulate 1: *Closure.* If a and b are in S then $a * b$ is in S.

Postulate 2: *Associativity.* If a, b, c are in S then $(a * b) * c = a * (b * c)$.

Postulate 3: *Identity element.* There exists a unique element (called the identity element) e in S such that for any element x in S, $x * e = e * x = x$.

Postulate 4: *Inverse.* For every element x in S there exists a unique element x' in S such that $x * x' = x' * x = e$. The element x' is called the inverse of x w.r.t. $*$.

Postulate 5: *Commutativity.* If $a, b \in S$ then $a * b = b * a$.

It may be noted that a binary operation may satisfy none of the above five postulates. For example, let $S = \{1, 2, 3, 4, ...\}$, and let the binary operation be subtraction (i.e. $a * b = a - b$). Closure postulate is not satisfied since $2 - 3 = -1 \notin S$. $(2 - 3) - 4 \neq 2 - (3 - 4)$, and so associativity is not satisfied. As we cannot find a positive integer such that $x - e = e - x = x$, postulates 3 and 4 are not satisfied. Obviously, $a - b \neq b - a$. Therefore, commutativity is not satisfied.

Our interest lies in sets with a binary operation satisfying the postulates.

Definitions   (i) A set S with a binary operation $*$ is called a semigroup if postulates 1 and 2 are satisfied.

(ii) A set S with binary operation $*$ is called a *monoid* if postulates 1–3 are satisfied.

(iii) A set S with $*$ is called a *group* if postulates 1–4 are satisfied.

(iv) A semigroup (monoid or group) is called a commutative or abelian semigroup (monoid or group) if postulate 5 is satisfied.

Figure 1.1 gives the relationship between semigroups, monoids, groups, etc; the numbers refer to the postulate number.

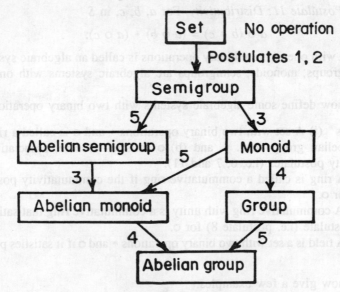

Fig. 1.1   Sets with one binary operation.

We interpret Fig. 1.1 as follows: A monoid satisfying postulate 4 is a group. A group satisfying postulate 5 is an abelian group etc.

We give a few examples as illustration.

(i) Z with addition is an abelian group.

(ii) Z with multiplication is an abelian monoid. (It is not a group since it does not satisfy postulate 4.)

(iii) $\{1, 2, 3, \ldots\}$ with addition is a commutative semigroup but not a monoid. (The identity element can be only 0, but 0 is not in the set.)

(iv) The power set 2^A of $A(A \neq \emptyset)$ with union is a commutative monoid. (The identity element is $\emptyset$.)

(v) The set of all 2×2 matrices under multiplication is a monoid but not an abelian monoid.

1.1.3   SETS WITH TWO BINARY OPERATIONS

Sometimes we come across sets with two binary operations defined on them (e.g. in the case of numbers we have addition and multiplication). Let S be a set with two binary operations $*$ and $\circ$. We give 11 postulates in the following way:

(i) Postulate 1–5 refer to $*$ postulates.

(ii) Postulates 6, 7, 8, 10 are simply postulates 1, 2, 3, 5 for the binary operation $\circ$.

(iii) *Postulate 9*: If S under $*$ satisfies postulates 1–5 then for every x in S, with $x \neq e$, there exists a unique element x' in S such that $x' \circ x = x \circ x' = e'$, where e' is the identity element corresponding to $\circ$.

(iv) *Postulate 11: Distributivity.* For a, b, c, in S

$$a \circ (b * c) = (a \circ b) * (a \circ c).$$

A set with one or more binary operations is called an algebraic system. For example, groups, monoids, semigroups are algebraic systems with one binary operation.

We now define some algebraic systems with two binary operations.

Definitions   (i) A set with two binary operations $*$ and $\circ$ is called a ring if (a) it is an abelian group w.r.t. $*$, and (b) $\circ$ satisfies closure, associativity and distributivity postulates (i.e. 6, 7 and 11).

(ii) A ring is called a commutative ring if the commutativity postulate is satisfied for $\circ$.

(iii) A commutative ring with unity is a commutative ring that satisfies the identity postulate (i.e. postulate 8) for $\circ$.

(iv) A field is a set with two binary operations $*$ and $\circ$ if it satisfies postulates 1–11.

We now give a few examples.

(i) Z with addition and multiplication (in place of $*$ and $\circ$) is a commutative ring with identity. (The identity element w.r.t. addition is 0, and the identity element w.r.t. multiplication is 1.)

(ii) The set of all rational numbers (i.e. fractions which are of the form a/b, where a is any integer and b is an integer different from zero) is a field. (The identity element w.r.t. multiplication is 1. The inverse of a/b, $a/b \neq 0$ is b/a.)

(iii) The set of all 2×2 matrices with matrix addition and matrix multiplication is a ring with identity, but not a field.

(iv) The power set 2^A ($A \neq \emptyset$) is also a set with two binary operations $\cup$ and $\cap$. The postulates satisfied by $\cup$ and $\cap$ are 1, 2, 3, 5, 6, 7, 8, 10 and 11. 2^A is not a group or a ring or a field. But it is an abelian monoid w.r.t. both the operations $\cup$ and $\cap$.

Figure 1.2 illustrates the relation between the various algebraic systems we have introduced. The interpretation is as given in Fig. 1.1. The numbers refer to

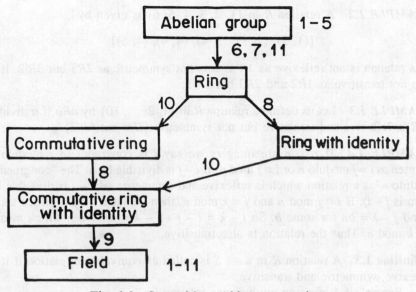

Fig. 1.2 Sets with two binary operations.

postulates. For example, an abelian group satisfying postulates 6, 7 and 11 is a ring.

1.1.4 RELATIONS

The concept of a relation is a basic concept in Computer Science as well as in real life. This concept arises when we consider a pair of objects and compare one with the other. For example, "being the father of" gives a relation between two persons. We can express the relation by ordered pairs (for instance, "a is the father of b" can be represented by the ordered pair (a, b)).

While executing a program, comparisons are made, and based on the result, different tasks are performed. Thus in Computer Science the concept of relation arises just as in the case of data structures.

Definition 1.2 A relation R in a set S is a collection of ordered pairs of elements in S (i.e. a subset of $S \times S$). When (x, y) is in R we write xRy. When (x, y) is not in R we write $xR'y$.

EXAMPLE 1.1 A relation R in Z can be defined by xRy if $x > y$.

Properties of Relations

  (i) A relation R in S is *reflexive* if xRx for every x in S.

  (ii) A relation R in S is *symmetric* if for x, y in S, yRx whenever xRy.

  (iii) A relation R in S is *transitive* if for x, y and z in S, xRz whenever xRy and yRz.

We note that the relation given in Example 1.1 is neither reflexive nor symmetric, but transitive.

EXAMPLE 1.2   A relation R in $\{1, 2, 3, 4, 5, 6\}$ is given by

$$\{(1, 2), (2, 3), (3, 4), (4, 4), (4, 5)\}$$

This relation is not reflexive as $1R'1$. It is not symmetric as $2R3$ but $3R'2$. It is also not transitive as $1R2$ and $2R3$ but $1R'3$.

EXAMPLE 1.3   Let us define a relation R in $\{1, 2, ..., 10\}$ by aRb if a divides b. R is reflexive and transitive but not symmetric ($3R6$ but $6R'3$).

EXAMPLE 1.4   If i, j, n are integers we say i is congruent to j modulo n (written as $i \equiv j$ modulo n or $i \equiv j$ mod n) if $i - j$ is divisible by n. The "congruence modulo n" is a relation which is reflexive and symmetric (if $i - j$ is divisible by n, so is $j - i$). If $i \equiv j$ mod n and $j \equiv k$ mod n, then we have $i - j = an$ for some a and $j - k = bn$ for some b. So $i - k = i - j + j - k = an + bn$, which means $i \equiv k$ mod n. Thus the relation is also transitive.

Definition 1.3   A relation R in a set S is called an equivalence relation if it is reflexive, symmetric and transitive.

Example 1.4 gives an equivalence relation in Z.

EXAMPLE 1.5   We can define an equivalence relation R on any set S by defining aRb if $a = b$. (Obviously, $a = a$ for every a. So, R is reflexive. If $a = b$ then $b = a$. So R is symmetric. Also, if $a = b$ and $b = c$, then $a = c$. So R is transitive.)

EXAMPLE 1.6   Define a relation R on the set of all persons in New Delhi by aRb if the persons a and b have the same date of birth. Then R is an equivalence relation.

Let us study this example more carefully. Corresponding to any day of the year (say, 4th February), we can associate the set of all persons born on that day. In this way the set of all persons in New Delhi can be partitioned into 366 subsets. In each of the 366 subsets any two elements are related. This leads to one more concept regarding equivalence relations.

Definition 1.4   Let R be an equivalence relation on a set S. Let $a \in S$. Then C_a is defined as

$$\{b \in S | aRb\}.$$

C_a is called an equivalence class containing a. In general, $C_a's$ are called equivalence classes.

EXAMPLE 1.7   For the congruence modulo 3 relation on $\{1, 2, ..., 7\}$,

$$C_2 = \{2, 5\}, \qquad C_1 = \{1, 4, 7\}$$

For the equivalence relation "having the same birth day" (discussed in Example 1.6), the set of persons born on 4th February is an equivalence class, and the number of equivalence classes is 366. Also, we may note that the union of all the 366 equivalence classes is the set of all persons in Delhi. This is true for any equivalence relation because of the following theorem.

Theorem 1.1 Any equivalence relation R on a set S partitions S into disjoint equivalence classes.

PROOF Let $\underset{a \in S}{\cup} C_a$ denote the union of distinct equivalence classes. We have to prove

(i) $S = \underset{a \in S}{\cup} C_a$,

(ii) $C_a \cap C_b = \emptyset$ if C_a and C_b are different, i.e. $C_a \neq C_b$.

Let $s \in S$. Then $s \in C_s$ (since sRs, R being reflexive). But $C_s \subseteq \underset{a \in S}{\cup} C_a$. So $S \subseteq \underset{a \in S}{\cup} C_a$. By definition of C_a, $C_a \subseteq S$ for every a in S. So $\underset{a \in S}{\cup} C_a \subseteq S$. Thus we have proved (i).

Before proving (ii), we may note the following:

$$C_a = C_b \quad \text{if } aRb \tag{1.1}$$

As aRb, we have bRa because R is symmetric. Let $d \in C_a$. By definition of C_a, we have aRd. As bRa and aRd, by transitivity of R, we get bRd. This means $d \in C_b$. Thus we have proved $C_a \subseteq C_b$. In a similar way we can show that $C_b \subseteq C_a$. Therefore, (1.1) is proved.

Now we prove (ii) by the method of contradiction (refer 1.4). We want to prove that $C_a \cap C_b = \emptyset$ if $C_a \neq C_b$. Suppose $C_a \cap C_b \neq \emptyset$. Then there exists some element d in S such that $d \in C_a$ and $d \in C_b$. As $d \in C_a$ we have aRd. Similarly, we have bRd. By symmetry of R, dRb. As aRd and dRb, by transitivity of R, we have aRb. Now we can use (1.1) to conclude that $C_a = C_b$. But this is a contradiction (as $C_a \neq C_b$). Therefore, $C_a \cap C_b = \emptyset$. Thus (ii) is proved. ∎

If we apply theorem 1.1 to the equivalence relation congruence modulo 3 on $\{1, 2, 3, 4, 5, 6, 7\}$, we get

$$C_1 = C_4 = C_7 = \{1, 4, 7\}$$
$$C_2 = C_5 = \{2, 5\}$$
$$C_3 = C_6 = \{3, 6\}$$

and, therefore,

$$\{1, 2, \ldots, 7\} = C_1 \cup C_2 \cup C_3$$

EXERCISE Let S denote the set of all students in a particular college. Define aRb if a and b study in the same class. What are the equivalence classes? In what way does R partition S?

1.1.5 CLOSURE OF RELATIONS

A given relation R may not be reflexive or transitive. By adding more ordered pairs to R we can make it reflexive or transitive. For example, consider a relation $R = \{(1, 2), (2, 3), (1, 1), (2, 2)\}$ in $\{1, 2, 3\}$. R is not reflexive as $3R'3$. But by adding $(3, 3)$ to R, we get a reflexive relation. Also, R is not transitive as $1R2$ and $2R3$ but $1R'3$. By adding the pair $(1, 3)$, we get a relation $T =$

$\{(1, 2), (2, 3), (1, 1), (2, 2), (1, 3)\}$ which is transitive. There are many transitive relations T containing R. But the smallest among them is interesting.

Definition 1.5   Let R be a relation in a set S. Then the transitive closure of R (denoted by R^+) is the smallest transitive relation containing R.

NOTE: We can define reflexive closure and symmetric closure in a similar way.

Definition 1.6   Let R be a relation in S. Then the reflexive-transitive closure of R (denoted by $R*$) is the smallest reflexive and transitive relation containing R.

For constructing R^+ and $R*$, we define the composite of two relations. Let R_1 and R_2 be relations in S. Then,

(i) $R_1 \circ R_2 = \{(a, c) \in S \times S \mid aR_1b \text{ and } bR_2c \text{ for some } b \in S\}$
(ii) $R_1^2 = R_1 \circ R_1$
(iii) $R_1^n = R_1^{n-1} \circ R_1$ for all $n \geq 2$

NOTE: For getting elements of $R_1 \circ R_2$, we combine (a, b) in R_1 and (b, c) in R_2 to get (a, c) in $R_1 \circ R_2$.

Theorem 1.2   Let S be a finite set and R be a relation in S. Then the transitive closure R^+ of R exists and $R^+ = R \cup R^2 \cup R^3 \dots$.

EXAMPLE 1.8   Let $R = \{(1, 2), (2, 3), (2, 4)\}$ be a relation in $\{1, 2, 3, 4\}$. Find R^+.

SOLUTION

$$R = \{(1, 2), (2, 3), (2, 4)\}$$

$$R^2 = \{(1, 2), (2, 3), (2, 4)\} \circ \{(1, 2), (2, 3), (2, 4)\}$$

$$= \{(1, 3), (1, 4)\}$$

(We combine (a, b) and (b, c) in R to get (a, c) in R^2).

$$R^3 = R^2 \circ R = \{(1, 3), (1, 4)\} \circ \{(1, 2), (2, 3), (2, 4)\} = \emptyset$$

(Here no pair (a, b) in R^2 can be combined with any pair in R.)

$$R^4 = R^5 = \dots = \emptyset$$

$$R^+ = R \cup R^2 = \{(1, 2), (2, 3), (2, 4), (1, 3), (1, 4)\}$$

EXAMPLE 1.9   Let $R = \{(a, b), (b, c), (c, a)\}$. Find R^+.

SOLUTION

$$R = \{(a, b), (b, c), (c, a)\}$$

$$R \circ R = \{(a, b), (b, c), (c, a)\} \circ \{(a, b), (b, c), (c, a)\}$$

$$= \{(a, c), (b, a), (c, b)\}$$

(This is obtained by combining the pairs: (a, b) and (b, c), (b, c) and (c, a), and (c, a) and (a, b).)

$$R^3 = R^2 \circ R = \{(a, c), (b, a), (c, b)\} \circ \{(a, b), (b, c), (c, a)\}$$

$$= \{(a, a), (b, b), (c, c)\}$$

$$R^4 = R^3 \circ R = \{(a, a), (b, b), (c, c)\} \circ \{(a, b), (b, c), (c, a)\}$$

$$= \{(a, b), (b, c), (c, a)\} = R$$

So,

$$R^5 = R^4 \circ R = R \circ R = R^2, \qquad R^6 = R^5 \circ R = R^2 \circ R = R^3$$

$$R^7 = R^6 \circ R = R^3 \circ R = R^4 = R \ldots$$

Then any R^n is one of R, R^2 or R^3. Hence,

$$R^+ = R \cup R^2 \cup R^3$$

$$= \{(a, b), (b, c), (c, a), (a, c), (b, a), (c, b), (a, a), (b, b), (c, c)\}$$

NOTE: $R^* = R^+ \cup \{(a, a) \mid a \in S\}$.

EXAMPLE 1.10 If $R = \{(a, b), (b, c), (c, a)\}$ is a relation in $\{a, b, c\}$, find R^*.

SOLUTION From Example 1.9,

$$R^* = R^+ \cup \{(a, a), (b, b), (c, c)\}$$

$$= \{(a, b), (b, c), (c, a), (a, c), (b, a), (c, b), (a, a), (b, b), (c, c)\}$$

EXAMPLE 1.11 What is the symmetric closure of relation R in S?

SOLUTION Symmetric closure of $R = R \cup \{(b, a) \mid aRb\}$.

1.1.6 FUNCTIONS

The concept of a function arises when we want to associate a unique value (or result) with a given argument (or input).

Definition 1.7 A function or map f from a set X to a set Y is a rule which associates to every element x in X a unique element in Y, which is denoted by $f(x)$. The element $f(x)$ is called the image of x under f. The function is denoted by $f: X \rightarrow Y$.

Functions can be defined either (a) by giving the images of all elements of X, or (b) by a computational rule which computes $f(x)$ once x is given.

EXAMPLES (a) $f: \{1, 2, 3, 4\} \rightarrow \{a, b, c\}$ can be defined by $f(1) = a$, $f(2) = c$, $f(3) = a$, $f(4) = b$.

(b) $f: R \rightarrow R$ can be defined by $f(x) = x^2 + 2x + 1$ for every x in R. (R denotes the set of all real numbers.)

Definition 1.8 $f : X \rightarrow Y$ is said to be one-to-one (or injective) if different elements in X have different images, i.e $f(x_1) \neq f(x_2)$ when $x_1 \neq x_2$.

NOTE: To prove f is one-to-one, we prove the following: Assume $f(x_1) = f(x_2)$ and show that $x_1 = x_2$.

Definition 1.9 $f : X \rightarrow Y$ is onto (surjective) if every element y in Y is the image of some element x in X.

Definition 1.10 $f : X \rightarrow Y$ is said to be a one-to-one correspondence or bijection if f is both one-to-one and onto.

EXAMPLE 1.12 $f : Z \rightarrow Z$ given by $f(n) = 2n$ is one-to-one but not onto.

SOLUTION   Suppose $f(n_1) = f(n_2)$. Then $2n_1 = 2n_2$. So $n_1 = n_2$. Hence f is one-to-one. It is not onto since no odd integer can be the image of any element in Z (as any image is even).

The following principle distinguishes a finite set from an infinite set.

Pigeon-hole Principle

Let S be a finite set. Then $f : S \rightarrow S$ is one-to-one iff it is onto.

NOTE: The above result is not true for infinite sets as Example 1.12 gives a one-to-one function $f : Z \rightarrow Z$ which is not onto.

EXAMPLE 1.13   Show that $f : R \rightarrow R - \{1\}$ given by $f(x) = (x + 1)/(x - 1)$ is onto.

SOLUTION   Let $y \in R$. Suppose $y = f(x) = (x + 1)/(x - 1)$. Then $y(x - 1) = x + 1$, i.e. $yx - x = 1 + y$. So, $x = (1 + y)/(y - 1)$. As $(1 + y)/(y - 1) \in R$ for all $y \neq 1$, y is the image of $(1 + y)/(y - 1)$ in $R - \{1\}$. Thus, f is onto.

1.2   GRAPHS AND TREES

The theory of graphs is widely applied in many areas of Computer Science— formal languages, compiler writing, artificial intelligence (AI), to mention only a few. Also, problems in Computer Science can be phrased as problems in graphs. Our interest lies mainly in trees (special types of graphs) and their properties.

1.2.1   GRAPHS

Definition 1.11   A graph (or undirected graph) consists of (a) a nonempty set V called the set of vertices, (b) a set E called the set of edges, and (c) a map Φ which assigns to every edge a unique unordered pair of vertices.

Representation of a Graph

Usually a graph, viz. undirected graph, is represented by a diagram where vertices are represented by points or small circles, and edges by arcs joining the vertices of the associated pair (given by the map Φ).

Figure 1.3, for example, gives an undirected graph. Thus, the unordered pair $\{v_1, v_2\}$ is associated with edge e_1; the pair $\{v_2, v_2\}$ is associated with e_6

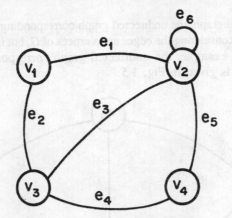

Fig. 1.3   An undirected graph.

(e_6 is a self loop. In general, an edge is called a self loop if the vertices in its associated pair coincide).

Definition 1.12   A directed graph (or digraph) consists of (a) a nonempty set V called the set of vertices, (b) a set E called the set of edges, and (c) a map Φ which assigns to every edge a unique ordered pair of vertices.

Representation of a Digraph

The representation is as in the case of undirected graphs except that edges are represented by directed arcs.

Figure 1.4, for example, gives a directed graph. The ordered pair (v_2, v_3), (v_3, v_4), (v_1, v_3) is associated with the edges e_3, e_4, e_2, respectively.

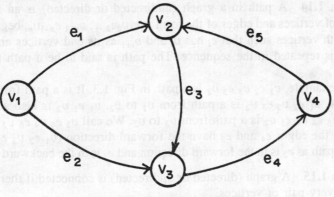

Fig. 1.4   A directed graph.

Definitions   (i) If (v_i, v_j) is associated with an edge e, then v_i and v_j are called end vertices of e; v_i is called a predecessor of v_j which is a successor of v_i.

In Fig. 1.3, v_2 and v_3 are end vertices of e_3. In Fig. 1.4, v_2 is a predecessor of v_3 which is a successor of v_2. Also, v_4 is a predecessor of v_2 and successor of v_3.

(ii) If G is a digraph, the undirected graph corresponding to G is the undirected graph obtained by considering the edges and vertices of G, but ignoring the 'direction' of the edges. For example, the undirected graph corresponding to the digraph given in Fig. 1.4 is given in Fig. 1.5.

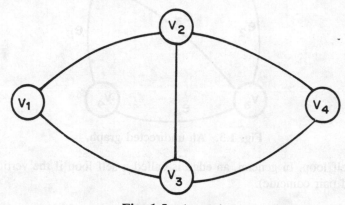

Fig. 1.5 A graph.

Definition 1.13 The degree of a vertex in a graph (directed or undirected) is the number of edges with v as an end vertex. (A self loop is counted twice while calculating the degree.) In Fig. 1.3, deg $(v_1) = 2$, deg $(v_3) = 3$, deg $(v_2) = 5$. In Fig. 1.4, deg $(v_2) = 3$, deg $(v_4) = 2$.

We mention the following theorem without proof.

Theorem 1.3 The number of vertices of odd degree in any graph (directed or undirected) is even.

Definition 1.14 A path in a graph (undirected or directed) is an alternating sequence of vertices and edges of the form $v_1 e_1 v_2 e_2 \ldots v_{n-1} e_{n-1} v_n$, beginning and ending with vertices such that e_i has v_i and v_{i+1} as its end vertices and no edge or vertex is repeated in the sequence. The path is said to be a path from v_1 to v_n.

For example, $v_1 e_2 v_3 e_3 v_2$ is a path in Fig. 1.3. It is a path from v_1 to v_2. In Fig. 1.4, $v_1 e_2 v_3 e_3 v_2$ is a path from v_1 to v_2. $v_1 e_1 v_2$ is also a path from v_1 to v_2. $v_3 e_4 v_4 e_5 v_2$ is a path from v_3 to v_2. We call $v_3 e_4 v_4 e_5 v_2$ a directed path since the edges e_4 and e_5 have the forward direction ($v_1 e_2 v_3 e_3 v_2$ is not a directed path as e_2 is in the forward direction and e_3 is in the backward direction).

Definition 1.15 A graph (directed or undirected) is connected if there is a path between every pair of vertices.

The graphs given by Figs. 1.3 and 1.4, for example, are connected.

Definition 1.16 A circuit in a graph is an alternating sequence $v_1 e_1 v_2 e_2 \ldots e_{n-1} v_1$ of vertices and edges starting and ending in the same vertex such that

e_i has v_i and v_{i+1} as end vertices and no edge or vertex other than v_1 is repeated.

In Fig. 1.3, for example, $v_3\,e_3\,v_2\,e_5\,v_4\,e_4\,v_3$, $v_1\,e_2\,v_3\,e_4\,v_4\,e_5\,v_2\,e_1\,v_1$ are circuits. In Fig. 1.4, $v_1\,e_2\,v_3\,e_3\,v_2\,e_1\,v_1$ and $v_2\,e_3\,v_3\,e_4\,v_4\,e_5\,v_2$ are circuits.

1.2.2 TREES

Definition 1.17 A graph (directed or undirected) is called a tree if it is connected and has no circuits.

The graphs given in Figs. 1.6 and 1.7, for example, are trees. The graphs given in Figs. 1.3 and 1.4 are not trees.

NOTE: A directed graph G is a tree iff the corresponding undirected graph is a tree.

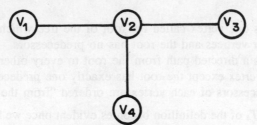

Fig. 1.6 A tree with four vertices.

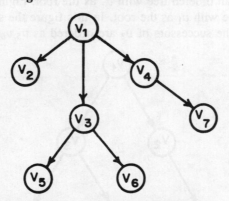

Fig. 1.7 A tree with seven vertices.

We now discuss some properties of trees (both directed and undirected) used in developing transition systems and studying grammar rules.

Property 1 A tree is a connected graph with no circuits or loops.

Property 2 In a tree there is one and only one path between every pair of vertices.

Property 3 If in a graph there is a unique (i.e. one and only one) path between every pair of vertices then the graph is a tree.

Property 4   A tree with n vertices has $n - 1$ edges.

Property 5   If a connected graph with n vertices has $n - 1$ edges then it is a tree.

Property 6   If a graph with no circuits has n vertices and $n - 1$ edges then it is a tree.

A leaf in a tree can be defined as a vertex of degree one. Vertices other than leaves are called internal vertices.

In Fig. 1.6, for example, v_1, v_3, v_4 are leaves and v_2 is an internal vertex. In Fig. 1.7, v_2, v_5, v_6, v_7 are leaves and v_1, v_3, v_4 are internal vertices.

The following definition of ordered trees will be used for representing derivations in context-free grammars.

Definition 1.18   An ordered directed tree is a digraph satisfying the following conditions:

T_1: There is one vertex called the root of the tree which is distinguished from all the other vertices and the root has no predecessors.

T_2: There is a directed path from the root to every other vertex.

T_3: Every vertex except the root has exactly one predecessor.

T_4: The successors of each vertex are ordered "from the left".

NOTE: Condition T_4 of the definition becomes evident once we have the diagram of the graph.

Figure 1.7 is an ordered tree with v_1 as the root. Figure 1.8 also gives an ordered directed tree with v_1 as the root. In this figure the successors of v_1 are ordered as v_2 v_3. The successors of v_3 are ordered as v_5 v_6.

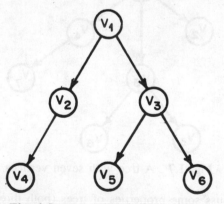

Fig. 1.8   An ordered directed tree.

By adopting the following convention, we can simplify Fig. 1.8. The root is at the top. The directed edges are represented by arrows pointing downwards. As all the arrows point downwards, the directed edges can be simply represented by lines sloping downwards, as illustrated in Fig. 1.9.

NOTE: An ordered directed tree is connected (which follows from T_2). It has no circuits (because of T_3). Hence an ordered directed tree is a tree (see Definition 1.17).

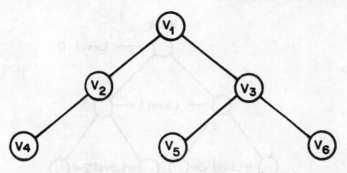

Fig. 1.9 Representation of an ordered directed tree.

As we use only ordered directed trees in applications to grammars, we refer to ordered directed trees as simply trees.

Definition 1.19 A binary tree is a tree in which the degree of the root is 2 and the remaining vertices are of degree 1 or 3.

NOTE: In a binary tree any vertex has at most two successors. For example, the trees given by Figs. 1.11 and 1.12 are binary trees. The tree given by Fig. 1.9 is not a binary tree.

Theorem 1.4 The number of vertices in a binary tree is odd.

PROOF Let n be the number of vertices. The root is of degree 2 and the remaining $n - 1$ vertices are of odd degree (by Definition 1.19) By Theorem 1.3, $n - 1$ is even and hence n is odd. ∎

We introduce some more terminology regarding trees:

(i) A son of a vertex v is a successor of v.

(ii) The father of v is the predecessor of v.

(iii) If there is a directed path from v_1 to v_2, v_1 is called an ancestor of v_2, and v_2 is called a descendant of v_1. (Convention: v_1 is an ancestor of itself and also a descendant of itself.)

(iv) The number of edges in a path is called the length of the path.

(v) The height of a tree is the length of a longest path from the root. For example, for the tree given by Fig. 1.9, the height is 2. (Actually there are three longest paths, $v_1 \rightarrow v_2 \rightarrow v_4$, $v_1 \rightarrow v_3 \rightarrow v_5$, $v_1 \rightarrow v_3 \rightarrow v_6$. Each is of length 2.)

(vi) A vertex v in a tree is at level k if there is a path of length k from the root to the vertex v (the maximum possible level in a tree is the height of the tree).

Figure 1.10, for example, gives a tree where the levels of vertices are indicated.

EXAMPLE 1.14 For a binary tree T with n vertices, show that the minimum possible height is $\lceil \log_2 (n + 1) - 1 \rceil$ ($\lceil k \rceil$ is the smallest integer $\geq k$), and the maximum possible height is $(n - 1)/2$.

SOLUTION In a binary tree the root is at level 0. As every vertex can have

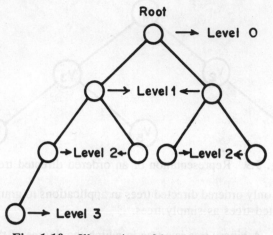

Fig. 1.10   Illustration of levels of vertices.

atmost two successors, we have atmost two vertices at level 1, atmost 4 vertices at level 2, etc. So the maximum number of vertices in a binary tree of height k is $1 + 2 + 2^2 + \ldots + 2^k$. As T has n vertices, $1 + 2 + 2^2 + \ldots + 2^k \geq n$, i.e. $(2^{k+1} - 1)/(2 - 1) \geq n$. So $k \geq \log_2 (n + 1) - 1$. As k is an integer, the smallest possible value for k is $\lceil \log_2 (n + 1) - 1 \rceil$. Thus the minimum possible height is $\lceil \log_2 (n + 1) - 1 \rceil$.

To get the maximum possible height, we proceed in a similar way. In a binary tree we have the root at zero level and at least two vertices at level 1, 2, ... When T is of height k, we have at least $1 + 2 + \ldots + 2$ (2 repeated k times) vertices. So $1 + 2k \leq n$, i.e. $k \leq (n - 1)/2$. But, n is odd by Theorem 1.3. So $(n - 1)/2$ is an integer. Hence the maximum possible value for k is $(n - 1)/2$.

EXAMPLE 1.15   When $n = 9$, the trees with minimum and maximum height are given by Figs. 1.11 and 1.12. The height of the tree given by Fig. 1.11 is $\lceil \log_2 (9 + 1) - 1 \rceil = 3$. For the tree given by Fig. 1.12, the height $= (9 - 1)/2 = 4$.

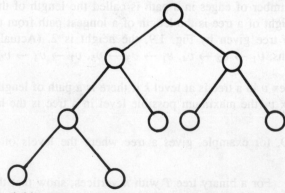

Fig. 1.11   Binary tree of minimum height with 9 vertices.

EXAMPLE 1.16   Prove that the number of leaves in a binary tree T is $(n + 1)/2$, where n is the number of vertices.

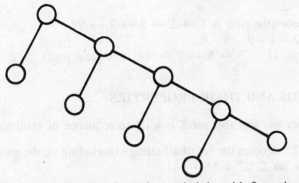

Fig. 1.12 Binary tree of maximum height with 9 vertices.

SOLUTION Let m be the number of leaves in a tree with n vertices. The root is of degree 2 and the remaining $n - m - 1$ vertices are of degree 3. As T has n vertices, it has $n - 1$ edges (by Property 4). As each edge is counted twice while calculating the degrees of its end vertices, $2(n - 1)$ = the sum of degrees of all vertices = $2 + m + 3 (n - m - 1)$. Solving for m, we get $m = (n + 1)/2$.

EXAMPLE 1.17 For the tree given by Fig. 1.13, answer the following questions:
    (a) Which vertices are leaves and which are internal vertices?
    (b) Which vertices are the sons of 5?
    (c) Which vertex is the father of 5?
    (d) What is the length of the path from 1 to 9?
    (e) What is the left-right order of leaves?
    (f) What is the height of the tree?

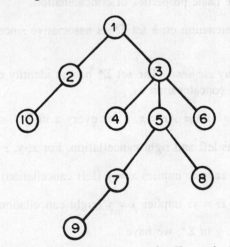

Fig. 1.13 The directed tree for Example 1.17.

SOLUTIONS (a) 10, 4, 9, 8, 6 are leaves. 1, 2, 3, 5, 7 are internal vertices.
    (b) 7 and 8 are sons of 5.
    (c) 3 is the father of 5.

(d) Four (the path is $1 \to 3 \to 5 \to 7 \to 9$).

(e) $10 - 4 - 9 - 8 - 6$.

(f) Four ($1 \to 3 \to 5 \to 7 \to 9$ is a longest path).

1.3 STRINGS AND THEIR PROPERTIES

A string over an alphabet set Σ is a finite sequence of symbols from Σ.

NOTATION: Σ^* denotes the set of all strings (including Λ, the empty string) over the alphabet set Σ. $\Sigma^+ = \Sigma^* - \{\Lambda\}$.

1.3.1   OPERATION ON STRINGS

The basic operation for strings is binary concatenation operation. We define the operation as follows: Let x and y be two strings in Σ^*. Let us form a new string z by placing y after x, i.e. $z = xy$. The string z is said to be obtained by concatenation of x and y.

EXAMPLE 1.18   Find xy and yx, where

(a) $x = 010$, $y = 1$

(b) $x = a \Lambda$ string Λ is, $y = $ ALGOL

SOLUTION   (a) $xy = 0101$, $yx = 1010$.

(b) $xy = a \Lambda$ string Λ is ALGOL

$yx = $ ALGOL $a \Lambda$ string Λ is

We give some basic properties of concatenation.

Property 1   Concatenation on a set Σ^* is associative since for each x, y, z in Σ^*, $x(yz) = (xy)z$.

Property 2   *Identity element*   The set Σ^* has an identity element Λ w.r.t. the binary operation of concatenation as

$$x\Lambda = \Lambda x = x \quad \text{for every } x \text{ in } \Sigma^*$$

Property 3 Σ^* has left and right cancellation. For x, y, z in Σ^*,

$$zx = zy \text{ implies } x = y \text{ (left cancellation)}$$

$$xz = yz \text{ implies } x = y \text{ (right cancellation)}$$

Property 4   For x, y in Σ^*, we have

$$|xy| = |x| + |y|$$

where $|x|$, $|y|$, $|xy|$ denote the lengths of the strings x, y, xy, respectively.

We introduce some more operations on strings.

Transpose Operation

We extend the concatenation operation to define the transpose operation as follows:
For any x in Σ^* and a in Σ,

$$(xa)^T = a(x)^T$$

For example, $(aaabab)^T$ is $babaaa$.

Palindrome. A palindrome is a string which is the same whether written forward or backward, e.g. Malayalam. A palindrome of even length can be obtained by concatenation of a string and its transpose.

Prefix and suffix of a string. A prefix of a string is a substring of leading symbols of that string. w is a prefix of y if there exists y' in Σ^* such that $y = wy'$. Then we write $w < y$. For example, the string 123 has 4 prefixes Λ, 1, 12, 123.

Similarly, a suffix of a string is a substring of trailing symbols of that string. w is a suffix of y if there exists $y' \in \Sigma^*$ such that $y = y'w$. For example, the string 123 has 4 suffixes Λ, 3, 23, 123.

Theorem 1.5 (Levi theorem)   Let v, w, x and $y \in \Sigma^*$ and $vw = xy$. Then:

(i) there exists a unique string z in Σ^* such that $v = xz$ and $y = zw$ if $|v| > |x|$;

(ii) $v = x$, $y = w$, i.e. $z = \Lambda$ if $|v| = |x|$;

(iii) there exists a unique string z in Σ^* such that $x = vz$, and $w = zy$ if $|v| < |x|$.

PROOF   We shall give a very simple proof by representing the strings by a diagram (see Fig. 1.14).   ∎

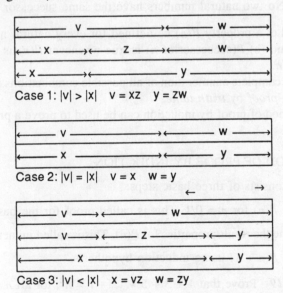

Case 1: $|v| > |x|$ $v = xz$ $y = zw$

Case 2: $|v| = |x|$ $v = x$ $w = y$

Case 3: $|v| < |x|$ $x = vz$ $w = zy$

Fig. 1.14 Illustration of Levis theorem.

The following definitions will be used in subsequent chapters.

1.3.2 TERMINAL AND NONTERMINAL SYMBOLS

A terminal symbol is a unique indivisible object used in generation of strings.

Nonterminal symbol is a unique object but divisible, used in generation of strings. Nonterminal symbol will be constructed from the terminal symbols; the number of terminal symbols in a nonterminal symbol may vary; it is also called a variable. In a natural language, e.g. English, the letters a, b, A, B, etc. are terminals and the words boy, cat, dog, go are nonterminal symbols. In programming languages, A, B, C, ..., Z, :, =, begin, and, if, then, etc. are terminal symbols. The following will be variable in Pascal:

$$< \text{For statement} > \rightarrow \text{for} < \text{control variable} > : =$$
$$< \text{for list} > \text{do} < \text{statement} >$$

1.4 PRINCIPLE OF INDUCTION

The process of reasoning from general observations to specific truths is called *induction*.

The following are properties regarding the set N of natural numbers and the principle of induction.

Property 1   Zero is a natural number.

Property 2   The successor of any natural number is also a natural number.

Property 3   Zero is not the successor of any natural number.

Property 4   No two natural numbers have the same successor.

Property 5   Let a property $P(n)$ be defined for every natural number n. If (a) $P(0)$ is true, and (b) $P(\text{successor of } n)$ is true whenever $P(n)$ is true, then $P(n)$ is true for all n.

Proof by complete enumeration of all possible combinations is called *perfect induction*, e.g. *proof by truth table*.

The method of proof by induction can be used to prove a property $P(n)$ for all n.

1.4.1 METHOD OF PROOF BY INDUCTION

This method consists of three basic steps:

Step 1   Prove $P(n)$ for $n = 0/1$. This is called proof for the basis.

Step 2   Assume the result/properties for $P(n)$. This is called induction hypothesis.

Step 3   Prove $P(n + 1)$ using induction hypothesis.

EXAMPLE 1.19   Prove that $1 + 3 + 5 + ... + r = n^2$, for all $n > 0$, where r is an odd integer and n is the number of terms in the sum. (Note: $r = 2n - 1$.)

SOLUTION (a) *Proof for the basis* For $n = 1$, L.H.S. $= 1$ and R.H.S. $= 1^2 = 1$. Hence the result is true for $n = 1$.

(b) By induction hypothesis we have $1 + 3 + 5 + ... + r = n^2$. As $r = 2n - 1$, L.H.S. $1 + 3 + 5 + ... + (2n - 1) = n^2$.

(c) We have to prove $1 + 3 + 5 + ... + r + r + 2 = (n + 1)^2$:

$$\text{L.H.S.} = (1 + 3 + 5 + ... + r + (r + 2))$$

$$= n^2 + r + 2 = n^2 + 2n - 1 + 2 = (n + 1)^2 = \text{R.H.S.}$$

EXAMPLE 1.20 Prove the following theorem by induction:

$$1 + 2 + 3 + ... + n = n(n + 1)/2$$

SOLUTION (a) *Proof for the basis* For $n = 1$, L.H.S. $= 1$ and R.H.S. $= 1(1 + 1)/2 = 1$.

(b) Assume $1 + 2 + 3 + ... + n = n(n + 1)/2$.

(c) We have to prove

$$1 + 2 + 3 + ... + (n + 1) = (n + 1)(n + 2)/2$$

$$1 + 2 + 3 + ... + n + (n + 1)$$

$$= n(n + 1)/2 + (n + 1) \quad \text{(by induction hypothesis)}$$

$$= (n + 1)(n + 2)/2 \quad \text{(on simplification)}.$$

The proof by induction can be modified in the following way.

1.4.2 MODIFIED METHOD OF INDUCTION

Three steps are involved in the modified proof by induction.

Step 1 Proof for the basis ($n = 0/1$).

Step 2 Assume the result/properties for all positive integers $< n + 1$.

Step 3 Prove the result/properties using induction hypothesis (i.e. step 2), for $n + 1$.

Example 1.21 illustrates the modified method of induction. The method we shall apply will be clear once we mention the induction hypothesis.

EXAMPLE 1.21 Prove the following theorem by induction: A tree with n vertices has $(n - 1)$ edges.

SOLUTION For $n = 1, 2$, the following trees can be drawn (see Fig. 1.15). So the theorem is true for $n = 1, 2$. Thus there is basis for induction.

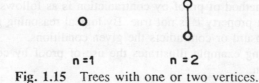

n =1   n = 2

Fig. 1.15 Trees with one or two vertices.

Consider a tree T with $(n + 1)$ vertices as shown in Fig. 1.16. Let e be an edge connecting the vertices v_i and v_j. There is a unique path between v_i and v_j through the edge e. (Property of a tree: There is a unique path between every pair of vertices in a tree.) Thus deletion of e from the graph will disconnect the graph

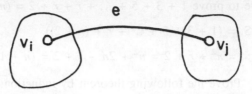

Fig. 1.16   Tree T with $(n + 1)$ vertices.

into two subtrees. Let n_1 and n_2 be the number of vertices in the subtrees. As $n_1 \leq n$ and $n_2 \leq n$, by induction hypothesis, the total number of edges in the subtrees is $n_1 - 1 + n_2 - 1$, i.e. $n - 2$. So, the number of edges in T is $n - 2 + 1 = n - 1$ (by including the deleted edge e). By induction the result is true for all trees.

EXAMPLE 1.22   Two definitions of palindromes are given below: Prove by induction that the two definitions are equivalent.

Definition 1   A palindrome is a string that reads the same forward and backward.

Definition 2   (a) Λ is a palindrome.
(b) If a is any symbol, the string a is a palindrome.
(c) If a is any symbol and x is a palindrome, then axa is a palindrome.
(d) Nothing is a palindrome unless it follows from (a)–(c).

SOLUTION   Let x be a string which satisfies definition 1, i.e. x reads the same forward and backward. By induction on the length of x we prove that x satisfies definition 2.

If $|x| \leq 1$, then $x = a$ or Λ. Since x is a palindrome by definition 1, Λ and a are also palindromes (hence (a) and (b)), i.e. there is basis for induction. If $|x| > 1$, then $x = awa$, where w, by definition 1 is a palindrome; hence rule (c). Thus, if x satisfies definition 1, then it satisfies definition 2.

Let x be a string which is constructed using definition 2. We show by induction on $|x|$ that it satisfies definition 1. There is basis for induction by rule (b). Assume the result for all strings with length $< n$. Let x be a string of length n. As x has to be constructed using rule (c), $x = aya$, where y is a palindrome. As y is a palindrome by definition 2 and $|y| < n$, it satisfies definition 1. So, $x = aya$ also satisfies definition 1.

We conclude this chapter with the method of proof by contradiction.

Proof by contradiction.   Suppose we want to prove a property P under certain conditions. The method of proof by contradiction is as follows:

Assume that property P is not true. By logical reasoning get a conclusion which is either absurd or contradicts the given conditions.

The following example illustrates the use of proof by contradiction and proof by induction.

EXAMPLE 1.23   Prove that there is no string x in $\{a, b\}^*$ such that $ax = xb$. (For definition of strings, refer Section 1.3.)

PROOF   We prove the result by induction on the length of x. When $|x| = 1$, $x = a$ or $x = b$. In both cases $ax \neq xb$. So there is basis for induction. Assume the result for any string whose length is less than n. Let x be any string of length n. We prove that $ax \neq xb$ through proof by contradiction. Suppose $ax = xb$. As a is the first symbol on the L.H.S., the first symbol of x is a. As b is the last symbol on R.H.S., the last symbol of x is b. So, we can write x as ayb with $|y| = n - 2$. This means $aayb = aybb$ which implies $ay = yb$. This contradicts the induction hypothesis. Thus, $ax \neq xb$. By induction the result is true for all strings.

EXERCISES

1. If $A = \{a, b\}$ and $B = \{b, c\}$, find (a) $(A \cup B)^*$, (b) $(A \cap B)^*$, (c) $A^* \cup B^*$, (d) $A^* \cap B^*$, (e) $(A - B)^*$, (f) $(B - A)^*$.

2. Let $S = \{a, b\}^*$. For $x, y \in S$, define $x \circ y = xy$, i.e. $x \circ y$ is obtained by concatenating x and y.

   (a) Is S closed under $\circ$?

   (b) Is $\circ$ associative?

   (c) Does S have the identity element with respect to $\circ$?

   (d) Is $\circ$ commutative?

3. Let $S = 2^X$, where X is any nonempty set. For $A, B \subseteq X$, let $A \circ B = A \cup B$. Is $\circ$ commutative associative? Does S have the identity element with respect to $\circ$? If $A \circ B = A \circ C$, does it imply that $B = C$?

4. Test whether the following statements are true or false. Justify your answer.

   (a) The set of all odd integers is a monoid under multiplication.

   (b) The set of all complex numbers is a group under multiplication.

   (c) The set of all integers under the operation $\circ$ given by $a \circ b = a + b - ab$ is a monoid.

   (d) 2^S under symmetric difference $\bar{V}$ defined by $A \bar{V} B = (A - B) \cup (B - A)$ is an abelian group.

5. Show that the following relations are equivalence relations:

   (a) On a set S, aRb if $a = b$.

   (b) On the set of all lines in the plane, $l_1 R l_2$ if l_1 is parallel to l_2.

   (c) On $N = \{0, 1, 2, ...\}$, mRn if m differs from n by a multiple of 3.

6. Show that the following are not equivalence relations

   (a) On a set S, aRb if $a \neq b$

   (b) On the set of lines in the plane, $l_1 R l_2$ if l_1 is perpendicular to l_2.

   (c) On $N = \{0, 1, 2, ...\}$ mRn if m divides n.

   (d) On $S = \{1, 2, ..., 10\}$, aRb if $a + b = 10$.

7. For x, y in $\{a, b\}^*$, define a relation R by xRy if $|x| = |y|$. Show that R is an equivalence relation. What are the equivalence classes?

8. For x, y in $\{a, b\}^*$, define a relation R by xRy if x is a substring of y (x is a substring of y if $y = z_1xz_2$ for some string z_1, z_2). Is R an equivalence relation?

9. Let $R = \{(1, 2), (2, 3), (1, 4), (4, 2), (3, 4)\}$. Find R^+, R^*

10. Find R^* for the following relations:

    (a) $R = \{(1, 1), (1, 2), (2, 1), (2, 3), (3, 2)\}$.

    (b) $R = \{(1, 1), (2, 3), (3, 4), (3, 2)\}$.

    (c) $R = \{(1, 1), (2, 2), (3, 3), (4, 4)\}$.

    (d) $R = \{(1, 2), (2, 3), (3, 1), (4, 4)\}$.

11. If R is an equivalence relation on S, what can you say about R^+, R^*?

12. Let $f:\{a, b\}^* \to \{a, b\}^*$ be given by $f(x) = ax$ for every $x \in \{a, b\}^*$. Show that f is one-to-one but not onto.

13. Let $g:\{a, b\}^* \to \{a, b\}^*$ be given by $g(x) = x^T$. Show that g is one-to-one and onto.

14. Give an example of (a) a tree with 6 vertices and (b) a binary tree with 7 vertices.

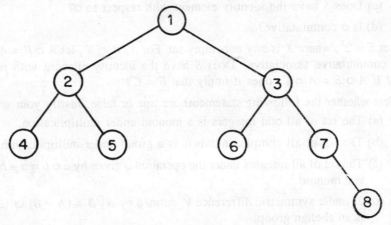

Fig. 1.17   A tree for Exercise 15.

15. For the tree T given in Fig. 1.17, answer the following:

    (a) Is T a binary tree?

    (b) Which vertices are leaves of T?

    (c) How many internal vertices are in T?

    (d) What is the height of T?

    (e) What is the left-to-right ordering of leaves?

    (f) Which vertex is the father of 5?

    (g) Find out the sons of 3.

16. In a get-together show that the number of persons who know odd number of persons is even.

[*Hint*: Use a graph.]

17. If X is a finite set, show that $|2^X| = 2^{|X|}$

18. Prove the following by principle of induction:

(a) $\displaystyle \sum_{k=1}^{n} k^2 = \frac{n(n+1)(2n+1)}{6}$.

(b) $\displaystyle \sum_{k=1}^{n} \frac{1}{k(k+1)} = \frac{n}{(n+1)}$.

(c) $10^{2n} - 1$ is divisible by 11 for all $n > 1$.

19. Prove the following by the Principle of Induction:

(a) $1 + 4 + 7 + \ldots + (3n - 2) = \dfrac{n(3n-1)}{2}$.

(b) $2^n > n$ for all $n > 1$.

(c) If $f(2) = 2$ and $f(2^k) = 2f(2^{k-1}) + 3$, then $f(2^k) = 5/2 \cdot 2^k - 3$.

20. The Fibonacci numbers are defined in the following way:
$$F(0) = 1, \; F(1) = 1, \; F(n+1) = F(n) + F(n-1).$$
Prove by induction that

(i) $\displaystyle F(2n+1) = \sum_{k=0}^{n} F(2k)$.

(ii) $\displaystyle F(2n+2) = \sum_{k=1}^{n} F(2k+1) + 1$.

21. Show that the maximum number of edges in a simple graph (i.e. a graph having no self-loops or parallel edges) is $\dfrac{n(n-1)}{2}$.

22. If $w \in \{a, b\}^*$ satisfies $abw = wab$, show that $|w|$ is even.

23. There are infinite number of envelopes arranged one after another and each envelope contains the instruction "open the next envelope". If a person opens an envelope he has to follow the instruction contained therein. Show that if a person opens the first envelope, he has to open all the envelopes.

2

The Theory of Automata

In this chapter we begin with the study of automaton. We deal with transition systems which are more general than finite automata. We define the acceptability of strings by finite automata and prove that nondeterministic finite automata have the same capability as the deterministic automata as far as acceptability is concerned. Besides, we discuss the equivalence of Mealy and Moore models. Finally, in the last section, we give an algorithm to construct a minimum state automaton equivalent to a given finite automaton.

2.1 DEFINITION OF AN AUTOMATON

We shall give the most general definition of an automaton and later modify it to computer applications. An automaton is defined as a system where energy, materials and information are transformed, transmitted and used for performing some functions without direct participation of man. Examples are automatic machine tools, automatic packing machines, and automatic photo printing machines.

In Computer Science the term 'automaton' means "discrete automaton" and is defined in a more abstract way as shown in Fig. 2.1.

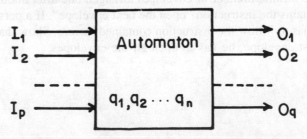

Fig. 2.1 Model of a discrete automaton.

Its characteristics are now described.

(i) *Input*. At each of the discrete instants of time t_1, t_2 ..., input values I_1, I_2 ..., each of which can take a finite number of fixed values from the input alphabet Σ, are applied to the input side of model shown in Fig. 2.1.

(ii) *Output*. O_1, O_2, ..., O_q are the outputs of the model, each of which can take finite numbers of fixed values from an output O.

(iii) *States.* At any instant of time the automaton can be in one of the states $q_1, q_2, ..., q_n$.

(iv) *State relation.* The next state of an automaton at any instant of time is determined by the present state and the present input.

(v) *Output relation.* Output is related to either state only or to both the input and the state. It should be noted that at any instant of time the automaton is in some state. On 'reading' an input symbol, the automaton moves to a next state which is given by the state relation.

NOTE: An automaton in which the output depends only on the input is called an automaton without a memory. An automaton in which the output depends on the states also is called automaton with a finite memory. An automaton in which the output depends only on the states of the machine is called a *Moore machine*. An automaton in which the output depends on the state and the input at any instant of time is called a *Mealy machine*.

EXAMPLE 2.1 Consider the simple shift register shown in Fig. 2.2.

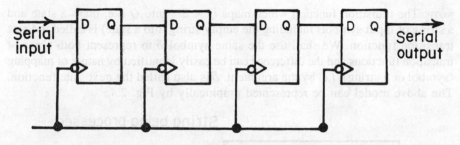

Fig. 2.2 4-bit serial shift register using D-flip flaps.

Consider the shift register as a finite-state machine.

SOLUTION The shift register (Fig. 2.2) can have $2^4 = 16$ states ($0000, 0001 \ldots 1111$), and one serial input and one serial output. The input alphabet is $\Sigma = \{0, 1\}$, and the output alphabet is $O = \{0, 1\}$. The above 4-bit serial shift register can be represented as in Fig. 2.3.

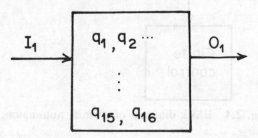

Fig. 2.3 A shift register as finite-state machine.

From the operation, it is clear that the output will depend upon both the input and the state and so it is a Mealy machine.

In general, any sequential machine behaviour can be represented by an automaton.

2.2 DESCRIPTION OF A FINITE AUTOMATON

Definition 2.1 Analytically, a finite automaton can be represented by a 5-tuple $(Q, \Sigma, \delta, q_0, F)$, where

    (i) Q is a finite nonempty set of states;

    (ii) Σ is a finite nonempty set of inputs called input alphabet;

    (iii) δ is a function which maps $Q \times \Sigma$ into Q and is usually called direct transition function. This is the function which describes the change of states during the transition. This mapping is usually represented by a transition table or a transition diagram.

    (iv) $q_0 \in Q$ is the initial state; and

    (v) $F \subseteq Q$ is the set of final states. It is assumed here that there may be more than one final state.

NOTE: The transition function which maps $Q \times \Sigma^*$ into Q (i.e. maps a state and a string of input symbols including the empty string into a state) is called indirect transition function. We shall use the same symbol δ to represent both types of transition functions and the difference can be easily identified by nature of mapping (symbol or a string), i.e. by the argument. δ is also called the next state function. The above model can be represented graphically by Fig. 2.4.

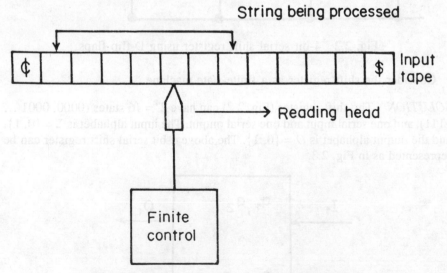

Fig. 2.4   Block diagram of a finite automaton.

Figure 2.4 is the block diagram for a finite automaton. The various components are explained as follows:

(i) *Input tape.* The input tape is divided into squares, each square containing a single symbol from the input alphabet Σ. The end squares of the tape contain end-markers $\mathcal{C}$ at the left end and $\mathcal{S}$ at the right end. Absence of end-markers indicates that the tape is of infinite length. The left-to-right sequence of symbols between the end-markers is the input string to be processed.

(ii) *Reading head.* The head examines only one square at a time and can move one square either to the left or to the right. For further analysis, we restrict the movement of R-head only to the right side.

(iii) *Finite control.* The input to the finite control will be usually: symbol under the R-head, say a, or the present state of the machine, say q, to give the following outputs: (a) A motion of R-head along the tape to the next square (In some a null move, i.e. R-head remaining to the same square is permitted); (b) the next state of the finite state machine given by $\delta(q, a)$.

2.3 TRANSITION SYSTEMS

A transition graph or a transition system is a finite directed labelled graph in which each vertex (or node) represents a state and the directed edges indicate the transition of a state and the edges are labelled with input/output.

A typical transition system is shown in Fig. 2.5. In the figure, the initial state is represented by a circle with an arrow pointing towards it, the final state by two

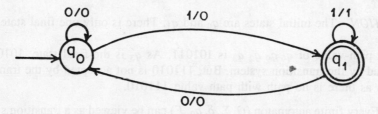

Fig. 2.5 A transition system.

concentric circles, and the other states are represented by just a circle. The edges are labelled by input/output (e.g. by 1/0 or 1/1). For example, if the system is in state q_0 and the input 1 is applied, the system moves to state q_1 as there is a directed edge from q_0 to q_1 with label 1/0. It outputs 0.

We now give the (analytical) definition of a transition system.

Definition 2.2 A transition system is a 5-tuple $(Q, \Sigma, \delta, Q_0, F)$, where (a) Q, Σ and F are the finite nonempty set of states, the input alphabet, and the set of final states, respectively, as in the case of finite automata; (b) $Q_0 \subseteq Q$, and Q_0 is nonempty; and (c) δ is a finite subset of $Q \times \Sigma^* \times Q$. In other words, if (q_1, w, q_2) is in δ, it means the following: The graph starts at the vertex q_1, goes along a set of edges, and reaches the vertex q_2. The concatenation of the label of all the edges thus encountered is w.

Definition 2.3 A transition system accepts a string w in Σ^* if (a) there exists a path which originates from some initial state, goes along the arrows, and terminates at some final state, and (b) the path value obtained by concatenation of all edge-labels of the path is equal to w.

EXAMPLE 2.2   Consider the transition system given in Fig. 2.6.

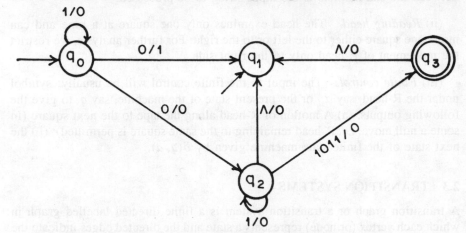

Fig. 2.6   Transition system for Example 2.2.

Determine the initial states, final states, and the acceptability of 101011, 111010.

SOLUTION   The initial states are q_0 and q_1. There is only one final state, viz., q_3.

The path-value of $q_0\, q_0\, q_2\, q_3$ is 101011. As q_3 is the final state, 101011 is accepted by the transition system. But, 111010 is not accepted by the transition system as there is no path with path value 111010.

NOTE: Every finite automaton $(Q, \Sigma, \delta, q_0, F)$ can be viewed as a transition system $(Q, \Sigma, \delta', Q_0, F)$ if we take $Q_0 = \{q_0\}$ and $\delta' = \{(q, w, \delta(q, w)) \mid q \in Q, w \in \Sigma^*\}$. But, a transition system need not be a finite automaton. For example, a transition system may contain more than one initial state.

2.4   PROPERTIES OF TRANSITION FUNCTIONS

Property 1 $\delta(q, \Lambda) = q$ in a finite automaton. This means the state of the system can be changed only by an input symbol.

Property 2   For all strings w and input symbols a,

$$\delta(q, aw) = \delta(\delta(q, a), w)$$

$$\delta(q, wa) = \delta(\delta(q, w), a)$$

This property gives the state after the automaton consumes or reads the first symbol of a string aw and the state after the automaton consumes a prefix of the string wa.

EXAMPLE 2.3   Prove that for any transition function δ and for any two input strings x and y,

$$\delta(q, xy) = \delta(\delta(q, x), y) \qquad (2.1)$$

PROOF By the method of induction on $|y|$, i.e. length of y.
Basis: when $|y| = 1$, $y = a \in \Sigma$,

$$\text{L.H.S. of (2.1)} = \delta(q, xa) = \delta(\delta(q, x), a) \quad \text{by Property 2}$$

$$= \text{R.H.S. of (2.1)}$$

Assume the result, i.e. (2.1) for all strings x and strings y with $|y| = n$. Let y be a string of length $n + 1$. Write $y = y_1 a$ where $|y_1| = n$.

$$\text{L.H.S. of (2.1)} = \delta(q, xy_1 a) = \delta(q, x_1 a), \qquad x_1 = xy_1$$

$$= \delta(\delta(q, x_1), a) \qquad \text{by Property 2}$$

$$= \delta(\delta(q, xy_1), a)$$

$$= \delta(\delta(\delta(q, x), y_1), a) \quad \text{by induction hypothesis}$$

$$\text{R.H.S. of (2.1)} = \delta(\delta(q, x), y_1 a)$$

$$= \delta(\delta(\delta(q, x), y_1), a) \quad \text{by Property 2}$$

Hence, L.H.S. = R.H.S. This proves (2.1) for any string y of length $n + 1$. By the principle of induction, (2.1) is true for all strings. ∎

EXAMPLE 2.4   Prove that if $\delta(q, x) = \delta(q, y)$, then $\delta(q, xz) = \delta(q, yz)$ for all strings z in Σ^+.
SOLUTION

$$\delta(q, xz) = \delta(\delta(q, x), z) \quad \text{by Example 2.3}$$

$$= \delta(\delta(q, y), z) \qquad (2.2)$$

By Example 2.3,

$$\delta(q, yz) = \delta(\delta(q, y), z) = \delta(q, xz) \qquad (2.3)$$

2.5 ACCEPTABILITY OF A STRING BY A FINITE AUTOMATON

Definition 2.4   A string x is accepted by a finite automaton $M = (Q, \Sigma, \delta, q_0, F)$ if $\delta(q_0, x) = q$ for some $q \in F$. This is basically the acceptability of a string by the final state.

NOTE: A final state is also called an accepting state.

EXAMPLE 2.5   Consider the finite state machine whose transition function δ is given in Table 2.1 in the form of a transition table. Here, $Q = \{q_0, q_1, q_2, q_3\}$, $\Sigma = \{0, 1\}$, $F = \{q_0\}$. Give the entire sequence of states for the input string 110001.

Table 2.1 Transition Function Table

	Inputs	
States	0	1
→ $\bigcirc q_0$	q_2	q_1
q_1	q_3	q_0
q_2	q_0	q_3
q_3	q_1	q_2

SOLUTION

$$\delta(q_0, 110101) = \delta(q_1, 10101)$$
$$= \delta(q_0, 0101)$$
$$= \delta(q_2, 101)$$
$$= \delta(q_3, 01)$$
$$= \delta(q_1, 1)$$
$$= \delta(q_0, \Lambda) = q_0$$

Hence,

$$q_0 \xrightarrow{1} q_1 \xrightarrow{1} q_0 \xrightarrow{0} q_2 \xrightarrow{1} q_3 \xrightarrow{0} q_1 \xrightarrow{1} q_0$$

The symbol $\downarrow$ indicates the current input symbol being processed by the machine.

2.6 NONDETERMINISTIC FINITE STATE MACHINES

We explain the concept of nondeterministic finite automaton using a transition
diagram (Fig. 2.7).

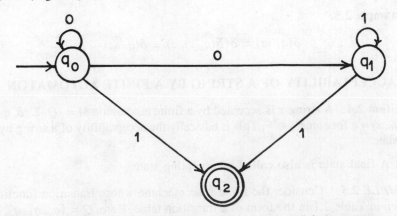

Fig. 2.7 Transition system representing nondeterministic automaton.

If the automaton is in a state $\{q_0\}$ and the input symbol is 0, what will be the next state? From the figure it is clear that the next state will be either $\{q_0\}$ or $\{q_1\}$. Thus some moves of the machine cannot be determined uniquely by the input symbol and the present state. Such machines are called nondeterministic automata, the formal definition of which is now given.

Definition 2.5   A nondeterministic finite automaton (NDFA) is a 5-tuple $(Q, \Sigma, \delta, q_0, F)$, where

> (i) Q is a finite nonempty set of states;
> (ii) Σ is a finite nonempty set of inputs;
> (iii) δ is the transition function mapping from $Q \times \Sigma$ into 2^Q which is the power set of Q, the set of all subsets of Q;
> (iv) $q_0 \in Q$ is the initial state; and
> (v) $F \subseteq Q$ is the set of final states.

We note that the difference between the deterministic and nondeterministic automata is only in δ. For deterministic automaton (DFA), the outcome is a state, i.e. an element of Q; for nondeterministic automaton the outcome is a subset of Q.

Consider, for example, the nondeterministic automaton whose transition diagram is given in Fig. 2.8.

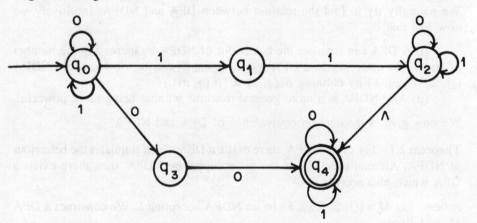

Fig. 2.8   Transition system for a nondeterministic automaton.

The sequence of states for the input string 0100 is given in Fig. 2.9. Hence,

$$\delta(q_0, 0100) = \{q_0, q_3, q_4\}$$

Since q_4 is an accepting state, the input string 0100 will be accepted by the nondeterministic automaton.

Definition 2.6   A string $w \in \Sigma^*$ is accepted by NDFA M if $\delta(q_0, w)$ contains some final state.

NOTE: As M is nondeterministic, $\delta(q_0, w)$ may have more than one state. So w

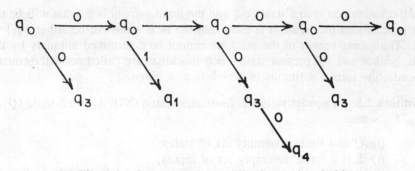

Fig. 2.9 States reached while processing 0100.

is accepted by M if a final state is *one* among the possible states M can reach on application of w.

Definition 2.7 The set accepted by an automaton M (deterministic or nondeterministic) is the set of all input strings accepted by M. It is denoted by $T(M)$.

2.7 THE EQUIVALENCE OF DFA AND NDFA

We naturally try to find the relation between DFA and NDFA. Intuitively we now feel that:

(i) A DFA can simulate the behaviour of NDFA by increasing the number of states. (In other words, a DFA $(Q, \Sigma, \delta, q_0, F)$ can be viewed as an NDFA $(Q, \Sigma, \delta', q_0, F)$ by defining $\delta'(q, a) = \{\delta(q, a)\}$.)
(ii) Any NDFA is a more general machine without being more powerful.

We now give a theorem on equivalence of DFA and NDFA.

Theorem 2.1 For every NDFA, there exists a DFA which simulates the behaviour of NDFA. Alternatively, if L is the set accepted by NDFA, then there exists a DFA which also accepts L.

PROOF   Let $M = (Q, \Sigma, \delta, q_0, F)$ be an NDFA accepting L. We construct a DFA M' as follows:

$$M' = (Q', \Sigma, \delta, q'_0, F')$$

where
(i) $Q' = 2^Q$ (any state in Q' is denoted by $[q_1, q_2 \ldots q_j]$, where $q_1, q_2 \ldots q_j \in Q$);
(ii) $q'_0 = [q_0]$;
(iii) F' is the set of all subsets of Q containing an element of F.

Before defining δ', let us look at the construction of Q', q'_0 and F'. M is initially at q_0. But, on application of an input symbol, say a, M can reach any of the states in $\delta(q_0, a)$. To describe M, just after the application of the input symbol a, we require all the possible states that M can reach after the application of a. So, M'

has to remember all these possible states at any instant of time. Hence the states of M' are defined as subsets of Q. As M starts with initial state q_0, q'_0 is defined as $[q_0]$. A string w belongs to $T(M)$ if a final state is one of the possible states M reaches on processing w. So, a final state in M' (i.e. an element of F') is any subset of Q containing some final state of M.

Now we can define δ':

(iv) $\delta'([q_1, q_2, ..., q_i], a) = \delta(q_1, a) \cup \delta(q_2, a) \cup ... \cup \delta(q_i, a)$.

Equivalently, $\delta'([q_1, q_2 ... q_i], a) = [p_1 ... p_j]$ if and only if

$$\delta(\{q_1, ..., q_i\}, a) = \{p_1, p_2, ..., p_j\}$$

Before proving $L = T(M')$, we prove an auxiliary result:

$$\delta'(q'_0, x) = [q_1, ..., q_i]$$

if and only if $\delta(q_0, x) = \{q_1, ..., q_i\}$ for all x in Σ^* (2.4)

We prove by induction on $|x|$, the "if" part, i.e.

$$\delta'(q'_0, x) = [q_1, q_2, ..., q_i], \text{ if } \delta(q_0, x) = \{q_1, ..., q_i\}$$ (2.5)

When $|x| = 0$, $\delta(q_0, \Lambda) = \{q_0\}$, and by definition of δ', $\delta'(q'_0, \Lambda) = q'_0 = [q_0]$. So, (2.5) is true for x with $|x| = 0$. Thus there is basis for induction.

Assume (2.5) is true for all strings y with $|y| \le m$. Let x be a string of length $m + 1$. We can write x as ya, where $|y| = m$ and $a \in \Sigma$. Let $\delta(q_0, y) = \{p_1, ..., p_j\}$ and $\delta(q_0, ya) = \{r_1, r_2, ..., r_k\}$. As $|y| \le m$, by induction hypothesis we have

$$\delta'(q'_0, y) = [p_1, ..., p_j]$$ (2.6)

Also, $\{r_1, r_2, ..., r_k\} = \delta(q_0, ya) = \delta(\delta(q_0, y), a) = \delta(\{p_1, ..., p_j\}, a)$. By definition of δ',

$$\delta'([p_1, ..., p_j], a) = [r_1, ..., r_k]$$ (2.7)

Hence,

$$\delta'(q'_0, ya) = \delta'(\delta'(q'_0, y), a) = \delta'([p_1, ..., p_j], a) \text{ by (2.6)}$$

$$= [r_1, ..., r_k] \text{ by (2.7)}$$

Thus we have proved (2.5) for $x = ya$.

By induction, (2.5) is true for all strings x. The other part (i.e. "only if" part) can be proved similarly, and so (2.4) is established.

Now, $x \in T(M)$ if and only if $\delta(q, x)$ contains a state of F. By (2.4), $\delta(q_0, x)$ contains a state of F if and only if $\delta'(q'_0, x)$ is in F'. Hence, $x \in T(M)$ if and only if $x \in T(M')$. This proves that DFA M' accepts L. ∎

NOTE: In the construction of a deterministic finite automaton M_1 equivalent to a given nondeterministic automaton M, the only difficult part is the construction of

δ' for M_1. By definition, $\delta'([q_1 \ldots q_k], a) = \bigcup_{i=1}^{k} \delta(q_i, a)$. So we have to apply δ to (q_i, a) for each $i = 1, 2, \ldots, k$ and take their union to get $\delta'([q_1 \ldots q_k], a)$.

When δ for M is given in terms of a state table, the construction is simpler. $\delta(q_i, a)$ is given by the row corresponding to q_i and column corresponding to a. To construct $\delta'([q_1 \ldots q_k], a)$, consider the states appearing in the rows corresponding to $q_1, \ldots, q_k$, and the column corresponding to a. These states constitute $\delta'([q_1 \ldots q_k], a)$.

NOTE: We write δ' as δ itself when there is no ambiguity. We also mark the initial state with $\rightarrow$ and final state with circle in the state table.

Table 2.2 State Table for Example 2.6

State/Σ	0	1
$\rightarrow \text{\textcircled{q_0}}$	q_0	q_1
q_1	q_1	q_0, q_1

EXAMPLE 2.6 Construct a deterministic automaton equivalent to $M = (\{q_0, q_1\}, \{0, 1\}, \delta, q_0, \{q_0\})$. δ is given by its state table (Table 2.2).

SOLUTION For the deterministic automaton M_1,

(i) the states are subsets of $\{q_0, q_1\}$, i.e. $\emptyset$, $[q_0]$, $[q_0, q_1]$, $[q_1]$;
(ii) $[q_0]$ is the initial state;
(iii) $[q_0]$ and $[q_0, q_1]$ are the final states as these are the only states containing q_0; and
(iv) δ is defined by the state table given by Table 2.3.

Table 2.3 State Table of M_1

States/Σ	0	1
$\emptyset$	$\emptyset$	$\emptyset$
$[q_0]$	$[q_0]$	$[q_1]$
$[q_1]$	$[q_1]$	$[q_0, q_1]$
$[q_0, q_1]$	$[q_0, q_1]$	$[q_0, q_1]$

q_0 and q_1 appear in the rows corresponding to q_0 and q_1 and the column corresponding to 0. So, $\delta([q_0, q_1], 0) = [q_0, q_1]$.

When M has n states, the corresponding finite automaton has 2^n states. However, we need not construct δ for all these 2^n states, but only for those states reachable from $[q_0]$. This is because our interest is only in constructing M_1 accepting $T(M)$. So, we start the construction of δ for $[q_0]$. We continue by considering only states appearing earlier under input columns and constructing δ for such states. We halt when no more new states appear under the input columns.

EXAMPLE 2.7   Find a deterministic acceptor equivalent to

$$M = (\{q_0, q_1, q_2\}, \{a, b\}, \delta, q_0, \{q_2\})$$

δ is given in Table 2.4.

Table 2.4   State Table for Example 2.7

States/Σ	a	b
$\rightarrow q_0$	q_0, q_1	q_2
q_1	q_0	q_1
$\textcircled{$q_2$}$		q_0, q_1

SOLUTION   The deterministic automaton M_1 equivalent to M is defined as follows:

$$M_1 = (2^Q, \{a, b\}, \delta, [q_0], F')$$

where

$$F = \{[q_2], [q_0, q_2], [q_1, q_2], [q_0, q_1, q_2]\}$$

We start the construction by considering $[q_0]$ first. We get $[q_2]$ and $[q_0, q_1]$. Then we construct δ for $[q_2]$ and $[q_0, q_1]$. $[q_1, q_2]$ is a new state appearing under input columns. After constructing δ for $[q_1, q_2]$, we do not get any new states and so we terminate the construction of δ. The state table is given in Table 2.5.

Table 2.5   State Table of M_1

States/Σ	a	b
$[q_0]$	$[q_0, q_1]$	$[q_2]$
$[q_2]$	$\emptyset$	$[q_0, q_1]$
$[q_0, q_1]$	$[q_0, q_1]$	$[q_1, q_2]$
$[q_1, q_2]$	$[q_0]$	$[q_0, q_1]$

EXAMPLE 2.8   Construct a deterministic finite automaton equivalent to $M = (\{q_0, q_1, q_2, q_3\}, \{0, 1\}, \delta, q_0, \{q_3\})$. δ is given in Table 2.6.

Table 2.6   State Table for Example 2.8

States/Σ	a	b
$\rightarrow q_0$	q_0, q_1	q_0
q_1	q_2	q_1
q_2	q_3	q_3
$\textcircled{$q_3$}$		q_2

SOLUTION   Let $Q = \{q_0, q_1, q_2, q_3\}$. Then the deterministic automaton M_1 equivalent to M is given by $M_1 = (2^Q, \{a, b\}, \delta, [q_0], F)$, where F consists of $[q_3]$, $[q_0, q_3]$, $[q_1, q_3]$, $[q_2, q_3]$, $[q_0, q_1, q_3]$, $[q_0, q_2, q_3]$, $[q_1, q_2, q_3]$ and $[q_0, q_1, q_2, q_3]$. δ is given in Table 2.7.

Table 2.7   State Table of M_1

States/Σ	a	b
$[q_0]$	$[q_0, q_1]$	$[q_0]$
$[q_0, q_1]$	$[q_0, q_1, q_2]$	$[q_0, q_1]$
$[q_0, q_1, q_2]$	$[q_0, q_1, q_2, q_3]$	$[q_0, q_1, q_3]$
$[q_0, q_1, q_3]$	$[q_0, q_1, q_2]$	$[q_0, q_1, q_2]$
$[q_0, q_1, q_2, q_3]$	$[q_0, q_1, q_2, q_3]$	$[q_0, q_1, q_2, q_3]$

2.8   MEALY AND MOORE MODELS

2.8.1   FINITE AUTOMATA WITH OUTPUTS

The finite automata which we considered in the earlier sections have binary output, i.e. they accept the string or do not accept the string. This acceptability was decided on the basis of reachability of the final state by the initial state. Now, we remove this restriction and consider the model where the outputs can be chosen from some other alphabet. The value of the output function $Z(t)$ in the most general case is a function of the present state $q(t)$ and the present input $x(t)$, i.e.

$$Z(t) = \lambda(q(t), x(t))$$

where λ is called the output function. This generalised model is usually called *Mealy machine*. If the output function $Z(t)$ depends only on the present state and is independent of the current input, the output function may be written as

$$Z(t) = \lambda(q(t))$$

This restricted model is called *Moore machine*. It is more convenient to use Moore machine in automata theory. We now give the most general definitions of these machines.

Definition 2.8   The Moore machine is a six-tuple $(Q, \Sigma, \Delta, \delta, \lambda, q_0)$, where

   (i) Q is a finite set of states;
  (ii) Σ is the input alphabet;
 (iii) Δ is the output alphabet;
 (iv) δ is the transition function $\Sigma \times Q$ into Q;
  (v) λ is the output function mapping Q into Δ; and
 (vi) q_0 is the initial state.

Definition 2.9   A Mealy machine is a six-tuple $(Q, \Sigma, \Delta, \delta, \lambda, q_0)$, where all the symbols except λ have the same meaning as in the Moore machine. λ is the output function mapping $\Sigma \times Q$ into Δ.

For example, Table 2.8 gives a Moore machine. The initial state q_0 is marked with an arrow. The table defines δ and λ.

Table 2.8 A Moore Machine

Present state	Next state δ		Output
	$a = 0$	$a = 1$	λ
$\rightarrow q_0$	q_3	q_1	0
q_1	q_1	q_2	1
q_2	q_2	q_3	0
q_3	q_3	q_0	0

For the input string 0111, the transition of states is given by $q_0 \rightarrow q_3 \rightarrow q_0 \rightarrow q_1 \rightarrow q_2$. The output string is 00010. For the input string Λ, the output is $\lambda (q_0) = 0$.

Transition Table 2.9, for example, describes a Mealy machine. (Note: For the input string 0011, the transition of states is given by $q_1 \rightarrow q_3 \rightarrow q_2 \rightarrow q_4 \rightarrow q_3$, and the output string is 0100. In the case of a Mealy machine, we get an output only on the application of an input symbol. So for the input string Λ, the output is only Λ. It may be observed that in the case of Moore machine, we get $\lambda(q_0)$ for the input string Λ.)

Table 2.9 A Mealy Machine

Present state	Next state			
	$a = 0$		$a = 1$	
	state	output	state	output
$\rightarrow q_1$	q_3	0	q_2	0
q_2	q_1	1	q_4	0
q_3	q_2	1	q_1	1
q_4	q_4	1	q_3	0

Remark: An FA can be converted into a Moore machine by introducing $\Delta = \{0, 1\}$ and defining $\lambda(q) = 1$ if $q \in F$ and $\lambda(q) = 0$ if $q \notin F$.

For a Moore machine if the input string is of length n, the output string is of length $n + 1$. The first output is $\lambda(q_0)$ for all output strings. In the case of Mealy machine if the input string is of length n, the output string is also of the same length n.

2.8.2 PROCEDURE FOR TRANSFORMING A MEALY MACHINE INTO A MOORE MACHINE

We develop procedures for transforming a Mealy machine into a Moore machine and vice versa so that for a given input string the output strings are the same (except for the first symbol) in both the machines.

EXAMPLE 2.9 Consider the Mealy machine described by the transition table given in Table 2.10. Construct a Moore machine which is equivalent to the Mealy machine.

Table 2.10 Mealy Machine of Example 2.9

| Present state | Next state | | | |
| | input $a = 0$ | | input $a = 1$ | |
	state	output	state	output
$\rightarrow q_1$	q_3	0	q_2	0
q_2	q_1	1	q_4	0
q_3	q_2	1	q_1	1
q_4	q_4	1	q_3	0

SOLUTION At the first stage we develop the procedure so that both machines accept exactly the same set of input sequences. We look into the next state column for any state, say q_i, and determine the number of different outputs associated with q_i in that column.

We split q_i into several different states, the number of such states being equal to the number of different outputs associated with q_i. For example, in this problem, q_1 is associated with one output 1 and q_2 is associated with two different outputs 0 and 1. Similarly, q_3 and q_4 are associated with the outputs 0 and 0, 1, respectively. So, we split q_2 into q_{20} and q_{21}. Similarly, q_4 is split into q_{40} and q_{41}. Now Table 2.10 can be reconstructed for the new states as in Table 2.11.

Table 2.11 State Table for Example 2.9

| Present state | Next state | | | |
| | input $a = 0$ | | input $a = 1$ | |
	state	output	state	output
$\rightarrow q_1$	q_3	0	q_{20}	0
q_{20}	q_1	1	q_{40}	0
q_{21}	q_1	1	q_{40}	0
q_3	q_{21}	1	q_1	1
q_{40}	q_{41}	1	q_3	0
q_{41}	q_{41}	1	q_3	0

The pair of states and outputs in the next state column can be rearranged as given in Table 2.12.

Table 2.12 Revised State Table for Example 2.9

| Present state | Next state | | Output |
	$a = 0$	$a = 1$	
$\rightarrow q_1$	q_3	q_{20}	1
q_{20}	q_1	q_{40}	0
q_{21}	q_1	q_{40}	1
q_3	q_{21}	q_1	0
q_{40}	q_{41}	q_3	0
q_{41}	q_{41}	q_3	1

Table 2.12 gives the Moore machine. Here we observe that the initial state q_1 is associated with output 1. This means that with input Λ we get an output of 1, if the machine starts at state q_1. Thus this Moore machine accepts a zero-length sequence (null sequence) which is not accepted by the Mealy machine. To overcome this situation, either we must neglect the response of a Moore machine to input Λ, or we must add a new starting state q_0, whose state transitions are identical with those of q_1 but whose output is 0. So Table 2.12 is transformed to Table 2.13.

Table 2.13   Moore Machine of Example 2.9

Present state	Next state		Output
	$a = 0$	$a = 1$	
$\rightarrow q_0$	q_3	q_{20}	0
q_1	q_3	q_{20}	1
q_{20}	q_1	q_{40}	0
q_{21}	q_1	q_{40}	1
q_3	q_{21}	q_1	0
q_{40}	q_{41}	q_3	0
q_{41}	q_{41}	q_3	1

From the foregoing procedure it is clear that if we have m-output, n-state Mealy machine, the corresponding m-output Moore machine has no more than $mn + 1$ states.

2.8.3 PROCEDURE FOR TRANSFORMING A MOORE MACHINE TO CORRESPONDING MEALY MACHINE

We modify the acceptability of input string by a Moore machine by neglecting the response of the Moore machine to input Λ. We thus define that Mealy Machine M and Moore Machine M' are equivalent if for all input strings w, $bZ_M(w) = Z_{M'}(w)$, where b is the output of Moore machine for its initial state. We give the following result: Let $M_1 = (Q, \Sigma, \Delta, \delta, \lambda, q_0)$ be a Moore machine. Then the following procedure may be adopted to construct an equivalent Mealy machine M_2.

Construction

(a) We have to define the output function λ' for Mealy machine as a function of present state and input symbol. We define λ' by

$$\lambda'(q, a) = \lambda(\delta(q, a)) \quad \text{for all states } q \text{ and input symbols } a.$$

(b) the transition function is the same as that of the given Moore machine.

EXAMPLE 2.10 Construct a Mealy Machine which is equivalent to the Moore machine given in Table 2.14.

SOLUTION   We must follow the reverse procedure of converting Mealy machine

Table 2.14 Moore Machine of Example 2.10

Present state	Next state		Output
	$a = 0$	$a = 1$	
$\rightarrow q_0$	q_3	q_1	0
q_1	q_1	q_2	1
q_2	q_2	q_3	0
q_3	q_3	q_0	0

into Moore machine. In the case of the Moore machine, for every input symbol we form the pair consisting of the next state and the corresponding output and reconstruct the table for Mealy Machine. For example, the states q_3 and q_1 in the next state column should be associated with outputs 0 and 1, respectively. The transition table for Mealy machine is given in Table 2.15.

Table 2.15 Mealy Machine of Example 2.10

Present state	Next state			
	$a = 0$		$a = 1$	
	state	output	state	output
$\rightarrow q_0$	q_3	0	q_1	1
q_1	q_1	1	q_2	0
q_2	q_2	0	q_3	0
q_3	q_3	0	q_0	0

NOTE: We can reduce the number of states in any model by considering states with identical transitions. If two states have identical transitions (i.e. the rows corresponding to these two states are identical), then we can delete one of them.

EXAMPLE 2.11 Consider the Moore machine described by the transition table given in Table 2.16. Construct the corresponding Mealy machine.

Table 2.16 Moore Machine of Example 2.11

Present state	Next state		Output
	$a = 0$	$a = 1$	
$\rightarrow q_1$	q_1	q_2	0
q_2	q_1	q_3	0
q_3	q_1	q_3	1

SOLUTION We construct the transition table in Table 2.17 by associating the output with the transitions.

In Table 2.17 the rows corresponding to q_2 and q_3 are identical. So, we can delete one of the two states, i.e., q_2 or q_3. We delete q_3. Table 2.18 gives the reconstructed table.

Table 2.17 Transition Table of Example 2.11

| Present state | Next state | | | |
| | $a = 0$ | | $a = 1$ | |
	state	output	state	output
$\rightarrow q_1$	q_1	0	q_2	0
q_2	q_1	0	q_3	1
q_3	q_1	0	q_3	1

Table 2.18 Mealy Machine of Example 2.11

| Present state | Next state | | | |
| | $a = 0$ | | $a = 1$ | |
	state	output	state	output
$\rightarrow q_1$	q_1	0	q_2	0
q_2	q_1	0	q_2	1

In Table 2.17, we have deleted q_3-row and replaced q_3 by q_2 in the other rows.

EXAMPLE 2.12   Consider a Mealy machine represented by Fig. 2.10. Construct a Moore machine equivalent to this Mealy machine.

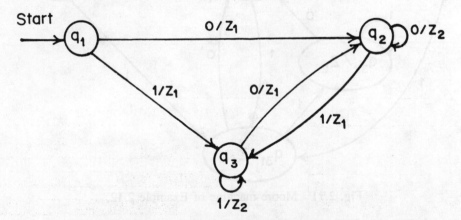

Fig. 2.10   Mealy machine of Example 2.12.

SOLUTION   Let us convert the transition diagram into the transition Table 2.19. For the given problem: q_1 is not associated with any output. q_2 is associated with two different outputs Z_1 and Z_2; q_3 is associated with two different outputs Z_1 and Z_2. Thus we must split q_2 into q_{21} and q_{22} with outputs Z_1 and Z_2, respectively and q_3 into q_{31} and q_{32} with outputs Z_1 and Z_2, respectively. Table 2.19 may be reconstructed as Table 2.20.

Table 2.19 Transition Table for Example 2.12

Present state	Next state			
	$a = 0$		$a = 1$	
	state	output	state	output
$\rightarrow q_1$	q_2	Z_1	q_3	Z_1
q_2	q_2	Z_2	q_3	Z_1
q_3	q_2	Z_1	q_3	Z_2

Table 2.20 Transition Table of Moore Machine

Present state	Next state		Output
	$a = 0$	$a = 1$	
$\rightarrow q_1$	q_{21}	q_{31}	
q_{21}	q_{22}	q_{31}	Z_1
q_{22}	q_{22}	q_{31}	Z_2
q_{31}	q_{21}	q_{32}	Z_1
q_{32}	q_{21}	q_{32}	Z_2

Figure 2.11 gives the transition diagram of the required Moore machine.

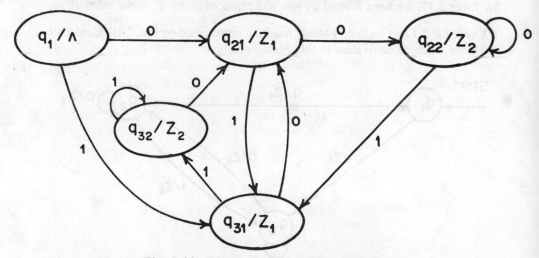

Fig. 2.11 Moore machine of Example 2.12.

2.9 MINIMISATION OF FINITE AUTOMATA

In this section we construct an automaton with minimum number of states equivalent to a given automaton M.

As our interest lies only in strings accepted by M, what really matters is whether a state is a final state or not. We define some relations in Q.

Definition 2.8 Two states q_1 and q_2 are equivalent (denoted by $q_1 \equiv q_2$) if both $\delta(q_1, x)$ and $\delta(q_2, x)$ are final states, or both of them are nonfinal states for all $x \in \Sigma^*$.

As it is difficult to construct $\delta(q_1, x)$ and $\delta(q_2, x)$ for all $x \in \Sigma^*$ (there are infinite number of strings in Σ^*), we give one more definition.

Definition 2.9   Two states q_1 and q_2 are k-equivalent ($k \geq 0$) if both $\delta(q_1, x)$ and $\delta(q_2, x)$ are final states or both nonfinal states for all strings x of length k or less. In particular, any two final states are 0-equivalent and any two nonfinal states are also 0-equivalent.

We mention some of the properties of these relations.

Property 1   The relations we have defined, i.e. equivalence and k-equivalence, are equivalence relations, i.e. they are reflexive, symmetric and transitive.

Property 2   By Theorem 1.1, these induce partitions of Q. These partitions can be denoted by π and π_k, respectively. Elements of π_k are k-equivalence classes.

Property 3   If q_1 and q_2 are k-equivalent for all $k \geq 0$, then they are equivalent.

Property 4   If q_1 and q_2 are $(k + 1)$-equivalent, then they are k-equivalent.

Property 5 $\pi_n = \pi_{n+1}$ for some n. (π_n denotes the set of equivalence classes under n-equivalence.)

The following result is the key to the construction of minimum state automaton.

RESULT   Two states q_1 and q_2 are $(k + 1)$-equivalent if (a) they are k-equivalent; (b) $\delta(q_1, a)$ and $\delta(q_2, a)$ are also k-equivalent for every $a \in \Sigma$.

PROOF   We prove the result by contradiction. Suppose q_1 and q_2 are not $(k + 1)$-equivalent. Then there exists a string $w = aw_1$ of length $k + 1$ such that $\delta(q_1, aw_1)$ is a final state and $\delta(q_2, aw_1)$ is not a final state (or vice versa; the proof is similar). So $\delta(\delta(q_1, a), w_1)$ is a final state and $\delta(\delta(q_2, a), w_1)$ is not a final state. As w_1 is a string of length k, $\delta(q_1, a)$ and $\delta(q_2, a)$ are not k-equivalent. This is a contradiction, and hence the result is proved.   ∎

Using the previous result we can construct $(k + 1)$-equivalence classes once k-equivalence classes are known.

2.9.1   CONSTRUCTION OF MINIMUM AUTOMATON

Step 1   (Construction of π_0). By definition of 0-equivalence, $\pi_0 = \{Q_1^0, Q_2^0\}$, where Q_1^0 is the set of all final states and $Q_2^0 = Q - Q_1^0$.

Step 2   (Construction of π_{k+1} from π_k). Let Q_i^k be any subset in π_k. If q_1 and q_2 are in Q_i^k, they are $(k + 1)$-equivalent provided $\delta(q_1, a)$ and $\delta(q_2, a)$ are k-equivalent. Find out whether $\delta(q_1, a)$ and $\delta(q_2, a)$ are in the same equivalence class in π_k for every $a \in \Sigma$. If so, q_1 and q_2 are $(k + 1)$-equivalent. In this way, Q_i^k is further divided into $(k + 1)$-equivalence classes. Repeat this for every Q_i^k in π_k to get all the elements of π_{k+1}.

Step 3   Construct π_n for $n = 1, 2, \ldots$ until $\pi_n = \pi_{n+1}$.

Step 4   (Construction of minimum automaton). For the required minimum state automaton, the states are the equivalence classes obtained in step 3, i.e. the elements of π_n. The state table is obtained by replacing a state q by the corresponding equivalence class $[q]$.

Remark: In the above construction, the crucial part is the construction of equivalence classes; for, after getting the equivalence classes, the table for minimum automaton is obtained by replacing states by the corresponding equivalence classes. The number of equivalence classes is less than or equal to $|Q|$. Consider an equivalence class $[q_1] = \{q_1, q_2, ..., q_k\}$. If q_1 is reached while processing w_1w_2 $\in T(M)$ with $\delta(q_0, w_1) = q_1$, then $\delta(q_1, w_2) \in F$. So, $\delta(q_i, w_2) \in F$ for $i = 2, ...,$ k. Thus we see that $q_i, i = 2, ..., k$ is reached on processing some $w \in T(M)$ iff q_1 is reached on processing w, i.e. q_1 of $[q_1]$ can play the role of $q_2, ..., q_k$. The above argument explains why we replace a state by the corresponding equivalence class.

NOTE: The construction of π_0, π_1, π_2, etc. is easy when the transition table is given. $\pi_0 = \{Q_1^0, Q_2^0\}$, where $Q_1^0 = F$ and $Q_2^0 = Q - F$. The subsets in π_1 are obtained by partitioning subsets of π_0 further. If $q_1, q_2 \in Q_1^0$, consider the states in each a-column, where $a \in \Sigma$ corresponding to q_1 and q_2. If they are in the same subset of π_0, q_1 and q_2 are 1-equivalent. If the states under some a-column are in different subsets of π_0, then q_1 and q_2 are not 1-equivalent. In general, $(k + 1)$-equivalent states are obtained by applying the above method for q_1 and q_2 in Q_i^k.

EXAMPLE 2.13 Construct a minimum state automaton equivalent to the finite automaton given in Fig. 2.12.

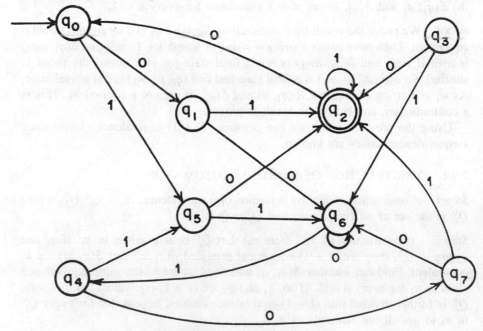

Fig. 2.12 FA of Example 2.13.

SOLUTION It will be easier if we construct the transition table given in Table 2.21.

Table 2.21   Transition Table for Example 2.13

State/Σ	0	1
$\rightarrow q_0$	q_1	q_5
q_1	q_6	q_2
$\textcircled{q_2}$	q_0	q_2
q_3	q_2	q_6
q_4	q_7	q_5
q_5	q_2	q_6
q_6	q_6	q_4
q_7	q_6	q_2

By applying step 1, we get

$$Q_1^0 = F = \{q_2\}, \qquad Q_2^0 = Q - Q_1^0$$

So,

$$\pi_0 = \{\{q_2\}, \{q_0, q_1, q_3, q_4, q_5, q_6, q_7\}\}$$

$\{q_2\}$ in π_0 cannot be further partitioned. So, $Q_1' = \{q_2\}$. Consider q_0 and $q_1 \in Q_2^0$. The entries under 0-column corresponding to q_0 and q_1 are q_1 and q_6; they lie in Q_2^0. The entries under 1-column are q_5 and q_2. $q_2 \in Q_1^0$ and $q_5 \in Q_2^0$. Therefore, q_0 and q_1 are not 1-equivalent. Similarly, q_0 is not 1-equivalent to q_3, q_5 and q_7.

Now, consider q_0 and q_4. The entries under 0-column are q_1 and q_7. Both are in Q_2^0. The entries under 1-column are q_5, q_5. So q_4 and q_0 are 1-equivalent. Similarly, q_0 is 1-equivalent to q_6. $\{q_0, q_4, q_6\}$ is a subset in π_1. So, $Q_2' = \{q_0, q_4, q_6\}$.

Repeat the construction by considering q_1 and any one of the states q_3, q_5, q_7. q_1 is not 1-equivalent to q_3 or q_5 but 1-equivalent to q_7. Hence, $Q_3' = \{q_1, q_7\}$. The elements left over in Q_2^0 are q_3 and q_5. By considering the entries under 0-column and 1-column, we see that q_3 and q_5 are 1-equivalent. So $Q_4' = \{q_3, q_5\}$. Therefore,

$$\pi_1 = \{\{q_2\}, \{q_0, q_4, q_6\}, \{q_1, q_7\}, \{q_3, q_5\}\}$$

$\{q_2\}$ is also in π_2 as it cannot be partitioned further. Now the entries under 0-column corresponding to q_0 and q_4 are q_1 and q_7, and these lie in the same equivalence class in π_1. The entries under 1-column are q_5, q_5. So q_0 and q_4 are 2-equivalent. But q_0 and q_6 are not 2-equivalent. Hence, $\{q_0, q_4, q_6\}$ is partitioned into $\{q_0, q_4\}$ and $\{q_6\}$. q_1 and q_7 are 2-equivalent. q_3 and q_5 are also 2-equivalent. Thus, $\pi_2 = \{\{q_2\}, \{q_0, q_4\}, \{q_6\}, \{q_1, q_7\}, \{q_3, q_5\}\}$ q_0 and q_4 are 3-equivalent. q_1 and q_7 are 3-equivalent. Also, q_3 and q_5 are 3-equivalent. Therefore,

$$\pi_3 = \{\{q_2\}, \{q_0, q_4\}, \{q_6\}, \{q_1, q_7\}, \{q_3, q_5\}\}$$

As $\pi_2 = \pi_3$, π_2 gives the equivalence classes, the minimum state automaton is

$$M' = (Q', \{0, 1\}, \delta', q_0', F')$$

where

$$Q' = \{[q_2], [q_0, q_4], [q_6], [q_1, q_7], [q_3, q_5]\}$$

$$q_0' = [q_0, q_4], \qquad F' = [q_2]$$

and δ' is given by Table 2.22.

Table 2.22   Transition Table of Minimum
State Automaton

State/Σ	0	1
$[q_0, q_4]$	$[q_1, q_7]$	$[q_3, q_5]$
$[q_1, q_7]$	$[q_6]$	$[q_2]$
$[q_2]$	$[q_0, q_4]$	$[q_2]$
$[q_3, q_5]$	$[q_2]$	$[q_6]$
$[q_6]$	$[q_6]$	$[q_0, q_4]$

NOTE: The transition diagram for the minimum state automaton is given in Fig. 2.13. The states q_0 and q_4 are identified and treated as one state. (So also are q_1, q_7 and q_3, q_5.) But the transitions in both the diagrams (i.e. Figs. 2.12 and

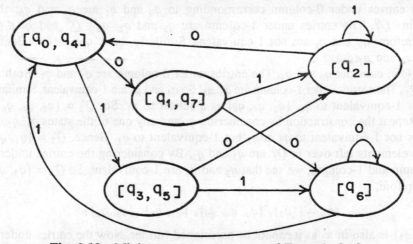

Fig. 2.13   Minimum state automaton of Example 2.13.

2.13) are the same. If there is an arrow from q_i to q_j with label a, then there is an arrow from $[q_i]$ to $[q_j]$ with the same label in the diagram for minimum state automaton. Symbolically, if $\delta(q_i, a) = q_j$, then $\delta'([q_i], a) = [q_j]$.

EXAMPLE 2.14   Construct the minimum state automaton equivalent to the transition diagram given in Fig. 2.14.

SOLUTION   We construct the transition table given in Table 2.23.

Since there is only one final state q_3, $Q_1^0 = \{q_3\}$, $Q_2^0 = Q - Q_1^0$. Hence, $\pi_0 = \{\{q_3\}, \{q_0, q_1, q_2, q_4, q_5, q_6, q_7\}\}$. As $\{q_3\}$ cannot be partitioned further, $Q_1' =$

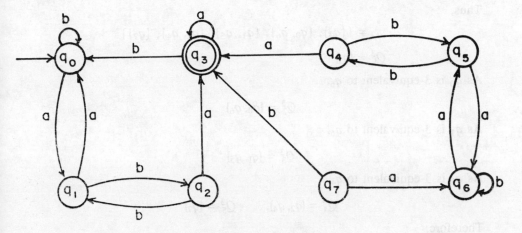

Fig. 2.14   FA of Example 2.14.

Table 2.23   Transition Table of Example 2.14

State/Σ	a	b
→ q_0	q_1	q_0
q_1	q_0	q_2
q_2	q_3	q_1
(q_3)	q_3	q_0
q_4	q_3	q_5
q_5	q_6	q_4
q_6	q_5	q_6
q_7	q_6	q_3

$\{q_3\}$. Now q_0 is 1-equivalent to q_1, q_5, q_6, but not to q_2, q_4, q_7, and so $Q'_2 = \{q_0, q_1, q_5, q_6\}$. q_2 is 1-equivalent to q_4. Hence, $Q'_3 = \{q_2, q_4\}$. The only element left over in Q_2^0 is q_7. Therefore, $Q'_4 = \{q_7\}$. Thus,

$$\pi_1 = \{\{q_3\}, \{q_0, q_1, q_5, q_6\}, \{q_2, q_4\}, \{q_7\}\}$$

$$Q_1^2 = \{q_3\}$$

q_0 is 2-equivalent to q_6 but not to q_1 or q_5. So,

$$Q_2^2 = \{q_0, q_6\}$$

As q_1 is 2-equivalent to q_5,

$$Q_3^2 = \{q_1, q_5\}$$

As q_2 is 2-equivalent to q_4,

$$Q_4^2 = \{q_2, q_4\}, \qquad Q_5^2 = \{q_7\}$$

Thus,

$$\pi_2 = \{\{q_3\}, \{q_0, q_6\}, \{q_1, q_5\}, \{q_2, q_4\}, \{q_7\}\}$$

$$Q_1^3 = \{q_3\}$$

As q_0 is 3-equivalent to q_6,

$$Q_2^3 = \{q_0, q_6\}$$

As q_1 is 3-equivalent to q_5,

$$Q_3^3 = \{q_1, q_5\}$$

As q_2 is 3-equivalent to q_4,

$$Q_4^3 = \{q_2, q_4\}, \qquad Q_5^3 = \{q_7\}$$

Therefore,

$$\pi_3 = \{\{q_3\}, \{q_0, q_6\}, \{q_1, q_5\}, \{q_2, q_4\}, \{q_7\}\}$$

As $\pi_3 = \pi_2$, π_2 gives us the equivalence classes, the minimum state automaton is $M' = (Q', \{a, b\}, \delta', q'_0, F')$, where

$$Q' = \{[q_3], [q_0, q_6], [q_1, q_5], [q_2, q_4], [q_7]\}$$

$$q'_0 = [q_0, q_6], \qquad F' = [q_3]$$

δ' is given by Table 2.24.

Table 2.24 Transition Table of Minimum
State Automaton

State/Σ	a	b
$[q_0, q_6]$	$[q_1, q_5]$	$[q_0, q_6]$
$[q_1, q_5]$	$[q_0, q_6]$	$[q_2, q_4]$
$[q_2, q_4]$	$[q_3]$	$[q_1, q_5]$
$[q_3]$	$[q_3]$	$[q_0, q_6]$
$[q_7]$	$[q_0, q_6]$	$[q_3]$

NOTE: The transition diagram for M' is given in Fig. 2.15.

EXERCISES

1. For the finite state machine M given in Table 2.1, find out the strings among the following strings which are accepted by M: (a) 101101, (b) 11111, (c) 000000.

2. For the transition system M given in Fig. 2.8, obtain the sequence of states for the input sequence 000101. Also find an input sequence not accepted by M.

3. Test whether 110011, 110110 are accepted by the transition system given in Fig. 2.6.

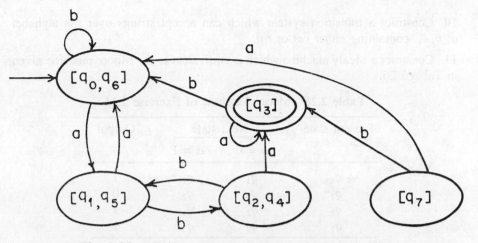

Fig. 2.15   Minimum state automaton of Example 2.14.

4. Let $M = (Q, \Sigma, \delta, q_0, F)$ be a finite automaton. Let R be a relation in Q defined by $q_1 R q_2$ if $\delta(q_1, a) = \delta(q_2, a)$ for some $a \in \Sigma$. Is R an equivalence relation?

5. Construct a nondeterministic finite automaton accepting $\{ab, ba\}$, and use it to find a deterministic automaton accepting the same set.

6. Construct a nondeterministic finite automaton accepting the set of all strings over $\{a, b\}$ ending in aba. Use it to construct a DFA accepting the same set of strings.

7. The transition table of a nondeterministic finite automaton M is given in Table 2.25. Construct a deterministic finite automaton equivalent to M.

Table 2.25   Transition Table for Exercise 2.7

State	0	1	2
$\rightarrow q_0$	$q_1 q_4$	q_4	$q_2 q_3$
q_1		q_4	
q_2			$q_2 q_3$
$\textcircled{q_3}$		q_4	
q_4			

8. Construct a DFA equivalent to the NDFA given in Fig. 2.8.

9. $M = (\{q_1, q_2, q_3\}, \{0, 1\}, \delta, q_1, \{q_3\})$ is a nondeterministic finite automaton, where δ is given by

$$\delta(q_1, 0) = \{q_2, q_3\} \quad \delta(q_1, 1) = \{q_1\}$$

$$\delta(q_2, 0) = \{q_1, q_2\} \quad \delta(q_2, 1) = \emptyset$$

$$\delta(q_3, 0) = \{q_2\} \quad \delta(q_3, 1) = \{q_1, q_2\}$$

Construct an equivalent DFA.

10. Construct a transition system which can accept strings over the alphabet $a, b, \ldots$ containing either *cat* or *rat*.

11. Construct a Mealy machine which is equivalent to the Moore machine given in Table 2.26.

Table 2.26 Moore Machine of Exercise 2.11

Present state	Next state		Output
	$a = 0$	$a = 1$	
$\rightarrow q_0$	q_1	q_2	1
q_1	q_3	q_2	0
q_2	q_2	q_1	1
q_3	q_0	q_3	1

12. Construct a Moore machine equivalent to the Mealy machine M given in Table 2.27.

Table 2.27 Mealy Machine of Exercise 2.12

Present state	Next state			
	$a = 0$		$a = 1$	
	state	output	state	output
$\rightarrow q_1$	q_1	1	q_2	0
q_2	q_4	1	q_4	1
q_3	q_2	1	q_3	1
q_4	q_3	0	q_1	1

13. Construct a Mealy machine which can output EVEN, ODD according as the total number of 1's encountered is even or odd. The input symbols are 0 and 1.

14. Construct a minimum state automaton equivalent to a given automaton M whose transition table is given in Table 2.28.

Table 2.28 FA of Exercise 2.14

States	Input	
	a	b
$\rightarrow q_0$	q_0	q_3
q_1	q_2	q_5
q_2	q_3	q_4
q_3	q_0	q_5
q_4	q_0	q_6
q_5	q_1	q_4
$\textcircled{q_6}$	q_1	q_3

3

Formal Languages

In this chapter we introduce the concepts of grammars and formal languages and discuss Chomsky classification of languages. We also study the inclusion relation between the four classes of languages. Finally, we discuss the closure properties of these classes under various operations.

3.1 BASIC DEFINITIONS AND EXAMPLES

The theory of formal languages is an area with a number of applications in Computer Science. Linguists were trying in the early 50s to define precisely valid sentences and give structural descriptions of sentences. They wanted to define a formal grammar (i.e., to describe the rules of grammar in a rigorous mathematical way) to describe English. They thought such description of natural languages (the languages we use in everyday life such as English, Hindi, French, etc.) would make language translation using computers easy. It was Noam Chomsky who gave a mathematical model of a grammar in 1956. Although it was not useful for describing natural languages such as English, it turned out to be useful for computer languages. In fact, the Backus-Naur form used to describe ALGOL followed the definition of grammar (a context-free grammar) given by Chomsky.

Before giving the definition of grammar, we shall study, for the sake of simplicity, two types of sentences in English with a view to formalising the construction of these sentences. The sentences we consider are those with a noun and a verb, or those with a noun-verb and adverb (such as "Ram ate quickly" or "Sam ran"). The sentence "Ram ate quickly" has the words 'Ram', 'ate', 'quickly' written in that order. If we replace 'Ram' by 'Sam', 'Tom', 'Gita' etc., i.e. by any noun, 'ate' by 'ran', 'walked', etc., i.e. by any verb in the past tense, and 'quickly' by 'slowly', i.e. by any adverb, we get other grammatically correct sentences. So the structure of "Ram ate quickly" can be given as ⟨noun⟩ ⟨verb⟩ ⟨adverb⟩. For ⟨noun⟩ we can substitute 'Ram', 'Sam', 'Tom', 'Gita', etc. Similarly, we can substitute 'ate', 'walked', 'ran', etc. for ⟨verb⟩, and 'quickly', 'slowly' for ⟨adverb⟩. Similarly, the structure of "Sam ran" can be given in the form ⟨noun⟩ ⟨verb⟩.

We have to note that ⟨noun⟩ ⟨verb⟩ ⟨adverb⟩ is not a sentence but only the description of a particular type of sentence. If we replace ⟨noun⟩, ⟨verb⟩ and ⟨adverb⟩ by suitable words, we get actual grammatically correct sentences. Let us call ⟨noun⟩, ⟨verb⟩, ⟨adverb⟩ as variables. Words like 'Ram', 'Sam', 'ate', 'ran', 'quickly', 'slowly' which form sentences can be called terminals. So our sentences turn out to be strings of terminals. Let S be a variable denoting a sentence. Now, we can form the following rules to generate two types of sentences:

$S \rightarrow \langle \text{noun} \rangle \langle \text{verb} \rangle \langle \text{adverb} \rangle$

$S \rightarrow \langle \text{noun} \rangle \langle \text{verb} \rangle$

$\langle \text{noun} \rangle \rightarrow \text{Sam}$

$\langle \text{noun} \rangle \rightarrow \text{Ram}$

$\langle \text{noun} \rangle \rightarrow \text{Gita}$

$\langle \text{verb} \rangle \rightarrow \text{ran}$

$\langle \text{verb} \rangle \rightarrow \text{ate}$

$\langle \text{verb} \rangle \rightarrow \text{walked}$

$\langle \text{adverb} \rangle \rightarrow \text{slowly}$

$\langle \text{adverb} \rangle \rightarrow \text{quickly}$

(Each arrow represents a rule meaning that the word on the right side of the arrow can replace the word on the left side of the arrow.) Let us denote the collection of the rules given above by P.

If our vocabulary is thus restricted to 'Ram', 'Sam', 'Gita', 'ate', 'ran', 'walked', 'quickly' and 'slowly', and our sentences are of the form $\langle \text{noun} \rangle$ $\langle \text{verb} \rangle \langle \text{adverb} \rangle$ and $\langle \text{noun} \rangle \langle \text{verb} \rangle$, we can describe the grammar by a 4-tuple (V_N, Σ, P, S), where

$$V_N = \{\langle \text{noun} \rangle, \langle \text{verb} \rangle, \langle \text{adverb} \rangle\}$$

$$\Sigma = \{\text{Ram, Sam, Gita, ate, ran, walked, quickly, slowly}\}$$

P is the collection of rules described above (the rules may be called productions), and S is the special symbol denoting a sentence. The sentences are obtained by (a) starting with S, (b) replacing words using the productions, and (c) terminating when a string of terminals is obtained.

With this background we can give the definition of a grammar. As mentioned earlier, the definition is due to Noam Chomsky.

3.1.1 DEFINITION OF A GRAMMAR

Definition 3.1 A phrase-structure grammar (or simply a grammar) is (V_N, Σ, P, S), where

 (i) V_N is a finite nonempty set whose elements are called variables,
 (ii) Σ is a finite nonempty set whose elements are called terminals,
 (iii) $V_N \cap \Sigma = \emptyset$,
 (iv) S is a special variable (i.e. an element of V_N) called the start symbol, and
 (v) P is a finite set whose elements are $\alpha \rightarrow \beta$, where α and β are strings on $V_N \cup \Sigma$. α has at least one symbol from V_N. Elements of P are called productions or production rules or rewriting rules.

NOTE: The set of productions is the kernel of grammars and language specification. We observe the following regarding the production rules.

(i) Reverse substitution is not permitted. For example, if $S \to AB$ is a production, then we can replace S by AB, but we cannot replace AB by S.

(ii) No inversion operation is permitted. For example, if $S \to AB$ is a production, it is not necessary that $AB \to S$ is a production.

EXAMPLE 3.1

$$G = (V_N, \Sigma, P, S) \text{ is a grammar}$$

where

$$V_N = \{\langle\text{sentence}\rangle, \langle\text{noun}\rangle, \langle\text{verb}\rangle, \langle\text{adverb}\rangle\}$$

$$\Sigma = \{\text{Ram, Sam, ate, sang, well}\}$$

$$S = \langle\text{sentence}\rangle$$

P consists of the following productions:

$\langle\text{sentence}\rangle \to \langle\text{noun}\rangle \ \langle\text{verb}\rangle$

$\langle\text{sentence}\rangle \to \langle\text{noun}\rangle \ \langle\text{verb}\rangle \ \langle\text{adverb}\rangle$

$\langle\text{noun}\rangle \to \text{Ram}$

$\langle\text{noun}\rangle \to \text{Sam}$

$\langle\text{verb}\rangle \to \text{ate}$

$\langle\text{verb}\rangle \to \text{sang}$

$\langle\text{adverb}\rangle \to \text{well}$

NOTATION: (a) If A is any set, then A^* denotes the set of all strings over A. A^+ denotes $A^* - \{\Lambda\}$, where Λ is the empty string.

(b) $A, B, C, A_1, A_2 \ldots$ denote variables.

(c) $a, b, c, \ldots$ denote terminals.

(d) $x, y, z, w \ldots$ denote strings of terminals.

(e) $\alpha, \beta, r, \ldots$ denote elements of $(V_N \cup \Sigma)^*$.

(f) $X^0 = \Lambda$ for any symbol X in $V_N \cup \Sigma$.

3.1.2 DERIVATIONS AND THE LANGUAGE GENERATED BY A GRAMMAR

Productions are used to derive one string over $V_N \cup \Sigma$ from another string. We give a formal definition of derivation as follows:

Definition 3.2 If $\alpha \to \beta$ is a production in a grammar G and γ, δ are any two strings on $V_N \cup \Sigma$, then we say $\gamma \alpha \delta$ directly derives $\gamma \beta \delta$ in G (we write $\gamma \alpha \delta \underset{G}{\Rightarrow} \gamma \beta \delta$). This process is called one-step derivation. In particular, if $\alpha \to \beta$ is a production, then $\alpha \underset{G}{\Rightarrow} \beta$.

NOTE: If α is a part of a string and $\alpha \to \beta$ is a production, we can replace α by β in that string (without altering the remaining parts). In this case we say the string we started with directly derives the new string.

For example,

$$G = (\{S\}, \{0, 1\}, \{S \rightarrow 0S1, S \rightarrow 01\}, S)$$

has the production $S \rightarrow 0S1$. So, S in $0^4 S 1^4$ can be replaced by $0S1$. The resulting string is $0^4 0S11^4$. Thus we have $0^4 S1^4 \underset{G}{\Rightarrow} 0^4 0S11^4$.

NOTE: $\underset{G}{\Rightarrow}$ induces a relation R on $(V_N \cup \Sigma)^*$, i.e. $\alpha R \beta$ if $\alpha \underset{G}{\Rightarrow} \beta$.

Definition 3.3   If α and β are strings on $V_N \cup \Sigma$, then we say α derives β if $\alpha \underset{G}{\overset{*}{\Rightarrow}} \beta$. Here $\underset{G}{\overset{*}{\Rightarrow}}$ denotes the reflexive-transitive closure of the relation $\underset{G}{\Rightarrow}$ in $(V_N \cup \Sigma)^*$ (refer Section 1.1.5).

NOTE: We can note in particular that $\alpha \underset{G}{\overset{*}{\Rightarrow}} \alpha$. Also, if $\alpha \underset{G}{\overset{*}{\Rightarrow}} \beta$, $\alpha \neq \beta$, then there exist strings $\alpha_1, \alpha_2, \ldots, \alpha_n$, where $n \geq 2$ such that $\alpha = \alpha_1 \underset{G}{\Rightarrow} \alpha_2 \underset{G}{\Rightarrow} \alpha_3 \ldots \underset{G}{\Rightarrow} \alpha_n = \beta$. When $\alpha \underset{G}{\overset{*}{\Rightarrow}} \beta$ in n steps we write $\alpha \underset{G}{\overset{n}{\Rightarrow}} \beta$.

Consider, for example, $G = (\{S\}, \{0, 1\}, \{S \rightarrow 0S1, S \rightarrow 01\}, S)$.

As $S \underset{G}{\Rightarrow} 0S1 \underset{G}{\Rightarrow} 0^2 S 1^2 \underset{G}{\Rightarrow} 0^3 S 1^3, S \underset{G}{\overset{*}{\Rightarrow}} 0^3 S 1^3$. We also have $0^3 S 1^3 \underset{G}{\overset{*}{\Rightarrow}} 0^3 S 1^3$ (as $\alpha \underset{G}{\overset{*}{\Rightarrow}} \alpha$).

Definition 3.4   The language generated by a grammar G (denoted by $L(G)$) is defined as $\{w \in \Sigma^* \mid S \underset{G}{\overset{*}{\Rightarrow}} w\}$. The elements of $L(G)$ are called sentences.

Stated in another way, $L(G)$ is the set of all terminal strings derived from the start symbol S.

Definition 3.5   If $S \underset{G}{\overset{*}{\Rightarrow}} \alpha$, then α is called a sentential form. We can note that elements of $L(G)$ are sentential forms but not vice versa.

Definition 3.6 G_1 and G_2 are equivalent if $L(G_1) = L(G_2)$.

Remarks on Derivation

1. Any derivation involves the application of productions. When the number of times we apply productions is one, we write $\alpha \underset{G}{\Rightarrow} \beta$; when it is more than one, we write $\alpha \underset{G}{\overset{*}{\Rightarrow}} \beta$ (Note: $\alpha \underset{G}{\overset{*}{\Rightarrow}} \alpha$).

2. The string generated by the most recent application of production is called the working string.

3. The derivation of a string is complete when the working string cannot be modified. If the final string does not contain any variable, it is a sentence in the language. If the final string contains a variable, it is a sentential form and in this case the production generator gets 'stuck'.

NOTATION: (a) We write $\alpha \underset{G}{\overset{*}{\Rightarrow}} \beta$ simply as $\alpha \overset{*}{\Rightarrow} \beta$ if G is clear from the context.

(b) If $A \rightarrow \alpha$ is a production where $A \in V_N$, then it is called an A-production.

(c) If $A \rightarrow \alpha_1, A \rightarrow \alpha_2, \ldots, A \rightarrow \alpha_m$ are A-productions, these productions are written as $A \rightarrow \alpha_1 \mid \alpha_2 \mid \ldots \mid \alpha_m$.

We give several examples of grammars and languages generated by them.

EXAMPLE 3.2   If $G = (\{S\}, \{0, 1\}, \{S \to 0S1, S \to \Lambda\}, S)$, find $L(G)$.

SOLUTION   As $S \to \Lambda$ is a production, $S \underset{G}{\Rightarrow} \Lambda$. So Λ is in $L(G)$. Also, for all $n \geq 1$,

$$S \underset{G}{\Rightarrow} 0S1 \underset{G}{\Rightarrow} 0^2 S1^2 \underset{G}{\Rightarrow} \ldots \underset{G}{\Rightarrow} 0^n S1^n \underset{G}{\Rightarrow} 0^n1^n$$

Therefore,

$$0^n1^n \in L(G) \quad \text{for } n \geq 0$$

(Note that in the above derivation $S \to 0S1$ is applied at every step except in the last step. In the last step we apply $S \to \Lambda$). Hence, $\{0^n1^n | n \geq 0\} \subseteq L(G)$.

To show that $L(G) \subseteq \{0^n1^n \mid n \geq 0\}$, we start with w in $L(G)$. The derivation of w starts with S. If $S \to \Lambda$ is applied first, we get Λ. In this case $w = \Lambda$. Otherwise the first production to be applied is $S \to 0S1$. At any stage if we apply $S \to \Lambda$, we get a terminal string. Also, the terminal string is obtained only by applying $S \to \Lambda$. Thus the derivation of w is of the form $S \overset{*}{\underset{G}{\Rightarrow}} 0^n S1^n \underset{G}{\Rightarrow} 0^n1^n$, i.e.

$$L(G) \subseteq \{0^n1^n \mid n \geq 0\}$$

Therefore,

$$L(G) = \{0^n1^n | n \geq 0\}$$

EXAMPLE 3.3   If $G = (\{S\}, \{a\}, \{S \to SS\}, S)$, find the language generated by G.

SOLUTION $L(G) = \emptyset$, since the only production $S \to SS$ in G has no terminal on the right-hand side.

EXAMPLE 3.4   Let $G = (\{S, C\}, \{a, b\}, P, S)$, where P consists of $S \to aCa$, $C \to aCa \mid b$. Find $L(G)$.

SOLUTION $S \Rightarrow aCa \Rightarrow aba$. So $aba \in L(G)$

$$S \Rightarrow aCa \quad \text{(by application of } S \to aCa)$$

$$\overset{*}{\Rightarrow} a^n Ca^n \quad \text{(by application of } C \to aCa \ (n-1) \text{ times)}$$

$$\Rightarrow a^n ba^n \quad \text{(by application of } C \to b)$$

Hence, $a^n ba^n \in L(G)$, where $n \geq 1$. Therefore,

$$\{a^n ba^n | n \geq 1\} \subseteq L(G)$$

As the only S-production is $S \to aCa$, this is the first production we have to apply in the derivation of any terminal string. If we apply $C \to b$, we get aba. Otherwise we have to apply only $C \to aCa$, either once or several times. So we get a^nCa^n with a single variable C. To get a terminal string we have to replace C by b, by applying $C \rightarrow b$. So any derivation is of the form $S \overset{*}{\Rightarrow} a^n ba^n$ with $n \geq 1$. Therefore, $L(G) \subseteq \{a^n ba^n | n \geq 1\}$. Thus, $L(G) = \{a^n ba^n | n \geq 1\}$.

EXERCISE Construct a grammar G so that $L(G) = \{a^n ba^m | n, m \geq 1\}$.

Remark. By applying the convention regarding the notation of variables, terminals and the start symbol, it will be clear from the context whether a symbol denotes a variable or terminal. We can specify a grammar by its productions alone.

EXAMPLE 3.5 If G is $S \rightarrow aS | bS | a | b$, find $L(G)$.

SOLUTION We show that $L(G) = \{a, b\}^+$. As we have only two terminals $a, b, L(G) \subseteq \{a, b\}^*$. All productions are S-productions, and so Λ can be in $L(G)$ only when $S \rightarrow \Lambda$ is a production in the grammar G. Thus,

$$L(G) \subseteq \{a, b\}^* - \{\Lambda\} = \{a, b\}^+$$

To show $\{a, b\}^+ \subseteq L(G)$, consider any string $a_1 a_2 \ldots a_n$, where each a_i is either a or b. The first production in the derivation of $a_1 a_2 \ldots a_n$ is $S \rightarrow aS$ or $S \rightarrow bS$ according as $a_1 = a$ or $a_1 = b$. The subsequent productions are obtained in a similar way. The last production is $S \rightarrow a$ or $S \rightarrow b$ according as $a_n = a$ or $a_n = b$. So $a_1 a_2 \ldots a_n \in L(G)$. Thus we have $L(G) = \{a, b\}^+$.

EXERCISE If G is $S \rightarrow aS | a$, then show that $L(G) = \{a\}^+$.

Some of the following examples illustrate the method of constructing a grammar G generating a given subset of strings over Σ. The difficult part is the construction of productions. We try to define the given set by recursion and then develop productions generating the strings in the given subset of Σ^*.

EXAMPLE 3.6 Let L be the set of all palindromes over $\{a, b\}$. Construct G generating L.

SOLUTION For constructing a grammar G generating the set of all palindromes, we use the recursive definition (given in Section 1.4) to observe the following:

    (i) Λ is a palindrome.
    (ii) a, b are palindromes.
    (iii) If x is a palindrome axa, bxb are palindromes.

So we define P as the set consisting of:

    (i) $S \rightarrow \Lambda$.
    (ii) $S \rightarrow a$ and $S \rightarrow b$.
    (iii) $S \rightarrow aSa$ and $S \rightarrow bSb$.

Let $G = (\{S\}, \{a, b\}, P, S)$. Then

$$S \Rightarrow \Lambda, \quad S \Rightarrow a, \quad S \Rightarrow b.$$

Therefore,

$$\Lambda, a, b, \in L(G)$$

If x is a palindrome of even length, then $x = a_1a_2 \ldots a_ma_m \ldots a_1$, where each a_i is a or b. Then $S \overset{*}{\Rightarrow} a_1a_2 \ldots a_ma_ma_{m-1} \ldots a_1$ by applying $S \to aSa$ or $S \to bSb$. Thus, $x \in L(G)$.

If x is a palindrome of odd length, then $x = a_1a_2 \ldots a_nca_n \ldots a_1$, where a_i's and c are either a or b. So $S \overset{*}{\Rightarrow} a_1 \ldots a_n Sa_n \ldots a_1 \Rightarrow x$ by applying $S \to aSa$, $S \to bSb$ and finally, $S \to a$ or $S \to b$. Thus $x \in L(G)$. This proves $L = L(G)$.

EXAMPLE 3.7   Construct a grammar generating $L = \{wcw^T \mid w \in \{a, b\}^*\}$.

SOLUTION   Let $G = (\{S\}, \{a, b, c\}, P, S)$, where P is defined as $S \to aSa$ $\mid bSb \mid c$. It is easy to see the idea behind the construction. Any string in L is generated by recursion as follows: (a) $c \in L$; (b) if $x \in L$ then $wxw^T \in L$. So, as in the earlier example, we have the productions $S \to aSa \mid bSb \mid c$.

EXAMPLE 3.8   Find a grammar generating $L = \{a^nb^nc^i \mid n \geq 1, i \geq 0\}$.

SOLUTION

$$L = L_1 \cup L_2, \ L_1 = \{a^nb^n \mid n \geq 1\}$$

$$L_2 = \{a^nb^nc^i \mid n \geq 1, i \geq 1\}$$

We construct L_1 by recursion and L_2 by concatenating elements of L_1 and c^i, $i \geq 1$. We define P as the set of the following productions:

$$S \to A, \qquad A \to ab, \qquad A \to aAb, \qquad S \to Sc$$

Let $G = (\{S, A\}, \{a, b, c\}, P, S)$. For $n \geq 1$, $i \geq 0$, we have

$$S \overset{*}{\Rightarrow} Sc^i \Rightarrow Ac^i \overset{*}{\Rightarrow} a^{n-1}Ab^{n-1}c^i \Rightarrow a^{n-1}abb^{n-1}c^i = a^nb^nc^i$$

Thus,

$$\{a^nb^nc^i \mid n \geq 1, i \geq 0\} \subseteq L(G).$$

To prove the reverse inclusion, we note that the only S-productions are $S \to Sc$ and $S \to A$. If we start with $S \to A$, we have to apply $A \Rightarrow a^{n-1}Ab^{n-1} \overset{*}{\Rightarrow} a^nb^n$, and so $a^nb^nc^0 \in L(G)$. If we start with $S \to Sc$, we have to apply $S \to Sc$ repeatedly to get Sc^i. But to get a terminal string, we have to apply $S \to A$. As $A \overset{*}{\Rightarrow} a^nb^n$, the resulting terminal string is $a^nb^nc^i$. Thus we have shown that

$$L(G) \subseteq \{a^nb^nc^i \mid n \geq 1, i \geq 0\}$$

Therefore,

$$L(G) = \{a^nb^nc^i \mid n \geq 1, i \geq 0\}$$

EXAMPLE 3.9   Find a grammar generating $\{a^jb^nc^n \mid n \geq 1, j \geq 0\}$.

SOLUTION   Let $G = (\{S, A\}, \{a, b, c\}, P, S)$, where P consists of $S \to aS$, $S \to A$, $A \to bAc \mid bc$. As in the previous example, we can prove that G is the required grammar.

EXAMPLE 3.10   Let $G = (\{S, A_1\}, \{0, 1, 2\}, P, S)$, where P consists of $S \to 0SA_12$, $S \to 012$, $2A_1 \to A_12$, $1A_1 \to 11$. Show that

$$L(G) = \{0^n 1^n 2^n \mid n \geq 1\}$$

SOLUTION   As $S \to 012$ is a production we have $S \Rightarrow 012$, i.e. $012 \in L(G)$. Also,

$$S \overset{*}{\Rightarrow} 0^{n-1} S(A_1 2)^{n-1} \quad \text{by applying } S \to 0SA_12 \quad (n-1) \text{ times}$$

$$\Rightarrow 0^n 12 (A_1 2)^{n-1} \quad \text{by applying } S \to 012$$

$$\overset{*}{\Rightarrow} 0^n 1 A_1^{n-1} 2^n \quad \text{by applying } 2A_1 \to A_12 \text{ several times}$$

$$\overset{*}{\Rightarrow} 0^n 1^n 2^n \quad \text{by applying } 1A_1 \to 11 \quad (n-1) \text{ times}$$

Therefore,

$$0^n 1^n 2^n \in L(G) \quad \text{for all } n \geq 1.$$

To prove that $L(G) \subseteq \{0^n 1^n 2^n \mid n \geq 1\}$, we proceed as follows: If the first production we apply is $S \to 012$, we get 012. Otherwise we have to apply $S \to 0SA_12$ once or several times to get $0^{n-1} S(A_1 2)^{n-1}$. To eliminate S we have to apply $S \to 012$. Thus we arrive at a sentential form $0^n 12 (A_1 2)^{n-1}$. To eliminate the variable A_1, we have to apply $2A_1 \to A_12$ or $1A_1 \to 11$. $2A_1 \to A_12$ interchanges 2 and A_1. Only $1A_1 \to 11$ eliminates A_1. The sentential form we have obtained is $0^n 12 A_1 2 A_1 2 \ldots A_1 2$. If we use $1A_1 \to 11$ before taking all 2's to the right, we will get 12 in the middle of the string. A_1's appearing subsequently cannot be eliminated. So we have to bring all 2's to the right by applying $2A_1 \to A_12$ several times. Then we can apply $1A_1 \to 11$ repeatedly and get $0^n 1^n 2^n$ (as derived in the first part of the proof). Thus

$$L(G) \subseteq \{0^n 1^n 2^n \mid n \geq 1\}$$

This shows that $L(G) = \{0^n 1^n 2^n \mid n \geq 1\}$.

In the next example we construct a grammar generating

$$\{a^n b^n c^n \mid n \geq 1\}$$

EXAMPLE 3.11   Construct a grammar G generating $\{a^n b^n c^n \mid n \geq 1\}$.

SOLUTION   Let $L = \{a^n b^n c^n \mid n \geq 1\}$. We try to construct L by recursion. We already know how to construct $a^n b^n$ recursively.

As it is difficult to construct $a^n b^n c^n$ recursively, we do it in two stages: (i) we construct $a^n \alpha^n$, and (ii) we convert α^n into $b^n c^n$. For stage (i), we can have the following productions $S \to aS\alpha \mid a\alpha$. A natural choice for α (to execute stage (ii)) is bc. But converting $(bc)^n$ into $b^n c^n$ is not possible as $(bc)^n$ has no variables. So we can take $\alpha = BC$, where B and C are variables. To bring B's together we introduce $CB \to BC$. We introduce some more productions to convert B's into b's and C's into c's. So we define G as follows: Let $G = (\{S, B, C\}, \{a, b, c\}, P, S)$, where P consists of $S \to aSBC \mid aBC$, $CB \to BC$, $aB \to ab$, $bB \to bb$, $bC \to bc$, $cC \to cc$. $S \Rightarrow aBC \Rightarrow abC \Rightarrow abc$. Thus, $abc \in L(G)$. Also,

$$S \overset{*}{\Rightarrow} a^{n-1} S(BC)^{n-1} \qquad \text{by applying } S \to aSBc \quad (n-1) \text{ times}$$

$$\Rightarrow a^{n-1} aBC(BC)^{n-1} \qquad \text{by applying } S \to aBC$$

$$\overset{*}{\Rightarrow} a^n B^n C^n \qquad \text{by applying } CB \to BC \text{ several times}$$
$$\text{since } CB \to BC \text{ interchanges } B \text{ and } C$$

$$\Rightarrow a^{n-1} abB^{n-1} C^n \qquad \text{by applying } aB \to ab \text{ once}$$

$$\overset{*}{\Rightarrow} a^n b^n C^n \qquad \text{by applying } bB \to bb \text{ several times}$$

$$\Rightarrow a^n b^{n-1} bcC^{n-1} \qquad \text{by applying } bC \to bc \text{ once}$$

$$\Rightarrow a^n b^n c^n \qquad \text{by applying } cC \to cc \text{ several times}$$

Therefore,

$$L(G) \subseteq \{a^n b^n c^n \mid n \geq 1\}$$

To show that $\{a^n b^n c^n \mid n \geq 1\} \subseteq L(G)$, it is enough to prove that the only way to arrive at a terminal string is to proceed as above in deriving $a^n b^n c^n$ $(n \geq 1)$.

To start with, we have to apply only S-production. If we apply $S \to aBC$, first we get abc. Otherwise we have to apply $S \to aSBC$ once or several times and get the sentential form $a^{n-1} S(BC)^{n-1}$. At this stage the only production we can apply is $S \to aBC$, and the resulting string is $a^n (BC)^n$.

In the derivation of $a^n b^n c^n$, we converted all B's into b's and only then converted C's into c's. We show that this is the only way of arriving at a terminal string.

$a^n (BC)^n$ is a string of terminals followed by a string of variables. The productions we can apply to $a^n (BC)^n$ are either $CB \to BC$ or one of $aB \to ab$, $bB \to bb$, $bC \to bc$, $cC \to cc$. By application of any one of these productions we get a sentential form which is a string of terminals followed by a string of variables. Suppose a C is converted before converting all B's. Then we have $a^n (BC)^n \overset{*}{\Rightarrow} a^n b^i c\alpha$, where $i < n$ and α is a string of B's and C's containing at least one B. In $a^n b^i c\alpha$, variables appear only in α. As c appears just before α, the only production we can apply is $cC \to cc$. If α starts with B, we cannot proceed. Otherwise we apply $cC \to cc$ repeatedly until we obtain the string of the form $a^n b^i c^j B\alpha'$. But the only productions involving B are $aB \to ab$ and $bB \to bb$. As B is preceded by c in $a^n b^i c^j B\alpha'$, we cannot convert B, and so we cannot get a terminal string. So $L(G) \subseteq \{a^n b^n c^n \mid n \geq 1\}$. Thus we have proved that

$$L(G) = \{a^n b^n c^n \mid n \geq 1\}$$

EXAMPLE 3.12   Construct a grammar G generating $\{xx \mid x \in \{a, b\}^*\}$.

SOLUTION   We construct G as follows:

$$G = (\{S, S_1, S_2, S_3, A, B\}, \{a, b\}, P, S),$$

where P consists of

$$P_1: S \to S_1S_2S_3$$

$$P_2, P_3: S_1S_2 \to aS_1A, \qquad S_1S_2 \to bS_1B$$

$$P_4, P_5: AS_3 \to S_2aS_3, \qquad BS_3 \to S_2bS_3$$

$$P_6, P_7, P_8, P_9: Aa \to aA, \qquad Ab \to bA, \qquad Ba \to aB, \qquad Bb \to bB$$

$$P_{10}, P_{11}: aS_2 \to S_2a, \qquad bS_2 \to S_2b$$

$$P_{12}, P_{13}: S_1S_2 \to \Lambda, \qquad S_3 \to \Lambda$$

Remarks: The following remarks give us an idea about the construction of productions P_1–P_{13}.

1. P_1 is the only S-production.
2. Using $S_1S_2 \to aS_1A$, we can add terminal a to the left of S_1 and variable A to the right. A is used to make us remember that we have added the terminal a to the left of S_1. Using $AS_3 \to S_2aS_3$, we add a to the right of S_2.
3. Using $S_1S_2 \to bS_1B$, we add b to the left of S_1 and variable B to the right. Using $BS_3 \to S_2bS_3$ we add b to the right of S_2.
4. S_2 acts as a centre-marker.
5. We can add terminals only by using $P_2 - P_5$.
6. $P_6 - P_9$ simply interchange symbols. They push A or B to the right. This enables us to place A or B to the left of S_3. (Only then we can apply P_4 or P_5).
7. $S_1S_2 \to \Lambda$, $S_3 \to \Lambda$ are used to completely eliminate S_1, S_2, S_3.
8. P_{10}, P_{11} are used to push S_2 to the left. This enables us to get S_2 to the right of S_1 (so that we can apply P_{12}).

Let $L = \{xx | x \in \{a, b\}^*\}$. We first prove that $L \subseteq L(G)$. So we have

$$S \Rightarrow S_1S_2S_3 \Rightarrow aS_1AS_3 \Rightarrow aS_1S_2aS_3 \qquad (3.1)$$

or

$$S \Rightarrow S_1S_2S_3 \Rightarrow bS_1BS_3 \Rightarrow bS_1S_2bS_3 \qquad (3.2)$$

Let us start with xx with $x \in \{ab\}^*$. We can apply (3.1) or (3.2), depending on the first symbol of x. If the first two symbols in x are ab (other cases are similar), we have $S \overset{*}{\Rightarrow} aS_1\underline{S_2aS_3} \Rightarrow abS_1\underline{BaS_3} \Rightarrow abS_1a\underline{BS_3} \Rightarrow abS_1\underline{aS_2}bS_3 \Rightarrow abS_1S_2abS_3$. Repeating the construction for every symbol in x, we get $xS_1S_2xS_3$. On application of P_{12} and P_{13}, we get $S \overset{*}{\Rightarrow} xS_1S_2xS_3 \overset{*}{\Rightarrow} x\Lambda x\Lambda = xx$. Thus, $L \subseteq L(G)$.

To prove that $L(G) \subseteq L$, we note that the first three steps in any derivation of $L(G)$ are given by (3.1) or (3.2). Thus in any derivation (except $S \to \Lambda$), we get $aS_1S_2aS_3$ or $bS_1S_2bS_3$ as a sentential form.

We can discuss the possible ways of reducing $aS_1S_2aS_3$ (the other case is similar) to a terminal string. The first production we can apply to $aS_1S_2aS_3$ is one of $S_1S_2 \to \Lambda$, $S_3 \to \Lambda$, $S_1S_2 \to aS_1A$, $S_1S_2 \to bS_1B$.

Case 1 We apply $S_1S_2 \rightarrow \Lambda$ to $aS_1S_2aS_3$. In this case we get $a \Lambda aS_3$. As the productions involving S_3 on the left are P_4, P_5 or P_{13}, we have to apply only $S_3 \rightarrow \Lambda$ to aaS_3 and get $aa \in L$.

Case 2 We apply $S_3 \rightarrow \Lambda$ to $aS_1S_2aS_3$. In this case we get $aS_1S_2 a\Lambda$. If we apply $S_1S_2 \rightarrow \Lambda$, we get $a\Lambda a\Lambda = aa \in L$; or we can apply $S_1S_2 \rightarrow aS_1A$ to aS_1S_2a to get aaS_1Aa. In the latter case, we can apply only $Aa \rightarrow aA$ to aaS_1Aa. The resulting string is aaS_1aA which cannot be reduced further.

From cases 1 and 2 we see that either we have to apply both P_{12} and P_{13} or neither of them.

Case 3 In this case we apply $S_1S_2 \rightarrow aS_1A$ or $S_1S_2 \rightarrow bS_1B$. If we apply $S_1S_2 \rightarrow aS_1A$ to $aS_1S_2aS_3$ we get aaS_1AaS_3. By the nature of productions we have to follow only $aaS_1AaS_3 \Rightarrow aaS_1aAS_3 \Rightarrow a^2S_1aS_2aS_3 \Rightarrow a^2S_1S_2a^2S_3$. If we apply $S_1S_2 \rightarrow bS_1B$, we get $abS_1S_2abS_3$. Thus the effect of applying $S_1S_2 \rightarrow aS_1A$ is to add a to the left of S_1S_2 and S_3.

If we apply $S_1S_2 \rightarrow \Lambda$, $S_3 \rightarrow \Lambda$ (By cases 1 and 2 we have to apply both) we get $abab \in L$. Otherwise, by application of P_2 or P_3, we add the same terminal symbol to the left of S_1S_2 and S_3. The resulting string is of the form $xS_1S_2xS_3$. Ultimately, we have to apply P_{12} and P_{13} and get $x\Lambda x\Lambda = xx \in L$. So $L(G) \subseteq L$. Hence, $L(G) = L$.

EXAMPLE 3.13 Let $G = (\{S, A_1, A_2\}, \{a, b\}, P, S)$, where P consists of $S \rightarrow aA_1A_2a$, $A_1 \rightarrow baA_1A_2b$, $A_2 \rightarrow A_1ab$, $aA_1 \rightarrow baa$, $bA_2b \rightarrow abab$. Test whether $w = baabbabaaabbaba$ is in $L(G)$.

SOLUTION We have to start with an S-Production. At every stage we apply a suitable production which is likely to derive w. In this example, we underline the substring to be replaced by the use of a production.

$$S \Rightarrow a\underline{A_1}A_2a$$
$$\Rightarrow baa\underline{A_2}a$$
$$\Rightarrow baa\underline{A_1}aba$$
$$\Rightarrow baaba\underline{A_1}A_2baba$$
$$\Rightarrow baabbaa\underline{A_2}baba$$
$$\Rightarrow baabbaa\underline{A_1}abbaba$$
$$\Rightarrow baabbabaaabbaba = w$$

Therefore,

$$w \in L(G)$$

EXAMPLE 3.14 If the grammar G given by the productions $S \rightarrow aSa \mid bSb \mid aa \mid bb \mid \Lambda$, show that (a) $L(G)$ has no strings of odd length, (b) any string in $L(G)$ is of length $2n$, $n \geq 0$, and (c) the number of strings of length $2n$ is 2^n.

SOLUTION On application of any production (except $S \rightarrow \Lambda$), a variable is replaced by two terminals and at the most one variable. So, every step in any derivation increases the number of terminals by 2 except that involving $S \to \Lambda$. Thus, we have proved (a) and (b).

To prove (c), consider any string w of length $2n$. Then it is of the form $a_1 a_2 \ldots a_n a_n \ldots a_1$ involving n 'parameters' $a_1, a_2, \ldots, a_n$. Each a_i can be either a or b. So the number of such strings is 2^n. This proves (c).

3.2 CHOMSKY CLASSIFICATION OF LANGUAGES

In the definition of a grammar (V_N, Σ, P, S), V_N and Σ are sets of symbols and $S \in V_N$. So if we want to classify grammars, we have to do it only by considering the form of productions. Chomsky classified the grammars into four types in terms of productions (types 0–3).

A type 0 grammar is any phrase structure grammar without any restrictions. (All the grammars we have considered are type 0 grammars.)

To define the other types we need a definition.

In a production of the form $\phi A \psi \to \phi \alpha \psi$, where A is a variable, ϕ is called the left context ψ, the right context, and $\phi \alpha \psi$ the replacement string.

EXAMPLE 3.15   (a) In $ab\underline{A}bcd \to ab\underline{AB}bcd$, ab is the left context, bcd is the right context, $\alpha = AB$.

(b) In $A\underline{C} \to A$, A is the left context, Λ is the right context. $\alpha = \Lambda$. The production simply erases C when the left context is A and the right context is Λ.

(c) For $C \to \Lambda$, the left and right contexts are Λ. $\alpha = \Lambda$. The production simply erases C in any context.

A production without any restrictions is called a type 0 production.

A production of the form $\phi A \psi \to \phi \alpha \psi$ is called a type 1 production if $\alpha \neq \Lambda$. In type 1 productions erasing of A is not permitted.

EXAMPLE 3.16   (a) $a\underline{A}bcD \to a\underline{bcD}bcD$ is a type 1 production. a, bcD are the left context and right context, respectively. A is replaced by $bcD \neq \Lambda$.

(b) $A\underline{B} \to A\underline{bBc}$ is a type 1 production. The left context is A, right context is Λ.

(c) $A \to abA$ is a type 1 production. Here both the left and right contexts are Λ.

Definition 3.7   A grammar is called type 1 or context-sensitive or context-dependent if all its productions are type 1 productions. The production $S \to \Lambda$ is also allowed in a type 1 grammar, but in this case S does not appear on the right-hand side of any production.

Definition 3.8   The language generated by a type 1 grammar is called a type 1 or context-sensitive language.

NOTE: In a context-sensitive grammar G, we allow $S \to \Lambda$ for including Λ in $L(G)$. Apart from $S \to \Lambda$, all the other productions do not decrease the length of the working string.

A type 1 production $\phi A \psi \to \phi \alpha \psi$ does not increase the length of the working string. In other words, $|\phi A \psi| \le |\phi \alpha \psi|$ as $\alpha \ne \Lambda$. But if $\alpha \to \beta$ is a production such that $|\alpha| \le |\beta|$, then it need not be a type 1 production. For example, $BC \to CB$ is not of type 1. We prove that such productions can be replaced by a set of type 1 productions (Theorem 3.2).

Theorem 3.1 Let G be a type .0 grammar. Then we can find an equivalent grammar G_1 in which each production is *either* of the form $\alpha \to \beta$, where α and β are strings of variables only, or of the form $A \to a$, where A is a variable and a is a terminal. G_1 is of type 1, type 2 or type 3 according as G is of type 1, type 2 or type 3.

PROOF   We construct G_1 as follows: For constructing productions of G_1, consider a production $\alpha \to \beta$ in G, where α or β has some terminals. In both α and β we replace every terminal by a new variable C_a and get α' and β'. Thus, corresponding to every $\alpha \to \beta$, where α or β contains some terminal, we construct $\alpha' \to \beta'$ and productions of the form $C_a \to a$ for every terminal a appearing in α or β. The construction is performed for every such $\alpha \to \beta$. The productions for G_1 are the new productions we have obtained through the above construction. For G_1 the variables are the variables of G together with the new variables (of the form C_a). The terminals and the start symbol of G_1 are those of G. G_1 satisfies the required conditions and is equivalent to G. So $L(G) = L(G_1)$. ∎

Definition 3.9 A grammar $G = (V_N, \Sigma, P, S)$ is monotonic (or length-increasing) if every production in P is of the form $\alpha \to \beta$ with $|\alpha| \le |\beta|$ or $S \to \Lambda$. In the second case, S does not appear on the right-hand side of any production in P.

Theorem 3.2 Every monotonic grammar G is equivalent to a type 1 grammar.

PROOF   We apply Theorem 3.1 to get an equivalent grammar G_1. We construct G' equivalent to grammar G_1 as follows: Consider a production $A_1 A_2 \dots A_m \to B_1 B_2 \dots B_n$ with $n \ge m$ in G_1. If $m = 1$, then the above production is of type 1 (with left and right context being Λ). Suppose $m \ge 2$. Corresponding to $A_1 A_2 \dots A_m \to B_1 B_2 \dots B_n$, we construct the following type 1 productions introducing new variables $C_1, C_2, \dots, C_m$.

$$A_1 A_2 \dots A_m \to C_1 A_2 \dots A_m,$$

$$C_1 A_2 \dots A_m \to C_1 C_2 A_3 \dots A_m,$$

$$C_1 C_2 A_3 \dots A_m \to C_1 C_2 C_3 A_4 \dots A_m, \dots$$

$$C_1 C_2 \dots C_{m-1} A_m \to C_1 C_2 \dots C_m B_{m+1} B_{m+2} \dots B_n$$

$$C_1 C_2 \dots C_m B_{m+1} \dots B_n \to B_1 C_2 \dots C_m B_{m+1} \dots B_n,$$

$$B_1 C_2 C_3 \dots B_n \to B_1 B_2 C_3 \dots B_n, \dots$$

$$B_1 B_2 \dots C_m B_{m+1} \dots B_n \to B_1 B_2 \dots B_m \dots B_n$$

The above construction can be explained as follows: $A_1A_2 \ldots A_m \rightarrow B_1B_2 \ldots B_n$ is not of type 1 as we replace more than one symbol on L.H.S. In the chain of productions we have constructed, we replace A_1 by C_1, A_2 by C_2 ..., A_m by $C_mB_{m+1} \ldots B_n$. Afterwards we start replacing C_1 by B_1, C_2 by B_2, etc. As we replace only one variable at a time, these productions are of type 1.

We repeat the construction for every production in G_1 which is not of type 1. For the new grammar G', the variables are the variables of G_1 together with the new variables. The productions of G' are the new type 1 productions obtained through the above construction. The terminals and the start symbol of G' are those of G_1.

G' is context-sensitive and from the construction it is easy to see that $L(G') = L(G_1) = L(G)$. ∎

Definition 3.10 A type 2 production is a production of the form $A \rightarrow \alpha$, where $A \in V_N$ and $\alpha \in (V_N \cup \Sigma)^*$. In other words, the L.H.S. has no left context or right context. For example, $S \rightarrow Aa, A \rightarrow a, B \rightarrow abc, A \rightarrow \Lambda$ are type 2 productions.

Definition 3.11 A grammar is called a type 2 grammar if it contains only type 2 productions. It is also called a context-free grammar (as A can be replaced by α in any context). A language generated by a context-free grammar is called a type 2 language or a context-free language.

Definition 3.12 A production of the form $A \rightarrow a$ or $A \rightarrow aB$, where $A, B \in V_N$ and $a \in \Sigma$, is called a type 3 production.

Definition 3.13 A grammar is called a type 3 or regular grammar if all its productions are type 3 productions. A production $S \rightarrow \Lambda$ is allowed in type 3 grammar, but in this case S does not appear on the right-hand side of any production.

EXAMPLE 3.17 Find the highest type number which can be applied to the following grammars:

(a) $S \rightarrow Aa$, $A \rightarrow c \,|\, Ba$, $B \rightarrow abc$.
(b) $S \rightarrow ASB \,|\, d$, $A \rightarrow aA$.
(c) $S \rightarrow aS \,|\, ab$.

SOLUTION   (a) $S \rightarrow Aa, A \rightarrow Ba, B \rightarrow abc$ are type 2 and $A \rightarrow c$ is type 3. So the highest type number is 2.

(b) $S \rightarrow ASB$ is type 2, $S \rightarrow d, A \rightarrow aA$ are type 3. Therefore, the highest type number is 2.

(c) $S \rightarrow aS$ is type 3 and $S \rightarrow ab$ is type 2. Hence the highest type number is 2.

3.3 LANGUAGES AND THEIR RELATION

In this section we discuss the relation between the classes of languages we have defined under Chomsky classification.

Let $\mathscr{L}_0$, $\mathscr{L}_{csl}$, $\mathscr{L}_{cfl}$ and $\mathscr{L}_{rl}$ denote the family of type 0 languages, context-sensitive languages, context-free languages and regular languages, respectively.

Property 1 From the definition, it follows that $\mathscr{L}_{rl} \subseteq \mathscr{L}_{cfl}, \mathscr{L}_{csl} \subseteq \mathscr{L}_0, \mathscr{L}_{cfl} \subseteq \mathscr{L}_0$.

Property 2 $\mathscr{L}_{cfl} \subseteq \mathscr{L}_{csl}$. The inclusion relation is not immediate as we allow $A \rightarrow \Lambda$ in context-free grammars even when $A \neq S$, but not in context-sensitive grammars (we allow only $S \rightarrow \Lambda$ in context-sensitive grammars). In Chapter 5 we prove that a context-free grammar G with productions of the form $A \rightarrow \Lambda$ is equivalent to a context-free grammar G_1 which has no productions of the form $A \rightarrow \Lambda$ (except $S \rightarrow \Lambda$). Also, when G_1 has $S \rightarrow \Lambda$, S does not appear on the right-hand side of any production. So G_1 is context-sensitive. This proves $\mathscr{L}_{cfl} \subseteq \mathscr{L}_{csl}$.

Property 3 $\mathscr{L}_{rl} \subseteq \mathscr{L}_{cfl} \subseteq \mathscr{L}_{csl} \subseteq \mathscr{L}_0$. This follows from properties 1 and 2.

Property 4 $\mathscr{L}_{rl} \subset \mathscr{L}_{cfl} \subset \mathscr{L}_{csl} \subset \mathscr{L}_0$.

In Chapter 4 we shall prove that $\mathscr{L}_{rl} \subset_{\neq} \mathscr{L}_{cfl}$. In Chapter 5 we shall prove that $\mathscr{L}_{cfl} \subset_{\neq} \mathscr{L}_{csl}$. In Section 7.7 we shall establish that $\mathscr{L}_{csl} \subset_{\neq} \mathscr{L}_0$.

Remarks: 1. The grammars given in Examples 3.1–3.4 and 3.6–3.9 are context-free but not regular. The grammar given in Example 3.5 is regular. The grammars given in Examples 3.10 and 3.11 are not context-sensitive as we have productions of the form $2A_1 \rightarrow A_1 2$, $CB \rightarrow BC$ which are not type 1 rules. But they are equivalent to context-sensitive grammar by Theorem 3.2.

2. Two grammars of different types may generate the same language. For example, consider the regular grammar G given in Example 3.5. It generates $\{a, b\}^+$. Let G' be given by $S \rightarrow SS|aS|bS|a|b$. Then $L(G') = L(G)$ as the production $S \rightarrow aS|bS|a|b$ is in G also and $S \rightarrow SS$ does not generate any more string.

3. The type of a given grammar is easily decided by the nature of productions. But to decide the type of a given subset of Σ^* is more difficult. By Remark 2, the same set of strings may be generated by a grammar of higher type. To prove that a given language is not regular or context-free, we need powerful theorems like Pumping Lemma.

3.4 RECURSIVE AND RECURSIVELY ENUMERABLE SETS

The results given in this section will be used to prove $\mathscr{L}_{csl} \subset \mathscr{L}_0$ in Section 7.7. For defining recursive sets, we need the definition of a procedure and an algorithm.

A *procedure* for solving a problem is a finite sequence of instructions which can be mechanically carried out given any input.

An *algorithm* is a procedure that terminates after a finite number of steps for any input.

Definition 3.14 A set X is recursive if we have an algorithm to determine whether a given element belongs to X or not.

Definition 3.15 A recursively enumerable set is a set X for which we have a procedure to determine whether a given element belongs to X or not.

It is clear that a recursive set is recursively enumerable.

Theorem 3.3 A context-sensitive language is recursive.

PROOF Let $G = (V_N, \Sigma, P, S)$ and $w \in \Sigma^*$. We have to construct an algorithm to test whether $w \in L(G)$ or not. If $w = \Lambda$, then $w \in L(G)$ iff $S \rightarrow \Lambda$ is in P. As there are only finite number of productions in P, we have to test whether $S \rightarrow \Lambda$ is in P or not.

Let $|w| = n \geq 1$. The algorithm is based on the construction of a sequence $\{W_i\}$ of subsets of $(V_N \cup \Sigma)^*$. W_i is simply the set of all sentential forms of length less than or equal to n derivable in atmost i steps. The construction is done recursively as follows:

    (i) $W_0 = \{S\}$.
    (ii) $W_{i+1} = W_i \cup \{\beta \in (V_N \cup \Sigma)^* | \text{there exists } \alpha \text{ in } W_i \text{ such that } \alpha \Rightarrow \beta \text{ and } |\beta| \leq n\}$.
    W_i's satisfy the following:
    (iii) $W_i \subseteq W_{i+1}$ for all $i \geq 0$.
    (iv) There exists k such that $W_k = W_{k+1}$.
    (v) If k is the smallest integer such that $W_k = W_{k+1}$, then $W_k = \{\alpha \in (V_N \cup \Sigma)^* | S \stackrel{*}{\Rightarrow} \alpha \text{ and } |\alpha| \leq n\}$.

Point (iii) follows from point (ii). To prove (iv), we consider the number N of strings over $V_N \cup \Sigma$ of length less than or equal to n. If $|V_N \cup \Sigma| = m$, then $N = 1 + m + m^2 + \ldots + m^n$ since m^i is the number of strings of length i over $V_N \cup \Sigma$, i.e., $N = (m^{n+1} - 1)/(m - 1)$, and N is fixed as it depends only on n and m. As any string in W_i is of length atmost n, $|W_i| \leq N$. Therefore, $W_k = W_{k+1}$ for some $k \leq N$. This proves point (iv).

From (ii) it follows that $W_k = W_{k+1}$ implies $W_{k+1} = W_{k+2}$.

$$\{\alpha \in (V_N \cup \Sigma)^* | S \stackrel{*}{\Rightarrow} \alpha, |\alpha| \leq n\} = W_1 \cup W_2 \cup \ldots \cup W_k \cup W_{k+1} \ldots$$
$$= W_1 \cup W_2 \cup \ldots \cup W_k$$
$$= W_k \text{ from (iii)}$$

This proves (v).

From (v) it follows that $w \in L(G)$ (i.e. $S \stackrel{*}{\Rightarrow} w$) if and only if $w \in W_k$. Also, $W_1, W_2, \ldots, W_k$ can be constructed in a finite number of steps. We give the required algorithm as follows:

Algorithm to test whether $w \in L(G)$. 1. Construct $W_1, W_2, \ldots$ using (i) and (ii). We terminate the construction when $W_{k+1} = W_k$ for the first time.

    2. If $w \in W_k$ then $w \in L(G)$. Otherwise, $w \notin L(G)$. (As $|W_k| \leq N$, testing whether w is in W_k requires atmost N steps). ∎

EXAMPLE 3.18 Consider the grammar G given by $S \rightarrow 0SA_12$, $S \rightarrow 012$, $2A_1 \rightarrow A_12$, $1A_1 \rightarrow 11$. Test whether (a) $00112 \in L(G)$ and (b) $001122 \in L(G)$.

SOLUTION (a) To test whether $w = 00112 \in L(G)$, we construct the sets W_0, W_1, W_2 etc. $|w| = 5$.

$$W_0 = \{S\}$$

$$W_1 = \{012, S, 0SA_12\}$$

$$W_2 = \{012, S, 0SA_12\}$$

As $W_2 = W_1$, we terminate. (Although $0SA_12 \Rightarrow 0012A_12$, we cannot include $0012A_12$ in W_1 as its length is > 5). $00112 \notin W_1$. Hence $00112 \notin L(G)$.

(b) To test whether $w = 001122 \in L(G)$. Here, $|w| = 6$. We construct W_0, W_1, W_2, etc.

$$W_0 = \{S\}$$

$$W_1 = \{012, S, 0SA_12\}$$

$$W_2 = \{012, S, 0SA_12, 0012A_12\}$$

$$W_3 = \{012, S, 0SA_12, 0012A_12, 001A_122\}$$

$$W_4 = \{012, S, 0SA_12, 0012A_12, 001A_122, 001122\}$$

$$W_5 = \{012, S, 0SA_12, 0012A_12, 001A_122, 001122\}$$

As $W_5 = W_4$, we terminate. Then $001122 \in W_4$. Thus $001122 \in L(G)$.

The following theorem is of theoretical interest, and shows that there exists a recursive set over $\{0, 1\}$ which is not a context sensitive-language. The proof is by diagonalisation method which is used quite often in Set theory.

Theorem 3.4   There exists a recursive set which is not a context-sensitive language over $\{0, 1\}$.

PROOF   Let $\Sigma = \{0, 1\}$. We write the elements of Σ^* as a sequence. (i.e. the elements of Σ^* are enumerated as the first element, second element, etc.) For example, one such way of writing is $\Lambda, 0, 1, 00, 01, 10, 11, 000, \ldots$. In this case, 010 will be the 10th element.

As every grammar is defined in terms of finite alphabet set and a finite set of productions, we can also write all context-sensitive grammars over Σ as a sequence, say $G_1, G_2, \ldots$

We define $X = \{w_i \in \Sigma^* \mid w_i \notin L(G_i)\}$. We can show that X is recursive. If $w \in \Sigma^*$, then we can find i such that $w = w_i$. This can be done in a finite number of steps (depending on $|w|$). For example, if $w = 0100$, then $w = w_{20}$. As G_{20} is context-sensitive, we have an algorithm to test whether $w = w_{20} \in L(G_{20})$ by Theorem 3.3. So X is recursive.

We prove by contradiction that X is not a context-sensitive language. If it is so, then $X = L(G_n)$ for some n. Consider w_n (the nth element in Σ^*). By definition of X, $w_n \in X$ implies $w_n \notin L(G_n)$. This contradicts $X = L(G_n)$. $w_n \notin X$ implies $w_n \in L(G_n)$ and once again, this contradicts $X = L(G_n)$. Thus, $X \neq L(G_n)$ for any n, i.e., X is not a context-sensitive language. ∎

3.5   OPERATIONS ON LANGUAGES

We consider the effect of applying set operations on $\mathscr{L}_0$, $\mathscr{L}_{csl}$, $\mathscr{L}_{cfl}$, $\mathscr{L}_{rl}$. Let A and B be any two sets of strings. The concatenation AB of A and B is defined by $AB = \{uv \mid u \in A, v \in B\}$. (Here, uv is the concatenation of the strings u and v.)

We define A^1 as A and A^{n+1} as $A^n A$ for all $n \geq 1$.

The transpose set A^T of A is defined by

$$A^T = \{u^T \mid u \in A\}$$

Theorem 3.5   Each of the classes $\mathscr{L}_0$, $\mathscr{L}_{csl}$, $\mathscr{L}_{cfl}$, $\mathscr{L}_{rl}$ is closed under union.

PROOF   Let L_1 and L_2 be two languages of the same type i. We can apply Theorem 3.1 to get grammars $G_1 = (V'_N, \Sigma_1, P_1, S_1)$ and $G_2 = (V''_N, \Sigma_2, P_2, S_2)$ of type i generating L_1 and L_2, respectively. So any production in G_1 or G_2 is either $\alpha \rightarrow \beta$, where α, β contain only variables or $A \rightarrow a$, where $A \in V_N$, $a \in \Sigma$.

We can further assume that $V'_N \cap V''_N = \emptyset$ (This is achieved by renaming the variables of V''_N if they occur in V'_N.)

Define a new grammar G_u as follows:

$$G_u = (V'_N \cup V''_N \cup \{S\}, \Sigma_1 \cup \Sigma_2, P_u, S)$$

where S is a new symbol, i.e., $S \notin V'_N \cup V''_N$.

$$P_u = P_1 \cup P_2 \cup \{S \rightarrow S_1, S \rightarrow S_2\}$$

We prove $L(G_u) = L_1 \cup L_2$ as follows: If $w \in L_1 \cup L_2$, then $S_1 \overset{*}{\underset{G_1}{\Rightarrow}} w$ or $S_2 \overset{*}{\underset{G_2}{\Rightarrow}} w$. Therefore,

$$S \underset{G_u}{\Rightarrow} S_1 \overset{*}{\underset{G_u}{\Rightarrow}} w \text{ or } S \underset{G_u}{\Rightarrow} S_2 \overset{*}{\underset{G_u}{\Rightarrow}} w, \text{ i.e. } w \in L(G_u)$$

Thus $L_1 \cup L_2 \subseteq L(G_u)$.

To prove that $L(G_u) \subseteq L_1 \cup L_2$, consider a derivation of w. The first step should be $S \Rightarrow S_1$ or $S \Rightarrow S_2$. If $S \Rightarrow S_1$ is the first step, in the subsequent steps S_1 is changed. As $V'_N \cap V''_N = \emptyset$, these steps should involve only variables of V'_N and the productions we apply are in P_1. So $S \overset{*}{\underset{G_1}{\Rightarrow}} w$. Similarly, if the first step is $S \Rightarrow S_2$, then $S \overset{*}{\underset{G_2}{\Rightarrow}} S_2 \overset{*}{\underset{G_2}{\Rightarrow}} w$. Thus, $L(G_u) = L_1 \cup L_2$. Also, $L(G_u)$ is of type 0 or type 2 according as L_1 and L_2 are of type 0 or type 2. If Λ is not in $L_1 \cup L_2$, then $L(G_u)$ is of type 3 or type 1 according as L_1 and L_2 are of type 1 or type 3.

Suppose $\Lambda \in L_1$. In this case, define

$$G_u = (V'_N \cup V''_N \cup \{S, S'\}, \Sigma_1 \cup \Sigma_2, P_u, S')$$

where (a) S' is a new symbol, i.e. $S' \notin V'_N \cup V''_N \cup \{S\}$, and (b) $P_u = P_1 \cup P_2 \cup \{S' \rightarrow S, S \rightarrow S_1, S \rightarrow S_2\}$. So, $L(G_u)$ is of type 1 or type 3 according as L_1 and L_2 are of type 1 or type 3. When $\Lambda \in L_2$, the proof is similar.   ∎

Theorem 3.6   Each of the classes $\mathscr{L}_0$, $\mathscr{L}_{csl}$, $\mathscr{L}_{cfl}$, $\mathscr{L}_{rl}$ is closed under concatenation.

PROOF Let L_1 and L_2 be two languages of type i. Then, as in Theorem 3.5, we get $G_1 = (V'_N, \Sigma_1, P_1, S_1)$ and $G_2 = (V''_N, \Sigma_2, P_2, S_2)$ of the same type i. We have to prove that L_1L_2 is of type i.

Construct a new grammar G_{con} as follows:

$$G_{con} = (V'_N \cup V''_N \cup \{S\}, \Sigma_1 \cup \Sigma_2, P_{con}, S)$$

where $\quad S \notin V'_N \cup V''_N$

$$P_{con} = P_1 \cup P_2 \cup \{S \to S_1 S_2\}$$

We prove $L_1L_2 = L(G_{con})$. If $w = w_1 w_2 \in L_1 L_2$, then

$$S_1 \overset{*}{\underset{G_1}{\Rightarrow}} w_1, \quad S_2 \overset{*}{\underset{G_2}{\Rightarrow}} w_2$$

So,

$$S \underset{G_{con}}{\Rightarrow} S_1 S_2 \overset{*}{\underset{G_{con}}{\Rightarrow}} w_1 w_2$$

Therefore,

$$L_1 L_2 \subseteq L(G_{con})$$

If $w \in L(G_{con})$, then the first step in the derivation of w is $S \Rightarrow S_1 S_2$. As $V'_N \cap V''_N = \emptyset$ and productions in G_1 or G_2 involve only variables (except those of the form $A \to a$), $w = w_1 w_2$, where $S \overset{*}{\underset{G_1}{\Rightarrow}} w_1$ and $S \overset{*}{\underset{G_2}{\Rightarrow}} w_2$. Thus $L_1 L_2 = L(G_{con})$. Also, G_{con} is of type 0 or type 2 according as G_1 and G_2 are of type 0 or type 2. The above construction is sufficient when G_1 and G_2 are also of type 3 or type 1 provided $\Lambda \notin L_1 \cup L_2$.

Suppose G_1 and G_2 are of type 1 or type 3 and $\Lambda \in L_1$ or $\Lambda \in L_2$. Let $L'_1 = L_1 - \{\Lambda\}$, $L'_2 = L_2 - \{\Lambda\}$. Then

$$L_1 L_2 = \begin{cases} L'_1 L'_2 \cup L'_2 & \text{if } \Lambda \text{ is in } L_1 \text{ but not in } L_2 \\ L'_1 L'_2 \cup L'_1 & \text{if } \Lambda \text{ is in } L_2 \text{ but not in } L_1 \\ L'_1 L'_2 \cup L'_1 \cup L'_2 \cup \{\Lambda\} & \text{if } \Lambda \text{ is in } L_1 \text{ and also in } L_2 \end{cases}$$

As we have already shown, $\mathscr{L}_{csl}$ and $\mathscr{L}_{rl}$ are closed under union, $L_1 L_2$ is of type 1 or type 3 according as L_1 and L_2 are of type 1 or type 3. ∎

Theorem 3.7 Each of the classes $\mathscr{L}_0$, $\mathscr{L}_{csl}$, $\mathscr{L}_{cfl}$, $\mathscr{L}_{rl}$ is closed under transpose operation.

PROOF Let L be a language of type i. Then $L = L(G)$, where G is of type i.

We construct a new grammar G^T as follows: $G^T = (V_N, \Sigma, P^T, S)$, where productions of P^T are constructed by reversing the symbols on L.H.S. and R.H.S. of every production in P. Symbolically, $\alpha^T \to \beta^T$ is in P^T if $\alpha \to \beta$ is in P.

From the construction it is obvious that G^T is of type 0, 1 or 2 according as G is of type 0, 1 or 2 and $L(G^T) = L^T$. For regular grammar, the proof is given in Chapter 4.

It is more difficult to establish closure property under intersection at present as we need the properties of families of languages under consideration. We state the results without proof. We prove some of them in Chapter 8.

Theorem 3.8   (i) Each of the families $\mathscr{L}_0$, $\mathscr{L}_{csl}$, $\mathscr{L}_{rl}$ is closed under intersection.

(ii) $\mathscr{L}_{cfl}$ is not closed under intersection. But the intersection of a context-free language and regular language is context-free.

3.6   LANGUAGES AND AUTOMATA

In Chapters 6 and 7, we shall construct accepting devices for the four types of languages. Figure 3.1 describes the relation between the four types of languages and automata: TM, LBA, pda, and FA stand for Turing machine, linear bounded automaton, pushdown automaton and finite automaton, respectively.

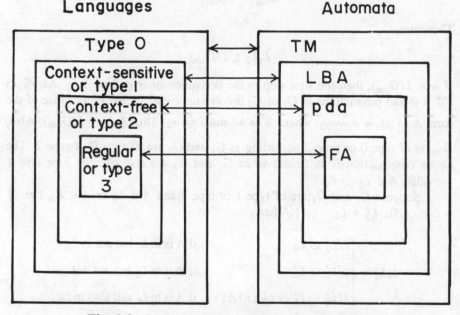

Fig. 3.1   Languages and corresponding automata.

EXERCISES

1. Find the language generated by the following grammars:
   (a) $S \rightarrow 0S1|0A1, A \rightarrow 1A|1$
   (b) $S \rightarrow 0S1|0A|0|1B|1, A \rightarrow 0A|0, B \rightarrow 1B|1$
   (c) $S \rightarrow 0SBA \mid 01A, AB \rightarrow BA, 1B \rightarrow 11, 1A \rightarrow 10, 0A \rightarrow 00$
   (d) $S \rightarrow 0S1|0A1, A \rightarrow 1A0|10$
   (e) $S \rightarrow 0A|1S|0|1, A \rightarrow 1A|1S|1.$

2. Construct the grammar, accepting each of the following sets:
   (a) The set of all strings over $\{0, 1\}$ consisting of equal number of 0's and 1's.
   (b) $\{0^n 1^m 0^m 1^n \mid m, n \geq 1\}$.
   (c) $\{0^n 1^{2n} \mid n \geq 1\}$.
   (d) $\{0^n 1^n \mid n \geq 1\} \cup \{1^m 0^m \mid m \geq 1\}$.
   (e) $\{0^n 1^m 0^n \mid m, n \geq 1\} \cup \{0^n 1^m 2^m \mid m, n \geq 1\}$.

3. Test whether $001100, 001010, 01010$ are in the language generated by the grammar given in Exercise 1(b).

4. Let $G = (\{A, B, S\}, \{0, 1\}, P, S)$, where P consists of $S \to 0AB, A0 \to S0B$, $A1 \to SB1, B \to SA, B \to 01$. Show that $L(G) = \emptyset$.

5. Find the language generated by the grammar $S \to AB, A \to A1 \mid 0$, $B \to 2B \mid 3$. Can the above language be generated by a grammar of higher type?

6. State whether the following statements are true or false. Justify your answer with a proof or a counter-example.
   (a) If G_1 and G_2 are equivalent, then they are of the same type.
   (b) If L is a finite subset of Σ^*, then L is a context-free language.
   (c) If L is a finite subset of Σ^*, then L is a regular language.

7. Show that $\{a^{n^2} \mid n \geq 1\}$ is generated by the grammar $S \to a, S \to A_3A_4, A_3 \to A_1A_3A_2, A_3 \to A_1A_2, A_1A_2 \to aA_2A_1, A_1a \to aA_1, A_2a \to aA_2, A_1A_4 \to A_4a, A_2A_4 \to A_5a, A_2A_5 \to A_5a, A_5 \to a$.

8. Construct (i) a context-sensitive but not context-free grammar, (ii) a context-free but not regular grammar, (iii) a regular grammar to generate $\{a^n \mid n \geq 1\}$.

9. Construct a grammar which generates all even integers up to 998.

10. Construct context-free grammars to generate the following:
    (a) $\{0^m 1^n \mid m \neq n, m, n \geq 1\}$.
    (b) $\{a^l b^m c^n \mid \text{one of } l, m, n \text{ equals 1 and the remaining two are equal}\}$.
    (c) $\{0^m 1^n \mid 1 \leq m \leq n\}$.
    (d) $\{a^l b^m c^n \mid l + m = n\}$.
    (e) The set of all strings over $\{0, 1\}$ containing twice as many 0's as 1's.

11. Construct regular grammars to generate the following:
    (a) $\{a^{2n} \mid n \geq 1\}$.
    (b) The set of all strings over $\{a, b\}$ ending in a.
    (c) The set of all strings over $\{a, b\}$ beginning with a.
    (d) $\{a^l b^m c^n \mid l, m, n \geq 1\}$.
    (e) $\{(ab)^n \mid n \geq 1\}$.

12. Is $\underset{G}{\Rightarrow}$ an equivalence relation on $(V_N \cup \Sigma)^*$.

13. Show that $G_1 = (\{S\}, \{a, b\}, P_1, S)$, where $P_1 = \{S \to aSb \mid ab\}$ is equivalent to $G_2 = (\{S, A, B, C\}, \{a, b\}, P_2, S)$. Here P_2 consists of $S \to AC$, $C \to SB, S \to AB, A \to a, B \to b$.

14. If each production in a grammar G has some variable on its right-hand side, what can you say about $L(G)$?

15. Show that $\{abc, bca, cab\}$ can be generated by a regular grammar whose terminal set is $\{a, b, c\}$.

16. Construct a grammar to generate $\{(ab)^n \mid n \geq 1\} \cup \{(ba)^n \mid n \geq 1\}$.

17. Show that a grammar consisting of productions of the form $A \to xB \mid y$, where x, y are in Σ^* and $A, B \in V_N$ is equivalent to a regular grammar.

4

Regular Sets and Regular Grammars

In this chapter, we first define regular expressions as a means of representing certain subsets of strings over Σ and prove that regular sets are precisely those accepted by finite automata or transition systems. We use pumping lemma for regular sets to prove that certain sets are not regular. We then discuss closure properties of regular sets. Finally, we give the relation between regular sets and regular grammars.

4.1 REGULAR EXPRESSIONS

Regular expressions are useful for representing certain sets of strings in an algebraic fashion. Actually these describe the languages accepted by finite state automata.

We give a formal recursive definition of regular expressions over Σ as follows:

1. Any terminal symbol (i.e. an element of Σ), Λ and $\emptyset$ are regular expressions. When we view a in Σ as a regular expression, we denote it by **a**.

2. The union of two regular expressions R_1 and R_2, written as $R_1 + R_2$, is also a regular expression.

3. The concatenation of two regular expressions R_1 and R_2, written as R_1R_2, is also a regular expression.

4. The iteration (or closure) of a regular expression R, written as R^*, is also a regular expression.

5. If R is a regular expression, then (R) is also a regular expression.

6. The regular expressions over Σ are precisely those obtained recursively by the application of the rules 1–5 once or several times.

NOTE: (a) We use **x** for a regular expression just to distinguish it from the symbol (or string) x.

(b) The parentheses used in rule 5 influence the order of evaluation of a regular expression.

(c) In the absence of parentheses, we have the hierarchy of operations as follows: iteration (closure), concatenation, and union. That is, in evaluating a regular expression involving various operations, we perform iteration first, then concatenation, and finally union. This hierarchy is similar to that followed for arithmetic expressions (exponentiation, multiplication and addition).

Definition 4.1   Any set represented by a regular expression is called a regular set.

If, for example, $a, b \in \Sigma$, then (a) **a** denotes the set $\{a\}$, (b) **a + b** denotes $\{a, b\}$, (c) **ab** denotes $\{ab\}$, (d) **a*** denotes the set $\{\Lambda, a, aa, aaa, \ldots\}$ and (e) $(\mathbf{a + b})\mathbf{*}$ denotes $\{a, b\}\mathbf{*}$.

Now we shall explain the evaluation procedure for the three basic operations. Let $\mathbf{R}_1$ and $\mathbf{R}_2$ denote any two regular expressions. Then (a) a string in $\mathbf{R}_1 + \mathbf{R}_2$ is a string from $\mathbf{R}_1$ or a string from $\mathbf{R}_2$; (b) a string in $\mathbf{R}_1\mathbf{R}_2$ is a string from $\mathbf{R}_1$ followed by a string from $\mathbf{R}_2$, and (c) a string in $\mathbf{R}^*$ is a string obtained by concatenating n elements for some $n \geq 0$. Consequently, (a) the set represented by $\mathbf{R}_1 + \mathbf{R}_2$ is the union of the sets represented by $\mathbf{R}_1$ and $\mathbf{R}_2$, (b) the set represented by $\mathbf{R}_1\mathbf{R}_2$ is the concatenation of the sets represented by $\mathbf{R}_1$ and $\mathbf{R}_2$ (Recall that the concatenation AB of sets A and B of strings over Σ is given by $AB = \{w_1w_2 | w_1 \in A, w_2 \in B\}$, and (c) the set represented by $\mathbf{R}^*$ is $\{w_1w_2 \ldots w_n | w_i$ is in the set represented by $\mathbf{R}$ and $n \geq 0\}$.

NOTE: By the definition of regular expressions, the class of regular sets over Σ is closed under union, concatenation and closure (iteration) by the conditions 2, 3, 4 of the definition.

EXAMPLE 4.1   Describe the following sets by regular expressions: (a) $\{101\}$, (b) $\{abba\}$, (c) $\{01, 10\}$, (d) $\{\Lambda, ab\}$, (e) $\{abb, a, b, bba\}$, (f) $\{\Lambda, 0, 00, 000, \ldots\}$, and (g) $\{1, 11, 111, \ldots\}$.

SOLUTION   (a) Now, $\{1\}, \{0\}$ are represented by **1** and **0**, respectively. 101 is obtained by concatenating 1, 0 and 1. So, $\{101\}$ is represented by **101**.

(b) **abba** represents $\{abba\}$.

(c) As $\{01, 10\}$ is the union of $\{01\}$ and $\{10\}$, $\{01, 10\}$ is represented by **01 + 10**.

(d) The set $\{\Lambda, ab\}$ is represented by $\Lambda + \mathbf{ab}$.

(e) The set $\{abb, a, b, bba\}$ is represented by **abb + a + b + bba**.

(f) As $\{\Lambda, 0, 00, 000, \ldots\}$ is simply $\{0\}\mathbf{*}$, it is represented by $\mathbf{0*}$.

(g) Any element in $\{1,11, 111, \ldots\}$ can be obtained by concatenating 1 and any element of $\{1\}\mathbf{*}$. Hence $\mathbf{1(1)*}$ represents $\{1, 11, 111, \ldots\}$.

EXAMPLE 4.2   Describe the following sets by regular expressions:

(a) L_1 = the set of all strings of 0's and 1's ending in 00.

(b) L_2 = the set of all strings of 0's and 1's beginning with 0 and ending with 1.

(c) $L_3 = \{\Lambda, 11, 1111, 111111, \ldots\}$.

SOLUTION   (a) Any string in L_1 is obtained by concatenating any string over $\{0, 1\}$ and the string 00. $\{0, 1\}$ is represented by $\mathbf{0 + 1}$. Hence L_1 is represented by $(\mathbf{0 + 1})\mathbf{* \, 00}$.

(b) As any element of L_2 is obtained by concatenating 0, any string over $\{0, 1\}$ and 1, L_2 can be represented by $\mathbf{0(0 + 1)* \, 1}$.

(c) Any element of L_3 is either Λ or a string of even number of 1's, i.e. a string of the form $(11)^n$, $n \geq 0$. So L_3 can be represented by $(\mathbf{11})\mathbf{*}$.

4.1.1 IDENTITIES FOR REGULAR EXPRESSIONS

Two regular expressions P and Q are equivalent (we write $P = Q$) if P and Q represent the same set of strings.

We now give the identities for regular expressions; these are useful for simplifying regular expressions.

$$I_1 \quad \varnothing + R = R$$

$$I_2 \quad \varnothing R = R\varnothing = \varnothing$$

$$I_3 \quad \Lambda R = R\Lambda = R$$

$$I_4 \quad \Lambda^* = \Lambda \text{ and } \varnothing^* = \Lambda$$

$$I_5 \quad R + R = R$$

$$I_6 \quad R^*R^* = R^*$$

$$I_7 \quad RR^* = R^*R$$

$$I_8 \quad (R^*)^* = R^*$$

$$I_9 \quad \Lambda + RR^* = R^* = \Lambda + R^*R$$

$$I_{10} \quad (PQ)^*P = P(QP)^*$$

$$I_{11} \quad (P + Q)^* = (P^*Q^*)^* = (P^* + Q^*)^*$$

$$I_{12} \quad (P + Q)R = PR + QR \text{ and } R(P + Q) = RP + RQ$$

NOTE: By the 'set P' we mean the set represented by the regular expression P.

The following theorem is very much useful in simplifying regular expressions (i.e. replacing a given regular expression P by a simpler regular expression equivalent to P).

Theorem 4.1 (Arden's theorem) Let P and Q be two regular expressions over Σ. If P does not contain Λ, then the following equation in R, viz.

$$R = Q + RP \tag{4.1}$$

has a unique solution (i.e. one and only one solution) given by $R = QP^*$.

PROOF

$$Q + (QP^*)\,P = Q(\Lambda + P^*P) = QP^* \text{ by } I_9$$

Hence (4.1) is satisfied when $R = QP^*$. This means $R = QP^*$ is a solution of (4.1).

To prove uniqueness, consider (4.1). Here, replacing R by $Q + RP$ on the R.H.S., we get the equation

$$Q + RP = Q + (Q + RP)P$$

$$= \mathbf{Q} + \mathbf{QP} + \mathbf{RPP}$$

$$= \mathbf{Q} + \mathbf{QP} + \mathbf{RP}^2$$

$$= \mathbf{Q} + \mathbf{QP} + \mathbf{QP}^2 + \dots + \mathbf{QP}^i + \mathbf{RP}^{i+1}$$

$$= \mathbf{Q}(\Lambda + \mathbf{P} + \mathbf{P}^2 + \dots + \mathbf{P}^i) + \mathbf{RP}^{i+1}$$

From (4.1),

$$\mathbf{R} = \mathbf{Q}(\Lambda + \mathbf{P} + \mathbf{P}^2 + \dots + \mathbf{P}^i) + \mathbf{RP}^{i+1} \quad \text{for } i \geq 0 \qquad (4.2)$$

We now show that any solution of (4.1) is equivalent to $\mathbf{QP}^*$. Suppose $\mathbf{R}$ satisfies (4.1), then it satisfies (4.2). Let w be a string of length i in the set $\mathbf{R}$. Then w belongs to the set $\mathbf{Q}(\Lambda + \mathbf{P} + \mathbf{P}^2 + \dots + \mathbf{P}^i) + \mathbf{RP}^{i+1}$. As $\mathbf{P}$ does not contain Λ, $\mathbf{RP}^{i+1}$ has no string of length less than $i + 1$ and so w is not in the set $\mathbf{RP}^{i+1}$. This means w belongs to the set $\mathbf{Q}(\Lambda + \mathbf{P} + \mathbf{P}^2 + \dots + \mathbf{P}^i)$, and hence to $\mathbf{QP}^*$.

Consider a string w in the set $\mathbf{QP}^*$. Then w is in the set $\mathbf{QP}^k$ for some $k \geq 0$, and hence in $\mathbf{Q}(\Lambda + \mathbf{P} + \mathbf{P}^2 + \dots + \mathbf{P}^k)$. So w is on the R.H.S. of (4.2). Therefore, w is in $\mathbf{R}$ (L.H.S. of (4.2)). Thus $\mathbf{R}$ and $\mathbf{QP}^*$ represent the same set. This proves the uniqueness of the solution of (4.1). $\blacksquare$

NOTE: Henceforward in this text, regular expressions are abbreviated as r.e.

EXAMPLE 4.3 (a) Give an r.e. for representing the set L of strings in which every 0 is immediately followed by at least two 1's.

(b) Prove that the regular expression $\mathbf{R} = \Lambda + 1^*(011)^*(1^* (011)^*)^*$ also describes the same set of strings.

SOLUTION (a) If w is in L, then either (i) w does not contain any 0, or (ii) it contains a 0 preceded by 1 and followed by 11. So w can be written as $w_1 w_2 \dots w_n$, where each w_i is either 1 or 011. So L is represented by the r.e. $(1 + 011)^*$.

$$\text{(b)} \quad \mathbf{R} = \Lambda + \mathbf{P}_1 \mathbf{P}_1^*, \quad \text{where } \mathbf{P}_1 = 1^* (011)^*$$

$$= \mathbf{P}_1^* \text{ using } I_9$$

$$= (1^* (011)^*)^*$$

$$= (\mathbf{P}_2^* \mathbf{P}_3^*)^* \text{ letting } \mathbf{P}_2 = 1, \mathbf{P}_3 = 011$$

$$= (\mathbf{P}_2 + \mathbf{P}_3)^* \text{ using } I_{11}$$

$$= (1 + 011)^*$$

EXAMPLE 4.4 Prove $(1 + 00^*1) + (1 + 00^*1) (0 + 10^*1)^* (0 + 10^*1) = 0^*1(0 + 10^*1)^*$.

SOLUTION L.H.S. $= (1 + 00^*1) (\Lambda + (0 + 10^*1^* (0 + 10^*1))$ using I_{12}

$$= (1 + 00^*1) (0 + 10^*1)^* \text{ using } I_9$$

$$= (\Lambda + 00^*)1 (0 + 10^*1)^* \text{ using } I_{12} \text{ for } 1 + 00^*1$$

$$= 0*1(0 + 10*1)* \text{ using } I_9$$

$$= \text{R.H.S.}$$

4.2 FINITE AUTOMATA AND REGULAR EXPRESSIONS

In this section we study the relation between regular expressions and finite automata and that between regular expressions and transition systems.

4.2.1 TRANSITION SYSTEMS AND REGULAR EXPRESSIONS

The following theorem describes the relation between transition systems and regular expressions.

Theorem 4.2 Every regular expression **R** can be recognised by a transition system, i.e. for every string w in the set **R**, there exists a path from the initial state to a final state with path value w.

PROOF   The proof is by the principle of induction on the total number of characters in **R**. By 'character' we mean elements of Σ, Λ, $\emptyset$, * and +. For example, if **R** $= \Lambda + 10*11*0$, the characters are Λ, +, 1, 0, *, 1, 1, *, 0, and the number of characters is 9.

Basis.   Let the number of characters in **R** be 1. Then **R** $= \Lambda$, or **R** $= \emptyset$, or **R** $= a_i$, $a_i \in \Sigma$. The transition systems given in Fig. 4.1 will recognise these regular expressions.

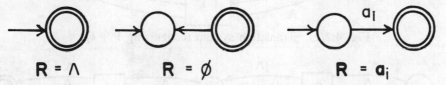

R = Λ   **R = $\emptyset$**   **R = a_i**

Fig. 4.1   Transition systems recognising elementary regular sets.

Induction step.   Assume the theorem is true for regular expressions with n characters or less. We must prove that it is also true for $n + 1$ characters. Let **R** have $n + 1$ characters. Then,

$$\mathbf{R} = \mathbf{P} + \mathbf{Q} \quad \text{or} \quad \mathbf{R} = \mathbf{PQ} \quad \text{or} \quad \mathbf{R} = \mathbf{P}*$$

where **P** and **Q** are regular expressions, each having n characters or less. By induction hypothesis, **P** and **Q** can be recognised by transition systems G and H, respectively, as shown in Figs. 4.2(a) and 4.2(b).

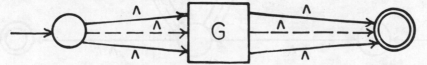

Fig. 4.2(a)   Transition system recognising **P**.

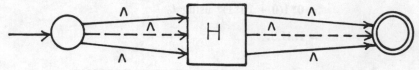

Fig. 4.2(b)   Transition system recognising Q.

The regular expression **R** = **P** + **Q** can be recognised by the transition system formed using G and H. We introduce a new initial state q_0 and a new unique final state q_f. q_0 is connected to the initial states of G and H by Λ-moves. The final states of G and H are connected to q_f by Λ-moves. The transition system recognising **P** + **Q** is given in Fig. 4.2(c). Similar constructions for **PQ** and **P*** are given in Figs. 4.2(d) and 4.2(e). Thus **R** is recognised by a transition system. Therefore, by induction every r.e. is recognised by a transition system. ∎

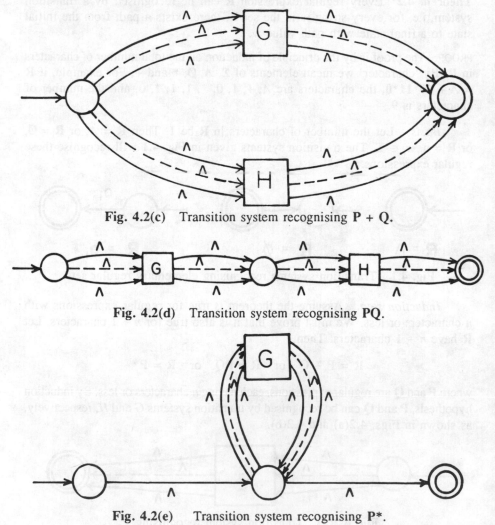

Fig. 4.2(c)   Transition system recognising **P** + **Q**.

Fig. 4.2(d)   Transition system recognising **PQ**.

Fig. 4.2(e)   Transition system recognising **P***.

Theorem 4.1 gives a method of constructing a transition system recognising (accepting) an r.e. (regular set). In the later sections we give a method of converting a transition system recognising an r.e. into a finite automaton recognising the same r.e. Thus, if a regular expression **P** is given, we can construct an FA accepting the regular set given by **P**. (The following theorem is regarding the converse; Theorems 4.2 and 4.3 prove the equivalence of regular expressions (or regular sets) and the sets accepted by FA.)

Theorem 4.3 Any set L accepted by a finite automaton M is represented by a regular expression.

PROOF Let

$$M = (\{q_1 \ldots q_m\}, \Sigma, \delta, q_1, F)$$

The construction that we give can be better understood in terms of the state diagram of M. If a string $w \in \Sigma^*$ is accepted by M, then there is a path from q_1 to some final state with path value w. So to each final state, say q_j, there corresponds a subset of Σ^* consisting of path values of paths from q_0 to q_j. As $T(M)$ is the union of such subsets of Σ^*, it is enough to represent them by regular expressions. So the main part of the proof lies in the construction of subsets of path values of paths from the state q_i to the state q_j.

Let P_{ij}^k denote the set of path values of paths from q_i to q_j whose intermediate vertices lie in $\{q_1, \ldots, q_k\}$. We construct P_{ij}^k for $k = 0, 1, \ldots, n$ recursively as follows:

$$P_{ij}^0 = \{a \in \Sigma \mid \delta(q_i, a) = q_j\} \tag{4.3}$$

$$P_{ii}^0 = \{a \in \Sigma \mid \delta(q_i, a) = q_i\} \cup \{\Lambda\} \tag{4.4}$$

$$P_{ij}^k = P_{ik}^{k-1} (P_{kk}^{k-1})^* P_{kj}^{k-1} \cup P_{ij}^{k-1} \tag{4.5}$$

In terms of the state diagram, the construction can be understood better. P_{ij}^0 simply denotes the set of path values (i.e. labels) of edges from q_i to q_j. In P_{ii}^0 we include Λ in addition to labels of self loops from q_i. This explains (4.3) and (4.4).

Consider a path from q_i to q_j whose intermediate vertices lie in $\{q_1, \ldots, q_k\}$. If the path does not pass through q_k, then its path value lies in P_{ij}^{k-1}. Otherwise, the path passes through q_k possibly more than once. The path can be split into several paths with path values $w_1, w_2 \ldots w_l$ as in Fig. 4.3. $w = w_1 w_2 \ldots w_l$. w_1 is the path value of the path from q_i to q_k (without passing through q_k, i.e. q_k is

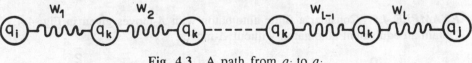

Fig. 4.3 A path from q_i to q_j.

not an intermediate vertex). $w_2, \ldots, w_{l-1}$ are the path values of paths from q_k to itself without passing through q_k. w_l is the path value of the path from q_k to q_j without passing through q_k. So w_1 is in P_{ik}^{k-1}, $w_2, \ldots, w_{l-1}$ are in (P_{kk}^{k-1}), and w_l is in P_{kj}^{k-1}. This explains (4.5).

We prove that the sets introduced by (4.3)–(4.5) are represented by regular expressions by induction on k (for all i and j). P_{ij}^0 is a finite subset of Σ, say $\{a_1, \ldots, a_t\}$. Then, $\mathbf{P}_{ij}^0$ is represented by $\mathbf{P}_{ij}^0 = a_1 + a_2 + \ldots + a_t$. Similarly, we can construct $\mathbf{P}_{ii}^0$ representing P_{ii}^0. Thus there is basis for induction.

Let us assume the result for $k - 1$, i.e., P_{ij}^{k-1} is represented by an r.e. $\mathbf{P}_{ij}^{k-1}$ for all i and j. From (4.5) we have $P_{ij}^k = P_{ik}^{k-1}(P_{kk}^{k-1})^* P_{kj}^{k-1} \cup P_{ij}^{k-1}$. So it is obvious that P_{ij}^k is represented by $\mathbf{P}_{ij}^k = \mathbf{P}_{ik}^{k-1}(\mathbf{P}_{kk}^{k-1})^* \mathbf{P}_{kj}^{k-1} \cup \mathbf{P}_{ij}^{k-1}$. Therefore, the result is true for all k. By the principle of induction, the sets constructed by (4.3)–(4.5) are represented by regular expressions.

As $Q = \{q_1, \ldots, q_m\}$, $\mathbf{P}_{1j}^m$ denotes the set of path values of all paths from q_1 to q_j. If $F = \{q_{f_1}, \ldots, q_{f_n}\}$ then $T(M) = \bigcup_{j=1}^{n} P_{1f_j}^m$. So $T(M)$ is represented by the regular expression $\mathbf{P}_{1f_1}^m + \ldots + \mathbf{P}_{1f_n}^m$. Thus, $L = T(M)$ is represented by a regular expression.

NOTE: P_{ij}^0 and P_{ii}^0 are subsets of $\Sigma \cup \{\Lambda\}$, and so they are finite sets. So every P_{ij}^k is obtained by applying union, concatenation and closure to the set of all singletons in $\Sigma \cup \{\Lambda\}$. Using this we can prove Kleene's theorem (Theorem 4.4) at the end of this section. Kleene's theorem characterises regular sets in terms of subsets of Σ and operations (union, concatenation, closure) on singletons in $\Sigma \cup \{\Lambda\}$.

4.2.2   TRANSITION SYSTEM CONTAINING Λ-MOVES

The transition systems can be generalised by permitting Λ-transitions or Λ-moves which are associated with a null symbol Λ. These transitions can occur when no input is applied. But it is possible to convert a transition system with Λ-moves into an equivalent transition system without Λ-moves. We shall give a simple method of doing it with the help of an example.

Suppose we want to replace a Λ-move from vertex v_1 to vertex v_2. Then we proceed as follows:

Step 1   Find all the edges starting from v_2.

Step 2   Duplicate all these edges starting from v_1, without changing the edge labels.

Step 3   If v_1 is an initial state, make v_2 also as initial state.

Step 4   If v_2 is a final state, make v_1 as the final state.

EXAMPLE 4.5   Consider a finite automaton with Λ-moves given in Fig. 4.4. Obtain an equivalent automaton without Λ-moves.

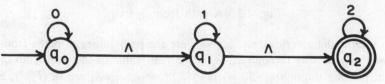

Fig. 4.4   FA of Example 4.5.

SOLUTION We first eliminate the Λ-move from q_0 to q_1 to get Fig. 4.5(a). q_1 is made an initial state. Then we eliminate the Λ-move from q_0 to q_2 in Fig. 4.5(a) to get Fig. 4.5(b). As q_2 is a final state, q_0 is also made a final state. Finally, the Λ-move from q_1 to q_2 is eliminated in Fig. 4.5(c).

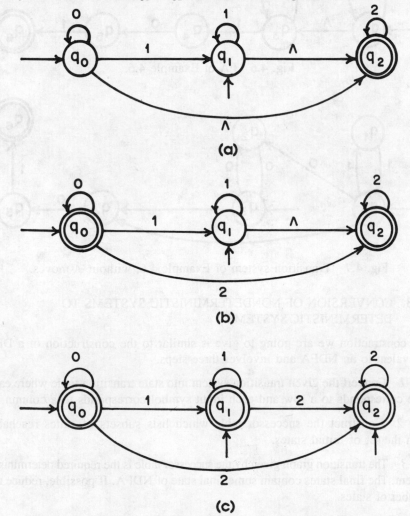

Fig. 4.5 Transition system without Λ-moves of Example 4.5.

EXAMPLE 4.6 Consider a graph (i.e. transition system) containing a Λ-move given in Fig. 4.6. Obtain an equivalent graph (i.e. transition system) without Λ-moves.

SOLUTION There is a Λ-move from q_0 to q_3. There are two edges, one from q_3 to q_2 with label 0 and another from q_3 to q_4 with label 1. We duplicate these edges from q_0. As q_0 is an initial state, q_3 is made an initial state. The resulting transition graph is given in Fig. 4.7.

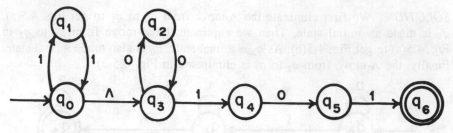

Fig. 4.6   FA of Example 4.6.

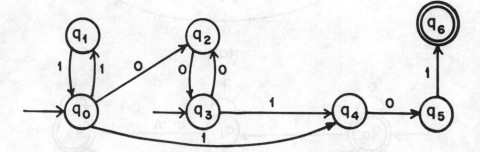

Fig. 4.7   Transition system of Example 4.6, without Λ-moves.

4.2.3   CONVERSION OF NONDETERMINISTIC SYSTEMS TO DETERMINISTIC SYSTEMS

The construction we are going to give is similar to the construction of a DFA equivalent to an NDFA and involves three steps.

Step 1   Convert the given transition system into state transition table where each state corresponds to a row and each input symbol corresponds to a column.

Step 2   Construct the successor table which lists subsets of states reachable from the set of initial states.

Step 3   The transition graph given by the successor table is the required deterministic system. The final states contain some final state of NDFA. If possible, reduce the number of states.

NOTE: The construction is similar to that given in Section 2.7 for automata except for the initial step. In the earlier method for automata, we started with $[q_0]$. Here we start with the set of all initial states. The other steps are similar.

EXAMPLE 4.7   Obtain the deterministic graph (system) equivalent to the transition system given in Fig. 4.8.

SOLUTION   We construct the transition table corresponding to the given nondeterministic system. It is given in Table 4.1.

We construct the successor table by starting with $[q_0, q_1]$. From Table 4.1 we see that $[q_0, q_1, q_2]$ is reachable from $[q_0, q_1]$ by a b-path. There are no

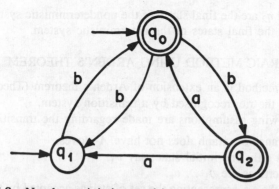

Fig. 4.8 Nondeterministic transition system of Example 4.7.

Table 4.1 Transition Table for Example 4.7

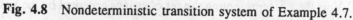

State/Σ	a	b
→ q_0		q_1, q_2
q_1		q_0
q_2	q_0, q_1	

a-paths from $[q_0, q_1]$. Similarly, $[q_0, q_1]$ is reachable from $[q_0, q_1, q_2]$ by an a-path and $[q_0, q_1, q_2]$ is reachable from itself. We proceed with the construction for all the elements in Q_a for every $a \in \Sigma$.

Table 4.2 Deterministic Transition Table of Example 4.7

Q	Q_a	Q_b
$[q_0, q_1]$	$\emptyset$	$[q_0, q_1, q_2]$
$[q_0, q_1, q_2]$	$[q_0, q_1]$	$[q_0, q_1, q_2]$
$\emptyset$	$\emptyset$	$\emptyset$

We terminate the construction when all the elements Q_a, $a \in \Sigma$ are already in Q. Table 4.2 gives the successor table. From the successor table it is easy to construct the deterministic transition system given in Fig. 4.9.

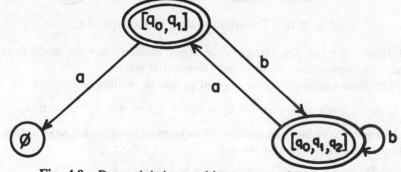

Fig. 4.9 Deterministic transition system of Example 4.7.

As q_0 and q_2 are the final states of the nondeterministic system $[q_0, q_1]$ and $[q_0, q_1, q_2]$ are the final states of the deterministic system.

4.2.4 ALGEBRAIC METHOD USING ARDEN'S THEOREM

The following method is an extension of Arden's theorem (Theorem 4.1). This is used to find the r.e. recognised by a transition system.

The following assumptions are made regarding the transition system:

(i) The transition graph does not have Λ-moves.

(ii) It has only one initial state, say v_1.

(iii) Its vertices are $v_1 \ldots v_n$.

(iv) V_i is the r.e. representing the set of strings accepted by the system even though v_i is a final state.

(v) α_{ij} denotes the r.e. representing the set of labels of edges from v_i to v_j. When there is no such edge, $\alpha_{ij} = \emptyset$. Consequently, we can get the following set of equations in $V_1 \ldots V_n$:

$$V_1 = V_1 \, \alpha_{11} + V_2 \, \alpha_{21} + \ldots + V_n \, \alpha_{n1} + \Lambda$$

$$V_2 = V_1 \, \alpha_{12} + V_2 \, \alpha_{22} + \ldots + V_n \, \alpha_{n2}$$

$$V_n = V_1 \, \alpha_{1n} + V_2 \, \alpha_{2n} + \ldots + V_n \, \alpha_{nn}$$

By repeatedly applying substitutions and Theorem 4.1 (Arden's theorem), we can express V_i in terms of α_{ij}'s.

For getting the set of strings recognised by the transition system, we have to take the 'union' of all V_i's corresponding to final states.

EXAMPLE 4.8 Consider the transition system given in Fig. 4.10. Prove that the strings recognised are $(a + a(b + aa)*b)* \, a(b + aa)* \, a$.

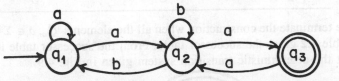

Fig. 4.10 Transition system of Example 4.8.

SOLUTION We can directly apply the above method since the graph does not contain any Λ-move and there is only one initial state.

The three equations for q_1, q_2 and q_3 can be written as

$$q_1 = q_1 a + q_2 b + \Lambda, \qquad q_2 = q_1 a + q_2 b + q_3 a, \qquad q_3 = q_2 a$$

It is necessary to reduce the number of unknowns by repeated substitution. By substituting q_3 in q_2-equation, we get

$$q_2 = q_1 a + q_2 b + q_2 aa$$

$$= q_1a + q_2(b + aa)$$

$$= q_1a \ (b + aa)^*$$

by applying Theorem 4.1. Substituting q_2 in q_1, we get

$$q_1 = q_1a + q_1a(b + aa)^*b + \Lambda$$

$$= q_1(a + a(b + aa)^*b) + \Lambda$$

Hence

$$q_1 = \Lambda(a + a(b + aa)^*b)^*$$

$$q_2 = (a + a(b + aa)^*b)^* \ a(b + aa)^*$$

$$q_3 = (a + a(b + aa)^*b)^* \ a(b + aa)^*a$$

Since q_3 is a final state, the set of strings recognised by the graph is given by

$$(a + a(b + aa)^*b)a(b + aa)^*a$$

EXAMPLE 4.9   Prove that the FA whose transition diagram is given in Fig. 4.11 accepts the set of all strings over the alphabet $\{a, b\}$ with an equal number of

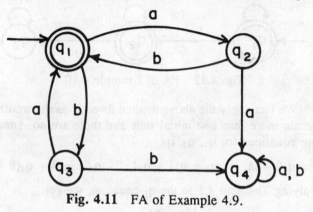

Fig. 4.11   FA of Example 4.9.

a's and b's, such that each prefix has atmost one more a than b's and atmost one more b than a's.

SOLUTION   We can apply the above method directly since the graph does not contain Λ-move and there is only one initial state. We get the following equations for q_1, q_2, q_3, q_4:

$$q_1 = q_2b + q_3a + \Lambda$$

$$q_2 = q_1a,$$

$$q_3 = q_1b$$

$$q_4 = q_2a + q_3b + q_4a + q_4b$$

As q_1 is the only final state and the q_1-equation involves only q_2 and q_3, we use only q_2- and q_3-equations (the q_4-equation is redundant for our purposes). Substituting for q_2 and q_3, we get

$$q_1 = q_1ab + q_1ba + \Lambda = q_1(ab + ba) + \Lambda$$

By applying Theorem 4.1, we get

$$q_1 = \Lambda(ab + ba)^* = (ab + ba)^*$$

As q_1 is the only final state, the strings accepted by the given FA are strings given by $(ab + ba)^*$. As any such string is a string of ab's and ba's we get equal number of a's and b's. If a prefix x of a sentence accepted by the FA has even number of symbols, then it should have equal number of a's and b's since x is a substring formed by ab's and ba's. If the prefix x has odd number of symbols, then we can write x as ya or yb. As y has even number of symbols, y has equal number of a's and b's. Thus x has one more a than b or vice versa.

EXAMPLE 4.10 Describe in English the set accepted by FA whose transition diagram is given in Fig. 4.12.

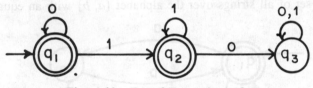

Fig. 4.12   FA of Example 4.10.

SOLUTION We can apply the above method directly as the transition diagram does not contain more than one initial state and there are no Λ-moves. We get the following equations for q_1, q_2, q_3.

$$q_1 = q_10 + \Lambda, \qquad q_2 = q_11 + q_21, \qquad q_3 = q_20 + q_3(0 + 1)$$

By applying Theorem 4.1 to the q_1-equation, we get

$$q_1 = \Lambda0^* = 0^*$$

So,

$$q_2 = q_11 + q_21 = 0^*1 + q_21$$

Therefore,

$$q_2 = (0^*1)1^*$$

As the final states are q_1 and q_2, we need not solve for q_3:

$$q_1 + q_2 = 0^* + 0^*(11^*) = 0^*(\Lambda + 11^*) = 0^*(1^*) \text{ by } I_9$$

The strings represented by the transition graph are 0^*1^*. We can interpret the strings in the English language in the following way. The strings accepted by the FA are precisely the strings of any number of 0's (possibly Λ) followed by a string of any number of 1's (possibly Λ).

EXAMPLE 4.11 Construct a regular expression corresponding to the state diagram given in Fig. 4.13.

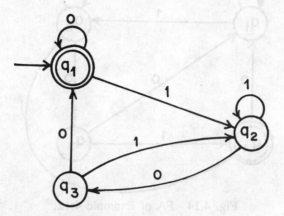

Fig. 4.13 FA of Example 4.11.

SOLUTION There is only one initial state. Also, there are no Λ-moves. The equations are

$$q_1 = q_1 0 + q_3 0 + \Lambda, \qquad q_2 = q_1 1 + q_2 1 + q_3 1, \qquad q_3 = q_2 0$$

So,

$$q_2 = q_1 1 + q_2 1 + (q_2 0)1 = q_1 1 + q_2(1 + 01)$$

By applying Theorem 4.1, we get

$$q_2 = q_1 1(1 + 01)^*$$

Also,

$$q_1 = q_1 0 + q_3 0 + \Lambda = q_1 0 + q_2 00 + \Lambda$$

$$= q_1 0 + (q_1 1(1 + 01)^*)\, 00 + \Lambda$$

$$= q_1(0 + 1(1 + 01)^*\, 00) + \Lambda$$

Once again applying Theorem 4.1, we get

$$q_1 = \Lambda(0 + 1(1 + 01)^*\, 00)^* = (0 + 1(1 + 01)^*\, 00)^*$$

As q_1 is the only final state, the regular expression corresponding to the given diagram is $(0 + 1(1 + 01)^*\, 00)^*$.

EXAMPLE 4.12 Find the regular expression corresponding to Fig. 4.14.

SOLUTION There is only one initial state, and there are no Λ-moves. So we form the equations corresponding to q_1, q_2, q_3, q_4:

$$q_1 = q_1 0 + q_3 0 + q_4 0 + \Lambda$$

$$q_2 = q_1 1 + q_2 1 + q_4 1$$

$$q_3 = q_2 0$$

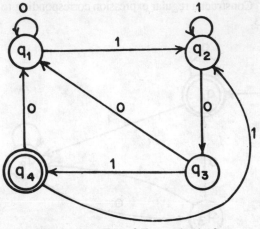

Fig. 4.14   FA of Example 4.12.

$$q_4 = q_3 1$$

Now,

$$q_4 = q_3 1 = (q_2 0)1 = q_2 01$$

Thus we are able to write q_3, q_4 in terms of q_2. Using the q_2-equation, we get

$$q_2 = q_1 1 + q_2 1 + q_2 011 = q_1 1 + q_2 (1 + 011)$$

By applying Theorem 4.1, we obtain

$$q_2 = (q_1 1)(1 + 011)^* = q_1 (1(1 + 011)^*)$$

From the q_1-equation we have

$$q_1 = q_1 0 + q_2 00 + q_2 010 + \Lambda$$

$$= q_1 0 + q_2 (00 + 010) + \Lambda$$

$$= q_1 0 + q_1 1(1 + 011)^* (00 + 010) + \Lambda$$

Again, by applying Theorem 4.1, we obtain

$$q_1 = \Lambda (0 + 1(1 + 011)^* (00 + 010))^*$$

$$q_4 = q_2 01 = q_1 1(1 + 011)^* 01$$

$$= (0 + 1(1 + 011)^*(00 + 010))^*(1(1 + 011)^* 01)$$

4.2.5   CONSTRUCTION OF FINITE AUTOMATA EQUIVALENT TO A REGULAR EXPRESSION

The method we are going to give for constructing an FA equivalent to a given regular expression is called the subset method which involves two steps.

Step 1   Construct a transition graph (transition system) equivalent to the given regular expression using Λ-moves. This is done by using Theorem 4.2.

Step 2   Construct the transition table for the transition graph obtained in step 1. Using the method given in Section 4.2.3, construct the equivalent DFA. We reduce the number of states if possible.

EXAMPLE 4.13   Construct an FA equivalent to the regular expression.

$$(0 + 1)^*(00 + 11)(0 + 1)^*$$

SOLUTION: *Step 1* (Construction of transition graph). First of all we construct the transition graph with Λ-moves using the constructions of Theorem 4.2. Then we eliminate Λ-moves as discussed in Section 4.2.2.

We start with Fig. 4.15(a).

We eliminate the concatenations in the given r.e. by introducing new vertices q_1 and q_2 and get Fig. 4.15(b).

We eliminate * operations in Fig. 4.15(b) by introducing two new vertices q_5 and q_6 and Λ-moves as shown in Fig. 4.15(c).

We eliminate concatenations and + in Fig. 4.15(c) and get Fig. 4.15(d).

We eliminate Λ-moves in Fig. 4.15(d) and get Fig. 4.15(e) which gives the NDFA equivalent to the given r.e.

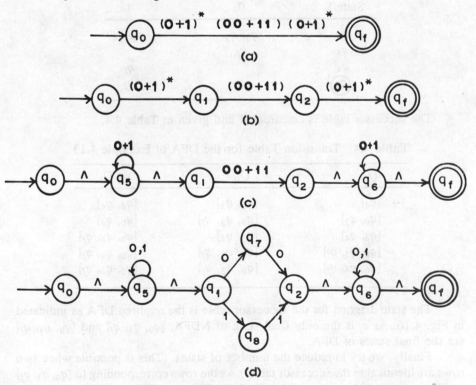

Fig. 4.15   Construction of FA equivalent to $(0 + 1)^* (00 + 11) (0 + 1)^*$ *(cont.).*

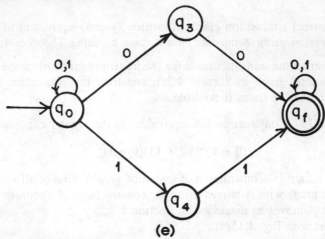

(e)

Fig. 4.15   Construction of FA equivalent to $(0 + 1)^* (00 + 11) (0 + 1)^*$.

Step 2   (Construction of DFA) We construct the transition table for NDFA as given in Table 4.3.

Table 4.3   Transition Table for Example 4.13

State/Σ	0	1
→ q_0	q_0, q_3	q_0, q_4
q_3	q_f	
q_4		q_f
$\textcircled{$q_f$}$	q_f	q_f

The successor table is constructed and given in Table 4.4.

Table 4.4   Transition Table for the DFA of Example 4.13

Q	Q_0	Q_1
→ $[q_0]$	$[q_0, q_3]$	$[q_0, q_4]$
$[q_0, q_3]$	$[q_0, q_3, q_f]$	$[q_0, q_4]$
$[q_0, q_4]$	$[q_0, q_3]$	$[q_0, q_4, q_f]$
$[q_0, q_3, q_f]$	$[q_0, q_3, q_f]$	$[q_0, q_4, q_f]$
$[q_0, q_4, q_f]$	$[q_0, q_3, q_f]$	$[q_0, q_4, q_f]$

The state diagram for the successor table is the required DFA as indicated in Fig. 4.16. As q_f is the only final state of NDFA, $[q_0, q_3, q_f]$ and $[q_0, q_4, q_f]$ are the final states of DFA.

Finally, we try to reduce the number of states. (This is possible when two rows are identical in the successor table.) As the rows corresponding to $[q_0, q_3, q_f]$ and $[q_0, q_4, q_f]$ are identical, we identify them. The state diagram for the equivalent automaton, where the number of states is reduced, is given in Fig. 4.17.

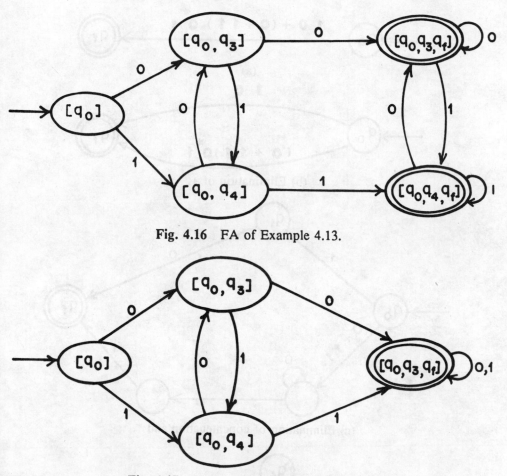

Fig. 4.16   FA of Example 4.13.

Fig. 4.17   Reduced FA of Example 4.13.

NOTE: While constructing the transition graph equivalent to a given r.e., the operation (concatenation, *, +) that is eliminated first, depends on the regular expression.

EXAMPLE 4.14   Construct a DFA with reduced states equivalent to the r.e. $10 + (0 + 11)0^* 1$.

SOLUTION: *Step 1* (Construction of transition graph). The transition graph is constructed by eliminating the operation +, concatenation and *, and the Λ-moves in successive steps. The step-by-step construction is given in Figs. 4.18(a)–4.18(e).

Step 2   (Construction of DFA) For the NDFA given in Fig. 4.18(e), the corresponding transition table is given in Table 4.5.

The successor table is constructed and given in Table 4.6.

In Table 4.6 the columns corresponding to $[q_f]$ and Ø are identical. So we can identify $[q_f]$ and Ø.

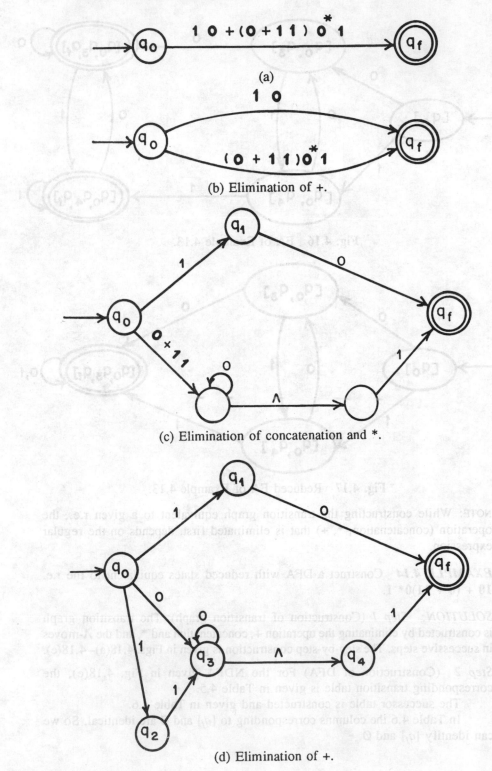

(a)

(b) Elimination of +.

(c) Elimination of concatenation and *.

(d) Elimination of +.

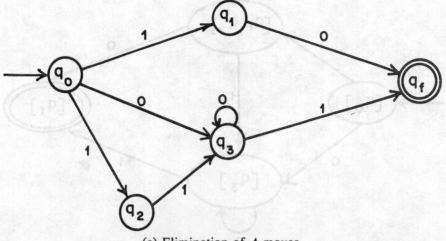

(e) Elimination of Λ-moves.

Fig. 4.18   Construction of FA of Example 4.14.

Table 4.5   Transition Table for Example 4.14

State/Σ	0	1
$\rightarrow q_0$	q_3	q_1, q_2
q_1	q_f	
q_2		q_3
q_3	q_3	q_f
(q_f)		

Table 4.6   Transition Table of DFA for Example 4.14

Q	Q_0	Q_1
$\rightarrow [q_0]$	$[q_3]$	$[q_1, q_2]$
$[q_3]$	$[q_3]$	$[q_f]$
$[q_1, q_2]$	$[q_f]$	$[q_3]$
$([q_f])$	$\emptyset$	$\emptyset$
$\emptyset$	$\emptyset$	$\emptyset$

The DFA with reduced number of states corresponding to Table 4.6 is given in Fig. 4.19.

4.2.6   EQUIVALENCE OF TWO FINITE AUTOMATA

Two finite automata over Σ are equivalent if they accept the same set of strings over Σ. When two FAs are not equivalent, there is some string w over Σ satisfying the following: One automaton reaches a final state on application of w, whereas the other automaton reaches a nonfinal state.

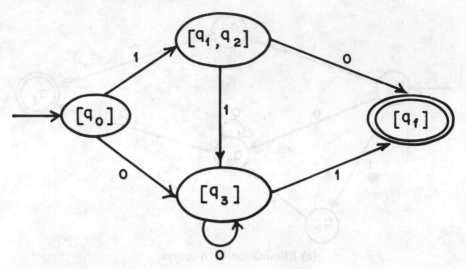

Fig. 4.19   Reduced DFA of Example 4.14.

We give a method, called *comparison method*, to test the equivalence of two FAs over Σ.

Comparison Method

Let M and M' be two FAs over Σ. We construct comparison table consisting of $n + 1$ columns, where n is the number of input symbols. The first column consists of pairs of vertices of the form (q, q'), where $q \in M$ and $q' \in M'$. If (q, q') appears in some row of the first column, then the corresponding entry in the a-column $(a \in \Sigma)$ is (q_a, q'_a), where q_a and q'_a are reachable from q and q', respectively on application of a (i.e. by a-paths).

The comparison table is constructed by starting with the pair of initial vertices q_{in}, q'_{in} of M and M' in the first column. The first elements in the subsequent columns are (q_a, q'_a), where q_a and q'_a are reachable by a-paths from q_{in} and q'_{in}. We repeat the construction by considering the pairs in the second and subsequent columns which are not in the first column.

The row-wise construction is repeated. There are two cases:

Case 1   If we reach a pair (q, q') such that q is a final state of M, and q' is a nonfinal state of M' or vice versa, we terminate the construction and conclude that M and M' are not equivalent.

Case 2   Here the construction is terminated when no new element appears in the second and subsequent columns which are not in the first column (i.e. when all the elements in the second and subsequent columns appear in the first column). In this case we conclude that M and M' are equivalent.

EXAMPLE 4.15   Consider the following two DFAs M and M' over $\{0, 1\}$ given in Fig. 4.20. Find out whether M and M' are equivalent.

SOLUTION   The initial states in M and M' are q_1 and q_4, respectively. Hence

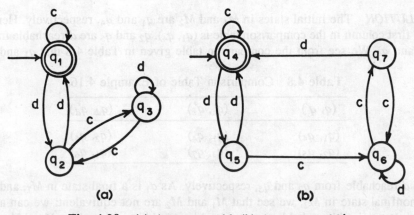

Fig. 4.20 (a) Automaton M, (b) Automaton M'.

the first element of the first column in the comparison table must be (q_1, q_4). The first element in the second column is (q_1, q_4) since both q_1 and q_4 are c-reachable from the respective initial states. The complete table is given in Table 4.7.

Table 4.7 Comparison Table of Example 4.15

(q, q')	(q_c, q'_c)	(q_d, q'_d)
(q_1, q_4)	(q_1, q_4)	(q_2, q_5)
(q_2, q_5)	(q_3, q_6)	(q_1, q_4)
(q_3, q_6)	(q_2, q_7)	(q_3, q_6)
(q_2, q_7)	(q_3, q_6)	(q_1, q_4)

As we do not get a pair (q, q'), where q is a final state and q' is a nonfinal state (or vice versa) at every row, we proceed until all the elements in the second and third columns are also in the first column. Therefore, M and M' are equivalent.

EXAMPLE 4.16 Show that the automata M_1 and M_2 given in Fig. 4.21 are not equivalent.

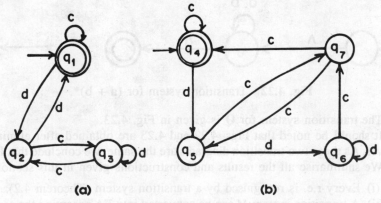

Fig. 4.21 (a) Automaton M_1, (b) Automaton M_2.

SOLUTION The initial states in M_1 and M_2 are q_1 and q_4, respectively. Hence the first column in the comparison table is (q_1, q_4). q_2 and q_5 are d-reachable from q_1 and q_4. We see from the comparison table given in Table 4.8 that q_1 and q_6

Table 4.8   Comparison Table of Example 4.16

(q, q')	(q_c, q'_c)	(q_d, q'_d)
(q_1, q_4)	(q_1, q_4)	(q_2, q_5)
(q_2, q_5)	(q_3, q_7)	(q_1, q_6)

are d-reachable from q_2 and q_5, respectively. As q_1 is a final state in M_1, and q_6 is nonfinal state in M_2, we see that M_1 and M_2 are not equivalent: we can also note that q_1 is dd-reachable from q_1, and hence dd is accepted by M_1. dd is not accepted by M_2 as only q_6 is dd-reachable from q_4, but q_6 is nonfinal.

4.2.7   EQUIVALENCE OF TWO REGULAR EXPRESSIONS

Suppose we are interested in testing the equivalence of two regular expressions, say **P** and **Q**. **P** and **Q** are equivalent iff they represent the same set. Also, **P** and **Q** are equivalent iff the corresponding FAs are equivalent.

To prove the equivalence of **P** and **Q**, (a) we prove that the sets **P** and **Q** are the same. (For nonequivalence we find a string in one set but not in the other.) Or (b) we use the identities to prove the equivalence of **P** and **Q**. Or (c) We construct the corresponding FA M and M' and prove that M and M' are equivalent. (For nonequivalence we prove that M and M' are not equivalent.)

The method to be chosen depends on the problem.

EXAMPLE 4.17   Prove $(a + b)^* = a^*(ba^*)^*$.

SOLUTION   Let **P** and **Q** denote $(a + b)^*$ and $a^*(ba^*)^*$, respectively. Using the construction in Section 4.2.5, **P** is given by the transition system given in Fig. 4.22.

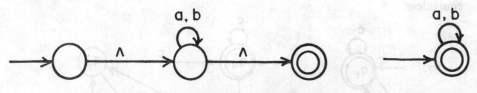

Fig. 4.22   Transition system for $(a + b)^*$.

The transition system for **Q** is given in Fig. 4.23.

It should be noted that Figs. 4.22 and 4.23 are obtained after eliminating Λ-moves. As these two transition diagrams are the same, we conclude that **P** = **Q**. We summarise all the results and constructions given in this section.

  (i) Every r.e. is recognised by a transition system (Theorem 4.2).
 (ii) A transition system M can be converted into FA accepting the same set as M (Section 4.2.3).

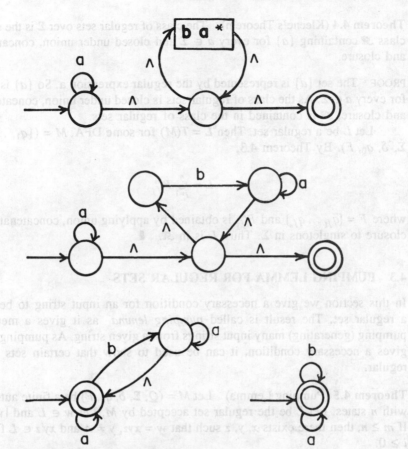

Fig. 4.23 Transition system for a*(ba*)*.

(iii) Any set accepted by FA is represented by an r.e. (Theorem 4.3).
(iv) A set accepted by a transition system is represented by an r.e. (from (ii) and (iii)).
(v) To get the r.e. representing a set accepted by a transition system, we can apply algebraic method using Arden's theorem (see Section 4.2.4).
(vi) If P is an r.e., then to construct an FA accepting the set P, we can apply the construction given in Section 4.2.5.
(vii) A subset L of Σ* is a regular set (or represented by an r.e.) iff it is accepted by an FA (From (i), (ii) and (iii)).
(viii) A subset L of Σ* is a regular set iff it is recognised by a transition system (from (i) and (iv)).
(ix) The capabilities of FA and transition systems are the same as far as acceptability of subsets of strings is concerned.
(x) To test the equivalence of two DFAs, we can apply the comparison method given in Section 4.2.6.

We conclude this section with Kleene's theorem.

Theorem 4.4 (Kleene's Theorem)   The class of regular sets over Σ is the smallest class $\mathcal{R}$ containing $\{a\}$ for every $a \in \Sigma$ and closed under union, concatenation and closure.

PROOF   The set $\{a\}$ is represented by the regular expression **a**. So $\{a\}$ is regular for every $a \in \Sigma$. As the class of regular sets is closed under union, concatenation, and closure, $\mathcal{R}$ is contained in the class of regular sets.

Let L be a regular set. Then $L = T(M)$ for some DFA, $M = (\{q_1, \dots , q_m\}, \Sigma, \delta, q_0, F)$. By Theorem 4.3,

$$L = \bigcup_{j=1}^{n} P_{1f_j}^{m}$$

where $F = \{q_{f_1} \dots q_{f_n}\}$ and $P_{1f_j}^{m}$ is obtained by applying union, concatenation and closure to singletons in Σ. Thus, L is in $\mathcal{R}$. ∎

4.3   PUMPING LEMMA FOR REGULAR SETS

In this section we give a necessary condition for an input string to belong to a regular set. The result is called *pumping lemma* as it gives a method of pumping (generating) many input strings from a given string. As pumping lemma gives a necessary condition, it can be used to show that certain sets are not regular.

Theorem 4.5 (Pumping Lemma)   Let $M = (Q, \Sigma, \delta, q_0, F)$ be a finite automaton with n states. Let L be the regular set accepted by M. Let $w \in L$ and $|w| \geq m$. If $m \geq n$, then there exists x, y, z such that $w = xyz$, $y \neq \Lambda$ and $xy^i z \in L$ for each $i \geq 0$.

PROOF   Let

$$w = a_1 a_2 \dots a_m, \qquad m \geq n$$

$$\delta(q_0, a_1 a_2 \dots a_i) = q_i \quad \text{for } i = 1, 2, \dots, m; \ Q_1 = \{q_0, q_1, \dots, q_m\}$$

That is, Q_1 is the sequence of states in the path with path value $w = a_1 a_2 \dots a_m$. As there are only n distinct states, at least two states in Q_1 must coincide. Among various pairs of repeated states, we take the first pair. Let us take them as q_j and q_k $(q_j = q_k)$. Then j and k satisfy the condition $0 \leq j < k \leq n$.

The string w can be decomposed into three substrings $a_1 a_2 \dots a_j, a_{j+1} \dots a_k$ and $a_{k+1} \dots a_m$. Let x, y, z denote these strings $a_1 a_2 \dots a_j, a_{j+1} \dots a_k, a_{k+1} \dots a_m$, respectively. As $k \leq n$, $|xy| \leq n$ and $w = xyz$. The path with path value w in the transition diagram of M is shown in Fig. 4.24.

The automaton M starts from the initial state q_0. On applying the string x, it reaches $q_j(= q_k)$. On applying the string y, it comes back to $q_j(= q_k)$. So after application of y^i for each $i \geq 0$, the automaton is in the same state q_j. On applying z, it reaches q_m, a final state. Hence $xy^i z \in L$. As every state in Q_1 is obtained by applying an input symbol, $y \neq \Lambda$. ∎

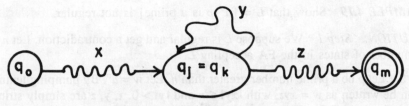

Fig. 4.24   String accepted by M.

NOTE: The decomposition is valid only for strings of length greater than or equal to the number of states. For such a string $w = xyz$, we can 'iterate' the substring y in xyz as many times as we like and get strings of the form $xy^i z$ which are longer than xyz and are in L. By considering the path from q_0 to q_k and then the path from q_k to q_m (without going through the loop), we get a path ending in a final state with path value xz. (This corresponds to the case when $i = 0$.)

4.4 APPLICATION OF PUMPING LEMMA

This theorem can be used to prove that certain sets are not regular. We now give the steps needed for proving that a given set is not regular.

Step 1 Assume L is regular. Let n be the number of states in the corresponding FA.

Step 2 Choose a string w such that $|w| \geq n$. Use pumping lemma to write $w = xyz$, with $|xy| \leq n$ and $|y| > 0$.

Step 3 Find a suitable integer i such that $xy^i z \notin L$. This contradicts our assumption. Hence L is not regular.

NOTE: The crucial part of the procedure is to find i such that $xy^i z \notin L$. In some cases we prove $xy^i z \notin L$ by considering $|xy^i z|$. In some cases we may have to use the 'structure' of strings in L.

EXAMPLE 4.18   Show that the set $L = \{a^{i^2} \mid i \geq 1\}$ is not regular.

SOLUTION   Step 1   Suppose L is regular and we get a contradiction. Let n be the number of states in FA accepting L.

Step 2   Let $w = a^{n^2}$. Then $|w| = n^2 > n$. By pumping lemma we can write $w = xyz$ with $|xy| \leq n$ and $|y| > 0$.

Step 3   Consider $xy^2 z$. $|xy^2 z| = |x| + 2|y| + |z| > |x| + |y| + |z|$ as $|y| > 0$. This means $n^2 = |xyz| = |x| + |y| + |z| < |xy^2 z|$. As $|xy| \leq n$, $|y| \leq n$. Therefore, $|xy^2 z| = |x| + 2|y| + |z| \leq n^2 + n$, i.e.

$$n^2 < |xy^2 z| \leq n^2 + n < n^2 + n + n + 1$$

Hence, $|xy^2 z|$ strictly lies between n^2 and $(n + 1)^2$, but is not equal to any one of them. Thus $|xy^2 z|$ is not a perfect square and so $xy^2 z \notin L$. But by pumping lemma $xy^2 z \in L$. This is a contradiction.

EXAMPLE 4.19   Show that $L = \{a^p | p \text{ is a prime}\}$ is not regular.

SOLUTION: *Step 1*   We suppose L is regular and get a contradiction. Let n be the number of states in the FA accepting L.

Step 2   Let p be a prime number greater than n. Let $w = a^p$. By pumping lemma, w can be written as $w = xyz$, with $|xy| \le n$ and $|y| > 0$. x, y, z are simply strings of a's. So, $y = a^m$ for some $m \ge 1$ (and $\le n$).

Step 3   Let $i = p + 1$. Then $|xy^i z| = |xyz| + |y^{i-1}| = p + (i - 1)m = p + pm$. By pumping lemma, $xy^i z \in L$. But $|xy^i z| = p + pm = p(1 + m)$ and $p(1 + m)$ is not a prime. So $xy^i z \notin L$. This is a contradiction. Thus L is not regular.

EXAMPLE 4.20   Show that $L = \{0^i 1^i | i \ge 1\}$ is not regular.

SOLUTION: *Step 1*   Suppose L is regular and we get a contradiction. Let n be the number of states in FA accepting L.

Step 2   Let $w = 0^n 1^n$. Then $|w| = 2n > n$. By pumping lemma we write $w = xyz$ with $|xy| \le n$ and $|y| \ne 0$.

Step 3   We want to find i so that $xy^i z \notin L$ for getting a contradiction. The string y can be in any of the following forms:

Case 1 y has 0's, i.e. $y = 0^k$ for some $k \ge 1$.

Case 2 y has only 1's, i.e. $y = 1^l$ for some $l \ge 1$.

Case 3 y has both 0's and 1's i.e. $y = 0^k 1^j$ for some $k, j \ge 1$.

In case 1, we can take $i = 0$. As $xyz = 0^n 1^n$, $xz = 0^{n-k} 1^n$. As $k \ge 1$, $n - k \ne n$. So $xz \notin L$.

In case 2, take $i = 0$. As before, xz is $0^n 1^{n-l}$ and $n \ne n - l$. So $xz \notin L$.

In case 3, take $i = 2$. As $xyz = 0^{n-k} 0^k 1^j 1^{n-j}$, $xy^2 z = 0^{n-k} 0^k 1^j 0^k 1^j 1^{n-j}$. As $xy^2 z$ is not of the form $0^i 1^i$, $xy^2 z \notin L$.

Thus in all the cases we get a contradiction. Therefore, L is not regular.

EXAMPLE 4.21   Show that $L = \{ww | w \in \{a, b\}^*\}$ is not regular.

SOLUTION   We prove the result by the method of contradiction.

Step 1   Suppose L is regular. Let n be the number of states in the automaton M accepting L.

Step 2   Let us consider $ww = a^n b a^n b$ in L. $|ww| = 2(n + 1) > n$. We can apply pumping lemma to write $ww = xyz$ with $|y| \ne 0$, $|xy| \le n$.

Step 3   We want to find i so that $xy^i z \notin L$ for getting a contradiction. The string y can be in only one of the following forms:

Case 1 y has no b's, i.e. $y = a^k$ for some $k \ge 1$.

Case 2 y has only one b.

We may note that y cannot have two b's. If so, $|y| \ge n + 2$. But $|y| \le |xy| \le n$. In case 1, we can take $i = 0$. Then $xy^0 z = xz$ is of the form $a^m b a^n b$, where

$m = n - k < n$ (or $a^n b a^m b$). We cannot write xz in the form uu with $u \in \{a, b\}^*$, and so $xz \notin L$. In case 2 also, we can take $i = 0$. Then $xy^0 z = xz$ has only one b (as one b is removed from xyz, b being in y). So $xz \notin L$ as any element in L should have even number of a's and even number of b's.

Thus in both the cases we get a contradiction. Therefore, L is not regular.

NOTE: If a set L of strings over Σ is given and if we have to test whether L is regular or not, we try to write a regular expression representing L using the definition of L. If this is not possible, we use pumping lemma to prove that L is not regular.

EXAMPLE 4.22   Is $L = \{a^{2n} \mid n \geq 1\}$ regular?

SOLUTION   We can write a^{2n} as $a(a^2)^i a$, where $i \geq 0$. Now $\{(a^2)^i \mid i \geq 0\}$ is simply $\{a^2\}^*$. So L is represented by the regular expression $\mathbf{a(P)^*a}$, where $\mathbf{P}$ represents $\{a^2\}$. The corresponding FA (using the construction given in Section 4.2.5) is given in Fig. 4.25.

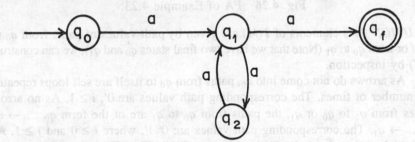

Fig. 4.25   FA of Example 4.22.

4.5   CLOSURE PROPERTIES OF REGULAR SETS

In this section we discuss the closure properties of regular sets under (a) set union, (b) concatenation, (c) closure (iteration), (d) transpose, (e) set intersection, and (f) complementation.

In Section 4.1, we have seen that the class of regular sets is closed under union, concatenation and closure.

Theorem 4.6   If L is regular then L^T is also regular.

PROOF   As L is regular by (vii), given at the end of Section 4.2, we can construct a FA $M = (Q, \Sigma, \delta, q_0, F)$ such that $T(M) = L$.

We construct a transition system M' by starting with the state diagram of M, and reversing the direction of the directed edges. The set of initial states of M' is defined as the set F, and q_0 is defined as the (only) final state of M', i.e. $M' = (Q, \Sigma, \delta', F, \{q_0\})$.

If $w \in T(M)$, we have a path from q_0, to some final state in F with path value w. By 'reversing the edges', we get a pair in M' from some final state in F to q_0. Its path value is w^T. So $w^T \in T(M')$. In a similar way, we can see that if $w_1 \in T(M')$, then $w_1^T \in T(M)$. Thus from the state diagram it is easy to see that $T(M') = T(M)^T$. We can prove rigorously that $w \in T(M)$ iff $w^T \in T(M')$ by induction on $|w|$. So $T(M)^T = T(M')$. By (viii) of Section 4.2, $T(M')$ is regular, i.e. $T(M)^T$ is regular. ∎

EXAMPLE 4.23   Consider the FA M given by Fig. 4.26. What is $T(M)$? Show that $T(M)^T$ is regular.

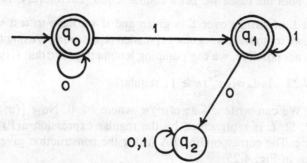

Fig. 4.26   FA of Example 4.23.

SOLUTION   As elements of $T(M)$ are given by path values of paths from q_0 to itself or from q_0 to q_1 (Note that we have two final states q_0 and q_1), we can construct $T(M)$ by inspection.

As arrows do not come into q_0, paths from q_0 to itself are self loops repeated any number of times. The corresponding path values are 0^i, $i \geq 1$. As no arrow comes from q_2 to q_0 or q_1, the paths from q_0 to q_1 are of the form $q_0 \ldots \rightarrow q_0$ $q_1 \ldots \rightarrow q_1$. The corresponding path values are $0^i 1^j$, where $i \geq 0$ and $j \geq 1$. As the initial state q_0 is also a final state, $\Lambda \in T(M)$. Thus $T(M)$ is

$$\{0^i 1^j \,|\, i, j \geq 0\}$$

Hence $T(M)^T = \{1^j 0^i \,|\, i, j \geq 0\}$.

The transition system M' is constructed as follows:

(i)   The initial states of M' are q_0 and q_1.
(ii) The (only) final state of M' is q_0.
(iii) The direction of the directed edges is reversed. M' is given in Fig. 4.27.

From (i)–(iii) it follows that

$$T(M') = T(M)^T.$$

Hence, $T(M)^T$ is regular.

NOTE: In Example 4.23, we can see by inspection that $T(M') = \{1^j 0^i \,|\, i, j \geq 0\}$. The strings of $T(M')$ are obtained as path values of paths from q_0 to itself or from q_1 to q_0.

Theorem 4.7   If L is a regular set over Σ, then $\Sigma^* - L$ is also regular over Σ.

PROOF   As L is regular by (vii), given at the end of Section 4.2, we can construct a DFA $M = (Q, \Sigma, \delta, q_0, F)$ accepting L, i.e. $L = T(M)$.

We construct another DFA $M' = (Q, \Sigma, \delta, q_0, F')$ by defining $F' = Q - F$, i.e. M and M' differ only in their final states. A final state of M' is a nonfinal state of M and vice versa. The state diagrams of M and M' are the same except for the final states.

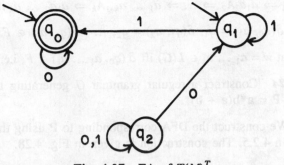

Fig. 4.27 FA of $T(M)^T$.

$w \in T(M')$ if and only if $\delta(q_0, w) \in F' = Q - F$, i.e. iff $w \notin L$. This proves $T(M') = \Sigma^* - X$. ∎

Theorem 4.8 If X and Y are regular sets over Σ, then $X \cap Y$ is also regular over Σ.

PROOF By De Morgan's law for sets, $X \cap Y = \Sigma^* - ((\Sigma^* - X) \cup (\Sigma^* - Y))$. By Theorem 4.7, $\Sigma^* - X$ and $\Sigma^* - Y$ are regular. So, $(\Sigma^* - X) \cup (\Sigma^* - Y)$ is also regular. By applying Theorem 4.7, once again $\Sigma^* - ((\Sigma^* - X) \cup (\Sigma^* - Y))$ is regular, i.e. $X \cap Y$ is regular. ∎

4.6 REGULAR SETS AND REGULAR GRAMMARS

We have seen that regular sets are precisely those accepted by DFA. In this section we show that the class of regular sets over Σ is precisely the regular languages over the terminal set Σ.

4.6.1 CONSTRUCTION OF A REGULAR GRAMMAR GENERATING $T(M)$ FOR A GIVEN DFA M

Let $M = (\{q_0, \ldots, q_n\}, \Sigma, \delta, q_0, F)$. If w is in $T(M)$, then it is obtained by concatenating the labels corresponding to several transitions, the first from q_0 and the last terminating at some final state. So for the grammar G to be constructed, productions should correspond to transitions. Also, there should be provision for terminating the derivation once a transition terminating at some final state is encountered. With these ideas in mind we construct G as:

$$G = (\{A_0, A_1, \ldots, A_n\}, \Sigma, P, A_0)$$

P is defined by the following rules:

(i) $A_i \rightarrow aA_j$ is included in P if $\delta(q_i, a) = q_j \notin F$.
(ii) $A_i \rightarrow aA_j$ and $A_i \rightarrow a$ are included in P if $\delta(q_i, a) = q_j \in F$.

We can show that $L(G) = T(M)$ by using the construction of P. Such a construction gives

$$A_i \Rightarrow aA_j \quad \text{iff} \quad \delta(q_i, a) = q_j$$
$$A_i \Rightarrow a \quad \text{iff} \quad \delta(q_i, a) \in F$$

So, $A_0 \Rightarrow a_1A_1 \Rightarrow a_1a_2A_2 \Rightarrow \ldots \Rightarrow a_1 \ldots a_{k-1}A_k \Rightarrow a_1a_2 \ldots a_k$ iff

$$\delta(q_0, a_1) = q_1, \delta(q_1, a_2) = q_2, \ldots, \delta(q_k, a_k) \in F$$

This proves that $w = a_1 \ldots a_k \in L(G)$ iff $\delta(q_0, a_1 \ldots a_k) \in F$, i.e. iff $w \in T(M)$.

EXAMPLE 4.24 Construct a regular grammar G generating the regular set represented by $\mathbf{P = a*b(a + b)*}$.

SOLUTION We construct the DFA corresponding to **P** using the construction given in Section 4.2.5. The construction is given in Fig. 4.28.

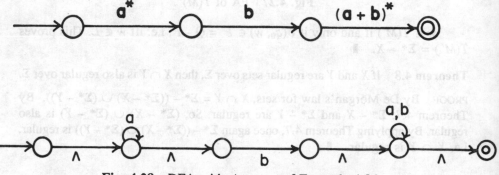

Fig. 4.28 DFA with Λ-moves of Example 4.24.

After eliminating Λ-moves, we get the DFA straightaway, as shown in Fig. 4.29.

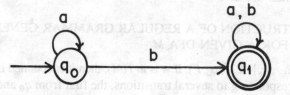

Fig. 4.29 DFA without λ-moves of Example 4.24.

Let $G = (\{A_0, A_1\}, \{a, b\}, P, A_0)$, where P is given by

$$A_0 \to aA_0, \qquad A_0 \to bA_1, \qquad A_0 \to b$$

$$A_1 \to aA_1, \qquad A_1 \to bA_1, \qquad A_1 \to a, \qquad A_1 \to b$$

G is the required regular grammar.

4.6.2 CONSTRUCTION OF A TRANSITION SYSTEM M ACCEPTING $L(G)$ FOR A GIVEN REGULAR GRAMMAR G

Let $G = (\{A_0, A_1, \ldots, A_n\}, \Sigma, P, A_0)$. We construct a transition system M whose (a) states correspond to variables, (b) initial state corresponds to A_0, (c) transitions in M correspond to productions in P. As the last production applied in any derivation is of the form $A_i \rightarrow a$, the corresponding transition terminates at a new state, and this is the unique final state.

We define M as $(\{q_0, ..., q_n, q_f\}, \Sigma, \delta, q_0, \{q_f\})$. δ is defined as follows:

(i) Each production $A_i \rightarrow aA_j$ induces a transition from q_i to q_j with label a.

(ii) Each production $A_k \rightarrow a$ induces a transition from q_k to q_f with label a.

From the construction it is easy to see that $A_0 \Rightarrow a_1A_1 \Rightarrow a_1a_2A_2 \Rightarrow ... \Rightarrow a_1 ... a_{n-1}A_{n-1} \Rightarrow a_1 ... a_n$ is a derivation of $a_1a_2 ... a_n$ iff there is a path in M starting from q_0 and terminating in q_f with path value $a_1a_2 ... a_n$. Therefore, $L(G) = T(M)$.

EXAMPLE 4.25 Let $G = (\{A_0, A_1\}, \{a, b\}, P, A_0)$, where P consists of $A_0 \rightarrow aA_1$, $A_1 \rightarrow bA_1$, $A_1 \rightarrow a$, $A_1 \rightarrow bA_0$. Construct a transition system M accepting $L(G)$.

SOLUTION Let $M = (\{q_0, q_1, q_f\}, \{a, b\}, \delta, q_0, \{q_f\})$, where q_0 and q_1 correspond to A_0 and A_1, respectively and q_f is the new (final) state introduced. $A_0 \rightarrow aA_1$ induces a transition from q_0 to q_1 with label a. Similarly, $A_1 \rightarrow bA_1$ and $A_1 \rightarrow bA_0$ induce transitions from q_1 to q_1 with label b and from q_1 to q_0 with label b, respectively. $A_1 \rightarrow a$ induces a transition from q_1 to q_f with label a. M is given in Fig. 4.30.

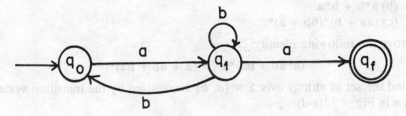

Fig. 4.30 Transition system of Example 4.25.

EXAMPLE 4.26 If a regular grammar G is given by $S \rightarrow aS | a$, find M accepting $L(G)$.

SOLUTION Let q_0 correspond to S and q_f which is the new (final) state. M is given in Fig. 4.31. Symbolically,

$$M = (\{q_0, q_f\}, \{a\}, \delta, q_0, \{q_f\}).$$

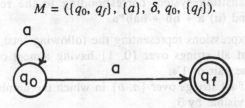

Fig. 4.31 Transition system of Example 4.26.

NOTE: If $S \rightarrow \Lambda$ is in P, the corresponding transition is from q_0 to q_f with label Λ.

By using the construction given in Section 4.2.3, we can construct a DFA M accepting $L(G)$ for a given regular grammar G.

EXERCISES

1. Represent the following sets by regular expressions:
   (a) $\{0, 1, 2\}$.
   (b) $\{1^{2n+1} | n > 0\}$.
   (c) $\{w \in \{a, b\}^* | w$ has only one $a\}$.
   (d) The set of all strings over $\{0, 1\}$ which has atmost two zeros.
   (e) $\{a^2, a^5, a^8, ...\}$.
   (f) $\{a^n | n$ is divisible by 2 or 3 or $n = 5\}$.
   (g) The set of all strings over $\{a, b\}$ beginning and ending with a.

2. Find all strings of length 5 or less in the regular set represented by the following:
   (a) $(ab + a)^*(aa + b)$.
   (b) $(a^*b + b^*a)^*a$.
   (c) $a^* + (ab + a)^*$.

3. Describe, in the English language, the sets represented by the following regular expressions:
   (a) $a(a + b)^*ab$.
   (b) $a^*b + b^*a$.
   (c) $(aa + b)^*(bb + a)^*$.

4. Prove the following identity:
$$(a^*ab + ba)^*a^* = (a + ab + ba)^*$$

5. Find the set of strings over $\Sigma = \{a, b\}$ recognised by the transition systems shown in Fig. 4.32(a-d).

6. Find the regular expression corresponding to the automaton given in Fig. 4.33.

7. Construct transition systems equivalent to the regular expressions given in Exercise 2.

8. Construct transition systems equivalent to the regular expressions given in Exercise 3.

9. Construct a transition system corresponding to the regular expression (i) $(ab + c^*)^* b$ and (ii) $a + bb + bab^*a$.

10. Find regular expressions representing the following sets:
   (a) The set of all strings over $\{0, 1\}$ having atmost one pair of 0's or atmost one pair of 1's.
   (b) The set of all strings over $\{a, b\}$ in which the number of occurrences of a is divisible by 3.
   (c) The set of all strings over $\{a, b\}$ in which there are at least two occurrences of b between any two occurrences of a.

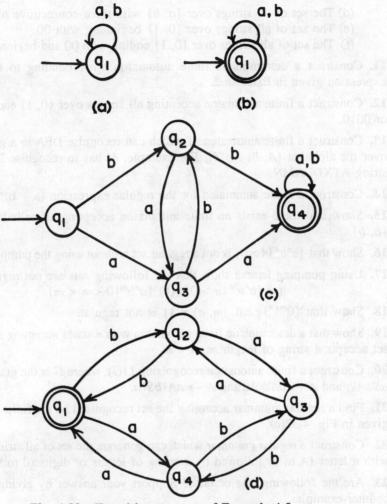

Fig. 4.32   Transition systems of Example 4.5.

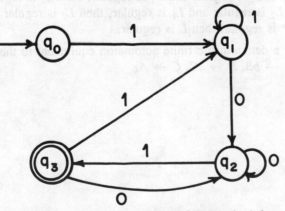

Fig. 4.33   Transition system of Example 4.6.

(d) The set of all strings over $\{a, b\}$ with three consecutive b's.

(e) The set of all strings over $\{0, 1\}$ beginning with 00.

(f) The set of all strings over $\{0, 1\}$ ending with 00 and beginning with 1.

11. Construct a deterministic finite automaton corresponding to the regular expression given in Exercise 2.

12. Construct a finite automaton accepting all strings over $\{0, 1\}$ ending in 010 or 0010.

13. Construct a finite automaton M which can recognise DFA in a given string over the alphabet $\{A, B, ..., Z\}$. For example, M has to recognise DFA in the string ATXDFAMN.

14. Construct a finite automaton for the regular expression (a + b)*abb.

15. Show that there exists no finite automaton accepting all palindromes over $\{a, b\}$.

16. Show that $\{a^n b^n \mid n > 0\}$ is not a regular set without using the pumping lemma.

17. Using pumping lemma show that the following sets are not regular:
(a) $\{a^n b^{2n} \mid n > 0\}$; (b) $\{a^n b^m \mid 0 < n < m\}$.

18. Show that $\{0^m 1^n \mid \text{g.c.d. } (m, n) = 1\}$ is not regular.

19. Show that a deterministic finite automaton with n states accepting a nonempty set accepts a string of length m, $m < n$.

20. Construct a finite automaton recognising $L(G)$, where G is the grammar $S \rightarrow aS \mid bA \mid b$ and $A \rightarrow aA \mid bS \mid a$. and $A \rightarrow aA \mid bS \mid a$.

21. Find a regular grammar accepting the set recognised by the finite automaton given in Fig. 4.32(c).

22. Construct a regular grammar which can generate the set of all strings starting with a letter (A to Z) followed by a string of letters or digits (0 to 9).

23. Are the following true or false? Support your answer by giving proofs or counter-examples.
(a) If $L_1 \cup L_2$ is regular and L_1 is regular, then L_2 is regular.
(b) If $L_1 L_2$ is regular and L_1 is regular, then L_2 is regular.
(c) If L^* is regular, then L is regular.

24. Construct a deterministic finite automaton equivalent to the grammar $S \rightarrow aS \mid bS \mid aA$, $A \rightarrow bB$, $B \rightarrow aC$, $C \rightarrow \Lambda$.

5
Context-Free Languages

In this chapter we study context-free grammars and languages. We define derivation trees and give methods of simplifying context-free grammars. The two normal forms—Chomsky normal form and Greibach normal form—are dealt with. We conclude this chapter after proving pumping lemma and giving some decision algorithms.

5.1 CONTEXT-FREE LANGUAGES AND DERIVATION TREES

Context-free languages are applied in parser design. It is also useful for describing block structure in programming languages. It is easy to visualise derivations in context-free languages as we can represent derivations using tree structures.

We recall the definition of a context-free grammar (CFG). G is context-free if every production is of the form $A \rightarrow \alpha$, where $A \in V_N$ and $\alpha \in (V_N \cup \Sigma)^*$.

EXAMPLE 5.1 Construct a context-free grammar G generating all integers (with sign).

SOLUTION Let

$$G = (V_N, \Sigma, P, S)$$

where

$$V_N = \{S, \langle \text{sign} \rangle, \langle \text{digit} \rangle, \langle \text{Integer} \rangle\}$$

$$\Sigma = \{0, 1, 2, 3, ..., 9, +, -\}$$

P consists of $S \rightarrow \langle \text{sign} \rangle \langle \text{integer} \rangle$, $\langle \text{sign} \rangle \rightarrow +|-$,

$$\langle \text{integer} \rangle \rightarrow \langle \text{digit} \rangle \langle \text{integer} \rangle | \langle \text{digit} \rangle$$

$$\langle \text{digit} \rangle \rightarrow 0|1|2|...|9$$

$L(G)$ = the set of all integers. For example, the derivation of −17 can be obtained as follows:

$$S \Rightarrow \langle \text{sign} \rangle \langle \text{integer} \rangle \Rightarrow - \langle \text{integer} \rangle$$

$$\Rightarrow - \langle \text{digit} \rangle \langle \text{integer} \rangle \Rightarrow - 1 \langle \text{integer} \rangle \Rightarrow - 1 \langle \text{digit} \rangle$$

$$\Rightarrow - 17$$

111

5.1.1   DERIVATION TREES

The derivation in a CFG can be represented using trees. Such trees representing derivations are called derivation trees. We give a rigorous definition of a derivation tree.

Definition 5.1   A derivation tree (also called a parse tree) for a CFG $G = (V_N, \Sigma, P, S)$ is a tree satisfying the following:

    (i)   Every vertex has a label which is a variable or terminal or Λ.
    (ii) The root has label S.
    (iii) The label of an internal vertex is a variable.
    (iv) If the vertices $n_1, n_2, \ldots, n_k$ written with labels $X_1, X_2, \ldots, X_k$ are the sons of vertex n with label A, then $A \rightarrow X_1 X_2 \ldots X_k$ is a production in P.
    (v) A vertex n is a leaf if its label is $a \in \Sigma$ or Λ; n is the only son of its father if its label is Λ.

    For example, let $G = (\{S, A\}, \{a, b\}, P, S)$, where P consists of $S \rightarrow aAS$ $|\, a\, |\, SS$, $A \rightarrow SbA\, |\, ba$. Figure 5.1 is an example of a derivation tree.

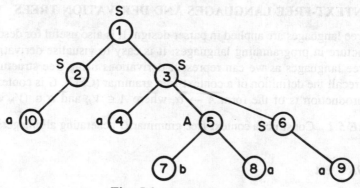

Fig. 5.1   Derivation tree.

NOTE: Vertices 4–6 are sons of 3 written from the left, and $S \rightarrow aAS$ is in P. Vertices 7 and 8 are sons of 5 written from the left, and $A \rightarrow ba$ is a production in P. Vertex 5 is an internal vertex and its label is A, which is a variable.

Ordering of Leaves from the Left

We can order all the vertices of a tree in the following way: The successors of the root (i.e. sons of the root) are ordered from the left by the definition (refer Section 1.2). So vertices at level 1 are ordered from the left. If v_1 and v_2 are any two vertices at level 1 and v_1 is to the left of v_2, then we say that v_1 is to the left of any son of v_2. Also, any son of v_1 is to the left of v_2 and to the left of any son of v_2. Thus we get a left-to-right ordering of vertices at level 2. Repeating the process up to level k, where k is the height of the tree, we have an ordering of all vertices from the left.

    Our main interest is in the ordering of leaves.

In Fig. 5.1, for example, the sons of the root are 2 and 3 ordered from the left. So, the son of 2, viz. 10, is to the left of any son of 3. The sons of 3 ordered from the left are 4-5-6. The vertices at level 2 in the left-to-right ordering are 10-4-5-6. 4 is to the left of 5. The sons of 5 ordered from the left are 7-8. So 4 is to the left of 7. Similarly, 8 is to the left of 9. Thus the order of the leaves from the left is 10-4-7-8-9.

NOTE: If we draw the sons of any vertex keeping in mind the left-to-right ordering, we get the left-to-right ordering of leaves by 'reading' the leaves in the anti-clockwise direction.

Definition 5.2 The yield of a derivation tree is the concatenation of the labels of the leaves without repetition in the left-to-right ordering.

The yield of the derivation tree of Fig. 5.1, for example, is *aabaa*.

NOTE: Consider the derivation tree in Fig. 5.2. As sons of 1 are 2-3 in the left-to-right ordering, by condition (iv) of Definition 5.1, we have production $S \rightarrow SS$. By applying condition (iv) to other vertices, we get the productions $S \rightarrow a$, $S \rightarrow aAS$, $A \rightarrow ba$ and $S \rightarrow a$. Using these productions we get the following derivation:

$$S \Rightarrow SS \Rightarrow aS \Rightarrow aaAS \Rightarrow aabaS \Rightarrow aabaa$$

Thus the yield of the derivation tree is a sentential form in G.

Definition A subtree of a derivation tree T is a tree (a) whose root is some vertex v of T, (b) whose vertices are the descendants of v together with their labels, and (c) whose edges are those connecting the descendants of v.

Figures 5.2 and 5.3, for example, give two subtrees of the derivation tree shown in Fig. 5.1.

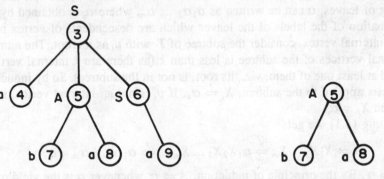

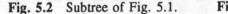

Fig. 5.2 Subtree of Fig. 5.1.　　　**Fig. 5.3** Another subtree of Fig. 5.1.

NOTE: A subtree looks like a derivation tree except that the label of the root may not be S. It is called an A-tree if the label of its root is A.

Remark When there is no need for numbering the vertices, we represent the vertices by points. The following theorem asserts that sentential forms in CFG G are precisely the yields of derivation trees for G.

Theorem 5.1 Let $G = (V_N, \Sigma, P, S)$ be a CFG. Then $S \overset{*}{\Rightarrow} \alpha$ if and only if there is a derivation tree for G with yield α.

PROOF   We prove that $A \overset{*}{\Rightarrow} \alpha$ if and only if there is an A-tree with yield α. Once this is proved, the theorem follows by assuming that $A = S$.

Let α be the yield of an A-tree T. We prove that $A \overset{*}{\Rightarrow} \alpha$ by induction on the number of internal vertices in T.

When the tree has only one internal vertex, the remaining vertices are leaves and are the sons of the root. This is illustrated in Fig. 5.4.

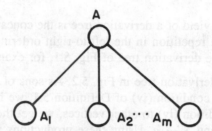

Fig. 5.4   A tree with only one internal vertex.

By condition (iv) of Definition 5.1, $A \to A_1 A_2 \ldots A_m = \alpha$ is a production in G, i.e., $A \Rightarrow \alpha$. Thus there is basis for induction. Now assume the result for all trees with atmost $k - 1$ internal vertices ($k > 1$).

Let T be an A-tree with k internal vertices ($k \geq 2$). Let $v_1, v_2, \ldots, v_m$ be the sons of the root in the left-to-right ordering. Let their labels be $X_1, X_2, \ldots, X_m$. By condition (iv) of Definition 5.1, $A \to X_1 X_2 \ldots X_m$ is in P, and so

$$A \Rightarrow X_1 X_2 \ldots X_m \qquad (5.1)$$

As $k \geq 2$, at least one of the sons is an internal vertex. By the left-to-right ordering of leaves, α can be written as $\alpha_1 \alpha_2 \ldots \alpha_m$, where α_i is obtained by the concatenation of the labels of the leaves which are descendents of vertex v_i. If v_i is an internal vertex, consider the subtree of T with v_i as its root. The number of internal vertices of the subtree is less than k (as there are k internal vertices in T and at least one of them, viz., its root, is not in the subtree). So by induction hypothesis applied to the subtree, $X_i \overset{*}{\Rightarrow} \alpha_i$. If v_i is not an internal vertex, i.e. a leaf, then $X_i = \alpha_i$.

Using (5.1) we get

$$A \Rightarrow X_1 X_2 \ldots X_m \overset{*}{\Rightarrow} \alpha_1 X_2 X_3 \ldots X_m \ldots \overset{*}{\Rightarrow} \alpha_1 \alpha_2 \ldots \alpha_m = \alpha,$$

i.e. $A \overset{*}{\Rightarrow} \alpha$. By the principle of induction, $A \overset{*}{\Rightarrow} \alpha$ whenever α is the yield of an A-tree.

To prove the "only if" part, let us assume that $A \overset{*}{\Rightarrow} \alpha$. We have to construct an A-tree whose yield is α. We do this by induction on the number of steps in $A \overset{*}{\Rightarrow} \alpha$.

When $A \Rightarrow \alpha$, $A \to \alpha$ is a production in P. If $\alpha = X_1 X_2 \ldots X_m$, the A-tree with yield α is constructed and given as in Fig. 5.5. So there is basis for induction. Assume the result for derivations in atmost k steps. Let $A \overset{k}{\Rightarrow} \alpha$; we can split this

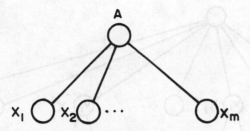

Fig. 5.5   Derivation tree for one-step derivation.

as $A \Rightarrow X_1 \ldots X_m \overset{k-1}{\Rightarrow} \alpha$. $A \Rightarrow X_1 \ldots X_m$ implies $A \to X_1 X_2 \ldots X_m$ is a production in P. In the derivation $X_1 X_2 \ldots X_m \overset{k-1}{\Rightarrow} \alpha$, either (i) X_i is not changed throughout the derivation, or (ii) X_i is changed in some subsequent step. Let α_i be the substring of α derived from X_i. Then $X_i \overset{*}{\Rightarrow} \alpha_i$ in (ii) and $X_i = \alpha_i$ in (i). As G is context-free, in every step of the derivation $X_1 X_2 \ldots X_m \overset{*}{\Rightarrow} \alpha$, we replace a single variable by a string. As $\alpha_1, \alpha_2, \ldots, \alpha_m$ account for all the symbols in α, $\alpha = \alpha_1 \alpha_2 \ldots \alpha_m$.

We construct the derivation tree with yield α as follows: As $A \to X_1 \ldots X_m$ is in P, we construct a tree with m leaves whose labels are $X_1, \ldots, X_m$ in the left-to-right ordering. The tree is given in Fig. 5.6. In (i) above, we leave the

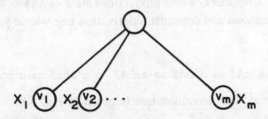

Fig. 5.6   Derivation tree with yield $X_1 X_2 \ldots X_m$.

vertex v_i as it is. In (ii), $X_i \overset{*}{\Rightarrow} \alpha_i$ in less than k steps (as $X_1 \ldots X_m \overset{n-1}{\Rightarrow} \alpha$). By induction hypothesis there exists an X_i-tree T_i with yield α_i. We attach the tree T_i at the vertex v_i (i.e. v_i is the root of T_i). The resulting tree is given in Fig. 5.7. In this figure, let i and j be the first and last indexes such that X_i and X_j satisfy (ii). So $\alpha_1 \ldots \alpha_{i-1}$ are the labels of leaves at level 1 in T. α_i is the yield of the X_i-tree T_i, etc.

Thus we get a derivation tree with yield α. By the principle of induction we get the result for any derivation. This completes the proof of "only if" part. ∎

NOTE: The derivation tree does not specify the order in which we apply the productions for getting α. So, the same derivation tree can induce several derivations.

The following remark is used quite often in proofs and constructions involving CFGs.

Remark: If A derives a terminal string w and if the first step in the derivation

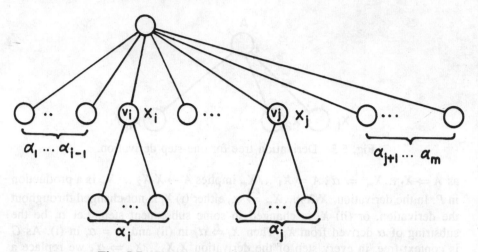

Fig. 5.7 Derivation tree with yield $\alpha_1\alpha_2 \ldots \alpha_n$.

is $A \Rightarrow A_1A_2 \ldots A_n$, then we can write w as $w_1w_2 \ldots w_n$ so that $A_i \overset{*}{\Rightarrow} w_i$. (Actually, in the derivation tree for w, the ith son of the root has label A_i, and w_i is the yield of the subtree whose root is the ith son.)

EXAMPLE 5.2 Consider G whose productions are $S \to aAS \mid a, A \to SbA \mid SS \mid ba$. Show that $S \overset{*}{\Rightarrow} aabbaa$ and construct a derivation tree whose yield is $aabbaa$.

SOLUTION

$$S \Rightarrow aAS \Rightarrow aSbAS \Rightarrow aabAS \Rightarrow a^2bbaS \Rightarrow a^2b^2a^2 \qquad (5.2)$$

Hence, $S \overset{*}{\Rightarrow} a^2b^2a^2$. The derivation tree is given in Fig. 5.8.

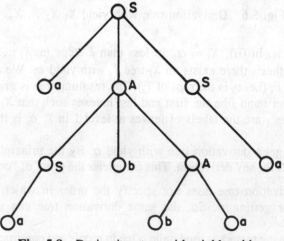

Fig. 5.8 Derivation tree with yield $aabbaa$.

NOTE: Consider G given in Example 5.2. We have seen that $S \overset{*}{\Rightarrow} a^2b^2a^2$, and (5.2) gives a derivation of $a^2b^2a^2$.

Another derivation of $a^2b^2a^2$ is

$$S \Rightarrow aAS \Rightarrow aAa \Rightarrow aSbAa \Rightarrow aSbbaa \Rightarrow aabbaa \qquad (5.3)$$

Yet another derivation of $a^2b^2a^2$ is

$$S \Rightarrow aAS \Rightarrow aSbAS \Rightarrow aSbAa \Rightarrow aabAa \Rightarrow aabbaa \qquad (5.4)$$

In derivation (5.2), whenever we replace a variable X using a production, there are no variables to the left of X. In derivation (5.3), there are no variables to the right of X. But in (5.4), no such conditions are satisfied. These lead to the following definitions.

Definition 5.3 A derivation $A \overset{*}{\Rightarrow} w$ is called a *leftmost* derivation if we apply a production only to the leftmost variable at every step.

Definition 5.4 A derivation $A \overset{*}{\Rightarrow} w$ is a *rightmost* derivation if we apply production to the rightmost variable at every step.

Relation (5.2), for example, is a leftmost derivation. Relation (5.3) is a rightmost derivation. But (5.4) is neither leftmost nor rightmost. In the second step of (5.4), the rightmost variable S is not replaced. So (5.4) is not a rightmost derivation. In the fourth step, the leftmost variable S is not replaced. So (5.4) is not a leftmost derivation.

Theorem 5.2 If $A \overset{*}{\Rightarrow} w$ in G, then there is a leftmost derivation of w.

PROOF We prove the result for every A in V_N by induction on the number of steps in $A \overset{*}{\Rightarrow} w$. $A \Rightarrow w$ is a leftmost derivation as L.H.S. has only one variable. So there is basis for induction. Let us assume the result for derivations in atmost k steps. Let $A \overset{k+1}{\Rightarrow} w$. The derivation can be split as $A \Rightarrow X_1 X_2 \dots X_m \overset{k}{\Rightarrow} w$.

The string w can be split as $w_1 w_2 \dots w_m$ such that $X_i \overset{*}{\Rightarrow} w_i$ (see remark before Example 5.2). As $X_i \overset{*}{\Rightarrow} w_i$ involves atmost k steps by induction hypothesis, we can find a leftmost derivation of w_i. Using these leftmost derivations, we get a leftmost derivation of w given by

$$A \Rightarrow X_1 X_2 \dots X_m \overset{*}{\Rightarrow} w_1 X_2 \dots X_m \overset{*}{\Rightarrow} w_1 w_2 X_3 \dots X_m \dots \overset{*}{\Rightarrow} w_1 w_2 \dots w_m$$

Hence by induction the result is true for all derivations $A \overset{*}{\Rightarrow} w$. ∎

Corollary Every derivation tree of w induces a leftmost derivation of w.

Once we get some derivation of w, it is easy to get a leftmost derivation of w in the following way: From the derivation tree for w, at every level consider the productions for the variables at that level, taken in the left-to-right ordering. The leftmost derivation is obtained by applying the productions in this order.

EXAMPLE 5.3 Let G be the grammar $S \to OB \mid 1A$, $A \to 0 \mid 0S \mid 1AA$, $B \to 1 \mid 1S \mid 0BB$. For the string 00110101, find (a) leftmost derivation, (b) rightmost derivation, and (c) derivation tree.

SOLUTION

(a) $S \Rightarrow 0B \Rightarrow 00BB \Rightarrow 001B \Rightarrow 0011S$

$\Rightarrow 0^2 1^2 0B \Rightarrow 0^2 1^2 01S \Rightarrow 0^2 1^2 010B \Rightarrow 0^2 1^2 0101$

(b) $S \Rightarrow 0B \Rightarrow 00BB \Rightarrow 00B1S \Rightarrow 00B10B$

$\Rightarrow 0^2 B101S \Rightarrow 0^2 B1010B \Rightarrow 0^2 B10101 \Rightarrow 0^2 110101.$

The derivation tree is given in Fig. 5.9.

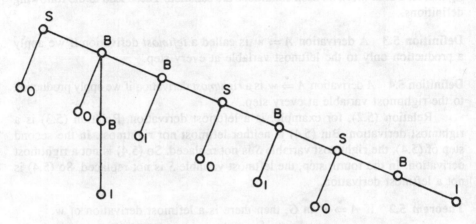

Fig. 5.9   Derivation tree with yield 00110101.

5.2   AMBIGUITY IN CONTEXT-FREE GRAMMARS

Sometimes we come across ambiguous sentences in the language we are using. Consider the following sentence in English: "In books selected information is given." The word 'selected' may refer to books or information. So the sentence may be parsed in two different ways. The same situation may arise in context-free languages. The same terminal string may be the yield of two derivation trees. So there may be two different leftmost derivations of w by Theorem 5.2. This leads to the definition of ambiguous sentences in a context-free language.

Definition 5.5   A terminal string $w \in L(G)$ is ambiguous if there exists two or more derivation trees for w (or there exist two or more leftmost derivation of w).

Consider, for example, $G = (\{S\}, \{a, b, +, *\}, P, S)$, where P consists of $S \rightarrow S + S | S * S | a | b$. We have two derivation trees for $a + a * b$ given in Fig. 5.10. The leftmost derivations of $a + a * b$ induced by the two derivation trees are

$$S \Rightarrow S + S \Rightarrow a + S \Rightarrow a + S * S \Rightarrow a + a * S \Rightarrow a + a * b$$
$$S \Rightarrow S * S \Rightarrow S + S * S \Rightarrow a + S * S \Rightarrow a + a * S \Rightarrow a + a * b$$

Therefore, $a + a * b$ is ambiguous.

Definition 5.6   A context-free grammar G is ambiguous if there exists some $w \in L(G)$, which is ambiguous.

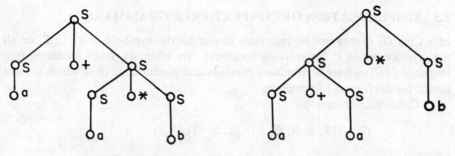

Fig. 5.10   Derivation trees for $a + a * b$.

EXAMPLE 5.4   If G is the grammar $S \rightarrow SbS \mid a$, show that G is ambiguous.

SOLUTION   To prove that G is ambiguous, we have to find a $w \in L(G)$, which is ambiguous. Consider $w = abababa \in L(G)$. Then we get two derivation trees for w (see Fig. 5.11). Thus, G is ambiguous.

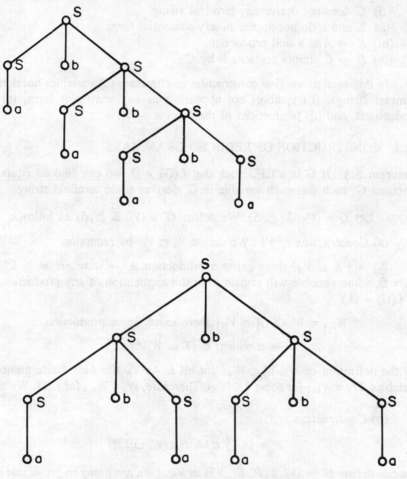

Fig. 5.11   Derivation tree for *abababa*.
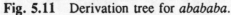

5.3   SIMPLIFICATION OF CONTEXT-FREE GRAMMARS

In a CFG G, it may not be necessary to use all the symbols in $V_N \cup \Sigma$, or all the productions in P for deriving sentences. So when we study a context-free language $L(G)$, we try to eliminate symbols and productions in G which are not useful for derivation of sentences.

Consider, for example,

$$G = (\{S, A, B, C, E\}, \{a, b, c\}, P, S)$$

where

$$P = \{S \to AB, A \to a, B \to b, B \to C, E \to c \mid \Lambda\}$$

It is easy to see that $L(G) = \{ab\}$. Let $G' = (\{S, A, B\}, \{a, b\}, P', S)$, where P' consists of $S \to AB, A \to a, B \to b$. $L(G) = L(G')$. We have eliminated the symbols C, E and c and the productions $B \to C, E \to c \mid \Lambda$. We note the following points regarding the symbols and productions which are eliminated:

    (i) C does not derive any terminal string.
    (ii) E and c do not appear in any sentential form.
    (iii) $E \to \Lambda$ is a null production.
    (iv) $B \to C$ simply replaces B by C.

In this section we give construction to eliminate (a) variables not deriving terminal strings, (b) symbols not appearing in any sentential form, (c) null productions, and (d) productions of the form $A \to B$.

5.3.1   CONSTRUCTION OF REDUCED GRAMMARS

Theorem 5.3   If G is a CFG such that $L(G) \neq \emptyset$, we can find an equivalent grammar G' such that each variable in G' derives some terminal string.

PROOF   Let $G = (V_N, \Sigma, P, S)$. We define $G' = (V'_N, \Sigma, P', S)$ as follows:

    (a) *Construction of V'_N*. We define $W_i \subseteq V_N$ by recursion:

$W_1 = \{A \in V_N \mid$ there exists a production $A \to w$ where $w \in \Sigma^*\}$. (If $W_1 = \emptyset$, some variable will remain after the application of any production, and so $L(G) = \emptyset$.)

$$W_{i+1} = W_i \cup \{A \in V_N \mid \text{there exists some production}$$

$$A \to \alpha \text{ with } \alpha \in (\Sigma \cup W_i)^*\}.$$

By the definition of W_i, $W_i \subseteq W_{i+1}$ for all i. As V_N has only finite number of variables, $W_k = W_{k+1}$ for some $k \leq |V_N|$. Therefore, $W_k = W_{k+j}$ for $j \geq 1$. We define $V'_N = W_k$.

    (b) *Construction of P'*

$$P' = \{A \to \alpha \mid A, \alpha \in (V'_N \cup \Sigma)^*\}$$

We can define $G' = (V'_N, \Sigma, P', S)$. S is in V'_N. (We are going to prove that every variable in V_N' derives some terminal string. So if $S \notin V_N'$, $L(G) = \emptyset$. But $L(G) \neq \emptyset$.)

Before proving that G' is the required grammar, we apply the construction to an example.

EXAMPLE 5.5 Let $G = (V_N, \Sigma, P, S)$ be given by the productions $S \to AB$, $A \to a$, $B \to b$, $B \to C$, $E \to c$. Find G' such that every variable in G' derives some terminal string.

SOLUTION   (a) *Construction of V_N'* $W_1 = \{A, B, E\}$ since $A \to a$, $B \to b$, $E \to c$ are productions with a terminal string on the R.H.S.

$$W_2 = W_1 \cup \{A_1 \in V_N \mid A_1 \to \alpha \text{ for some } \alpha \in (\Sigma \cup \{A, B, E\})^*\}$$

$$= W_1 \cup \{S\} = \{A, B, E, S\}$$

$$W_3 = W_2 \cup \{A_1 \in V_N \mid A_1 \to \alpha \text{ for some } \alpha \in (\Sigma \cup \{S, A, B, E\})^*\}$$

$$= W_2 \cup \emptyset = W_2$$

Therefore,

$$V_N' = \{S, A, B, E\}$$

(b) *Construction of P'*

$$P' = \{A_1 \to \alpha \mid A_1, \alpha \in (V_N' \cup \Sigma)^*\}$$

$$= \{S \to AB, A \to a, B \to b, E \to c\}$$

Therefore,

$$G' = (\{S, A, B, E\}, \{a, b, c\}, P', S)$$

Now we prove:

(i) If each $A \in V_N'$, then $A \underset{G'}{\overset{*}{\Rightarrow}} w$ for some $w \in \Sigma^*$; conversely, if $A \underset{G}{\overset{*}{\Rightarrow}} w$, then $A \in V_N'$.

(ii) $L(G') = L(G)$.

To prove (i) we note that $W_k = W_1 \cup W_2 \ldots \cup W_k$. We prove by induction on i that for $i = 1, 2, \ldots, k$, $A \in W_i$ implies $A \underset{G'}{\overset{*}{\Rightarrow}} w$ for some $w \in \Sigma^*$. If $A \in W_1$, then $A \underset{G}{\Rightarrow} w$. So the production $A \to w$ is in P'. Therefore, $A \underset{G'}{\overset{*}{\Rightarrow}} w$. Thus there is basis for induction. Let us assume the result for i. Let $A \in W_{i+1}$. Then either $A \in W_i$, in which case, $A \underset{G'}{\overset{*}{\Rightarrow}} w$ for some $w \in \Sigma^*$ by induction hypothesis. Or, there exists a production $A \to \alpha$ with $\alpha \in (\Sigma \cup W_i)^*$. By definition of P', $A \to \alpha$ is in P'. We can write $\alpha = X_1 X_2 \ldots X_m$, where $X_j \in \Sigma \cup W_i$. If $X_j \in W_i$ by induction hypothesis, $X_j \underset{G'}{\overset{*}{\Rightarrow}} w_j$ for some $w_j \in \Sigma^*$. So $A \underset{G'}{\overset{*}{\Rightarrow}} w_1 w_2 \ldots w_m \in \Sigma^*$ (when X_j is a terminal, $w_j = X_j$). By induction the result is true for $i = 1, 2 \ldots k$.

The converse part can be proved in a similar way by induction on the number of steps in the derivation $A \underset{G}{\overset{*}{\Rightarrow}} w$. We see immediately that $L(G') \subseteq L(G)$ as $V_N' \subseteq V_N$ and $P' \subseteq P$. To prove $L(G) \subseteq L(G')$, we need an auxiliary result

$$A \underset{G'}{\overset{*}{\Rightarrow}} w \quad \text{if } A \underset{G}{\overset{*}{\Rightarrow}} w \quad \text{for some } w \in \Sigma^* \tag{5.5}$$

We prove (5.5) by induction on the number of steps in the derivation $A \underset{G}{\overset{*}{\Rightarrow}} w$. If $A \underset{G}{\Rightarrow} w$, then $A \to w$ is in P and $A \in W_1 \subseteq V_N'$. As $A \in V_N'$ and $w \in \Sigma^*$, $A \to w$ is in P'. So $A \underset{G'}{\Rightarrow} w$, and there is basis for induction. Assume (5.5) for derivations in almost k steps. Let $A \underset{G}{\overset{k+1}{\Rightarrow}} w$. By Remark 5.1 we can split this as

$A \underset{G}{\Rightarrow} X_1 X_2 \dots X_m \underset{G}{\overset{k}{\Rightarrow}} w_1 w_2 \dots w_m$ such that $X_j \underset{G}{\overset{*}{\Rightarrow}} w_j$. If $X_j \in \Sigma$ then $w_j = X_j$.

If $X_j \in V_N$ then by (i) above, $X_j \in V_N'$. As $X_j \underset{G}{\overset{*}{\Rightarrow}} w_j$ in almost k steps, $X_j \underset{G'}{\overset{*}{\Rightarrow}} w_j$. Also, $X_1, X_2 \dots X_m \in (\Sigma \cup V_N')^*$ implies $A \to X_1 X_2 \dots X_m$ is in P'. Thus, $A \underset{G'}{\Rightarrow} X_1 X_2 \dots X_m \underset{G'}{\overset{*}{\Rightarrow}} w_1 w_2 \dots w_m$. Hence by induction, (5.5) is true for all derivations. In particular, $S \underset{G}{\overset{*}{\Rightarrow}} w$ implies $S \underset{G'}{\overset{*}{\Rightarrow}} w$. This proves that $L(G) \subseteq L(G')$, and (ii) is completely proved. ∎

Theorem 5.4 For every CFG $G = (V_N, \Sigma, P, S)$, we can construct an equivalent grammar $G' = (V_N', \Sigma', P', S)$ such that every symbol in $V_N' \cup \Sigma'$ appears in some sentential form (i.e. for every X in $V_N' \cup \Sigma'$ there exists α such that $S \underset{G'}{\overset{*}{\Rightarrow}} \alpha$ and X is a symbol in the string α).

PROOF We construct $G' = (V_N', \Sigma', P', S)$ as follows:

(a) *Construction of W_i for $i \geq 1$*

    (i) $W_1 = \{S\}$.
    (ii) $W_{i+1} = W_i \cup \{X \in V_N \cup \Sigma \mid \text{there exists a production } A \to \alpha \text{ with } A \in W_i \text{ and } \alpha \text{ containing the symbol } X\}$.

We may note that $W_i \subseteq V_N \cup \Sigma$ and $W_i \subseteq W_{i+1}$. As we have only finite number of elements in $V_N \cup \Sigma$, $W_k = W_{k+1}$ for some k. This means that $W_k = W_{k+j}$ for all $j \geq 0$.

(b) *Construction of V_N', Σ' and P'* We define

$$V_N' = V_N \cap W_k, \qquad \Sigma' = \Sigma \cap W_k$$
$$P' = \{A \to \alpha \mid A \in W_k\}.$$

Before proving that G' is the required grammar, we apply the construction to an example.

EXAMPLE 5.6 Consider $G = (\{S, A, B, E\}, \{a, b, c\}, P, S)$, where P consists of $S \to AB$, $A \to a$, $B \to b$, $E \to c$.

SOLUTION

$$W_1 = \{S\}$$

$$W_2 = \{S\} \cup \{X \in V_N \cup \Sigma | \text{there exists a production } A \to \alpha \text{ with}$$
$$A \in W_1 \text{ and } \alpha \text{ containing } X\}$$

$$= \{S\} \cup \{A, B\}$$

$$W_3 = \{S, A, B\} \cup \{a, b\}$$

$$W_4 = W_3$$

$$V_N' = \{S, A, B\} \quad \Sigma' = \{a, b\}$$

$$P' = \{S \to AB, A \to a, B \to b\}$$

Thus the required grammar is $G' = (V_N', \Sigma', P', S)$.

To complete the proof, we have to show that (a) every symbol in $V_N' \cup \Sigma'$ appears in some sentential form of G', and (b) conversely, $L(G') = L(G)$.

To prove (a), consider $X \in V_N' \cup \Sigma' = W_k$. By construction $W_k = W_1 \cup W_2 \ldots \cup W_k$. We prove that $X \in W_i$, $i \le k$, appears in some sentential form by induction on i. When $i = 1$, $X = S$ and $S \overset{*}{\underset{G'}{\Rightarrow}} S$. Thus there is basis for induction. Assume the result for all variables in W_i. Let $X \in W_{i+1}$. Then either $X \in W_i$, in which case, X appears in some sentential form by induction hypothesis. Otherwise, there exists a production $A \to \alpha$, where $A \in W_i$ and α contains the symbol X_i. A appears in some sentential form, say $\beta A \gamma$. Therefore,

$$S \overset{*}{\underset{G'}{\Rightarrow}} \beta A \gamma \underset{G'}{\Rightarrow} \beta \alpha \gamma$$

This means that $\beta \alpha \gamma$ is some sentential form and X is a symbol in $\beta \alpha \gamma$. Thus by induction the result is true for $X \in W_i$, $i \le k$.

Conversely, if X appears in some sentential form, say $\beta X \gamma$, then $S \overset{l}{\underset{G}{\Rightarrow}} \beta X \gamma$. This implies $X \in W_l$. If $l \le k$, then $W_l \subseteq W_k$. If $l > k$, then $W_l = W_k$. Hence X appears in $V_N' \cup \Sigma'$. This proves (a).

To prove (b), we note $L(G') \subseteq L(G)$ as $V_N' \subseteq V_N$, $\Sigma' \subseteq \Sigma$ and $P' \subseteq P$. Let w be in $L(G)$ and $S = \alpha_1 \underset{G}{\Rightarrow} \alpha_2 \underset{G}{\Rightarrow} \alpha_3 = \ldots \Rightarrow \alpha_{n-1} \underset{G}{\Rightarrow} w$. We prove that every symbol in α_{i+1} is in W_{i+1} and $\alpha_i \underset{G'}{\Rightarrow} \alpha_{i+1}$ by induction on i. $\alpha_1 = S \underset{G}{\Rightarrow} \alpha_2$ implies $S \to \alpha_2$ is a production in P. By construction, every symbol in α_2 is in W_2 and $S \to \alpha_2$ is in P', i.e. $S \underset{G'}{\Rightarrow} \alpha_2$. Thus there is basis for induction. Let us assume the result for i. Consider $\alpha_{i+1} \underset{G}{\Rightarrow} \alpha_{i+2}$. This one-step derivation can be written in the form

$$\beta_{i+1} A \gamma_{i+1} \Rightarrow \beta_{i+1} \alpha \gamma_{i+1}$$

where $A \to \alpha$ is the production we are applying. By induction hypothesis,

$A \in W_{i+1}$. By construction of W_{i+2}, every symbol in α is in W_{i+2}. As all the symbols in β_{i+1} and γ_{i+1} are also in W_{i+1} by induction hypothesis, every symbol in $\beta_{i+1}\alpha\gamma_{i+1} = \alpha_{i+2}$ is in W_{i+2}. By the construction of P', $A \to \alpha$ is in P'. This means that $\alpha_{i+1} \underset{G'}{\Rightarrow} \alpha_{i+2}$. Thus the induction procedure is complete. So $S = \alpha_1 \underset{G'}{\Rightarrow}$ $\alpha_2 \underset{G'}{\Rightarrow} \alpha_3 \Rightarrow \dots \alpha_{n-1} \underset{G'}{\Rightarrow} w$. Therefore, $w \in L(G')$. This proves (b). ∎

Definition 5.7 Let $G = (V_N, \Sigma, P, S)$ be a CFG. G is said to be reduced or nonredundant if every symbol in $V_N \cup \Sigma$ appears in the course of the derivation of some terminal string, i.e. for every X in $V_N \cup \Sigma$, there exists a derivation $S \overset{*}{\Rightarrow} \alpha X \beta \overset{*}{\Rightarrow} w \in L(G)$. (We can say X is useful in the derivation of terminal strings.)

Theorem 5.5 For every CFG G there exists a reduced grammar G' which is equivalent to G.

PROOF   We construct the reduced grammar in two steps.

Step 1   We construct a grammar G_1 equivalent to the given grammar G so that every variable in G_1 derives some terminal string (Theorem 5.3).

Step 2   We construct a grammar $G' = (V'_N, \Sigma', P', S)$ equivalent to G_1 so that every symbol in G' appears in some sentential form of G' which is equivalent to G_1 and hence to G. G' is the required reduced grammar.

By step 2 every symbol X in G' appears in some sentential form, say $\alpha X \beta$. By step 1 every symbol in $\alpha X \beta$ derives some terminal string. Therefore, $S \overset{*}{\Rightarrow} \alpha X \beta \overset{*}{\Rightarrow} w$ for some w in Σ^*, i.e. G' is reduced.

NOTE: To get a reduced grammar, we must first apply Theorem 5.3 and then Theorem 5.4. For, if we apply Theorem 5.4 first and then Theorem 5.3, we may not get a reduced grammar (refer Exercise 8 at the end of the chapter).

EXAMPLE 5.7   Find a reduced grammar equivalent to the grammar G whose productions are

$$S \to AB \mid CA, B \to BC \mid AB, A \to a, C \to aB \mid b$$

SOLUTION: *Step 1*

$W_1 = \{A, C\}$ as $A \to a$ and $C \to b$ are productions with a terminal string on R.H.S.

$W_2 = \{A, C\} \cup \{A_1 \mid A_1 \to \alpha$ with $\alpha \in (\Sigma \cup \{A, C\})^*\}$

$= \{A, C\} \cup \{S\}$ as we have $S \to CA$

$W_3 = \{A, C, S\} \cup \{A_1 \mid A_1 \to \alpha$ with $\alpha \in (\Sigma \cup \{S, A, C\})^*\}$

$= \{A, C, S\} \cup \varnothing$

As $W_3 = W_2$,

$$V_N' = W_2 = \{S, A, C\}$$
$$P' = \{A_1 \rightarrow \alpha \mid A_1, \alpha \in (V_N' \cup \Sigma)^*\}$$
$$= \{S \rightarrow CA, A \rightarrow a, C \rightarrow b\}$$

Thus,

$$G_1 = (\{S, A, C\}, \{a, b\}, \{S \rightarrow CA, A \rightarrow a, C \rightarrow b\}, S)$$

Step 2 We have to apply Theorem 5.4 to G_1. Thus,

$$W_1 = \{S\}$$

As we have production $S \rightarrow CA$ and $S \in W_1$, $W_2 = \{S\} \cup \{A, C\}$

As $A \rightarrow a$ and $C \rightarrow b$ are productions with $A, C \in W_2$, $W_3 = \{S, A, C, a, b\}$

$$\text{As } W_3 = V_N' \cup \Sigma, P'' = \{A_1 \rightarrow \alpha \mid A_1 \in W_3\} = P'$$

Therefore,

$$G' = (\{S, A, C\}, \{a, b\}, \{S \rightarrow CA, A \rightarrow a, C \rightarrow b\}, S)$$

is the reduced grammar.

EXAMPLE 5.8 Construct a reduced grammar equivalent to the grammar

$$S \rightarrow aAa, \quad A \rightarrow Sb \mid bCC \mid DaA, \quad C \rightarrow abb \mid DD,$$
$$E \rightarrow aC, \quad D \rightarrow aDA$$

SOLUTION: Step 1

$$W_1 = \{C\} \text{ as } C \rightarrow abb$$

is the only production with a terminal string on the R.H.S.

$$W_2 = \{C\} \cup \{E, A\}$$

as $E \rightarrow aC$ and $A \rightarrow bCC$ are productions with R.H.S. in $(\Sigma \cup \{C\})^*$

$$W_3 = \{C, E, A\} \cup \{S\} \quad \text{as } S \rightarrow aAa \text{ and } aAa \text{ is in } (\Sigma \cup W_2)^*$$
$$W_4 = W_3 \cup \emptyset$$

Hence,

$$V_N' = W_3 = \{S, A, C, E\}$$
$$P' = \{A_1 \rightarrow \alpha \mid \alpha \in (V_N' \cup \Sigma)^*\}$$
$$= \{S \rightarrow aAa, A \rightarrow Sb \mid bCC, C \rightarrow abb, E \rightarrow aC\}$$
$$G_1 = (V_N', \{a, b\}, P', S)$$

Step 2   We have to apply Theorem 5.4 to G_1. We start with

$$W_1 = \{S\}$$

As we have $S \rightarrow aAa$,

$$W_2 = \{S\} \cup \{A, a\}$$

As $A \rightarrow Sb \mid bCC$,

$$W_3 = \{S, A, a\} \cup \{S, b, C\} = \{S, A, C, a, b\}$$

As we have $C \rightarrow abb$,

$$W_4 = W_3 \cup \{a, b\} = W_3$$

Hence

$$P'' = \{A_1 \rightarrow \alpha \mid A_1 \in W_3\}$$

$$= \{S \rightarrow aAa, A \rightarrow Sb \mid bCC, C \rightarrow abb\}$$

Therefore,

$$G' = (\{S, A, C\}, \{a, b\}, P'', S)$$

is the reduced grammar.

5.3.2   ELIMINATION OF NULL PRODUCTIONS

A context-free grammar may have productions of the form $A \rightarrow \Lambda$. The production $A \rightarrow \Lambda$ is just used to erase A. So a production of the form $A \rightarrow \Lambda$, where A is a variable, is called a *null production*. In this section we give a construction to eliminate null productions.

As an example, consider G whose productions are $S \rightarrow aS \mid aA \mid \Lambda, A \rightarrow \Lambda$. We have two null productions $S \rightarrow \Lambda$ and $A \rightarrow \Lambda$. We can delete $A \rightarrow \Lambda$ provided we erase A whenever it occurs in the course of a derivation of a terminal string. So we can replace $S \rightarrow aA$ by $S \rightarrow a$. If G_1 denotes the grammar whose productions are $S \rightarrow aS \mid a \mid \Lambda$, then $L(G_1) = L(G) = \{a^n \mid n \geq 0\}$. Thus it is possible to eliminate the null production $A \rightarrow \Lambda$. If we eliminate $S \rightarrow \Lambda$, we cannot generate Λ in $L(G)$. But we can generate $L(G) - \{\Lambda\}$ even if we eliminate $S \rightarrow \Lambda$.

Before giving the construction we give a definition.

Definition 5.8   A variable A in a context-free grammar is nullable if $A \overset{*}{\Rightarrow} \Lambda$.

Theorem 5.6   If $G = (V_N, \Sigma, P, S)$ is a context-free grammar, then we can find a context-free grammar G_1 having no null productions such that $L(G_1) = L(G) - \{\Lambda\}$.

PROOF   We construct $G_1 = (V_N, \Sigma, P', S)$ as follows:

Step 1   *Construction of the set of nullable variables*: We find the nullable variables recursively:

(i) $W_1 = \{A \in V_N | A \rightarrow \Lambda \text{ is in } P\}$.

(ii) $W_{i+1} = W_i \cup \{A \in V_N | \text{there exists a production } A \rightarrow \alpha \text{ with } \alpha \in W_i^*\}$.

By definition of W_i, $W_i \subseteq W_{i+1}$ for all i. As V_N is finite, $W_{k+1} = W_k$ for some $k \leq |V_N|$. So $W_{k+j} = W_k$ for all j. Let $W = W_k$. W is the set of all nullable variables.

Step 2 (a) *Construction of P':* Any production whose R.H.S. does not have any nullable variable is included in P'.

(b) If $A \rightarrow X_1 X_2 \ldots X_k$ is in P, the productions of the form $A \rightarrow \alpha_1 \alpha_2 \ldots \alpha_k$ are included in P', where $\alpha_i = X_i$ if $X_i \notin W$. $\alpha_i = X_i$ or Λ if $X_i \in W$ and $\alpha_1 \alpha_2 \ldots \alpha_k \neq \Lambda$. Actually, (b) gives several productions in P'. The productions are obtained either by not erasing any nullable variable on the R.H.S. of $A \rightarrow X_1 X_2 \ldots X_k$ or by erasing some or all nullable variables provided some symbol appears on the R.H.S. after erasing.

Let $G_1 = (V_N, \Sigma, P', S)$ G_1 has no null productions.

Before proving that G_1 is the required grammar, we apply the construction to an example.

EXAMPLE 5.9 Consider the grammar G whose productions are $S \rightarrow aS | AB$, $A \rightarrow \Lambda, B \rightarrow \Lambda, D \rightarrow b$. Construct a grammar G_1 without null productions generating $L(G) - \{\Lambda\}$.

SOLUTION: *Step 1 Construction of the set W of all nullable variables*

$W_1 = \{A_1 \in V_N | A_1 \rightarrow \Lambda \text{ is a production in } G\}$

$\quad = \{A, B\}$

$W_2 = \{A, B\} \cup \{S\}$ as $S \rightarrow AB$ is a production with $AB \in W_1^*$

$\quad = \{S, A, B\}$

$W_3 = W_2 \cup \emptyset = W_2$

Thus,

$W = W_2 = \{S, A, B\}$

Step 2: Construction of P'

(i) $D \rightarrow b$ is included in P'.

(ii) $S \rightarrow aS$ gives rise to $S \rightarrow aS$ and $S \rightarrow a$.

(iii) $S \rightarrow AB$ gives rise to $S \rightarrow AB$, $S \rightarrow A$ and $S \rightarrow B$.

(NOTE: We cannot erase both the nullable variables A and B in $S \rightarrow AB$ as we will get $S \rightarrow \Lambda$ in that case.) Hence the required grammar without null productions is

$$G_1 = (\{S, A, B, D\}, \{a, b\}, P', S)$$

where P' consists of

$D \rightarrow b, \quad S \rightarrow aS, \quad S \rightarrow AB, \quad S \rightarrow a, \quad S \rightarrow A, \quad S \rightarrow B$

Step 3 $L(G_1) = L(G) - \{\Lambda\}$. To prove that $L(G_1) = L(G) - \{\Lambda\}$, we prove an auxiliary result given by the following relation:

For all $A \in V_N$ and $w \in \Sigma^*$,

$$A \underset{G_1}{\overset{*}{\Rightarrow}} w \quad \text{if and only if } A \underset{G}{\overset{*}{\Rightarrow}} w \text{ and } w \neq \Lambda \tag{5.6}$$

We prove the "if" part first. Let $A \underset{G}{\overset{*}{\Rightarrow}} w$ and $w \neq \Lambda$. We prove that $A \underset{G_1}{\overset{*}{\Rightarrow}} w$ by induction on the number of steps in the derivation $A \underset{G}{\overset{*}{\Rightarrow}} w$. If $A \underset{G}{\Rightarrow} w$ and $w \neq \Lambda$, $A \to w$ is a production in P', and so $A \underset{G_1}{\Rightarrow} w$. Thus there is basis for induction. Assume the result for derivations in atmost i steps. Let $A \underset{G}{\overset{i+1}{\Rightarrow}} w$ and $w \neq \Lambda$. We can split the derivation as $A \underset{G}{\Rightarrow} X_1 X_2 \dots X_k \underset{G}{\overset{i}{\Rightarrow}} w_1 w_2 \dots w_k$, where $w = w_1 w_2 \dots w_k$ and $A_j \underset{G}{\overset{*}{\Rightarrow}} w_j$. As $w \neq \Lambda$, not all w_j's are Λ. If $w_j \neq \Lambda$, then by induction hypothesis, $X_j \underset{G_1}{\overset{*}{\Rightarrow}} w_j$. If $w_j = \Lambda$ then $X_j \in W$. So using the production $A \to A_1 A_2 \dots A_k$ in P, we construct $A \to \alpha_1 \alpha_2 \dots \alpha_k$ in P', where $\alpha_j = X_j$ if $w_j \neq \Lambda$ and $\alpha_j = \Lambda$ if $w_j = \Lambda$ (i.e. $X_j \in W$). Therefore, $A \underset{G_1}{\Rightarrow} \alpha_1 \alpha_2 \dots \alpha_k \underset{G_1}{\overset{*}{\Rightarrow}} w_1 \alpha_2 \, \alpha_k \underset{G_1}{\overset{*}{\Rightarrow}} \dots \Rightarrow w_1 w_2 \dots w_k = w$. By the principle of induction, the "if" part of (5.6) is proved.

We prove the "only if" part by induction on the number of steps in the derivation of $A \underset{G_1}{\overset{*}{\Rightarrow}} w$. If $A \underset{G_1}{\Rightarrow} w$, then $A \to w$ is in P_1. By construction of P', $A \to w$ is obtained from some production $A \to X_1 X_2 \dots X_n$ in P by erasing some (or none of) nullable variables. Hence $A \underset{G}{\Rightarrow} X_1 X_2 \dots X_n \underset{G}{\overset{*}{\Rightarrow}} w$. So there is basis for induction. Assume the result for derivation in atmost j steps. Let $A \underset{G_1}{\overset{j+1}{\Rightarrow}} w$. This can be split as $A \underset{G_1}{\Rightarrow} X_1 X_2 \dots X_k \underset{G_1}{\overset{j}{\Rightarrow}} w_1 w_2 \dots w_k$, where $X_i \underset{G_1}{\overset{*}{\Rightarrow}} w_i$. The first production $A \to X_1 X_2 \dots X_k$ in P' is obtained from some production $A \to \alpha$ in P by erasing some (or none of) nullable variables in α. So $A \underset{G}{\Rightarrow} \alpha \underset{G}{\overset{*}{\Rightarrow}} X_1 X_2 \dots X_k$. If $X_i \in \Sigma$ then $X_i \underset{G}{\overset{0}{\Rightarrow}} X_i = w_i$. If $X_i \in V_N$ then by induction hypothesis, $X_i \underset{G}{\overset{*}{\Rightarrow}} w_i$. So we get $A \underset{G}{\overset{*}{\Rightarrow}} X_1 X_2 \dots X_k \underset{G}{\overset{*}{\Rightarrow}} w_1 w_2 \dots w_k$. Hence by the principle of induction whenever $A \underset{G_1}{\overset{*}{\Rightarrow}} w$, we have $A \underset{G}{\overset{*}{\Rightarrow}} w$ and $w \neq \Lambda$. Thus (5.6) is completely proved.

By applying (5.6) to S, we have $w \in L(G_1)$ if and only if $w \in L(G)$ and $w \neq \Lambda$. This implies $L(G_1) = L(G) - \{\Lambda\}$. ∎

Corollary 1 There exists an algorithm to decide whether $\Lambda \in L(G)$ for a given context-free grammar G.

PROOF $\Lambda \in L(G)$ if and only if $S \in W$, i.e. S is nullable. The construction given in Theorem 5.6 is recursive and terminates in a finite number of steps (actually in atmost $|V_N|$ steps). So the required algorithm is as follows: (i) construct W; (ii) test whether $S \in W$.

Corollary 2 If $G = (V_N, \Sigma, P, S)$ is a context-free grammar we can find an equivalent context-free grammar $G_1 = (V'_N, \Sigma, P, S_1)$ without null productions except $S_1 \to \Lambda$ when Λ is in $L(G)$. If $S_1 \to \Lambda$ is in P_1, S_1 does not appear on the R.H.S. of any production in P_1.

PROOF   By Corollary 1, we can decide whether Λ is in $L(G)$.

Case 1 If Λ is not in $L(G)$, G_1 obtained by using Theorem 5.6 is the required equivalent grammar.

Case 2 If Λ is in $L(G)$, construct $G' = (V_N, \Sigma, P', S)$ using Theorem 5.6. $L(G') = L(G) - \{\Lambda\}$. Define $G_1 = (V_N \cup \{S_1\}, \Sigma, P_1, S_1)$, where $P_1 = P' \cup \{S_1 \to S, S_1 \to \Lambda\}$. S_1 does not appear on the R.H.S. of any production in P_1, and so G_1 is the required grammar with $L(G_1) = L(G)$. ∎

5.3.3   ELIMINATION OF UNIT PRODUCTIONS

A context-free grammar may have productions of the form $A \to B$, $A, B \in V_N$.

Consider, for example, G as the grammar $S \to A, A \to B, B \to C, C \to a$. It is easy to see that $L(G) = \{a\}$. The productions $S \to A, A \to B, B \to C$ are useful just to replace S by C. To get a terminal string, we need $C \to a$. If G_1 is $S \to a$, then $L(G_1) = L(G)$.

The next construction eliminates productions of the form $A \to B$.

Definition 5.9   A unit production (or a chain rule) in a context-free grammar G is a production of the form $A \to B$, where A and B are variables in G.

Theorem 5.7   If G is a context-free grammar, we can find a context-free grammar G_1 which has no null productions or unit productions such that $L(G_1) = L(G)$.

PROOF   We can apply Corollary 2 of Theorem 5.6 to grammar G to get a grammar $G' = (V_N, \Sigma, P, S)$ without null productions such that $L(G') = L(G)$. Let A be any variable in V_N.

Step 1: *Construction of the set of variables derivable from* A. Define $W_i(A)$ recursively as follows:

$$W_0(A) = \{A\}$$
$$W_{i+1}(A) = W_i(A) \cup \{B \in V_N | C \to B \text{ is in } P \text{ with } C \in W_i(A)\}$$

By definition of $W_i(A)$, $W_i(A) \subseteq W_{i+1}(A)$. As V_N is finite, $W_{k+1}(A) = W_k(A)$ for some $k \leq |V_N|$. So $W_{k+j}(A) = W_k(A)$ for all $j \geq 0$. Let $W(A) = W_k(A)$. Then $W(A)$ is the set of all variables derivable from A.

Step 2: *Construction of A-productions in* G_1. The A-productions in G_1 are either (a) the nonunit production in G' or (b) $A \to \alpha$ whenever $B \to \alpha$ is in G with $B \in W(A)$ and $\alpha \notin V_N$. (Actually, (b) covers (a) as $A \in W(A)$). Now, we define $G_1 = (V_N, \Sigma, P_1, S)$, where P_1 is constructed using step 2 for every $A \in V_N$.

Before proving that G_1 is the required grammar, we apply the construction to an example.

EXAMPLE 5.10　Let G be $S \rightarrow AB$, $A \rightarrow a$, $B \rightarrow C|b$, $C \rightarrow D$, $D \rightarrow E$ and $E \rightarrow a$. Eliminate unit productions and get an equivalent grammar.

SOLUTION:　Step 1

$$W_0(S) = \{S\}, \quad W_1(S) = W_0(S) \cup \emptyset$$

Hence $W(S) = \{S\}$. Similarly,

$$W(A) = \{A\}, \quad W(E) = \{E\}$$

$$W_0(B) = \{B\}, \quad W_1(B) = \{B\} \cup \{C\} = \{B, C\}$$

$$W_2(B) = \{B, C\} \cup \{D\}, \quad W_3(B) = \{B, C, D\} \cup \{E\}, \quad W_4(B) = W_3(B)$$

Therefore,

$$W(B) = \{B, C, D, E\}$$

Similarly,

$$W_0(C) = \{C\}, \quad W_1(C) = \{C, D\}, \quad W_2(C) = \{C, D, E\} = W_3(C)$$

Therefore,

$$W(C) = \{C, D, E\}, \quad W_0(D) = \{D\}$$

Hence,

$$W_1(D) = \{D, E\} = W_2(D)$$

Thus

$$W(D) = \{D, E\}$$

Step 2　The productions in G_1 are

$$S \rightarrow AB, \quad A \rightarrow a, \quad E \rightarrow a$$

$$B \rightarrow b|a, \quad C \rightarrow a, \quad D \rightarrow a$$

By construction, G_1 has no unit productions.

To complete the proof we have to show that $L(G') = L(G_1)$.

Step 3　$L(G') = L(G)$. If $A \rightarrow \alpha$ is in $P_1 - P$, then it is induced by $B \rightarrow \alpha$ in P with $B \in W(A)$, $\alpha \notin V_N$. $B \in W(A)$ implies $A \underset{G'}{\overset{*}{\Rightarrow}} B$. Hence, $A \underset{G'}{\overset{*}{\Rightarrow}} B \underset{G'}{\Rightarrow} \alpha$. So, if $A \underset{G_1}{\Rightarrow} \alpha$, then $A \underset{G'}{\overset{*}{\Rightarrow}} \alpha$. This proves $L(G_1) \subseteq L(G')$.

To prove the reverse inclusion, we start with a leftmost derivation $S \underset{G}{\Rightarrow} \alpha_1 \underset{G}{\Rightarrow} \alpha_2 \dots \underset{G}{\Rightarrow} \alpha_n = w$ in G'. Let i be the smallest index such that $\alpha_i \underset{G}{\Rightarrow} \alpha_{i+1}$ is obtained by a unit production and j be the smallest index greater than i such that $\alpha_j \underset{G}{\Rightarrow} \alpha_{j+1}$ is obtained by a nonunit production. So, $S \underset{G_1}{\Rightarrow} \alpha_i$, and $\alpha_i \underset{G'}{\overset{*}{\Rightarrow}} \alpha_{j+1}$ can be written as

$$\alpha_i = w_i A_i \beta_i \Rightarrow w_i A_{i+1}\beta_i \Rightarrow \dots \Rightarrow w_i A_j\beta_i \Rightarrow w_i \gamma \beta_i = \alpha_{j+1}$$

$A_j \in W(A_i)$ and $A_j \rightarrow \gamma$ is a nonunit production. Therefore, $A_i \rightarrow \gamma$ is a production in P_1. Hence, $\alpha_i \underset{G_1}{\overset{*}{\Rightarrow}} \alpha_{j+1}$. Thus we have $S \underset{G_1}{\overset{*}{\Rightarrow}} \alpha_{j+1}$.

Repeating the argument whenever some unit production occurs in the remaining part of the derivation, we can prove that $S \underset{G_1}{\overset{*}{\Rightarrow}} \alpha_n = w$. This proves $L(G') \subseteq L(G)$. ∎

Corollary If G is a context-free grammar, we can construct an equivalent grammar G' which is reduced and has no null productions or unit productions.

PROOF We construct G_1 in the following way:

Step 1 Eliminate null productions to get G_1 (Theorem 5.6 or Corollary 2 of the theorem).

Step 2 Eliminate unit productions in G_1 to get G_2 (Theorem 5.7).

Step 3 Construct a reduced grammar G' equivalent to G_2 (Theorem 5.5).

G' is the required grammar equivalent to G.

NOTE: We have to apply the constructions only in the order given in Corollary 1 of Theorem 5.7 to simplify grammars. If we change the order we may not get the grammar in the most simplified form (refer Exercise 11).

5.4 NORMAL FORMS FOR CONTEXT-FREE GRAMMARS

In a context-free grammar, the R.H.S. of a production can be any string of variables and terminals. When the productions in G satisfy certain restrictions, then G is said to be in a 'normal form'. Among several 'normal forms' we study two of them—the Chomsky normal form (CNF) and Greibach normal form—in this section.

5.4.1 CHOMSKY NORMAL FORM

In the Chomsky normal form, we have restrictions on the length of R.H.S. and the nature of symbols in the R.H.S. of productions.

Definition 5.10 A context-free grammar G is in Chomsky normal form if every production is of the form $A \rightarrow a$, or $A \rightarrow BC$, and $S \rightarrow \Lambda$ is in G if $\Lambda \in L(G)$. When Λ is in $L(G)$, we assume that S does not appear on the R.H.S. of any production.

For example, consider G whose productions are $S \rightarrow AB \,|\, \Lambda$, $A \rightarrow a$, $B \rightarrow b$. Then G is in Chomsky normal form.

Remark For a grammar in CNF, the derivation tree has the following property: Every node has atmost two descendants—either two internal vertices or a single leaf.

When a grammar is in CNF, some of the proofs and constructions are simpler.

Reduction to Chomsky Normal Form

Now we develop a method of constructing a grammar in CNF equivalent to a given context-free grammar. Let us first consider an example. Let G be $S \rightarrow ABC \mid aC, A \rightarrow a, B \rightarrow b, C \rightarrow c$. Except $S \rightarrow aC \mid ABC$, all the other productions are in the form required for CNF. The terminal a in $S \rightarrow aC$ can be replaced by a new variable D. By adding a new production $D \rightarrow a$, the effect of applying $S \rightarrow aC$ can be achieved by $S \rightarrow DC$ and $D \rightarrow a$. $S \rightarrow ABC$ is not in the required form, and hence this production can be replaced by $S \rightarrow AE$ and $E \rightarrow BC$. Thus, an equivalent grammar is $S \rightarrow AE \mid DC, E \rightarrow BC, A \rightarrow a, B \rightarrow b, C \rightarrow c, D \rightarrow a$.

The techniques applied in this example are used in the following theorem.

Theorem 5.8 (Reduction to Chomsky normal form). For every context-free grammar, there is an equivalent grammar G_2 in Chomsky normal form.

PROOF (Construction of a grammar in CNF)

Step 1: Elimination of null productions and unit productions. We apply Theorem 5.6 to eliminate null productions. We then apply Theorem 5.7 to the resulting grammar to eliminate chain productions. Let the grammar thus obtained be $G = (V_N, \Sigma, P, S)$.

Step 2: Elimination of terminals on R.H.S. We define $G_1 = (V'_N, \Sigma, P_1, S)$, where P_1 and V'_N are constructed as follows:

(i) All the productions in P of the form $A \rightarrow a$ or $A \rightarrow BC$ are included in P_1. All the variables in V_N are included in V'_N.

(ii) Consider $A \rightarrow X_1 X_2 \ldots X_n$ with some terminal on R.H.S. If X_i is a terminal, say a_i, add a new variable C_{a_i} to V'_N and $C_{a_i} \rightarrow a_i$ to P_1. In production $A \rightarrow X_1 X_2 \ldots X_n$, every terminal on R.H.S. is replaced by the corresponding new variable and the variables on the R.H.S. are retained. The resulting production is added to P_1. Thus we get $G_1 = (V'_N, \Sigma, P_1, S)$.

Step 3: Restricting the number of variables on R.H.S. For any production in P_1, the R.H.S. consists of either a single terminal (or Λ in $S \rightarrow \Lambda$) or two or more variables. We define $G_2 = (V''_N, \Sigma, P_2, S)$ as follows:

(i) All productions in P_1 are added to P_2 if they are in the required form. All the variables in V'_N are added to V''_N.

(ii) Consider $A \rightarrow A_1 A_2 \ldots A_m$, where $m \geq 3$. We introduce new productions $A \rightarrow A_1 C_1, C_1 \rightarrow A_2 C_2, \ldots, C_{m-2} \rightarrow A_{m-1} A_m$, and new variables $C_1, C_2, \ldots, C_{m-2}$. These are added to P'' and V''_N, respectively.

Thus we get G_2 in Chomsky normal form.

Before proving that G_2 is the required equivalent grammar, we apply the construction to the context-free grammar given in Example 5.11.

EXAMPLE 5.11 Reduce the following grammar G to CNF. G is $S \rightarrow aAD$, $A \rightarrow aB \mid bAB, B \rightarrow b, D \rightarrow d$.

production $C_{a_i} \to a_i$ is applied to get $A_i \overset{*}{\Rightarrow} w_i$. The production $A \to A_1 A_2 \dots A_m$ is induced by a production $A \to X_1 X_2 \dots X_m$ in P where $X_i = A_i$ if $A_i \in V_N$ and $X_i = w_i$ if $A_i = C_{a_i}$. So $A \underset{G}{\Rightarrow} X_1 X_2 \dots X_m \underset{G}{\overset{*}{\Rightarrow}} w_1 w_2 \dots w_m$.

SOLUTION As there are no null productions or unit productions, we can proceed to step 2.

Step 2: Let $G_1 = (V_N', \{a, b, d\}, P_1, S)$, where P_1 and V_N' are constructed as follows:

(i) $B \to b, D \to d$ are included in P_1.
(ii) $S \to aAD$ gives rise to $S \to C_a AD$ and $C_a \to a$.
    $A \to aB$ gives rise to $A \to C_a B$.
    $A \to bAB$ gives rise to $A \to C_b AB$ and $C_b \to b$.
    $V_N' = \{S, A, B, D, C_a, C_b\}$.

Step 3: P_1 consists of $S \to C_a AD$, $A \to C_a B \mid C_b AB$, $B \to b$, $D \to d$, $C_a \to a$, $C_b \to b$.

$A \to C_a B$, $B \to b$, $D \to d$, $C_a \to a$, $C_b \to b$ are added to P_2.

$S \to C_a AD$ is replaced by $S \to C_a C_1$ and $C_1 \to AD$.

$A \to C_b AB$ is replaced by $A \to C_b C_2$ and $C_2 \to AB$.

Let

$$G_2 = (\{S, A, B, D, C_a, C_b, C_1, C_2\}, \{a, b, d\}, P_2, S)$$

where P_2 consists of $S \to C_a C_1$, $A \to C_a B \mid C_b C_2$, $C_1 \to AD$, $C_2 \to AB$, $B \to b$, $D \to d$, $C_a \to a$, $C_b \to b$. G_2 is in CNF and equivalent to G.

Step 4: $L(G) = L(G_2)$. To complete the proof we have to show that $L(G) = L(G_1)$ $= L(G_2)$.

To show that $L(G) \subseteq L(G_1)$, we start with $w \in L(G)$. If $A \to X_1 X_2 \dots X_n$ is used in the derivation of w, the same effect can be achieved by using the corresponding production in P_1 and the productions involving the new variables. Hence, $A \underset{G_1}{\overset{*}{\Rightarrow}} X_1 X_2 \dots X_n$. Thus, $L(G) \subseteq L(G_1)$.

Let $w \in L(G_1)$. To show that $w \in L(G)$, it is enough to prove the following:

$$A \underset{G}{\overset{*}{\Rightarrow}} w \quad \text{if } A \in V_N, A \underset{G_1}{\overset{*}{\Rightarrow}} w \tag{5.7}$$

We prove (5.7) by induction on the number of steps in $A \underset{G_1}{\overset{*}{\Rightarrow}} w$.

If $A \underset{G_1}{\Rightarrow} w$, then $A \to w$ is a production in P_1. By construction of P_1, w is a single terminal. So $A \to w$ is in P, i.e. $A \underset{G}{\Rightarrow} w$. Thus there is basis for induction.

Let us assume (5.7) for derivations in atmost k steps. Let $A \underset{G_1}{\overset{k+1}{\Rightarrow}} w$. We can split this derivation as $A \underset{G_1}{\Rightarrow} A_1 A_2 \dots A_m \underset{G_1}{\overset{k}{\Rightarrow}} w_1 \cdot w_m = w$ such that $A_i \underset{G_1}{\overset{*}{\Rightarrow}} w_i$. Each A_i is either in V_N or a new variable, say C_{a_i}. When $A_i \in V_N$, $A_i \underset{G_1}{\overset{*}{\Rightarrow}} w_i$ is a derivation in atmost k steps, and so by induction hypothesis, $A_i \underset{G}{\overset{*}{\Rightarrow}} w_i$. When $A_i = C_{a_i}$, the i.e. $A \underset{G}{\overset{*}{\Rightarrow}} w$. Thus, (5.7) is true for all derivations. Therefore, $L(G) = L(G_1)$.

The effect of applying $A \rightarrow A_1 A_2 \ldots A_m$ in a derivation for $w \in L(G_1)$ can be achieved by applying the productions $A \rightarrow A_1 C_1$, $C_1 \rightarrow A_2 C_2$, ..., $C_{m-2} \rightarrow A_{m-1} A_m$ in P_2. Hence it is easy to see that $L(G_1) \subseteq L(G_2)$.

To prove $L(G_2) \subseteq L(G_1)$, we can prove an auxiliary result:

$$A \underset{G_1}{\overset{*}{\Rightarrow}} w \quad \text{if } A \in V'_N, A \underset{G_2}{\overset{*}{\Rightarrow}} w \tag{5.8}$$

Condition (5.8) can be proved by induction on the number of steps in $A \underset{G_2}{\overset{*}{\Rightarrow}} w$. Applying (5.7) to S, we get $L(G_2) \subseteq L(G_1)$. Thus,

$$L(G) = L(G_1) = L(G_2). \quad \blacksquare$$

EXAMPLE 5.12 Find a grammar in Chomsky normal form equivalent to $S \rightarrow aAbB$, $A \rightarrow aA \mid a$, $B \rightarrow bB \mid b$.

SOLUTION As there are no unit productions or null productions, we need not carry out step 1. We proceed to step 2.

Step 2 Let $G_1 = (V'_N, \{a, b\}, P_1, S)$, where P_1 and V'_N are constructed as follows:

(i) $A \rightarrow a$, $B \rightarrow b$ are added to P_1.
(ii) $S \rightarrow aAbB$, $A \rightarrow aA$, $B \rightarrow bB$ yield $S \rightarrow C_a A C_b B$, $A \rightarrow C_a A$, $B \rightarrow C_b B$, $C_a \rightarrow a$, $C_b \rightarrow b$.

$$V'_N = \{S, A, B, C_a, C_b\}.$$

Step 3 P_1 consists of $S \rightarrow C_a A C_b B$, $A \rightarrow C_a A$, $B \rightarrow C_b B$, $C_a \rightarrow a$, $C_b \rightarrow b$, $A \rightarrow a$, $B \rightarrow b$.

$S \rightarrow C_a A C_b B$ is replaced by $S \rightarrow C_a C_1$, $C_1 \rightarrow A C_2$, $C_2 \rightarrow C_b B$.

The remaining productions in P_1 are added to P_2. Let

$$G_2 = (\{S, A, B, C_a, C_b, C_1, C_2\}, \{a, b\}, P_2, S),$$

where P_2 consists of $S \rightarrow C_a C_1$, $C_1 \rightarrow A C_2$, $C_2 \rightarrow C_b B$, $A \rightarrow C_a A$, $B \rightarrow C_b B$, $C_a \rightarrow a$, $C_b \rightarrow b$, $A \rightarrow a$, and $B \rightarrow b$.

G_2 is in CNF and equivalent to the given grammar.

EXAMPLE 5.13 Find a grammar in CNF equivalent to the grammar

$$S \rightarrow \sim S \mid [S \supset S] \mid p \mid q \quad (S \text{ being the only variable})$$

SOLUTION As the given grammar has no unit or null productions, we omit step 1 and proceed to step 2.

Step 2 Let $G_1 = (V'_N, \Sigma, P_1, S)$, where P_1 and V'_N are constructed as follows:

(i) $S \rightarrow p \mid q$ are added to P_1.
(ii) $S \rightarrow \sim S$ induces $S \rightarrow AS$ and $A \rightarrow \sim$.

(iii) $S \rightarrow [S \supset S]$ induces $S \rightarrow BSCSD, B \rightarrow [, C \rightarrow \supset, D \rightarrow]$

$$V'_N = \{S, A, B, C, D\}$$

Step 3 P_1 consists of $S \rightarrow p \,|\, q$, $S \rightarrow AS$, $A \rightarrow \sim$, $B \rightarrow [, C \rightarrow \supset, D \rightarrow]$, $S \rightarrow BSCSD$.

$S \rightarrow BSCSD$ is replaced by $S \rightarrow BC_1$, $C_1 \rightarrow SC_2$, $C_2 \rightarrow CC_3$, $C_3 \rightarrow SD$.

Let

$$G_2 = (\{S, A, B, C, D, C_1, C_2, C_3\}, \Sigma, P_2, S)$$

where P_2 consists of $S \rightarrow p \,|\, q \,|\, AS \,|\, BC_1$, $A \rightarrow \sim$, $B \rightarrow [$, $C \rightarrow \supset$, $D \rightarrow]$, $C_1 \rightarrow SC_2$, $C_2 \rightarrow CC_3$, $C_3 \rightarrow SD$. G_2 is in CNF and equivalent to the given grammar.

5.4.2   GREIBACH NORMAL FORM

Greibach normal form (GNF) is another normal form quite useful in some proofs and constructions. A context-free grammar generating the set accepted by a pushdown automaton is in Greibach normal form as will be seen in Theorem 6.4.

Definition 5.11   A context-free grammar is in Greibach normal form if every production is of the form $A \rightarrow a\alpha$, where $\alpha \in V_N^*$ and $a \in \Sigma$ (α may be Λ), and $S \rightarrow \Lambda$ is in G if $\Lambda \in L(G)$. When $\Lambda \in L(G)$, we assume that S does not appear on the R.H.S. of any production. For example, G given by $S \rightarrow aAB \,|\, \Lambda, A \rightarrow bC$, $B \rightarrow b, C \rightarrow c$ is in GNF.

NOTE: A grammar in GNF is a natural generalisation of a regular grammar. In a regular grammar the productions are of the form $A \rightarrow a\alpha$, where $a \in \Sigma$ and $\alpha \in V_N \cup \{\Lambda\}$, i.e. $A \rightarrow a\alpha$, with $\alpha \in V_N^*$ and $|\alpha| \leq 1$. So for a grammar in GNF or a regular grammar, we get a (single) terminal and a string of variables (possibly Λ) on application of a production (with the exception of $S \rightarrow \Lambda$).

The construction we give in this section depends mainly on the following two technical lemmas:

Lemma 5.1   Let $G = (V_N, \Sigma, P, S)$ be a CFG. Let $A \rightarrow B\gamma$ be an A-production in P. Let the B-productions be $B \rightarrow \beta_1 \,|\, \beta_2 \,|\, \ldots \,|\, \beta_s$. Define

$$P_1 = (P - \{A \rightarrow B\gamma\}) \cup \{A \rightarrow \beta_i \gamma \,|\, 1 \leq i \leq s\}.$$

Then $G_1 = (V_N, \Sigma, P_1, S)$ is a context-free grammar equivalent to G.

PROOF   If we apply $A \rightarrow B\gamma$ in some derivation for $w \in L(G)$, we have to apply $B \rightarrow \beta_i$ for some i at a later step. So $A \overset{*}{\underset{G}{\Rightarrow}} \beta_i \gamma$. The effect of applying $A \rightarrow B\gamma$ and eliminating B in grammar G is the same as applying $A \rightarrow \beta_i \gamma$ for some i in grammar G_1. Hence $w \in L(G_1)$, i.e. $L(G) \subseteq L(G_1)$. Similarly, instead of applying $A \rightarrow \beta_i \gamma$, we can apply $A \rightarrow B\gamma$ and $B \rightarrow \beta_i$ to get $A \overset{*}{\underset{G}{\Rightarrow}} \beta_i \gamma$. This proves $L(G_1) \subseteq L(G)$.   ∎

NOTE: Lemma 5.1 is useful for deleting a variable B appearing as the first symbol on the R.H.S. of some A-production provided no B-production has B as the first symbol on R.H.S.

The construction given in Lemma 5.1 is simple. To eliminate B in $A \rightarrow B\gamma$, we simply replace B by the right-hand side of every B-production.

For example, using Lemma 5.1, we can replace $A \rightarrow Bab$ by $A \rightarrow aAab$, $A \rightarrow bBab$, $A \rightarrow aaab$, $A \rightarrow ABab$ when the B-productions are $B \rightarrow aA \mid bB \mid aa \mid AB$.

The lemma is useful to eliminate A from the R.H.S. of $A \rightarrow A\alpha$.

Lemma 5.2   Let $G = (V_N, \Sigma, P, S)$ be a context-free grammar. Let the set of A-productions be $A \rightarrow A\alpha_1 \mid ... A\alpha_r \mid \beta_1 \mid ... \mid \beta_s$ (β_i's do not start with A). Let Z be a new variable. Let $G_1 = (V_N \cup \{Z\}, \Sigma, P_1, S)$, where P_1 is defined as follows:

(i) The set of A-productions in P_1 are $A \rightarrow \beta_1 \mid \beta_2 \mid ... \mid \beta_s$

$$A \rightarrow \beta_1 Z \mid \beta_2 Z \mid ... \mid \beta_s Z.$$

(ii) The set of Z-productions in P_1 are $Z \rightarrow \alpha_1 \mid \alpha_2 \mid ... \mid \alpha_r$

$$Z \rightarrow \alpha_1 Z \mid \alpha_2 Z ... \mid \alpha_r Z.$$

(iii) The productions for the other variables are as in P. Then G_1 is a CFG and equivalent to G.

PROOF   To prove $L(G) \subseteq L(G_1)$, consider a leftmost derivation of w in G. The only productions in $P - P_1$ are $A \rightarrow A\alpha_1 \mid A\alpha_2 \; ... \mid A\alpha_r$. If $A \rightarrow A\alpha_{i_1}$, $A \rightarrow A\alpha_{i_2}, ..., A \rightarrow A\alpha_{i_k}$ are used, then $A \rightarrow \beta_j$ should be used at a later stage (to eliminate A). So we have $A \underset{G}{\overset{*}{\Rightarrow}} \beta_j A\alpha_{i_1} ... \alpha_{i_k}$ while deriving w in G. However,

$$A \underset{G_1}{\Rightarrow} \beta_j Z \underset{G_1}{\Rightarrow} \beta_j \alpha_{i_1} Z ... \underset{G_1}{\Rightarrow} \beta_j \alpha_{i_1} \alpha_{i_2} ... \alpha_{i_k}$$

i.e.

$$A \underset{G_1}{\overset{*}{\Rightarrow}} \beta_j A\alpha_{i_1} ... \alpha_{i_k}$$

Thus, A can be eliminated by using productions in G_1. Therefore, $w \in L(G_1)$.

To prove $L(G_1) \subseteq L(G)$, consider a leftmost derivation of w in G_1. The only productions in $P_1 - P$ are $A \rightarrow \beta_1 Z \mid \beta_2 Z \mid ... \beta_s Z$, $Z \rightarrow \alpha_1 \mid ... \mid \alpha_r$, $Z \rightarrow \alpha_1 Z \mid \alpha_2 Z \mid ... \mid \alpha_r Z$. If the new variable Z appears in the course of the derivation of w, it is because of the application of $A \rightarrow \beta_j Z$ in some earlier step. Also, Z can be eliminated only by a production of the form $Z \rightarrow \alpha_i$ or $Z \rightarrow \alpha_j Z$ for some i and j in a later step. So we get $A \underset{G_1}{\overset{*}{\Rightarrow}} \beta_j \alpha_{i_1} \alpha_{i_2} ... \alpha_{i_k}$ in the course of the derivation of w. But, we know that $A \underset{G}{\overset{*}{\Rightarrow}} \beta_j \alpha_{i_1} \alpha_{i_2} ... \alpha_{i_k}$. Therefore, $w \in L(G)$. ∎

EXAMPLE 5.14   Apply Lemma 5.2 to the following A-productions in a context-free grammar G.

$$A \rightarrow aBD \mid bDB \mid c, \qquad A \rightarrow AB \mid AD$$

SOLUTION In this example, $\alpha_1 = B$, $\alpha_2 = D$, $\beta_1 = aBD$, $\beta_2 = bDB$, $\beta_3 = c$. So the new productions are:

(i) $A \to aBD \mid bDB \mid c$, $A \to aBDZ \mid bDBZ \mid cZ$.

(ii) $Z \to B$, $Z \to D$, $Z \to BZ \mid DZ$.

Theorem 5.9 (Reduction to Greibach normal form). Every context-free language L can be generated by a context-free grammar G in Greibach normal form.

PROOF We prove the theorem when $\Lambda \notin L$ and then extend the construction to L having Λ.

Case 1 Construction of G (when $\Lambda \notin L$): Step 1 We eliminate null productions and then construct a grammar G in Chomsky normal form generating L. We rename the variables as $A_1, A_2, ..., A_n$ with $S = A_1$. We write G as $(\{A_1, A_2, ..., A_n\}, \Sigma, P, A_1)$.

Step 2 To get the productions in the form $A_i \to a\gamma$ or $A_i \to A_j\gamma$, where $j > i$, convert the A_i-productions ($i = 1, 2, ..., n - 1$) to the form $A_i \to A_j\gamma$ such that $j > i$. Prove that such modification is possible by induction on i.

Consider A_1-productions. If we have some A_1-productions of the form $A_1 \to A_1\gamma$, then we can apply Lemma 5.2 to get rid of such productions. We get a new variable, say Z_1, and A_1-productions of the form $A_1 \to a$ or $A_1 \to A_j\gamma'$, where $j > 1$. Thus there is basis for induction.

Assume we have modified A_1-productions, A_2-productions ... A_i-productions. Consider A_{i+1}-productions. Productions of the form $A_{i+1} \to a\gamma$ required no modification. Consider the first symbol (this will be a variable) on the R.H.S. of the remaining A_{i+1}-productions. Let t be the smallest index among the indices of such symbols (variables). If $t > i + 1$, there is nothing to prove. Otherwise, apply induction hypothesis to A_t-productions for $t \leq i$. So any A_t-production is of the form $A_t \to A_j\gamma$, where $j > t$ or $A_t \to a\gamma'$. Now we can apply Lemma 5.1 to A_{i+1}-production whose R.H.S. starts with A_t. The resulting A_{i+1}-productions are of the form $A_{i+1} \to A_j\gamma$, where $j > t$ (or $A_{i+1} \to a\gamma'$).

We repeat the above construction by finding t for the new set of A_{i+1}-productions. Ultimately, the A_{i+1}-productions are converted to the form $A_{i+1} \to A_j\gamma$, where $j \geq i + 1$ or $A_{i+1} \to a\gamma'$. Productions of the form $A_{i+1} \to A_{i+1}\gamma$ can be modified by using Lemma 5.2. Thus we have converted A_{i+1}-productions to the required form. By the principle of induction, the construction can be carried out for $i = 1, 2, ..., n$. Thus for $i = 1, 2, ..., n - 1$, any A_i-production is of form $A_i \to A_j\gamma$, where $j > i$ or $A_i \to a\gamma'$. Any A_n-production is of the form $A_n \to A_n\gamma$ or $A_n \to a\gamma'$.

Step 3 Convert A_n-productions to the form $A_n \to a\gamma$. Here, productions of the form $A_n \to A_n\gamma$ are eliminated using Lemma 5.2. The resulting A_n-productions are of the form $A_n \to a\gamma$.

Step 4 Modify A_i-productions to the form $A_i \to a\gamma$ for $i = 1, 2, ..., n - 1$. At the end of step 3, the A_n-productions are of the form $A_n \to a\gamma$. The A_{n-1} -productions are of the form $A_{n-1} \to a\gamma'$ or $A_{n-1} \to A_n\gamma$. By applying Lemma 5.1, we eliminate productions of the form $A_{n-1} \to A_n\gamma$. The resulting A_{n-1}-productions are in the required form. We repeat the construction by considering A_{n-2}, A_{n-3}, ..., A_1.

Step 5 Modify Z_i-productions. Every time we apply Lemma 5.2, we get a new variable. (We take it as Z_i when we apply the Lemma for A_i-productions.) The Z_i-productions are of the form $Z_i \rightarrow \alpha Z_i$ or $Z_i \rightarrow \alpha$ (where α is obtained from $A_i \rightarrow A_i\alpha$), and hence of the form $Z_i \rightarrow a\gamma$ or $Z_i \rightarrow A_k\gamma$ for some k. At the end of step 4, the R.H.S. of any A_k-production starts with a terminal. So we can apply Lemma 5.1 to eliminate $Z_i \rightarrow A_k\gamma$. Thus at the end of step 5, we get an equivalent grammar G_1 in GNF.

It is easy to see that G_1 is in GNF. We start with G in CNF. In G any A-production is of the form $A \rightarrow a$ or $A \rightarrow AB$ or $A \rightarrow CD$. When we apply Lemma 5.1 or Lemma 5.2 in step 2, we get new productions of the form $A \rightarrow a\alpha$ or $A \rightarrow \beta$, where $\alpha \in V_N^*$ and $\beta \in V_N^+$ and $a \in \Sigma$. In steps 3–5, the productions are modified to the form $A \rightarrow a\alpha$ or $Z \rightarrow a'\alpha'$, where $a, a' \in \Sigma$ and $\alpha, \alpha' \in V_N^*$.

Case 2 (Construction of G when $\Lambda \in L$). By the previous construction we get $G' = (V_N', \Sigma, P_1, S)$ in GNF such that $L(G') = L - \{\Lambda\}$. Define a new grammar G_1 as

$$G_1 = (V_N' \cup \{S'\}, \Sigma, P_1 \cup \{S' \rightarrow S, S' \rightarrow \Lambda\}, S')$$

$S' \rightarrow S$ can be eliminated by using Theorem 5.7. As S-productions are in the required form, S'-productions are also in the required form. So $L(G) = L(G_1)$ and G_1 is in GNF. ∎

Remark Although we convert the given grammar to CNF in the first step, it is not necessary to convert all the productions to the form required for CNF. In steps 2–5, we do not disturb productions of the form $A \rightarrow a\alpha$, $a \in \Sigma$ and $\alpha \in V_N^*$. So such productions can be allowed in G (in step 1). If we apply Lemma 5.1 or 5.2 as in steps 2–5 to productions of the form $A \rightarrow \alpha$, where $\alpha \in V_N^*$ and $|\alpha| \geq 2$, the resulting productions at the end of step 5 are in the required form (for GNF). Hence we can allow productions of the form $A \rightarrow \alpha$, where $\alpha \in V_N^*$, and $|\alpha| \geq 2$.

Thus we can apply steps 2–5 to a grammar whose productions are either $A \rightarrow a\alpha$, where $\alpha \in V_N^*$, or $A \rightarrow \alpha \in V_N^*$, where $|\alpha| \geq 2$. To reduce the productions to the form $A \rightarrow \alpha \in V_N^*$, where $|\alpha| \geq 2$, we can apply step 2 of Theorem 5.8.

EXAMPLE 5.15 Construct a grammar in Greibach normal form equivalent to the grammar $S \rightarrow AA|a$, $A \rightarrow SS|b$.

SOLUTION The given grammar is in CNF. S and A are renamed as A_1 and A_2, respectively. So the productions are $A_1 \rightarrow A_2A_2|a$ and $A_2 \rightarrow A_1A_1|b$. As the given grammar has no null productions and is in CNF we need not carry out step 1. So we proceed to step 2.

Step 2 (a) A_1-productions are in the required form. They are $A_1 \rightarrow A_2A_2|a$.

(b) $A_2 \rightarrow b$ is in the required form. Apply Lemma 5.1 to $A_2 \rightarrow A_1A_1$. The resulting productions are $A_2 \rightarrow A_2A_2A_1$, $A_2 \rightarrow aA_1$. Thus the A_2-productions are

$$A_2 \to A_2A_2A_1, \qquad A_2 \to aA_1, \qquad A_2 \to b.$$

Step 3   We have to apply Lemma 5.2 to A_2-productions as we have $A_2 \to A_2A_2A_1$. Let Z_2 be the new variable. The resulting productions are

$$A_2 \to aA_1, \qquad A_2 \to b$$
$$A_2 \to aA_1Z_2, \qquad A_2 \to bZ_2$$
$$Z_2 \to A_2A_1, \qquad Z_2 \to A_2A_1Z_2.$$

Step 4   (a) A_2-productions are $A_2 \to aA_1 \,|\, b \,|\, aA_1Z_2 \,|\, bZ_2$.

(b) Among the A_1-productions we retain $A_1 \to a$ and eliminate $A_1 \to A_2A_2$ using Lemma 5.1. The resulting productions are $A_1 \to aA_1A_2 \,|\, bA_2$, $A_1 \to aA_1Z_2A_2$ $|\, bZ_2A_2$. The set of all (modified) A_1-productions are $A_1 \to a \,|\, aA_1A_2 \,|\, bA_2 \,|\, aA_1Z_2A_2$ $|\, bZ_2A_2$.

Step 5   The Z_2-productions to be modified are $Z_2 \to A_2A_1$, $Z_2 \to A_2A_1Z_2$. We apply Lemma 5.1 and get

$$Z_2 \to aA_1A_1 \,|\, bA_1 \,|\, aA_1Z_2A_1 \,|\, bZ_2A_1$$
$$Z_2 \to aA_1A_1Z_2 \,|\, bA_1Z_2 \,|\, aA_1Z_2A_1Z_2 \,|\, bZ_2A_1Z_2$$

Hence the equivalent grammar is

$$G' = (\{A_1, A_2, Z_2\}, \{a, b\}, P_1, A_1)$$

where P_1 consists of

$$A_1 \to a \,|\, aA_1A_2 \,|\, bA_2 \,|\, aA_1Z_2A_2 \,|\, bZ_2A_2$$
$$A_2 \to aA_1 \,|\, b \,|\, aA_1Z_2 \,|\, bZ_2$$
$$Z_2 \to aA_1A_1 \,|\, bA_1 \,|\, aA_1Z_2A_1 \,|\, bZ_2A_1$$
$$Z_2 \to aA_1A_1Z_2 \,|\, bA_1Z_2 \,|\, aA_1Z_2A_1Z_2 \,|\, bZ_2A_1Z_2$$

EXAMPLE 5.16   Convert the grammar $S \to AB$, $A \to BS \,|\, b$, $B \to SA \,|\, a$ into GNF.

SOLUTION   As the given grammar is in CNF we can omit step 1 and proceed to step 2 after renaming S, A, B as A_1, A_2, A_3, respectively. The productions are $A_1 \to A_2A_3$, $A_2 \to A_3A_1 \,|\, b$, $A_3 \to A_1A_2 \,|\, a$.

Step 2   (a) The A_1-production $A_1 \to A_2A_3$ is in the required form.

(b) The A_2-productions $A_2 \to A_3A_1 \,|\, b$ are in the required form.

(c) $A_3 \to a$ is in the required form.

Apply Lemma 5.1 to $A_3 \to A_1A_2$. The resulting productions are $A_3 \to A_2A_3A_2$. Applying the lemma once again to $A_3 \to A_2A_3A_2$, we get $A_3 \to A_3A_1A_3A_2 \,|\, bA_3A_2$.

Step 3   The A_3-productions are $A_3 \to a \,|\, bA_3A_2$ and $A_3 \to A_3A_1A_3A_2$. As we have $A_3 \to A_3A_1A_3A_2$, we have to apply Lemma 5.2 to A_3-productions. Let Z_3 be the new variable. The resulting productions are

$$A_3 \rightarrow a \mid bA_3A_2, \qquad A_3 \rightarrow aZ_3 \mid bA_3A_2Z_3$$

$$Z_3 \rightarrow A_1A_3A_2, \qquad Z_3 \rightarrow A_1A_3A_2Z_3$$

Step 4 (a) The A_3-productions are

$$A_3 \rightarrow a \mid bA_3A_2 \mid aZ_3 \mid bA_3A_2Z_3 \tag{5.9}$$

(b) Among A_2-productions, we retain $A_2 \rightarrow b$ and eliminate $A_2 \rightarrow A_3A_1$ using Lemma 5.1. The resulting productions are:

$$A_2 \rightarrow aA_1 \mid bA_3A_2A_1 \mid aZ_3A_1 \mid bA_3A_2Z_3A_1$$

The modified A_2-productions are

$$A_2 \rightarrow b \mid aA_1 \mid bA_3A_2A_1 \mid aZ_3A_1 \mid bA_3A_2Z_3A_1 \tag{5.10}$$

(c) We apply Lemma 5.1 to $A_1 \rightarrow A_2A_3$ to get

$$A_1 \rightarrow bA_3 \mid aA_1A_3 \mid bA_3A_2A_1A_3 \mid aZ_3A_1A_3 \mid bA_3A_2Z_3A_1A_3 \tag{5.11}$$

Step 5 The Z_3-productions to be modified are:

$$Z_3 \rightarrow A_1A_3A_2 \mid A_1A_3A_2Z_3$$

We apply Lemma 5.1 and get

$$Z_3 \rightarrow bA_3A_3A_2 \mid bA_3A_3A_2Z_3$$

$$Z_3 \rightarrow aA_1A_3A_3A_2 \mid aA_1A_3A_3A_2Z_3$$

$$Z_3 \rightarrow bA_3A_2A_1A_3A_3A_2 \mid bA_3A_2A_1A_3A_3A_2Z_3 \tag{5.12}$$

$$Z_3 \rightarrow aZ_3A_1A_3A_3A_2 \mid aZ_3A_1A_3A_3A_2Z_3$$

$$Z_3 \rightarrow bA_3A_2Z_3A_1A_3A_3A_2 \mid bA_3A_2Z_3A_1A_3A_3A_2Z_3$$

The required grammar in GNF is given by (5.9) – (5.12).

The following example uses the remark following Theorem 5.9. In the example we retain productions of the form $A \rightarrow a\alpha$ and replace the terminals only when they appear as the second or subsequent symbol on R.H.S. (Example 5.17 gives productions to generate arithmetic expressions involving a and operations like +, * and parentheses.)

EXAMPLE 5.17 Find a grammar in GNF equivalent to the grammar $E \rightarrow E + T \mid T, T \rightarrow T * F \mid F, F \rightarrow (E) \mid a$.

SOLUTION: Step 1 We first eliminate unit productions. Hence

$$W_0(E) = \{E\}, \qquad W_1(E) = \{E\} \cup \{T\} = \{E, T\}$$

$$W_2(E) = \{E, T\} \cup \{F\} = \{E, T, F\}$$

So,

$$W(E) = \{E, T, F\}$$

So,

$$W_0(T) = \{T\}, \; W_1(T) = \{T\} \cup \{F\} = \{T, F\}$$

Thus,

$$W(T) = \{T, F\}$$

$$W_0(F) = \{F\}, \qquad W_1(F) = \{F\} = W(F)$$

The equivalent grammar without unit productions is, therefore, $G_1 = (V_N, \Sigma, P_1, S)$, where P_1 consists of

(i) $E \rightarrow E + T | T * F | (E) | a$,
(ii) $T \rightarrow T * F | (E) | a$, and
(iii) $F \rightarrow (E) | a$.

We apply step 2 of reduction to CNF. We introduce new variables A, B, C corresponding to $+, *,)$. The modified productions are

(i) $E \rightarrow EAT | TBF | (EC \mid a$.
(ii) $T \rightarrow TBF | (EC \mid a$.
(iii) $F \rightarrow (EC | a$.
(iv) $A \rightarrow +, B \rightarrow *, C \rightarrow)$.

The variables A, B, C, F, T and E are renamed as $A_1, A_2, A_3, A_4, A_5, A_6$. Then the productions become

$$A_1 \rightarrow +, \qquad A_2 \rightarrow *, \qquad A_3 \rightarrow), \qquad A_4 \rightarrow (A_6 A_3 | a, \qquad (5.13)$$

$$A_5 \rightarrow A_5 A_2 A_4 | (A_6 A_3 | a,$$

$$A_6 \rightarrow A_6 A_1 A_5 | A_5 A_2 A_4 | (A_6 A_3 | a$$

Step 2 We have to modify only A_5- and A_6-productions. $A_5 \rightarrow A_5 A_2 A_4$ can be modified by using Lemma 5.2. The resulting productions are

$$A_5 \rightarrow (A_6 A_3 | a, \qquad A_5 \rightarrow (A_6 A_3 Z_5 | a Z_5 \qquad (5.14)$$

$$Z_5 \rightarrow A_2 A_4 | A_2 A_4 Z_5$$

$A_6 \rightarrow A_5 A_2 A_4$ can be modified by using Lemma 5.1. The resulting productions are

$$A_6 \rightarrow (A_6 A_3 A_2 A_4 | a A_2 A_4 | (A_6 A_3 Z_5 A_2 A_4 | a Z_5 A_2 A_4$$

$$A_6 \rightarrow (A_6 A_3 | a \text{ are in the proper form.}$$

Step 3 $A_6 \rightarrow A_6 A_1 A_5$ can be modified by using Lemma 5.2. The resulting productions give all the A_6-productions:

$$A_6 \rightarrow (A_6 A_3 A_2 A_4 | a A_2 A_4 | (A_6 A_3 Z_5 A_2 A_4$$

$$A_6 \rightarrow a Z_5 A_2 A_4 | (A_6 A_3 | a \qquad (5.15)$$

$$A_6 \rightarrow (A_6A_3A_2A_4Z_6 \,|\, aA_2A_4Z_6 \,|\, (A_6A_3Z_5A_2A_4Z_6$$

$$A_6 \rightarrow aZ_5A_2A_4Z_6 \,|\, (A_6A_3Z_6 \,|\, aZ_6 \qquad (5.16)$$

$$Z_6 \rightarrow A_1A_5 \,|\, A_1A_5Z_6$$

Step 4   This step is not necessary as A_i-productions for $i = 5, 4, 3, 2, 1$ are in the required form.

Step 5   The Z_5-productions are $Z_5 \rightarrow A_2A_4 \,|\, A_2A_4Z_5$. These can be modified as

$$Z_5 \rightarrow * A_4 \,|\, * A_4Z_5 \qquad (5.17)$$

The Z_6-productions are $Z_6 \rightarrow A_1A_5 \,|\, A_1A_5Z_6$. These can be modified as

$$Z_6 \rightarrow + A_5 \,|\, + A_5Z_6 \qquad (5.18)$$

The required grammar in GNF is given by (5.13)–(5.18).

5.5   PUMPING LEMMA FOR CONTEXT-FREE LANGUAGES

The pumping lemma for context-free languages gives a method of generating infinite number of strings from a given sufficiently long string in a context-free language L. It is used to prove that certain languages are not context-free. The construction we make use of in proving pumping lemma yields some decision algorithms regarding context-free languages.

Lemma 5.3   Let G be a context-free grammar in CNF and T be a derivation tree in G. If the length of the longest path in T is less than or equal to k, then the yield of T is of length less than or equal to 2^{k-1}.

PROOF   We prove the result by induction on k, the length of the longest path for all A-trees (Recall an A-tree is a derivation tree whose root has label A).

When the longest path in an A-tree is of length 1, the root has only one son whose label is a terminal (when the root has two sons, the labels are variables). So the yield is of length 1. Thus there is basis for induction.

Assume the result for $k - 1$ $(k > 1)$. Let T be an A-tree with a longest path of length less than or equal to k. As $k > 1$, the root of T has exactly two sons with labels A_1 and A_2. The two subtrees with the two sons as roots have longest paths of length less than or equal to $k - 1$ (see Fig. 5.12).

If w_1 and w_2 are their yields, then by induction hypothesis, $|w_1| \leq 2^{k-2}$, $|w_2| \leq 2^{k-2}$. So the yield of $T = w_1w_2$, $|w_1w_2| \leq 2^{k-2} + 2^{k-2} = 2^{k-1}$. By the principle of induction, the result is true for all A-trees, and hence for all derivation trees.

Theorem 5.10   (Pumping lemma for context-free languages). Let L be a context-free language. Then we can find a natural number n such that:

    (i) Every $z \in L$ with $|z| \geq n$ can be written as $uvwxy$ for some strings u, v, w, x, y.

    (ii) $|vx| \geq 1$.

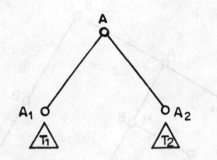

Fig. 5.12 Tree T with subtrees T_1 and T_2.

(iii) $|vwx| \leq n$.

(iv) $uv^k wx^k y \in L$ for all $k \geq 0$.

PROOF By Corollary 1 of Theorem 5.6, we can decide whether or not $\Lambda \in L$. When $\Lambda \in L$, we consider $L - \{\Lambda\}$ and construct a grammar $G = (V_N, \Sigma, P, S)$ in CNF generating $L - \{\Lambda\}$ (when $\Lambda \notin L$, we construct G in CNF generating L).

Let $|V_N| = m$ and $n = 2^m$. To prove that n is the required number, we start with $z \in L$, $|z| \geq 2^m$, and construct a derivation tree T (parse tree) of z. If the length of a longest path in T is atmost m, by Lemma 5.3, $|z| \leq 2^{m-1}$ (since z is the yield of T). But $|z| \geq 2^m > 2^{n-1}$. So T has a path, say Γ, of length greater than or equal to $m + 1$. Γ has at least $m + 2$ vertices and only the last vertex is a leaf. Thus in Γ all the labels except the last one are variables. As $|V_N| = m$, some label is repeated.

We choose a repeated label as follows: We start with the leaf of Γ and travel along Γ upwards. We stop when some label, say B, is repeated. (Among several repeated labels B is the first.) Let v_1 and v_2 be the vertices with label B, v_1 being nearer the root. In Γ, the portion of the path from v_1 to the leaf has only one label, viz., B, which is repeated, and so its length is atmost $m + 1$.

Let T_1 and T_2 be subtrees with v_1, v_2 as roots and z_1, w as yields, respectively. As Γ is a longest path in T, the portion of Γ from v_1 to the leaf is a longest path in T_1 and of length atmost $m + 1$. By Lemma 5.3, $|z_1| \leq 2^m$ (since z_1 is the yield of T_1).

For better understanding we illustrate the construction for the grammar whose productions are $S \to AB$, $A \to aB \,|\, a$, $B \to bA \,|\, b$, as in Fig. 5.13. In the figure,

$$\Gamma = S \to A \to B \to A \to B \to b$$

$$z = ababb, \qquad z_1 = bab, \qquad w = b$$

$$v = ba, \qquad x = \Lambda, \qquad u = a, \qquad y = b$$

As z and z_1 are the yields of T and a proper subtree T_1 of T, we can write $z = uz_1 y$. As z_1 and w are the yields of T_1 and a proper subtree T_2 of T_1, we can write $z_1 = vwx$. Also, $|vwx| > |w|$. So $|vx| \geq 1$. Thus we have $z = uvwxy$ with $|vwx| \leq n$ and $|vx| \geq 1$. This proves points (i)–(iii) of the theorem.

As T is an S-tree and T_1, T_2 are B-trees, we get $S \overset{*}{\Rightarrow} uBy$, $B \overset{*}{\Rightarrow} vBx$ and

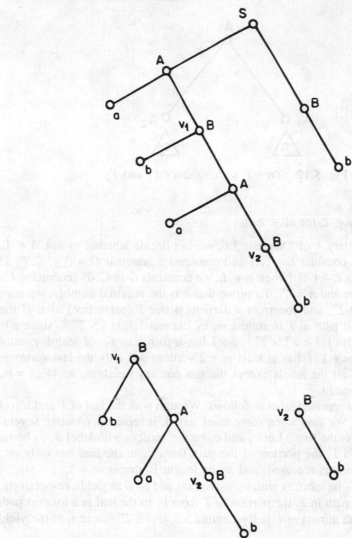

Fig. 5.13 Tree T and its subtrees T_1 and T_2.

$B \overset{*}{\Rightarrow} w$. As $S \overset{*}{\Rightarrow} uBy \Rightarrow uwy$, $uv^0wx^0y \in L$. For $k \geq 1$, $S \overset{*}{\Rightarrow} uBy \overset{*}{\Rightarrow} uv^kBx^ky \overset{*}{\Rightarrow} uv^kwx^ky \in L$. This proves point (iv) of the theorem. ∎

Corollary Let L be a context-free language and n be the natural number obtained by using pumping lemma. Then (a) $L \neq \emptyset$ if and only if there exists $w \in L$ with $|w| < n$, and (b) L is infinite if and only if there exists $z \in L$ such that $n \leq |z| < 2n$.

PROOF (a) We have to prove the "only if" part. If $z \in L$ with $|z| \geq n$, we apply pumping lemma to write $z = uvwxy$, where $1 \leq |vx| \leq n$. Also, $uwy \in L$ and $|uwy| < |z|$. Applying pumping lemma repeatedly, we can get $z' \in L$ such that $|z'| < n$. Thus (a) is proved.

(b) If $z \in L$ such that $n \le |z| < 2n$, by pumping lemma we can write $z = uvwxy$. Also, $uv^kwx^ky \in L$ for all $k \ge 0$. Thus we get infinite number of elements in L. Conversely, if L is infinite, we can find $z \in L$ with $|z| \ge n$. If $|z| < 2n$, there is nothing to prove. Otherwise, we can apply pumping lemma to write $z = uvwxy$ and get $uwy \in L$. Every time we apply pumping lemma we get a smaller string and the decrease in length is atmost n (being equal to $|vx|$). So we ultimately get a string z' in L such that $n \le |z'| < 2n$. This proves (b). ∎

NOTE: As the proof of the corollary depends only on the length of vx, we can have the corollary to regular sets also (refer pumping lemma for regular sets).

The corollary given above provides us algorithms to test whether a given context-free language is empty or infinite. But these algorithms are not efficient. We shall give some other algorithms in Section 5.6.

We use pumping lemma to show that a language L is not a context-free language. We assume that L is context-free. By applying pumping lemma we get a contradiction.

The procedure can be carried out by using the following steps:

Step 1 Assume L is context-free. Let n be the natural number obtained by using the pumping lemma.

Step 2 Choose $z \in L$ so that $|z| \ge n$. Write $z = uvwxy$ using the pumping lemma.

Step 3 Find a suitable k so that $uv^kwx^ky \notin L$. This is a contradiction, and so L is not context-free.

EXAMPLE 5.18   Show that $L = \{a^nb^nc^n \mid n \ge 1\}$ is not context-free but context-sensitive.

SOLUTION   We have already constructed a context-sensitive grammar G generating L (see Example 3.11). We note that in every string of L any symbol appears the same number of times as any other symbol. Also, a cannot appear after b and c cannot appear before b, and so on.

Step 1 Assume L is context-free. Let n be the natural number obtained by using pumping lemma.

Step 2 Let $z = a^nb^nc^n$. Then $|z| = 3n > n$. Write $z = uvwxy$, where $|vx| \ge 1$, i.e. at least one of v or x is not Λ.

Step 3 $uvwxy = a^nb^nc^n$. As $1 \le |vx| \le n$, v or x cannot contain all the three symbols a, b, c. So, (i) v or x is of the form a^ib^j (or b^ic^j) for some i, j such that $i + j \le n$. Or (ii) v or x is a string formed by the repetition of only one symbol among a, b, c.

When v or x is of the form a^ib^j, $v^2 = a^ib^ja^ib^j$ (or $x^2 = a^ib^ja^ib^j$). As v^2 is a substring of uv^2wx^2y, uv^2wx^2y cannot be of the form $a^mb^mc^m$. So, $uv^2wx^2y \notin L$.

When both v and x are formed by the repetition of a single symbol (e.g. $u = a^i$ and $v = b^j$ for some i and j, $i \le n$, $j \le n$), the string uwy will contain the remaining symbol, say a_1. Also, a_1^n will be a substring of uwy as a_1 does not occur in v or x. The number of occurrences of one of the other two symbols in uwy is less than n (recall $uvwxy = a^n b^n c^n$), and n is the number of occurrences of a_1. So $uv^0 wx^0 y = uwy \notin L$.

Thus for any choice of v or x, we get a contradiction. Therefore, L is not context-free.

EXAMPLE 5.19   Show that $L = \{a^p | p \text{ is a prime}\}$ is not a context-free language.

SOLUTION   We use the following property of L: If $w \in L$, then $|w|$ is a prime.

Step 1   Suppose $L = L(G)$ is context-free. Let n be the natural number obtained by using the pumping lemma.

Step 2   Let p be a prime number greater than n. Then $z = a^p \in L$. We write $z = uvwxy$.

Step 3   By pumping lemma, $uv^0 wx^0 y = uwy \in L$. So $|uwy|$ is a prime number, say q. Let $|vx| = r$. Then $|uv^q wx^q y| = q + qr$. As $q + qr$ is not a prime, $uv^q wx^q y \notin L$. This is a contradiction. Therefore, L is not context-free.

5.6   DECISION ALGORITHMS FOR CONTEXT-FREE LANGUAGES

In this section we give some decision algorithms for context-free languages and regular sets.

(*i*) *Algorithm for deciding whether a context-free language L is empty.* We can apply the construction given in Theorem 5.3 for getting $V_N' = W_k$. L is nonempty if and only if $S \in W_k$.

(*ii*) *Algorithm for deciding whether a context-free language L is finite.* Construct a nonredundant context-free grammar G in CNF generating $L - \{\Lambda\}$. We draw a directed graph whose vertices are variables in G. If $A \to BC$ is a production, there are directed edges from A to B and A to C. L is finite if and only if the directed graph has no cycles.

(*iii*) *Algorithm for deciding whether a regular language L is empty.* Construct a deterministic finite automaton M accepting L. We construct the set of all states reachable from the initial state q_0. We find the states which are reachable from q_0 by applying a single input symbol. These states are arranged as a row under columns corresponding to every input symbol. The construction is repeated for every state appearing in an earlier row. The construction terminates in a finite number of steps. If a final state appears in this tabular column, then L is nonempty. (Actually, we can terminate the construction as soon as some final state is obtained in the tabular column.) Otherwise, L is empty.

(*iv*) *Algorithm for deciding whether a regular language L is infinite.* Construct a deterministic finite automaton M accepting L. L is infinite if and only if M has a cycle.

EXERCISES

1. Find a derivation tree of $a * b + a * b$ given that $a * b + a * b$ is in $L(G)$, where G is given by $S \rightarrow S + S | S * S, S \rightarrow a | b$.

2. A context-free grammar G has the following productions:

$$S \rightarrow 0S0 | 1S1 | A, A \rightarrow 2B3, \quad B \rightarrow 2B3 | 3:$$

Describe the language generated by the parameters.

3. A derivation tree of a sentential form of a grammar G is given in Fig. 5.14.

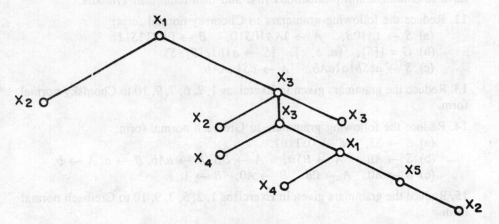

Fig. 5.14 Derivation tree of Example 5.3.

(a) What symbols are necessarily in V_N?
(b) What symbols are likely to be in Σ?
(c) Determine if the following strings are sentential forms (i) $X_4 X_2$, (ii) $X_2 X_2 X_3 X_2 X_3 X_3$, and (iii) $X_2 X_4 X_4 X_2$.

4. Find (i) a leftmost derivation, (ii) a rightmost derivation, and (iii) a derivation which is neither leftmost nor rightmost of *abababa* given that *abababa* is in $L(G)$, where G is the grammar given in Example 5.4.

5. Consider the following productions:

$$S \rightarrow aB | bA$$

$$A \rightarrow aS | bAA | a$$

$$B \rightarrow bS | aBB | b$$

For the string *aaabbabbba*, find
  (i) the leftmost derivation,
  (ii) the rightmost derivation, and
  (iii) Parse tree.

6. Show that the grammar $S \rightarrow a | abSb | aAb$, $A \rightarrow bS | aAAb$ is ambiguous.

7. Show that the grammar $S \to aB \,|\, ab,\ A \to aAB \,|\, a,\ B \to ABb \,|\, b$ is ambiguous.

8. Show that if we apply Theorem 5.4 first and then Theorem 5.3 to a grammar G, we may not get a reduced grammar.

9. Find a reduced grammar equivalent to the grammar $S \to aAa,\ A \to bBB,\ B \to ab,\ C \to aB$.

10. Given the grammar $S \to AB,\ A \to a,\ B \to C \,|\, b,\ C \to D,\ D \to E,\ E \to a$, find an equivalent grammar which is reduced and has no unit productions.

11. Show that for getting an equivalent grammar in the most simplified form, we have to eliminate unit productions first and then redundant symbols.

12. Reduce the following grammars to Chomsky normal form:
   (a) $S \to 1A \,|\, 0B,\quad A \to 1AA \,|\, 0S \,|\, 0,\quad B \to 0BB \,|\, 1S \,|\, 1$.
   (b) $G = (\{S\},\ \{a, b, c\},\ \{S \to a \,|\, b \,|\, cSS\},\ S)$.
   (c) $S \to abSb \,|\, a \,|\, aAb,\quad A \to bS \,|\, aAAb$.

13. Reduce the grammars given in Exercises 1, 2, 6, 7, 9, 10 to Chomsky normal form.

14. Reduce the following grammars to Greibach normal form:
   (a) $S \to SS,\quad S \to 0S1 \,|\, 01$.
   (b) $S \to AB,\quad A \to BSB,\quad A \to BB,\ B \to aAb,\ B \to a,\ A \to b$.
   (c) $S \to A0,\quad A \to 0B,\quad B \to A0,\quad B \to 1$.

15. Reduce the grammars given in Exercises 1, 2, 6, 7, 9, 10 to Greibach normal form.

16. Construct the grammars in Chomsky normal form generating the following:
   (a) $\{wcw^T \,|\, w \in \{a, b\}^*\}$,
   (b) the set of all strings over $\{a, b\}$ consisting of equal number of a's and b's,
   (c) $\{a^m b^n \,|\, m \neq n,\ m, n \geq 1\}$, and
   (d) $\{a^n b^m c^n \,|\, m, n \geq 1\}$.

17. Construct grammars in Greibach normal form generating the sets given in Exercise 16.

18. If $w \in L(G)$ and $|w| = k$, where G is in (i) Chomsky normal form, (ii) Greibach normal form, what can you say about the number of steps in the derivation of w?

19. Show that the language $\{a^{n^2} \,|\, n \geq 1\}$ is not context-free.

20. Show that the following are not context-free languages:
   (a) The set of all strings over $\{a, b, c\}$ in which the number of occurrences of a, b, c is the same.
   (b) $\{a^m b^m c^n \,|\, m \leq n \leq 2m\}$.
   (c) $\{a^m b^n \,|\, n = m^2\}$.

21. A context-free grammar G is called a right-linear grammar if each production is of the form $A \to wB$ or $A \to w$, where A, B are variables and $w \in \Sigma^*$. (G is said to be left-linear if the productions are of the form $A \to Bw$ or $A \to w$. G is linear if the productions are of the form $A \to vBw$ or $A \to w$.) Prove the following:

    (a) A right-linear or left-linear grammar is equivalent to a regular grammar

    (b) A linear grammar is not necessarily equivalent to a regular grammar.

22. A context-free grammar G is said to be self-embedding if there exists some useful variable A such that $A \stackrel{*}{\Rightarrow} uAv$, where $u, v \in \Sigma^*$, $u, v \neq \Lambda$. Show that a context-free language is regular iff it is generated by a nonselfembedding grammar.

23. Show that every context-free language without Λ is generated by a context-free grammar in which all productions are of the form $A \rightarrow a$, $A \rightarrow a\alpha b$.

6

Pushdown Automata

In this chapter we introduce pushdown automaton (pda). We discuss two types of acceptance of sets by pushdown automata. Finally, we prove that the sets accepted by pushdown automata are precisely the class of context-free languages.

6.1 BASIC DEFINITIONS

We have seen that the regular languages are precisely those accepted by finite automata. If M is a finite automaton accepting L, it is constructed in such a way that states act as a form of primitive memory. The states 'remember' the variables encountered in the course of derivation of a string. (In M, states correspond to variables.) Let us consider $L = \{a^n b^n \mid n \geq 1\}$. This is a context-free language but not regular. ($S \to aSb \mid ab$ generates L. Using pumping lemma we can show that L is not regular; cf. Example 4.20.)

A finite automaton cannot accept L, i.e. strings of the form $a^n b^n$ as it has to remember the number of a's in a string and so it will require infinite number of states. This difficulty can be avoided by adding an auxiliary memory in the form of a 'stack' (In a stack we add the elements in a linear way. While removing the elements we follow the last in first out (LIFO) basis, i.e. the most recently added element is removed first). The a's in the given string are added to the stack. When the symbol b is encountered in the input string an a is removed from the stack. Thus the matching of number of a's and number of b's is accomplished. This type of arrangement where a finite automaton has a stack leads to the generation of a pushdown automaton.

Before giving the rigorous definition, let us consider the components of a pushdown automaton and the way it operates. It has a read-only input tape, input alphabet, finite state control, a set of final states, and an initial state as in the case of an FA. In addition to these, it has a stack called the pushdown store (abbreviated as PDS). It is a read-write pushdown store as we add elements to PDS or remove elements from PDS. A finite automaton is in some state and on reading, an input symbol moves to a new state. The pushdown automaton is also in some state and on reading an input symbol and the topmost symbol in PDS, moves to a new state and writes (adds) a string of symbols in PDS. Figure 6.1 illustrates the pushdown automaton.

We now give a formal definition of a pushdown automaton.

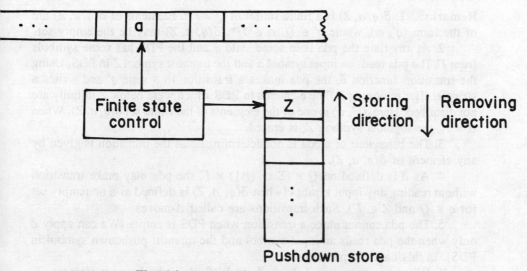

Fig. 6.1 Model of pushdown automaton.

Definition 6.1 A pushdown automaton consists of

  (i) a finite nonempty set of states denoted by Q,

  (ii) a finite nonempty set of input symbols denoted by Σ,

  (iii) a finite nonempty set of pushdown symbols denoted by Γ,

  (iv) a special state called the initial state denoted by q_0,

  (v) a special pushdown symbol called the *initial symbol* on the pushdown store denoted by Z_0,

  (vi) the set of final states, a subset of Q denoted by F, and

  (vii) the transition function δ from $Q \times (\Sigma \cup \{\Lambda\}) \times \Gamma$ to the set of finite subsets of $Q \times \Gamma^*$.

Symbolically, a pda is a 7-tuple, viz. $(Q, \Sigma, \Gamma, \delta, q_0, Z_0, F)$.

NOTE: When $\delta(q\,a, Z) = \emptyset$ for $(q, a, Z) \in Q \times (\Sigma \cup \{\Lambda\}) \times \Gamma$, we do not mention it.

EXAMPLE 6.1 Let

$$A = (Q, \Sigma, \Gamma, \delta, q_0, Z_0, F)$$

where

$$Q = \{q_0, q_1, q_f\}, \qquad \Sigma = \{a, b\}, \qquad \Gamma = \{a, Z_0\}, \qquad F = \{q_f\}$$

δ is given by

$$\delta(q_0, a, Z_0) = \{(q_0, aZ_0)\}, \, \delta(q_1, b, a) = \{(q_1, \Lambda)\}$$

$$\delta(q_0, a, a) = \{(q_0, aa)\}, \delta(q_1, \Lambda, Z_0) = \{(q_1, \Lambda)\}$$

$$\delta(q_0, b, a) = \{(q_1, \Lambda)\}$$

Remarks: 1. $\delta(q, a, Z)$ is a finite subset of $Q \times \Gamma^*$. Elements of $\delta(q, a, Z)$ are of the form (q', α), where $q' \in Q$, $\alpha \in \Gamma^*$. $\delta(q, a, Z)$ may be the empty set.

2. At any time the pda is in some state q and the PDS has some symbols from Γ. The pda reads an input symbol a and the topmost symbol Z in PDS. Using the transition function δ, the pda makes a transition to a state q' and writes a string α after removing Z. The elements in PDS which were below Z initially are not disturbed. Here, (q', α) is one of the elements of the finite set $\delta(q, a, Z)$. When $\alpha = \Lambda$, the topmost symbol, Z, is erased.

3. The behaviour of a pda is nondeterministic as the transition is given by any element of $\delta(q, a, Z)$.

4. As δ is defined on $Q \times (\Sigma \cup \{\Lambda\}) \times \Gamma$, the pda may make transition without reading any input symbol (when $\delta(q, \Lambda, Z)$ is defined as a nonempty set for $q \in Q$ and $Z \in \Gamma$). Such transitions are called Λ-moves.

5. The pda cannot make a transition when PDS is empty (We can apply δ only when the pda reads an input symbol and the topmost pushdown symbol in PDS). In this case the pda halts.

6. When we write $\alpha = Z_1 Z_2 \ldots Z_m$ in PDS, Z_1 is the topmost element, Z_2 is below Z_1, etc., and Z_m is below Z_{m-1}.

In the case of finite automaton, it is enough to specify the current state at any time and the remaining input string to be processed. But as we have the additional structure, viz., the PDS in pda, we have to specify the current state, the remaining input string to be processed, and the symbols in the PDS. This leads to the next definition.

Definition 6.2   Let $A = (Q, \Sigma, \Gamma, \delta, q_0, Z_0, F)$ be a pda. An instantaneous description (ID) is (q, x, α), where $q \in Q$, $x \in \Sigma^*$ and $\alpha \in \Gamma^*$.

For example, $(q, a_1 a_2 \ldots a_n, Z_1 Z_2 \ldots Z_m)$ is an ID. This describes the pda when the current state is q, the input string to be processed is $a_1 a_2 \ldots a_n$. The pda will process $a_1 a_2 \ldots a_n$ in that order. The PDS has $Z_1, Z_2, \ldots, Z_m$ with Z_1 at the top. Z_2 is the second element from the top, etc., and Z_m is the lowest element in PDS.

Definition 6.3   An initial ID is (q_0, x, Z_0). This means initially the pda is in the initial state q_0, the input string to be processed is x, and the PDS has only one symbol, viz. Z_0.

NOTE: In an ID (q, x, α), x may be Λ. In this case the pda makes a Λ-move.

For a finite automaton, the working can be described in terms of change of states. In the case of pda, because of its additional structure, viz. PDS, the working can be described in terms of change of IDs. So we have the following definition:

Definition 6.4   Let A be a pda. A move relation (denoted by $\vdash$) between IDs is defined as

$$(q, a_1 a_2 \ldots a_n, Z_1 Z_2 \ldots Z_n) \vdash (q', a_2 \ldots a_n, \beta Z_2 \ldots Z_m)$$

if $\delta(q, a_1, Z_1)$ contains (q', β).

NOTE: $(q, a_1a_2 \ldots a_n, Z_1Z_2 \ldots Z_m) \vdash (q', a_2a_3 \ldots a_n, \beta Z_2 \ldots Z_m)$ can be described as follows: The pda in state q with $Z_1Z_2 \ldots Z_m$ in PDS (Z_1 is at the top) reads the input symbol a_1. When $(q', \beta) \in \delta(q, a_1, Z_1)$, the pda moves to a state q' and writes β on the top of $Z_2 \ldots Z_m$. After this transition, the input string to be processed is $a_2a_3 \ldots a_n$.

If $\beta = Y_1Y_2 \ldots Y_k$, then Fig. 6.2 illustrates the move relation.

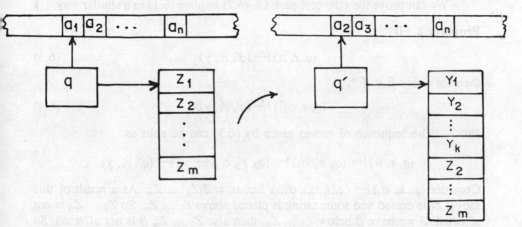

Fig. 6.2 An illustration of move relation.

Remark As $\vdash$ defines a relation in the set of all IDs of a pda, we can define the reflexive-transitive closure $\vdash^*$ which represents a definite sequence of n moves, where n is any non-negative integer.

If $(q, x, \alpha) \vdash^* (q', y, \beta)$ represents n moves, we write $(q, x, \alpha) \vdash^n (q', y, \beta)$. In particular, $(q, x, \alpha) \vdash^0 (q, x, \alpha)$. Also, $(q, x, \alpha) \vdash^* (q', y, \beta)$ can be split as

$$(q, x, \alpha) \vdash (q_1, x_1, \alpha_1) \vdash (q_2, x_2, \alpha_2) \vdash \ldots \vdash (q', y, \beta)$$

for some $x_1, x_2, \ldots, \in \Sigma^*$, $\alpha_1, \alpha_2, \ldots, \in \Gamma^*$.

NOTE: When we are dealing with more than one pda, we specify the pda also while describing the move relation. For example, a move relation in A is denoted by $\vdash_A$.

The next two results are properties of the relation $\vdash^*$ and are frequently used in constructions and proofs.

Property 1 If

$$(q_1, x, \alpha) \vdash^* (q_2, \Lambda, \beta) \tag{6.1}$$

then for every $y \in \Sigma^*$,

$$(q_1, xy, \alpha) \vdash^* (q_2, y, \beta) \tag{6.2}$$

Conversely, if $(q_1, xy, \alpha) \vdash^* (q_2, y, \beta)$ for some $y \in \Sigma^*$, then $(q_1, x, \alpha) \vdash^* (q_2, \Lambda, \beta)$.

PROOF   The result can be easily understood once we refer to Fig. 6.2 illustrating a move.

If the pda is in state q_1 with α in PDS, and the moves given by (6.1) are effected by processing the string x, the pda moves to state q_2 with β in PDS. The same transition is effected by starting with the input string xy and processing only x. In this case, y remains to be processed and hence we get (6.2).

We can prove the converse part, i.e. (6.2) implies (6.1) in a similar way.   ∎

Property 2   If

$$(q, x, \alpha) \vdash^* (q', \Lambda, \gamma) \tag{6.3}$$

then for every $\beta \in \Gamma^*$,

$$(q, x, \alpha\beta) \vdash^* (q', \Lambda, \gamma\beta) \tag{6.4}$$

PROOF   The sequence of moves given by (6.3) can be split as

$$(q, x, \alpha) \vdash (q_1, x_1, \alpha_1) \vdash (q_2, x_2, \alpha_2) \vdash ... \vdash (q', \Lambda, \gamma)$$

Consider $(q_i, x_i, \alpha_i) \vdash (q_{i+1}, x_{i+1}, \alpha_{i+1})$. Let $\alpha_i = Z_1 Z_2 ... Z_m$. As a result of this move, Z_1 is erased and some string is placed above $Z_2 ... Z_m$. So $Z_2 ... Z_m$ is not affected. If we have β below $Z_2 ... Z_m$, then also $Z_2 ... Z_m \beta$ is not affected. So we obtain $(q_i, x_i, \alpha_i\beta) \vdash (q_{i+1}, x_{i+1}, \alpha_{i+1}\beta)$. Therefore, we get a sequence of moves

$$(q, x, \alpha\beta) \vdash (q_1, x_1, \alpha_1\beta) \vdash ... \vdash (q', \Lambda, \gamma\beta)$$

i.e.

$$(q, x, \alpha\beta) \vdash^* (q', \Lambda, \gamma\beta)   ∎$$

NOTE: In general, (6.4) need not imply (6.3). Consider, for instance,

$$A = (\{q_0\}, \{a, b\}, \{Z_0\}, \delta, q_0, Z_0, \emptyset)$$

where

$$\delta(q_0, a, Z_0) = \{(q_0, \Lambda)\}, \delta(q_0, b, Z_0) = \{(q_0, Z_0 Z_0)\}$$

$$(q_0, aab, Z_0 Z_0 Z_0 Z_0)$$

$$\vdash (q_0, ab, Z_0 Z_0 Z_0)$$

$$\vdash (q_0, b, Z_0 Z_0)$$

$$\vdash (q_0, \Lambda, Z_0 Z_0 Z_0)$$

i.e.

$$(q_0, aab, Z_0 Z_0 Z_0 Z_0) \vdash^* (q_0, \Lambda, Z_0 Z_0 Z_0)$$

However, $(q_0, aab, Z_0) \vdash (q_0, ab, \Lambda)$; hence the pda cannot make any more transitions as the PDS is empty. This shows that (6.4) does not imply (6.3) if we assume $\alpha = Z_0 Z_0 Z_0$, $\beta = Z_0$, $\gamma = Z_0 Z_0$.

EXAMPLE 6.2

$$A = (\{q_0, q_1, q_f\}, \{a, b, c\}, \{a, b, Z_0\}, \delta, q_0, Z_0, \{q_f\}$$

is a pda, where δ is defined as

$$\delta(q_0, a, Z_0) = \{(q_0, aZ_0)\}, \qquad \delta(q_0, b, Z_0) = \{(q_0, bZ_0)\} \qquad (6.5)$$

$$\delta(q_0, a, a) = \{(q_0, aa)\}, \qquad \delta(q_0, b, a) = \{(q_0, ba)\} \qquad (6.6)$$

$$\delta(q_0, a, b) = \{(q_0, ab)\}, \qquad \delta(q_0, b, b) = \{(q_0, bb)\} \qquad (6.7)$$

$$\delta(q_0, c, a) = \{(q_1, a)\}, \qquad \delta(q_0, c, b) = \{(q_1, b)\}, \delta(q_0, c, Z_0)$$
$$= \{(q_1, Z_0)\} \qquad (6.8)$$

$$\delta(q_1, a, a) = \delta(q_1, b, b) = \{(q_1, \Lambda)\} \qquad (6.9)$$

$$\delta(q_1, \Lambda, Z_0) = \{(q_f, Z_0)\} \qquad (6.10)$$

We can explain δ as follows:

If A is in initial ID, then using Rule (6.5), A pushes the first symbol of the input string on PDS if it is a or b. By Rules (6.6) and (6.7), the symbols of the input string are pushed on PDS until it sees the centre-marker c. By Rule (6.8), on seeing c, the pda moves to state q_1 without making any changes in PDS. By Rule (6.9), the pda erases the topmost symbol if it coincides with the current input symbol (i.e. if they do not match, the pda halts). By Rule (6.10), the pda reaches the final state q_f only when the input string is exhausted, and the PDS has only Z_0.

We can explain the concepts of ID, moves etc., for this pda A. Suppose the input string is $acab$. We see how the pda processes the string. An initial configuration is $(q_0, bacab, Z_0)$. We get the following moves:

$$(q_0, bacab, Z_0) \vdash (q_0, acab, bZ_0) \quad \text{by Rule (6.5)}$$

$$\vdash (q_0, cab, abZ_0) \quad \text{by Rule (6.7)}$$

$$\vdash (q_1, ab, abZ_0) \quad \text{by Rule (6.8)}$$

$$\vdash (q_1, b, bZ_0) \quad \text{by Rule (6.9)}$$

$$\vdash (q_1, \Lambda, Z_0) \quad \text{by Rule (6.10)}$$

$$\vdash (q_f, \Lambda, Z_0) \quad \text{by Rule (6.10)}$$

i.e. $(q_0, bacab, Z_0) \vdash^* (q_f, Z_0)$

Proceeding in a similar way, we can show that

$$(q_0, wcw^T, Z_0) \vdash^* (q_f, \Lambda, Z_0) \quad \text{for all } w \in \{a, b\}^*$$

Suppose an initial configuration is $(q_0, abcbb, Z_0)$. Then we have

$$(q_0, abcbb, Z_0) \vdash (q_0, bcbb, aZ_0) \quad \text{by Rule (6.5)}$$

$$\vdash (q_0, cbb, baZ_0) \quad \text{by Rule (6.6)}$$

$$\vdash (q_1, bb, baZ_0) \quad \text{by Rule (6.8)}$$

$$\vdash (q_1, b, aZ_0) \quad \text{by Rule (6.9)}$$

Once the pda is in ID (q_1, b, aZ_0), it has to halt as $\delta(q_1, b, a) = \emptyset$. Hence we have

$$(q_0, abcbb, Z_0) \vdash^* (q_1, b, aZ_0)$$

As $\delta(q_0, c, Z_0) = \emptyset$, the pda cannot make any transition if it starts with an ID of the form (q_0, cw, Z_0).

NOTE: In Example 6.2, each $\delta(q, a, Z)$ is either empty or consists of a single element. So for making transitions, the pda has only one choice and the behaviour is deterministic.

In general, a deterministic pda can be defined as follows:

Definition 6.5 A pda $A = (Q, \Sigma, \Gamma, \delta, q_0, Z_0, F)$ is deterministic if (a) $\delta(q, a, Z)$ is either empty or a singleton, and (b) $\delta(q, \Lambda, Z) \neq \emptyset$ implies $\delta(q, a, Z) = \emptyset$ for each $a \in \Sigma$.

Consider the pda given in Example 6.2. $\delta(q, a, Z)$ given by Rules (6.5) – (6.10) are singletons. Also, $\delta(q_1, a, Z_0) = \emptyset$ and $\delta(q_1, a, Z_0) = \emptyset$ for all $a \in \Sigma$. So the pda given in Example 6.2 is deterministic.

6.2 ACCEPTANCE BY pda

A pda has final states like a nondeterministic finite automaton and has also the additional structure, viz., PDS. So we can define acceptance of input strings by pda in terms of final states or in terms of PDS.

Definition 6.6 Let $A = (Q, \Sigma, \Gamma, \delta, q_0, Z_0, F)$ be a pda. The set accepted by pda by final state is defined by

$$T(A) = \{w \in \Sigma^* | (q_0, w, Z_0) \vdash^* (q_f, \Lambda, \alpha) \quad \text{for some } q_f \in F \text{ and } \alpha \in \Gamma^*\}$$

EXAMPLE 6.3 Construct a pda A accepting $L = \{wcw^T \mid w \in \{a, b\}^*\}$ by final state.

SOLUTION Consider the pda given in Example 6.2. Let $wcw^T \in L$. Write $w = a_1a_2 \ldots a_n$, where each a_i is either a or b. Then we have

$$(q_0, a_1a_2 \ldots a_ncw^T, Z_0)$$

$$\vdash^* (q_0, cw^T, a_na_{n-1} \ldots a_1, Z_0) \quad \text{by Rules (6.5)–(6.7)}$$

$$\vdash (q_1, a_na_{n-1} \ldots a_1, a_na_{n-1} \ldots a_1, Z_0) \quad \text{by Rule (6.8)}$$

$$\vdash^* (q_1, \Lambda, Z_0) \quad \text{by Rule (6.9)}$$

$$\vdash (q_f, \Lambda, Z_0) \quad \text{by Rule (6.10)}$$

Therefore, $wcw^T \in T(A)$, i.e. $L \subseteq T(A)$.

To prove the reverse inclusion, it is enough to show that $L^c \subseteq T(A)^c$. Let $x \in L^c$.

Case 1 x does not have the symbol c. In this case the pda never makes a transition to q_1. So the pda cannot make a transition to q_f as we cannot apply Rule (6.10). Thus $x \in T(A)^c$.

Case 2

$$x = w_1 c w_2, \qquad w_2 \neq w_1^T$$

$$(q_0, w_1 c w_2, Z_0)$$

$$\overset{*}{\vdash} (q_0, c w_2, w_1^T Z_0) \quad \vdash (q_1, w_2, w_1^T Z_0)$$

As $w_2 \neq w_1^T$, the pda cannot reach an ID of the form (q_1, Λ, Z_0). So we cannot apply (6.10). Therefore, $x \in T(A)^c$.

Thus we have proved $L^c \subseteq T(A)^c$.

The next definition describes the second type of acceptance.

Definition 6.7   Let $A = (Q, \Sigma, \Gamma, \delta, q_0, Z_0, F)$ be a pda. The set $N(A)$ accepted by null store (or empty store) is defined by

$$N(A) = \{w \in \Sigma^* | (q_0, w, Z_0) \overset{*}{\vdash} (q, \Lambda, \Lambda) \quad \text{for some } q \in Q\}$$

In other words, w is in $N(A)$ if A is in initial ID (q_0, w, Z_0) and empties the PDS after processing all the symbols of w. So in defining $N(A)$, we consider the change brought about on PDS by application of w, and not the transition of states.

EXAMPLE 6.4   Consider the pda A given by Example 6.2 with an additional rule:

$$\delta(q_f, \Lambda, Z_0) = \{(q_f, \Lambda)\} \tag{6.11}$$

Then,

$$N(A) = \{wcw^T | w \in \{a, b\}^*\}$$

SOLUTION   From the construction of A, we see that Rules (6.5) – (6.10) cannot erase Z_0. We make a provision for erasing Z_0 from PDS by Rule (6.11). By Example 6.2, $wcw^T \in T(A)$ if and only if the pda reaches the ID (q_f, Λ, Z_0). By (6.11), PDS can be emptied by Λ-moves if and only if the pda reaches the ID (q_f, Λ, Z_0). Hence,

$$N(A) = \{wcw^T | w \in \{a, b\}^*\}$$

In the next theorem we prove that the set accepted by a pda A by null store is accepted by some pda B by final state.

Theorem 6.1   If $A = (Q, \Sigma, \Gamma, \delta, q_0, Z_0, F)$ is a pda accepting L by empty store, we can find a pda

$$B = (Q', \Sigma, \Gamma', \delta_B, q'_0, Z'_0, F')$$

which accepts L by final state, i.e. $L = N(A) = T(B)$.

PROOF B is constructed in such a way that (a) by the initial move of B, it reaches an initial ID of A, (b) by the final move of B, it reaches its final state, and (c) all intermediate moves of B are as in A.

Let us define B as follows:

$$B = (Q', \Sigma, \Gamma', \delta_B, q'_0, Z'_0, F)$$

where

q'_0 is a new state (not in Q),
$F' = \{q_f\}$, with q_f as a new state (not in Q),
$Q' = Q \cup \{q'_0, q_f\}$,
Z'_0 is a new start symbol for PDS of B,
$\Gamma' = \Gamma \cup \{Z'_0\}$, and
δ_B is given by the rules R_1, R_2, R_3

with

R_1: $\delta_B(q'_0, \Lambda, Z'_0) = \{(q_0, Z_0 Z'_0)\}$,
R_2: $\delta_B(q, a, Z) = \delta(q, a, Z)$ for all (q, a, Z) in $Q \times (\Sigma \cup \{\Lambda\}) \times \Gamma$
R_3: $\delta_B(q, \Lambda, Z'_0) = \{(q_f, \Lambda)\}$ for all $q \in Q$.

By R_1, the pda B moves from an initial ID of B to an initial ID of A. R_1 gives a Λ-move. As a result of R_1, B moves to the initial state of A with the start symbol Z_0 on the top of PDS.

R_2 is used to simulate A. Once B reaches an initial ID of A, R_2 can be used to simulate moves of A. We can repeatedly apply R_2 until Z'_0 is pushed to the top of PDS. As Z'_0 is a new pushdown symbol, we have to use R_3.

R_3 gives a Λ-move. Using R_3, B moves to the new (final) state q_f erasing Z'_0 in PDS.

Thus the behaviour of B and A are similar except for the Λ-moves given by R_1 and R_3. Also, $w \in T(B)$ if and only if B reaches q_f, i.e. if and only if the PDS has no symbols from Γ (since B can reach q_f only by the application of R_3). This suggests that $T(B) = N(A)$.

Now we prove rigorously that $N(A) = T(B)$. Suppose $w \in N(A)$. Then by the definition of $N(A)$, $(q_0, w, Z_0) \vdash^*_A (q, \Lambda, \Lambda)$ for some $q \in Q$. Using R_2 we see that

$$(q_0, w, Z_0) \vdash^*_B (q, \Lambda, \Lambda)$$

By result 2,

$$(q_0, w, Z_0 Z'_0) \vdash^*_B (q, \Lambda, Z'_0) \tag{6.12}$$

By R_1,

$$(q'_0, \Lambda, Z'_0) \vdash_B (q_0, \Lambda, Z_0 Z'_0)$$

By Result 1, we have

$$(q'_0, w, Z'_0) \vdash_{B} (q_0, w, Z_0 Z'_0) \tag{6.13}$$

By R_3,

$$(q, \Lambda, Z'_0) \vdash_{B} (q_f, \Lambda, \Lambda) \tag{6.14}$$

Combining (6.12)–(6.14), we have

$$(q'_0, w, Z'_0) \vdash_{B}^{*} (q_f, \Lambda, \Lambda)$$

This proves that $w \in T(B)$, i.e. $N(A) \subseteq T(B)$.

To prove $T(B) \subseteq N(A)$, start with $w \in T(B)$. Then

$$(q'_0, w, Z'_0) \vdash_{B}^{*} (q_f, \Lambda, \alpha) \tag{6.15}$$

But B can reach q_f only by application of R_3. To apply R_3, Z'_0 should be the topmost element on PDS. Z'_0 is placed initially, and so when it is on the top there are no other elements in PDS. So $\alpha = \Lambda$, and (6.15) actually reduces to

$$(q'_0, w, Z'_0) \vdash_{B}^{*} (q_f, \Lambda, \Lambda) \tag{6.16}$$

In (6.16), the initial and final steps are effected only by Λ-moves. The intermediate steps are induced by the corresponding moves of A. So (6.16) can be split as $(q'_0, \Lambda w, Z'_0) \vdash_{B} (q_0, w, Z_0 Z'_0) \vdash_{B}^{*} (q, \Lambda, Z'_0)$ for some $q \in Q$. Thus, $(q'_0, \Lambda w, Z'_0)$ $\vdash_{B} (q_0, w, Z_0 Z'_0) \vdash_{B}^{*} (q, \Lambda, Z'_0) \vdash_{B} (q_f, \Lambda, \Lambda)$. As we get $(q_0, w, Z_0 Z'_0) \vdash_{B}^{*} (q, \Lambda, Z'_0)$ by applying R_2 several times and R_2 does not affect Z'_0 at the bottom, we have $(q_0, w, Z_0) \vdash_{B}^{*} (q, \Lambda, \Lambda)$. By the construction of R_2, $(q_0, w, Z_0) \vdash_{A}^{*} (q, \Lambda, \Lambda)$, which means $w \in N(A)$. Thus, $T(B) \subseteq N(A)$, and hence $T(B) = N(A) = L$. ∎

NOTE: From the construction of B, it is easy to see that B is deterministic if and only if A is deterministic.

EXAMPLE 6.5 Consider the pda A given in Example 6.1 (Take $F = \varnothing$). Determine $N(A)$. Also construct a pda B such that $T(B) = N(A)$.

SOLUTION

$$A = (\{q_0, q_1\}, \{a, b\}, \{a, Z_0\}, \delta, q_0, Z_0, \varnothing),$$

where δ is given by

$$R_1: \delta(q_0, a, Z_0) = \{(q_0, a Z_0)\}$$

$$R_2: \delta(q_0, a, a) = \{(q_0, aa)\}$$

$$R_3: \delta(q_0, b, a) = \{(q_1, \Lambda)\}$$

$$R_4: \delta(q_1, b, a) = \{(q_1, \Lambda)\}$$

$$R_5: \delta(q_1, \Lambda, Z_0) = \{(q_1, \Lambda)\}$$

R_1 is used to store a in PDS if it is the first symbol of an input string. R_2 can be used repeatedly to store a^n in PDS. When b is encountered for the first time in the input string, a is erased (in PDS) using R_3. Also, the pda makes a transition to state q_1. After processing the entire input string, if Z_0 remains in PDS, it can be erased using the null move given by R_5. So, if $w = a^n b^n$, then we have

$$(q_0, a^n b^n, Z_0) \vdash^* (q_0, b^n, a^n Z_0) \quad \text{by applying } R_1 \text{ and } R_2$$

$$\vdash^* (q_1, \Lambda, Z_0) \qquad \text{by applying } R_3 \text{ and } R_4$$

$$\vdash (q_1, \Lambda, \Lambda) \qquad \text{by applying } R_5$$

Therefore, $a^n b^n \in N(A)$.

If $w \in N(A)$, then $(q_0, w, Z_0) \vdash^* (q_1, \Lambda, \Lambda)$. (Note that the PDS can be empty only when A is in state q_1.) Also, w should start with a. Otherwise, we cannot make any move. We store the symbol a in PDS if the current input symbol is a and the topmost symbol in PDS is a or Z_0. On seeing the input symbol b, the pda erases the symbol a in PDS. The pda enters the ID (q_1, Λ, Λ) only by the application of R_5. The pda can reach the ID (q_1, Λ, Z_0) only by erasing the a's in pda. This is possible only when the number of b's is equal to number of a's, and so $w = a^n b^n$. Thus we have proved that $N(A) = \{a^n b^n \mid n \geq 1\}$.

Now let

$$B = (Q', \{a, b\}, \Gamma', \delta_B, q_0', Z_0', F')$$

where

$$Q' = \{q_0, q_0', q_1, q_f\}, \qquad F' = \{q_f\}, \ \Gamma' = \{a, b, Z_0'\}$$

and δ_B is defined by

$$\delta_B(q_0', \Lambda, Z_0') = \{(q_0, Z_0 Z_0')\}$$

$$\delta_B(q_0, a, Z_0) = \{(q_0, a Z_0)\}$$

$$\delta_B(q_0, a, a) = \{(q_0, aa)\}$$

$$\delta_B(q_0, b, a) = \{(q_1, \Lambda)\}$$

$$\delta_B(q_1, b, a) = \{(q_1, \Lambda)\}$$

$$\delta_B(q_1, \Lambda, Z_0) = \{(q_1, \Lambda)\}$$

$$\delta_B(q_0, \Lambda, Z_0') = \{(q_f, \Lambda)\}$$

$$\delta_B(q_1, \Lambda, Z_0') = \{(q_f, \Lambda)\}$$

Thus,

$$T(B) = N(A) = \{a^n b^n \mid n \geq 1\}$$

The following theorem asserts that the set accepted by a pda A by final state is accepted by some pda B by null store.

Theorem 6.2   If $A = (Q, \Sigma, \Gamma, \delta, q_0, Z_0, F)$ accepts L by final state, we can find a pda B accepting L by empty store, i.e. $L = T(A) = N(B)$.

PROOF B is constructed from A in such a way that (a) by the initial move of B an initial ID of A is reached, (b) once B reaches an initial ID of A, it behaves like A until a final state of A is reached, and (c) when B reaches a final state of A, it guesses whether the input string is exhausted. Then B simulates A or it erases all the symbols in PDS.

The actual construction of B is as follows:

$$B = (Q \cup \{q_0', d\}, \Sigma, \Gamma \cup \{Z_0'\}, \delta_B, q_0', Z_0', \emptyset)$$

where q_0' is a new state (not in Q), d is a new (dead) state, and Z_0' is the new start symbol for PDS of B.

δ_B is defined by rules R_1, R_2, R_3 and R_4 as

R_1: $\delta_B(q_0', \Lambda, Z_0') = \{(q_0, Z_0 Z_0')\}$

R_2: $\delta_B(q, a, Z) = \delta(q, a, Z)$ $\qquad$ for all $a \in \Sigma, q \in Q, Z \in \Gamma$

R_3: $\delta_B(q, \Lambda, Z) = \delta(q, \Lambda, Z) \cup \{(d, \Lambda)\}$ $\quad$ for all $Z \in \Gamma \cup \{Z_0'\}$ and $q \in F$

R_4: $\delta_B(d, \Lambda, Z) = \{(d, \Lambda)\}$ $\qquad$ for all $Z \in \Gamma \cup \{Z_0'\}$

Using R_1, B enters an initial ID of A and the start symbol Z_0 is placed on top of PDS.

Using R_2, B can simulate A until it reaches a final state of A. On reaching a final state of A, B makes a guess whether the input string is exhausted or not. When the input string is not exhausted, B once again simulates A. Otherwise, B enters the dead state d. Rule R_4 gives a Λ-move. Using these Λ-moves, B erases all the symbols on PDS.

Now $w \in T(A)$ if and only if A reaches a final state. On reaching a final state of A, the pda can reach the state d and erase all the symbols in the PDS by Λ-moves. So, it is intuitively clear that $w \in T(A)$ if and only if $w \in N(B)$. We now prove rigorously that $T(A) = N(B)$.

Suppose $w \in T(A)$. Then for some $q \in F$, $\alpha \in \Gamma^*$,

$$(q_0, w, Z_0) \vdash_A^* (q, \Lambda, \alpha).$$

Using R_2, we get

$$(q_0, w, Z_0) \vdash_B^* (q, \Lambda, \alpha)$$

Applying Result 2, we obtain

$$(q_0, w, Z_0 Z_0') \vdash_{\overline{B}}^* (q, \Lambda, \alpha Z_0') \tag{6.17}$$

As

$$(q_0', \Lambda, Z_0') \vdash_{\overline{B}} (q_0, \Lambda, Z_0 Z_0')$$

using Result 1, we get

$$(q_0', w, Z_0') \vdash_{\overline{B}} (q_0, w, Z_0 Z_0') \tag{6.18}$$

From (6.18) and (6.17), we can deduce

$$(q_0', w, Z_0') \vdash_{\overline{B}}^* (q, \Lambda, \alpha Z_0') \tag{6.19}$$

By applying R_3 once and R_4 repeatedly, we get

$$(q, \Lambda, \alpha Z_0') \vdash_{\overline{B}}^* (d, \Lambda, \Lambda) \tag{6.20}$$

Relations (6.19) and (6.20) imply that $(q_0', w, Z_0') \vdash_{\overline{B}}^* (d, \Lambda, \Lambda)$. Thus we have proved $T(A) \subseteq N(B)$.

To prove that $N(B) \subseteq T(A)$, start with $w \in N(B)$. This means that for some state of B,

$$(q_0', w, Z_0') \vdash_{\overline{B}}^* (q, \Lambda, \Lambda) \tag{6.21}$$

As the initial move of B can be made only by using R_1, the first move of (6.21) is $(q_0', \Lambda w, Z_0') \vdash_{\overline{B}} (q_0, w, Z_0 Z_0')$.

Z_0' in the PDS can be erased only when B enters d; B can enter d only when it reaches a final state q of A in an earlier step. So (6.21) can be split as

$$(q_0, \Lambda w, Z_0) \vdash_{\overline{B}} (q_0, w, Z_0 Z_0') \vdash_{\overline{B}}^* (q, \Lambda, \alpha Z_0') \vdash_{\overline{B}}^* (q, \Lambda, \Lambda)$$

for some $q \in F$ and $\alpha \in \Gamma^*$. But, $(q_0, w, Z_0 Z_0') \vdash_{\overline{B}}^* (q, \Lambda, \alpha Z_0')$ can be obtained only by the application of R_2. So the moves involved are those induced by the moves of A. As Z_0' is not a pushdown symbol in A, Z_0' lying at the bottom is not affected by these moves. Hence

$$(q_0', \Lambda w, Z_0') \vdash_{\overline{A}}^* (q, \Lambda, \alpha), \qquad q \in F$$

So $w \in T(A)$ and $N(B) \subseteq T(A)$. Thus,

$$L = N(B) = T(A)$$

EXAMPLE 6.6   Construct a pda A accepting the set of all strings over $\{a, b\}$ with equal number of a's and b's.

SOLUTION Let

$$A = (\{q\}, \{a, b\}, \{Z_0, a, b\}, \delta, q, Z_0, \emptyset)$$

where δ is defined by the following rules:

$$\delta(q, a, Z_0) = \{(q, aZ_0)\} \quad \delta(q, b, Z_0) = \{(q, bZ_0)\}$$

$$\delta(q, a, a) = \{(q, aa)\} \quad \delta(q, b, b) = \{(q, bb)\}$$

$$\delta(q, a, b) = \{(q, \Lambda)\} \quad \delta(q, b, a) = \{(q, \Lambda)\}$$

$$\delta(q, \Lambda, Z_0) = \{(q, \Lambda)\}$$

The construction of δ is similar to that of the pda given in Example 6.2. But here we want to match the number of occurrences of a and b; so, the construction is simpler. We start by storing a symbol of the input string and continue storing until the other symbol occurs. If the topmost symbol in PDS is a and the current input symbol is b, a in PDS is erased. If w has equal number of a's and b's, then $(q, w, Z_0) \overset{*}{\vdash} (q, \Lambda, Z_0) \vdash (q, \Lambda, \Lambda)$. So $w \in N(A)$. We can show that $N(A)$ is the given set of strings over $\{a, b\}$ using the construction of δ.

6.3 PUSHDOWN AUTOMATA AND CONTEXT-FREE LANGUAGES

In this section we prove that the sets accepted by pda (by null store or final state) are precisely context-free languages.

Theorem 6.3 If L is a context-free language, then we can construct a pda A accepting L by empty store, i.e. $L = N(A)$.

PROOF We construct A by making use of productions in G.

Step 1 (Construction of A) Let $L = L(G)$, where $G = (V_N, \Sigma, P, S)$ is a context-free grammar. We construct a pda A as

$$A = (\{q\}, \Sigma, V_N \cup \Sigma, \delta, q, S, \emptyset)$$

where δ is defined by the following rules:

$$R_1: \delta(q, \Lambda, A) = \{(q, \alpha) \mid A \to \alpha \text{ is in } P\}$$

$$R_2: \delta(q, a, a) = \{(q, \Lambda)\} \quad \text{for every } a \text{ in } \Sigma$$

We can explain the construction in the following way: The pushdown symbols in A are variables and terminals. If the pda reads a variable A on the top of PDS, it makes a Λ-move by placing the R.H.S. of any A-production (after erasing A). If the pda reads a terminal a on PDS and if it matches with the current input symbol, then the pda erases a. In other cases the pda halts.

If $w \in L(G)$ is obtained by a left-most derivation

$$S \Rightarrow u_1 A_1 \alpha_1 \Rightarrow u_1 u_2 A_2 \alpha_2 \alpha_1 \Rightarrow \dots \Rightarrow w,$$

then A can empty the PDS on application of input string w. The first move of A is by a Λ-move corresponding to $S \to u_1 A_1 \alpha_1$. The pda erases S and stores $u_1 A_1 \alpha_1$. Then using R_2, the pda erases the symbols in u_1 by processing a prefix of w. Now, the topmost symbol in PDS is A_1. Once again by applying the Λ-move corresponding to $A_1 \to u_2 A_2 \alpha_2$, the pda erases A_2 and stores $u_2 A_2 \alpha_2$ above α_1. Proceeding in this way, the pda empties the PDS by processing the entire string w.

Before proving that $L(G) = N(A)$ (step 2), we apply the construction to an example.

EXAMPLE 6.7   Construct a pda A equivalent to the following context-free grammar: $S \to 0BB$, $B \to 0S \mid 1S \mid 0$. Test whether 010^4 is in $N(A)$.

SOLUTION   Define pda A as follows:

$$A = (\{q\}, \{0, 1\}, \{S, B, 0, 1\}, \delta, q, S, \emptyset)$$

δ is defined by the following rules:

$$R_1: \delta(q, \Lambda, S) = \{(q, 0BB)\}$$

$$R_2: \delta(q, \Lambda, B) = \{(q, 0S), (q, 1S), (q, 0)\}$$

$$R_3: \delta(q, 0, 0) = \{(q, \Lambda)\}$$

$$R_4: \delta(q, 1, 1) = \{(q, \Lambda)\}$$

$(q, 010^4, S) \vdash (q, 010^4, 0BB)$	by Rule R_1
$\vdash (q, 10^4, BB)$	by Rule R_3
$\vdash (q, 10^4, 1SB)$	by Rule R_2 since $(q, 1S) \in \delta(q, \Lambda, B)$
$\vdash (q, 0^4, SB)$	by Rule R_4
$\vdash (q, 0^4, 0BBB)$	by Rule R_1
$\vdash (q, 0^3, BBB)$	by Rule R_3
$\vdash^* (q, 0^3, 000)$	by Rule R_2 since $(q, 0) \in \delta(q, \Lambda, B)$
$\vdash^* (q, \Lambda, \Lambda)$	by Rule R_3

Thus,

$$010^4 \in N(A).$$

NOTE: After entering $(q, 10^4, BB)$, the pda may halt for a different sequence of moves, for example, $(q, 10^4, BB) \vdash (q, 10^4, 0B) \vdash (q, 10^4, 00)$. As $\delta(q, 1, 0)$ is the empty set, the pda halts.

Let us continue with the proof of the theorem.

Step 2   (Proof of the construction, i.e. $L(G) = N(A)$). First we prove $L(G) \subseteq N(A)$. Let $w \in L(G)$. Then it can be derived by a left most derivation. Any sentential form in a leftmost derivation is of the form $uA\alpha$, where $u \in \Sigma^*$, $A \in V_N$ and α $\in (V_N \cup \Sigma)^*$. We prove the following auxiliary result: If $S \stackrel{*}{\Rightarrow} uA\alpha$ by a leftmost derivation, then

$$(q, uv, S) \stackrel{*}{\vdash} (q, v, A\alpha) \quad \text{for every } v \in \Sigma^* \tag{6.22}$$

We prove (6.22) by induction on the number of steps in the derivation of $uA\alpha$. If $S \stackrel{0}{\Rightarrow} uA$, then $u = \Lambda$, $\alpha = \Lambda$, and $S = A$. As $(q, v, S) \stackrel{*}{\vdash} (q, v, S)$, there is basis for induction.

Suppose $S \stackrel{n+1}{\Rightarrow} uA\alpha$ by a leftmost derivation. This derivation can be split as $S \stackrel{n}{\Rightarrow} u_1 A_1 \alpha_1 \Rightarrow uA\alpha$. If the A_1-production we apply in the last step is $A_1 \rightarrow u_2 A \alpha_2$, then $u = u_1 u_2$, $\alpha = \alpha_2 \alpha_1$.

As $S \stackrel{n}{\Rightarrow} u_1 A_1 \alpha_1$, by induction hypothesis,

$$(q, u_1 u_2 v, S) \stackrel{*}{\vdash} (q, u_2 v, A_1 \alpha_1) \tag{6.23}$$

As $A_1 \rightarrow u_2 A \alpha_2$ is a production in P, by Rule R_1 we get $(q, \Lambda, A_1) \vdash (q, \Lambda, u_2 A \alpha_2)$. Applying properties 1 and 2 in Section 6.1, we get

$$(q, u_2 v, A_1 \alpha_1) \vdash (q, u_2 v, u_2 A \alpha_2 \alpha_1)$$

$$\vdash (q, v, A \alpha_2 \alpha_1) \quad \text{by Rule } R_2$$

Hence

$$(q, u_2 v, A_1 \alpha_1) \stackrel{*}{\vdash} (q, v, A \alpha_2 \alpha_1) \tag{6.24}$$

But $u_1 u_2 = u$ and $\alpha_2 \alpha_1 = \alpha$. So from (6.23) and (6.24), we have

$$(q, uv, S) \stackrel{*}{\vdash} (q, v, A\alpha)$$

Thus (6.22) is true for $S \stackrel{n+1}{\Rightarrow} uA\alpha$. By the principle of induction, (6.22) is true for any derivation. Now we prove that $L(G) \subseteq N(A)$. Let $w \in L(G)$. Then, w can be obtained from a leftmost derivation

$$S \stackrel{*}{\Rightarrow} uAv \Rightarrow uu'v = w$$

From (6.22),

$$(q, uu'v, S) \stackrel{*}{\vdash} (q, u'v, Av)$$

As $A \rightarrow u'$ is in P,

$$(q, u'v, Av) \stackrel{*}{\vdash} (q, u'v, u'v)$$

By Rule R_2,

$$(q, u'v, u'v) \stackrel{*}{\vdash} (q, \Lambda, \Lambda)$$

Therefore,

$$w = uu'v \in N(A) \quad \text{proving} \ L(G) \subseteq N(A)$$

Next we prove

$$N(A) \subseteq L(G)$$

Before proving the inclusion, let us prove the following auxiliary result:

$$S \overset{*}{\Rightarrow} u\alpha \quad \text{if} \ (q, uv, S) \overset{*}{\vdash} (q, v, \alpha) \tag{6.25}$$

We prove (6.25) by the number of moves in $(q, uv, S) \overset{*}{\vdash} (q, v, \alpha)$.

If $(q, uv, S) \overset{0}{\vdash} (q, v, \alpha)$, then $u = \Lambda, S = \alpha$; obviously, $S \overset{0}{\Rightarrow} \Lambda \alpha$. Thus there is basis for induction.

Let us assume (6.25) when the number of moves is n. Assume

$$(q, uv, S) \overset{n+1}{\vdash} (q, v, \alpha) \tag{6.26}$$

The last move in (6.26) is obtained either from $(q, \Lambda, A) \vdash (q, \Lambda, \alpha')$ or $(q, a, a) \vdash (q, \Lambda, \Lambda)$. In the first case, (6.26) can be split as

$$(q, uv, S) \overset{n}{\vdash} (q, v, A\alpha_2) \vdash (q, v, \alpha_1\alpha_2) = (q, v, \alpha)$$

By induction hypothesis, $S \overset{*}{\Rightarrow} uA\alpha_2$, and the last move is induced by $A \to \alpha_1$. Thus, $S \overset{*}{\Rightarrow} uA\alpha_2$ implies $\alpha_1\alpha_2 = \alpha$. So,

$$S \overset{*}{\Rightarrow} uA\alpha_2 \Rightarrow u\alpha_1\alpha_2 = u\alpha$$

In the second case, (6.26) can be split as

$$(q, uv, S) \overset{n}{\vdash} (q, av, a\alpha) \vdash (q, v, \alpha)$$

Also, $u = u'a$ for some $u' \in \Sigma$. So, $(q, u'av, S) \overset{n}{\vdash} (q, av, a\alpha)$ implies (by induction hypothesis) $S \overset{*}{\Rightarrow} u'a\alpha = u\alpha$. Thus in both the cases we have shown that $S \overset{*}{\Rightarrow} u\alpha$. By the principle of induction, (6.25) is true.

Now, we can prove that if $w \in N(A)$ then $w \in L(G)$. As $w \in N(A)$, $(q, w, S) \overset{*}{\vdash} (q, \Lambda, \Lambda)$. By taking $u = w, v = \Lambda, \alpha = \Lambda$ and applying (6.25), we get $S \overset{*}{\Rightarrow} w\Lambda = w$, i.e. $w \in L(G)$. Thus,

$$L(G) = N(A)$$

Theorem 6.4   If $A = (Q, \Sigma, \Gamma, \delta, q_0, Z_0, F)$ is a pda, then there exists a context-free grammar G such that $L(G) = N(A)$.

PROOF   We first give the construction of G and then prove that $N(A) = L(G)$.

Step 1   (Construction of G). We define $G = (V_N, \Sigma, P, S)$, where

$$V_N = \{S\} \cup \{[q, Z, q'] \mid q, q' \in Q, Z \in \Gamma\}$$

i.e. any element of V_N is either the new symbol S acting as the start symbol for G or an ordered triple whose first and third elements are states and the second element is a pushdown symbol.

The productions in P are induced by moves of pda as follows:

R_1: S-productions are given by $S \to [q_0, Z_0, q]$ for every q in Q.

R_2: Each move erasing a pushdown symbol given by $(q', \Lambda) \in \delta(q, a, Z)$ induces the production $[q, Z, q'] \to a$.

R_3: Each move not erasing a pushdown symbol given by $(q_1, Z_1 Z_2 \dots Z_m)$
$\in \delta(q, a, Z)$ induces many productions of the form

$$[q, Z, q'] \to a[q_1, Z_1, q_2][q_2, Z_2, q_3] \dots [q_m, Z_m, q']$$

where each of the states $q', q_2 \dots q_m$ can be any state in Q. Each move yields many productions because of R_3. We apply the construction to an example before proving that $L(G) = N(A)$.

EXAMPLE 6.8   Construct a context-free grammar G which accepts $N(A)$, where

$$A = (\{q_0, q_1\}, \{a, b\}, \{Z_0, Z\}, \delta, q_0, Z_0, \emptyset)$$

δ is given by

$$\delta(q_0, b, Z_0) = \{(q_0, ZZ_0)\}$$

$$\delta(q_0, \Lambda, Z_0) = \{(q_0, \Lambda)\}$$

$$\delta(q_0, b, Z) = \{(q_0, ZZ)\}$$

$$\delta(q_0, a, Z) = \{(q_1, Z)\}$$

$$\delta(q_1, b, Z) = \{(q_1, \Lambda)\}$$

$$\delta(q_1, a, Z_0) = \{(q_0, Z_0)\}$$

SOLUTION   Let

$$G = (V_N, \{a, b\}, P, S)$$

where V_N consists of S, $[q_0, Z_0, q_0]$, $[q_0, Z_0, q_1]$, $[q_0, Z, q_0]$, $[q_0, Z, q_1]$, $[q_1, Z_0, q_0]$, $[q_1, Z_0, q_1]$, $[q_1, Z, q_0]$, $[q_1, Z, q_1]$.

The productions are

$$P_1: S \to [q_0, Z_0, q_0]$$

$$P_2: S \to [q_0, Z_0, q_1]$$

$\delta(q_0, b, Z_0) = \{(q_0, ZZ_0)\}$ yields

$$P_3: [q_0, Z_0, q_0] \to b[q_0, Z, q_0][q_0, Z_0, q_0]$$

$$P_4: [q_0, Z_0, q_0] \to b[q_0, Z, q_1][q_1, Z_0, q_0]$$

$$P_5: [q_0, Z_0, q_1] \to b[q_0, Z, q_0][q_0, Z_0, q_1]$$

$$P_6: [q_0, Z_0, q_1] \to b[q_0, Z, q_1][q_1, Z_0, q_1]$$

$\delta(q_0, \Lambda, Z_0) = \{(q_0, \Lambda)\}$ gives

$$P_7: [q_0, Z_0, q_0] \to \Lambda$$

$\delta(q_0, b, Z) = \{(q_0, ZZ)\}$ gives

$$P_8: [q_0, Z, q_0] \to b[q_0, Z, q_0][q_0, Z, q_0]$$

$$P_9: [q_0, Z, q_0] \to b[q_0, Z, q_1][q_1, Z, q_0]$$

$$P_{10}: [q_0, Z, q_1] \to b[q_0, Z, q_0][q_0, Z, q_1]$$

$$P_{11}: [q_0, Z, q_1] \to b[q_0, Z, q_1][q_1, Z, q_1]$$

$\delta(q_0, a, Z) = \{(q_1, Z)\}$ yields

$$P_{12}: [q_0, Z, q_0] \to a[q_1, Z, q_0]$$

$$P_{13}: [q_0, Z, q_1] \to a[q_1, Z, q_1]$$

$\delta(q_1, b, Z) = \{(q_1, \Lambda)\}$ gives

$$P_{14}: [q_1, Z, q_1] \to b$$

$\delta(q_1, a, Z_0) = \{(q_0, Z_0)\}$ gives

$$P_{15}: [q_1, Z_0, q_0] \to a[q_0, Z_0, q_0]$$

$$P_{16}: [q_1, Z_0, q_1] \to a[q_0, Z_0, q_1]$$

P_1–P_{16} give the productions in P.

Using the techniques given in Chapter 5, we can reduce the number of variables and productions.

Step 2:   Proof of the construction, i.e. $N(A) = L(G)$.

Before proving that $N(A) = L(G)$, we note that a variable $[q, Z, q']$ indicates that for the pda the current state is q and the topmost symbol in PDS is Z. In the course of a derivation, a state q' is chosen in such a way that the PDS is emptied ultimately. This corresponds to applying R_2. (Note that the production given by R_2 replaces a variable by a terminal.)

To prove $N(A) = L(G)$, we need an auxiliary result:

$$[q, Z, q'] \underset{G}{\overset{*}{\Rightarrow}} w \tag{6.27}$$

if and only if

$$(q, w, Z) \overset{*}{\vdash} (q', \Lambda, \Lambda) \tag{6.28}$$

We prove the "if" part by induction on the number of steps in (6.28). If $(q, w, Z) \vdash (q', \Lambda, \Lambda)$, then w is either a in Σ or Λ. So we have

$$(q', \Lambda) \in \delta(q, w, Z)$$

By R_2 we get a production $[q, Z, q'] \rightarrow w$. So, $[q, Z, q'] \underset{G}{\Rightarrow} w$. Thus there is basis for induction.

Let us assume the result, viz. (6.28) implies (6.27) when the former has less than k moves. Consider $(q, w, Z) \overset{k}{\vdash} (q', \Lambda, \Lambda)$. This can be split as

$$(q, aw', Z) \vdash (q_1, w', Z_1 Z_2 \ldots Z_m) \overset{k-1}{\vdash} (q', \Lambda, \Lambda) \qquad (6.29)$$

where $w = aw'$ and $a \in \Sigma$ or $a = \Lambda$, depending on the first move.

Consider the second part of (6.29). This means that the PDS has $Z_1 Z_2 \ldots Z_m$ initially, and on application of w, the PDS is emptied. Each move of pda can either erase the topmost symbol on the PDS or replace the topmost symbol by some non-empty string. So several moves may be required for getting Z_2 on the top of PDS. Let w_1 be the prefix of w such that the PDS has $Z_2 Z_3 \ldots Z_m$ after the application of w_1. We can note that $Z_2 Z_3 \ldots Z_m$ are not disturbed while applying w_1. Let w_i be the substring of w such that the PDS has $Z_{i+1} \ldots Z_m$ on application of w_i. $Z_{i+1} \ldots Z_m$ is not disturbed while applying $w_1, w_2, \ldots, w_i$. The changes in PDS are illustrated in Fig. 6.3.

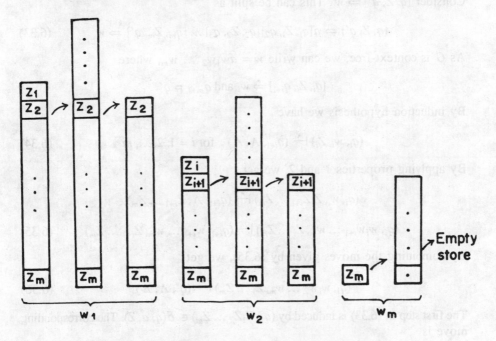

Fig. 6.3 Illustration of changes in pushdown store.

In terms of IDs, we have

$$(q_i, w_i, Z_i) \overset{*}{\vdash} (q_{i+1}, \Lambda, \Lambda) \quad \text{for} \quad i = 1, 2, \ldots, m, \ q_{m+1} = q' \qquad (6.30)$$

As each move in (6.30) requires less than k steps, by induction hypothesis we have

$$[q_i, Z_i, q_{i+1}] \overset{*}{\underset{G}{\Rightarrow}} w_i \quad \text{for } i = 1, 2, ..., m \tag{6.31}$$

The first part of (6.29) is given by $(q_1, Z_1 Z_2 \ldots Z_m) \in \delta(q, a, Z)$. By R_3 we get a production

$$[q, Z, q'] \rightarrow a[q_1, Z_1, q_2] [q_2, Z_2, q_3] \ldots [q_m, Z_m, q'] \tag{6.32}$$

From (6.31) and (6.32), we get

$$[q, Z, q'] \overset{*}{\Rightarrow} aw_1 w_2 \ldots w_m = w$$

By the principle of induction, (6.28) implies (6.27).

We prove the "only if" part by induction on the number of steps in the derivation of (6.27). Suppose $[q, Z, q'] \Rightarrow w$. Then $[q, Z, q'] \rightarrow w$ is a production in P. This production is obtained by R_2. So $w = \Lambda$ or $w \in \Sigma$ and $(q', \Lambda) \in \delta(q, w, Z)$. This gives the move $(q, w, Z) \vdash (q, \Lambda, \Lambda)$. Thus there is basis for induction.

Assume the result for derivations where the number of steps is less than k. Consider $[q, Z, q'] \overset{k}{\Rightarrow} w$. This can be split as

$$[q, Z, q'] \Rightarrow a[q_1, Z_1, q_2][q_2, Z_2, q_3] \ldots [q_m, Z_m, q'] \overset{k-1}{\Rightarrow} w \tag{6.33}$$

As G is context-free, we can write $w = aw_1 w_2 \ldots w_m$, where

$$[q_i, Z_i, q_{i+1}] \overset{*}{\underset{G}{\Rightarrow}} w_i \text{ and } q_{m+1} = q'$$

By induction hypothesis we have

$$(q_i, w_i, Z_i) \overset{*}{\vdash} (q_{i+1}, \Lambda, \Lambda) \quad \text{for } i = 1, 2, ..., m \tag{6.34}$$

By applying properties 1 and 2, we get

$$(q_i, w_i, Z_i Z_{i+1} \ldots Z_m) \overset{*}{\vdash} (q_{i+1}, \Lambda, Z_{i+1} \ldots Z_m)$$

$$(q_i, w_i w_{i+1} \ldots w_m, Z_i \ldots Z_m) \vdash (q_{i+1}, w_{i+1} \ldots w_m, Z_{i+1} \ldots Z_m) \tag{6.35}$$

By combining the moves given by (6.35), we get

$$(q_1, w_1 w_2 \ldots w_m, Z_1 \ldots Z_m) \overset{*}{\vdash} (q', \Lambda, \Lambda) \tag{6.36}$$

The first step in (6.33) is induced by $(q_1, Z_1 Z_2 \ldots Z_m) \in \delta(q, a, Z)$. The corresponding move is

$$(q, a, Z) \vdash (q_1, \Lambda, Z_1 Z_2 \ldots Z_m)$$

By applying property 1, we get

$$(q, aw_1 \ldots w_m, Z) \vdash (q_1, w_1 \ldots w_m, Z_1 \ldots Z_m) \tag{6.37}$$

From (6.37) and (6.36), we get $(q, w, Z) \overset{*}{\vdash} (q', \Lambda, \Lambda)$. By the principle of induction, (6.27) implies (6.28).

Thus we have proved the auxiliary result. In particular,

$$[q_0, Z_0, q'] \overset{*}{\Rightarrow} w \quad \text{iff} \ (q_0, w, Z_0) \overset{*}{\vdash} (q', \Lambda, \Lambda) \tag{6.38}$$

Now $w \in L(G)$

iff $S \overset{*}{\Rightarrow} w$

iff $S \Rightarrow [q_0, Z_0, q'] \overset{*}{\Rightarrow} w$ (for some q' by R_1)

iff $(q_0, w, Z_0) \overset{*}{\vdash} (q', \Lambda, \Lambda)$ by the auxiliary result

iff $w \in N(A)$

Thus, $N(A) = L(G)$.   ∎

Corollary   If A is a pda, then there exists a context-free grammar G such that $T(A) = L(G)$.

PROOF   By Theorem 6.2 we can find a pda A' such that $T(A) = N(A')$. By Theorem 6.4 we can construct G such that $N(A') = L(G)$. Thus $T(A) = L(G)$.   ∎

EXAMPLE 6.9   Construct a pda accepting $\{a^n b^m a^n \mid m, n \geq 1\}$ by null store. Construct the corresponding context-free grammar accepting the same set.

SOLUTION   The pda A accepting $\{a^n b^m a^n \mid m, n \geq 1\}$ is defined as follows:

$$A = (\{q_0, q_1\}, \{a, b\}, \{a, Z_0\}, \delta, q_0, Z_0, \emptyset)$$

where δ is defined by

$$R_1: \delta(q_0, a, Z_0) = \{(q_0, aZ_0)\}$$

$$R_2: \delta(q_0, a, a) = \{(q_0, aa)\}$$

$$R_3: \delta(q_0, b, a) = \{(q_1, a)\}$$

$$R_4: \delta(q_1, b, a) = \{(q_1, a)\}$$

$$R_5: \delta(q_1, a, a) = \{(q_1, \Lambda)\}$$

$$R_6: \delta(q_1, \Lambda, Z_0) = \{(q_1, \Lambda)\}$$

This is a modification of δ given in Example 6.2.

We start storing a's until a b occurs (Rules R_1 and R_2). When the current input symbol is b, the state changes, but no change in PDS occurs (Rule R_3). Once all the b's in the input string are exhausted (using Rule R_4), the remaining a's are erased (Rule R_5). Using R_6, Z_0 is erased. So

$$(q_0, a^n b^m a^n, Z_0) \overset{*}{\vdash} (q_1, \Lambda, Z_0) \vdash (q_1, \Lambda, \Lambda)$$

This means that $a^n b^m a^n \in N(A)$. We can show that

$$N(A) = \{a^n b^m a^n \mid m, n \geq 1\}$$

by using Rules R_1–R_5.

Define $G = (V_N, \{a, b\}, P, S)$, where V_N consists of

$$[q_0, Z_0, q_0], [q_1, Z_0, q_0], [q_0, a, q_0], [q_1, a, q_0]$$

$$[q_0, Z_0, q_1], [q_1, Z_0, q_1], [q_0, a, q_1], [q_1, a, q_1]$$

The productions in P are constructed as follows:

The S-productions are

$$P_1: S \rightarrow [q_0, Z_0, q_0], \qquad P_2: S \rightarrow [q_0, Z_0, q_1]$$

$\delta(q_0, a, Z_0) = \{(q_0, aZ_0)\}$ induces

$$P_3: [q_0, Z_0, q_0] \rightarrow a[q_0, a, q_0][q_0, Z_0, q_0]$$

$$P_4: [q_0, Z_0, q_0] \rightarrow a[q_0, a, q_1][q_1, Z_0, q_0]$$

$$P_5: [q_0, Z_0, q_1] \rightarrow a[q_0, a, q_0][q_0, Z_0, q_1]$$

$$P_6: [q_0, Z_0, q_1] \rightarrow a[q_0, a, q_1][q_1, Z_0, q_1]$$

$\delta(q_0, a, a) = \{(q_0, aa)\}$ yields

$$P_7: [q_0, a, q_0] \rightarrow a[q_0, a, q_0][q_0, a, q_0]$$

$$P_8: [q_0, a, q_0] \rightarrow a[q_0, a, q_1][q_1, a, q_0]$$

$$P_9: [q_0, a, q_1] \rightarrow a[q_0, a, q_0][q_0, a, q_1]$$

$$P_{10}: [q_0, a, q_1] \rightarrow a[q_0, a, q_1][q_1, a, q_1]$$

$\delta(q_0, b, a) = \{(q_1, a)\}$ gives

$$P_{11}: [q_0, a, q_0] \rightarrow b[q_1, a, q_0]$$

$$P_{12}: [q_0, a, q_1] \rightarrow b[q_1, a, q_1]$$

$\delta(q_1, b, a) = \{(q_1, a)\}$ yields

$$P_{13}: [q_1, a, q_0] \rightarrow b[q_1, a, q_0]$$

$$P_{14}: [q_1, a, q_1] \rightarrow b[q_1, a, q_1]$$

$\delta(q_1, a, a) = \{(q_1, \Lambda)\}$ gives

$$P_{15}: [q_1, a, q_1] \rightarrow a$$

$\delta(q_1, \Lambda, Z_0) = \{(q_1, \Lambda)\}$ yields

$$P_{16}: [q_1, Z_0, q_1] \rightarrow \Lambda$$

NOTE: When the number of states is a large number, it is neither necessary nor advisable to write all the productions. We construct productions involving those variables appearing in some sentential form. Using the constructions in Chapter 5, we can simplify the grammar further.

Theorem 6.5   The intersection of a context-free language L and a regular language R is a context-free language.

PROOF   Let L be accepted by a pda $A = (Q_A, \Sigma, \Gamma, \delta_A, q_0, Z_0, F_A)$ by final state and R by DFA $M = (Q_M, \Sigma, \delta_M, p_0, F_M)$.

We define a pda M' accepting $L \cap R$ by final state in such a way that M' simulates moves of A on input a in Σ and changes the state of M using δ_M. On input Λ, M' simulates A without changing the state of M. Let

$$M' = (Q_M \times Q_A, \Sigma, \Gamma, \delta, [p_0, q_0], Z_0, F_M \times F_A)$$

where δ is defined as follows:

$\delta([p, q], a, X)$ contains $([p', q'], \gamma)$ when $\delta_M(p, a) = p'$ and $\delta_A(q, a, X)$ contains (q', γ). $\delta([p, q], \Lambda, X)$ contains $([p, q'], \gamma)$ when $\delta_A (q, \Lambda, X)$ contains (q', γ).

To prove $T(M') = L \cap R$ we need an auxiliary result:

$$([p_0, q_0], w, Z_0) \overset{i}{\underset{M'}{\vdash}} ([p, q], \Lambda, \gamma) \tag{6.39}$$

if and only if

$$(q_0, w, Z_0) \overset{i}{\underset{A}{\vdash}} (q, \Lambda, \gamma) \text{ and } \delta_M(p_0, w) = p \tag{6.40}$$

We prove the 'only if' part by induction on i (the number of steps). If $i = 0$, the proof is trivial (In this case, $p = p_0$, $q = q_0$, $w = \Lambda$ and $\gamma = Z_0$). Thus there is basis for induction. Let us assume that (6.39) implies (6.40) when the former has $i - 1$ steps.

Let $([p_0, q_0], w'a, Z_0) \overset{i}{\underset{M'}{\vdash}} ([p, q], \Lambda, \gamma)$. This can be split into $([p_0, q_0], w'a,$ $Z_0) \overset{i-1}{\underset{M'}{\vdash}} ([p', q'], a, \beta) \underset{M'}{\vdash} ([p, q], \Lambda, \gamma)$, where $w = w'a$ and a is in Σ or $a = \Lambda$ depending on the last move. By induction hypothesis we have $(q_0, w', Z_0) \overset{i-1}{\underset{A}{\vdash}}$ (q', Λ, β) and $\delta_M(p_0, w') = p'$. By definition of δ, $([p', q'], a, \beta) \underset{M'}{\vdash} ([p, q], \Lambda, \gamma)$ implies $(q', a, \beta) \underset{M'}{\vdash} (q, \Lambda, \gamma)$ and $\delta_M(p', a) = p$. (Note: $p' = p$ when $a = \Lambda$.) So $\delta_M(p_0, w'a) = \delta_M(p', a) = p$. By combining the moves of A, we get $(q_0, w'a, Z_0)$ $\overset{i-1}{\underset{A}{\vdash}} (q', a, \beta) \underset{A}{\vdash} (q, \Lambda, \gamma)$ i.e. $(q_0, w, Z_0) \overset{i}{\underset{A}{\vdash}} (q, \Lambda, \gamma)$. So the result is true for i steps.

By the principle of induction 'only if' part is proved.

We prove the 'if' part also by induction on i. It is trivial to see that there is basis for induction.

Let us assume (6.40) with $i - 1$ steps. So $(q_0, w, Z_0) \overset{i}{\underset{A}{\vdash}} (q, \Lambda, \gamma)$ and $\delta_M(p_0, w') = p$. Writing w as $w'a$ and taking $\delta_M(p_0, w')$ as p' we get $(q_0, w'a, Z_0) \overset{i-1}{\underset{A}{\vdash}} (q', a, \beta) \overset{}{\underset{A}{\vdash}} (q, \Lambda, \gamma)$. So $(q_0, w', Z_0) \overset{i-1}{\underset{A}{\vdash}} (q', \Lambda, \beta)$.

By induction hypothesis we get $([p_0, q_0], w', Z_0) \overset{i-1}{\underset{M}{\vdash}} ([p', q'], \Lambda, \beta)$. Also, $\delta_M(p', a) = p$ and $(q', a, \beta) \overset{}{\underset{A}{\vdash}} (q, \Lambda, \gamma)$ implies $([p', q'], a, \beta) \overset{}{\underset{M}{\vdash}} ([p, q], \Lambda, \gamma)$.

Combining the moves we get $([p_0, q_0], w, Z_0) \overset{i}{\underset{M}{\vdash}} ([p, q], \Lambda \gamma)$.

Thus the result is true for i steps. By the principle of induction, the 'if' part is proved.

NOTE: In Chapter 8 we prove that the intersection of two context-free languages need not be context-free (property 3, Section 8.3).

6.4   PARSING AND PUSHDOWN AUTOMATA

In a natural language, parsing is the process of splitting a sentence into words. There are two types of parsing, viz., top-down parsing and bottom-up parsing. Suppose we want to parse the sentence "Ram ate a mango". If NP, VP, N, V, ART denote noun predicate, verb predicate, noun, verb and article, then the top-down parsing can be done as follows:

$S \rightarrow$ NPVP
$\rightarrow$ Name VP
$\rightarrow$ Ram VNP
$\rightarrow$ Ram ate ART N
$\rightarrow$ Ram ate a N
$\rightarrow$ Ram ate a mango

The bottom-up parsing for the same sentence is

Ram ate a mango $\rightarrow$ Name ate a mango
$\rightarrow$ Name verb a mango
$\rightarrow$ Name V ART N
$\rightarrow$ NP VN P
$\rightarrow$ NP VP
$\rightarrow$ S

In the case of formal languages, we derive a terminal string in $L(G)$ by applying the productions of G. If we know that $w \in \Sigma^*$ in $L(G)$, then $S \overset{*}{\Rightarrow} w$. The process of the reconstruction of the derivation of w is called parsing. Parsing is possible in the case of some context-free languages.

Parsing becomes important in the case of programming languages. If a statement in a programming language is given, only the derivation of the statement can give the meaning of the statement. (This is termed *semantics*).

As mentioned earlier, there are two types of parsing: top-down parsing and bottom-up parsing.

In top-down parsing, we attempt to construct the derivation (or the corresponding parse tree) of the input string, starting from the root (with label S) and ending in the given input string. This is equivalent to finding a leftmost derivation. On the other hand, in bottom-up parsing we build the derivation from the given input string to the top (root with label S).

6.4.1 TOP-DOWN PARSING

In this section we present certain techniques for top-down parsing which can be applied to certain subclass of context-free languages. We illustrate them by means of some examples. We discuss LL(1) parsing, LL(k) parsing, left factoring and technique to remove left recursion.

EXAMPLE 6.10 Let $G = (\{S, A, B\}, \{a, b\}, P, S)$ where P consists of $S \to aAB$, $S \to bBA$, $A \to bS$, $A \to a$, $B \to aS$, $B \to b$. $w = abbbab$ is in $L(G)$. Let us try to get a leftmost derivation of w. When we start with S we have two choices: $S \to aAB$ and $S \to bBA$. By looking at the first symbol of w, we see that $S \to bBA$ will not yield w. So we choose $S \to aAB$ as the production to be applied in step 1 and we get $S \Rightarrow aAB$. Now consider the leftmost variable A in the sentential form aAB. We have to apply an A-production among the productions $A \to bS$ and $A \to a$. $A \to a$ will not yield w subsequently since the second symbol in w is b. So we choose $A \to bS$ and get $S \Rightarrow aAB \Rightarrow abSB$. Also, the substring ab of w is also a substring of the sentential form $abSB$. By looking ahead for one symbol, viz., the symbol b, we decide to apply $S \to bBA$ in the third step. This leads to $S \Rightarrow aAB \Rightarrow abSB \Rightarrow abbBAB$. The leftmost variable in the sentential form $abbBAB$ is B. By looking ahead for one symbol which is b, we apply the B-production $B \to b$ in the fourth step. On similar considerations we apply $A \to a$ and $B \to b$ in the last two steps to get the leftmost derivation.

$$S \Rightarrow aAB \Rightarrow abSB \Rightarrow abbBAB \Rightarrow abbbAB \Rightarrow abbbaB \Rightarrow abbbab.$$

Thus in the case of the given grammar, we are able to construct a leftmost derivation of w by looking ahead for one symbol in the input string. In order to top-down parsing for a general string in $L(G)$, we prepare a table called *parsing table*. The table provides the production to be applied for a given variable with a particular look ahead for one symbol.

For convenience we denote the productions $S \to aAB$, $S \to bBA$, $A \to bS$, $A \to a$, $B \to aS$ and $B \to b$ by $P_1, P_2, ..., P_6$. Let E denote an error. It indicates that the given input string is not in $L(G)$. The table for the given grammar is given in Table 6.1.

Table 6.1 Parsing Table for Example 6.10

	Λ	a	b
S	E	P_1	P_2
A	E	P_4	P_3
B	E	P_5	P_6

For example, if A is the leftmost variable in a sentential form and the first symbol in unprocessed substring of the given input string is b, then we have to apply P_3.

A grammar possessing this property (by looking ahead for one symbol in the input string we can decide the production to be applied in the next step) is called an $LL(1)$ grammar.

EXAMPLE 6.11   Let G be a context-free grammar having the productions $S \to F + S$, $S \to F * S$, $S \to F$ and $F \to a$. Consider $w = a + a * a$. This is a string in $L(G)$. Let us try to get top-down parsing for w.

Looking ahead for one symbol will not help us. For the string $a + a * a$, we can apply $F \to a$ on seeing a. But if a is followed by $+$ or $*$, we cannot apply a. So in this case it is necessary to look ahead for two symbols.

When we start with S we have three productions $S \to F + S$, $S \to F * S$ and $S \to F$. The first two symbols in $a + a * a$ are $a+$. This forces us to apply only $S \to F + S$ and not other S-productions. So $S \Rightarrow F + S$. We can apply $F \to a$ now to get $S \Rightarrow F + S \Rightarrow a + S$. Now the remaining part of w is $a * a$. The first two symbols $a*$ suggest that we apply $S \to F * S$ in the third step. So $S \overset{*}{\Rightarrow} a + S \Rightarrow a + F * S$. As the third symbol in w is a, we apply $F \to a$, yielding $S \overset{*}{\Rightarrow} a + F * S \Rightarrow a + a * S$. The remaining part of the input string w is a. So we have to apply $S \to F$ and $F \to a$. Thus the leftmost derivation of $a + a * a$ is $S \Rightarrow F + S \Rightarrow a + S \Rightarrow a + F * S \Rightarrow a + a * S \Rightarrow a + a * F \Rightarrow a + a * a$.

As in Example 6.10, we can prepare a table (Table 6.2) which enables us to get a leftmost derivation for any input string. P_1, P_2, P_3 and P_4 denote the productions $S \to F + S$, $S \to F * S$, $S \to F$ and $F \to a$. E denotes an error.

Table 6.2   Parsing Table for Example 6.11

	Λ	a	$+$	$*$	aa	$a+$	$a*$
S	E	P_3	E	E	E	P_1	P_2
F	E	P_4	E	E	E	P_4	P_4

	$+a$	$++$	$+*$	$*a$	$*+$	$**$
S	E	E	E	E	E	E
F	E	E	E	E	E	E

For example, if the leftmost variable in a sentential form is F and the next two symbols to be processed are $a*$, then we apply P_4 i.e. $F \to a$. When we encounter $*a$ as the next two symbols, an error is indicated in the table and so the input string is not in $L(G)$.

A grammar G having the property (by looking ahead for k symbols we derive a given input string in $L(G)$), is called an LL(k) grammar.

The grammar given in Example 6.11 is an LL(2) grammar.

In the Examples 6.10 and 6.11 for getting a leftmost derivation, one production among several choices was obtained by look ahead for k symbols. This kind of nondeterminism cannot be resolved in some grammars even by looking ahead.

This is the case when a grammar has 2 A-productions of the form $A \rightarrow \alpha\beta$ and $A \rightarrow \alpha\gamma$. By a technique called 'left factoring', we resolve this nondeterminism. Another troublesome phenomenon in a context-free grammar which creates a problem is called left recursion. A variable A is called left recursive if there is an A-production of the form $A \rightarrow A\alpha$. Such a production can cause a top-down parser into an infinite loop. Left factoring and technique for avoiding left recursion are provided in Theorems 6.6 and 6.7.

Theorem 6.6 Let G be a context-free grammar having two A-productions of the form $A \rightarrow \alpha\beta$ and $A \rightarrow \alpha\gamma$. If $A \rightarrow \alpha\beta$ and $A \rightarrow \alpha\gamma$ are replaced by $A \rightarrow \alpha A'$. $A' \rightarrow \beta$ and $A' \rightarrow \gamma$, where A' is a new variable then the resulting grammar is equivalent to G.

PROOF The equivalence can be proved by showing that the effect of applying $A \rightarrow \alpha\beta$ and $A \rightarrow \alpha\gamma$ in a derivation can be realised by applying $A \rightarrow \alpha A'$. $A' \rightarrow \beta$ and $A' \rightarrow \gamma$ and vice versa.

NOTE: The technique of avoiding nondeterminism using theorem 6.6 is called left factoring.

Theorem 6.7 Let G be a contest-free grammar. Let the set of all A-productions be $\{A \rightarrow A\alpha_1, ..., A \rightarrow A\alpha_n, A \rightarrow \beta_1, ..., A \rightarrow \beta_m\}$. Then the grammar G' obtained by introducing a new variable A' and replacing all A-productions in G by $A \rightarrow \beta_1 A', ..., A \rightarrow \beta_m A', A' \rightarrow \alpha_1 A', ..., A' \rightarrow \alpha_n A'$ and $A' \rightarrow \Lambda$ is equivalent to G.

PROOF Similar to proof of Lemma 5.3.

Theorems 6.6 and 6.7 are useful to construct a top-down parser only for certain context-free grammars and not for all context-free grammars. We summarise our discussion as follows:

Construction of Top-Down Parser

Step 1 Eliminate left recursion in G by repeatedly applying Theorem 6.7 to all left recursive variables.

Step 2 Apply Theorem 6.6 to get left factoring wherever necessary.

Step 3 If the resulting grammar is LL(k) for some natural number k apply top-down parsing using techniques explained in Examples 6.10 and 6.11.

EXAMPLE 6.12 Consider the language consisting of all arithmetic expressions involving +, *, (and) over the variables $x1$ and $x2$. This language is generated by a grammar $G = (\{T, F, E\} \Sigma, P, E)$, where $\Sigma = (x, 1, 2, +, *, (,))\}$ and P consists of

$$E \rightarrow E + T \qquad F \rightarrow (E)$$
$$E \rightarrow T \qquad F \rightarrow x1$$
$$T \rightarrow T * F \qquad F \rightarrow x2$$
$$T \rightarrow F$$

Let us construct a top-down parser for $L(G)$.

Step 1 We eliminate left recursion by applying Theorem 6.7 to the left recursive variables E and T. We replace $E \rightarrow E + T$ and $E \rightarrow T$ by $E \rightarrow TE'$, $E' \rightarrow + TE'$ and $E' \rightarrow \Lambda$ (E' is a new variable). Similarly, $T \rightarrow T * F$ and $T \rightarrow F$ are replaced by $T \rightarrow FT'$, $T' \rightarrow * FT'$ and $T' \rightarrow \Lambda$. The resulting equivalent grammar is $G_1 = (\{T, F, E, T', E'\}, \Sigma, P', E)$, where P' consists of

$$
\begin{array}{ll}
E \rightarrow TE' & T' \rightarrow \Lambda \\
E' \rightarrow +TE' & F \rightarrow (E) \\
E' \rightarrow \Lambda & F \rightarrow x1 \\
T \rightarrow FT' & F \rightarrow x2 \\
T' \rightarrow *FT' &
\end{array}
$$

Step 2 We apply Theorem 6.6 for left factoring to $F \rightarrow x1$ and $F \rightarrow x2$ to get new productions $F \rightarrow xN$, $N \rightarrow 1$ and $N \rightarrow 2$.

The resulting equivalent grammar is
$$G_2 = (\{T, F, E, T', E'\}, \Sigma, P'', E) \text{ where } P'' \text{ consists of}$$

$$
\begin{array}{ll}
P_1 : E \rightarrow TE' & P_6 : T' \rightarrow \Lambda \\
P_2 : E' \rightarrow +TE' & P_7 : F \rightarrow (E) \\
P_3 : E' \rightarrow \Lambda & P_8 : F \rightarrow xN \\
P_4 : T \rightarrow FT' & P_9 : N \rightarrow 1 \\
P_5 : T' \rightarrow *FT' & P_{10} : N \rightarrow 2.
\end{array}
$$

Step 3 The grammar G_2 obtained in step 2 is an LL(1) grammar. The parsing table is given in Table 6.3.

Table 6.3 Parsing Table for Example 6.12

	Λ	x	1	2	+	*	(	)
E	E	P_1	E	E	E	E	P_1	E
T	E	P_4	E	E	E	E	P_4	E
F	E	P_8	E	E	E	E	P_7	E
T'	P_6	E	E	E	E	P_5	E	P_6
E'	P_3	E	E	E	P_2	E	E	P_3
N	E	E	P_9	P_{10}	E	E	E	E

6.4.2 TOP DOWN PARSING USING DETERMINISTIC pda's

We have seen that pda's are accepting devices for context-free languages. Theorem 6.3 gives us a method of constructing a pda accepting a given context-free language by empty store. In certain cases the construction can be modified in such a way that a leftmost derivation of a given input string can be obtained while testing whether the given string is accepted by the pda. This is the case when the given grammar is LL(1). We illustrate this by constructing a (deterministic) pda accepting the language given in Example 6.10 and a left most derivation of a given input string using the pda.

EXAMPLE 6.13 For the grammar given in Example 6.10, construct a deterministic pda accepting $L(G)$ and a leftmost derivaiton of *abbab*.

SOLUTION We construct a pda accepting $L(G)\$$ ($\$$ is a symbol indicating the end of the input string). This is done by using Theorem 6.3. The transitions are

$$\delta(q, \Lambda, A) = \{(q, \alpha)|A \rightarrow \alpha \text{ is in } P\}$$

$$\delta(q, t, t) = \{(q, \Lambda)\} \quad \text{for every } t \text{ in } \Sigma$$

This pda is not deterministic as we have two S-productions, two A-productions etc. In Example 6.10 we resolved the nondeterminism by looking ahead for one more symbol in the input string to be processed. In the construction of pda this can be achieved by changing state from q to q_a on reading a. When the pda is in state q_a and the current symbol is S we choose the transition resulting in (q, aAB). Now the deterministic pda accepting $L(G)\$$ by null store is

$$A = (\{p, q, q_a, q_b\}, \{a, b, \$\}, \{S, A, B, a, b, Z_0\}, \delta, p, Z_0, \varnothing)$$

where δ is defined by the following rules:

R_1 : $\delta(p, \Lambda, Z_0) = (q, s)$

R_2 : $\delta(q, a, \Lambda) = (q_a, \Lambda)$

R_3 : $\delta(q_a, \Lambda, a) = (q, e)$

R_4 : $\delta(q, b, \Lambda) = (q_b, \Lambda)$

R_5 : $\delta(q_a, \Lambda, b) = (q, e)$

R_6 : $\delta(q_a, \Lambda, S) = (q_a, aAB)$

R_7 : $\delta(q_b, \Lambda, S) = (q_b, bBA)$

R_8 : $\delta(q_a, \Lambda, A) = (q_a, a)$

R_9 : $\delta(q_b, \Lambda, A) = (q_b, bS)$

R_{10} : $\delta(q_a, \Lambda, B) = (q_a, aS)$

R_{11} : $\delta(q_b, \Lambda, B) = (q_b, b)$

R_{12} : $\delta(q, \$, Z_0) = (q, \Lambda)$

Here R_1 changes the initial ID (p, w, Z) into (q, w, SZ). R_2 and R_4 are for remembering the next symbol. R_6–R_{11} are simulating the productions. R_3 and R_5 are for matching the current input symbol and the topmost symbol on PDS and erasing it (in PDS). Finally, R_{12} is a move erasing Z and making the PDS empty when the last symbol $\$$ of the input string is read.

To get a leftmost derivation for a input string w, apply the unique transition given by R_1 to R_{12}. When we apply R_6 to R_{11}, we are using a corresponding production. By recording these productions we can test whether $w \in L(G)$ and get a leftmost derivation. The parsing for the input string *abbbab* is given in Table 6.4.

The last column of Table 6.4 gives us a leftmost derivation of *abbbab*. It is
$S \Rightarrow aAB \Rightarrow abSB \Rightarrow abbBAB \Rightarrow abbbAB \Rightarrow abbbaB \Rightarrow abbbab.$

Table 6.4 Top-down Parsing for w of Example 6.13

Step	State	Unread input	Pushdown stack	Transition used	Production applied
1	p	$abbbab\$$	Z_0	—	—
2	q	$abbbab\$$	SZ_0	R_1	
3	q_a	$bbbab\$$	SZ_0	R_2	
4	q_a	$bbbab\$$	$aABZ_0$	R_6	$S \to aAB$
5	q	$bbbab\$$	ABZ_0	R_3	
6	q_b	$bbab\$$	ABZ_0	R_4	
7	q_b	$bbab\$$	$bSBZ_0$	R_9	$A \to bS$
8	q	$bbab\$$	SBZ_0	R_5	
9	q_b	$bab\$$	SBZ_0	R_4	
10	q_b	$bab\$$	$bBABZ_0$	R_7	$S \to bBA$
11	q	$bab\$$	$BABZ_0$	R_5	
12	q_b	$ab\$$	$BABZ_0$	R_4	
13	q_b	$ab\$$	$bABZ_0$	R_{11}	$B \to b$
14	q	$ab\$$	ABZ_0	R_5	
15	q_a	$b\$$	ABZ_0	R_2	
16	q_a	$b\$$	aBZ_0	R_8	$A \to a$
17	q	$b\$$	BZ_0	R_3	
18	q_b	$\$$	BZ_0	R_4	
19	q_b	$\$$	bZ_0	R_{11}	$B \to b$
20	q	$\$$	Z_0	R_5	
21	q	Λ	Λ	R_{12}	

6.4.3 BOTTOM-UP PARSING

In bottom-up parsing we build the derivation tree from the given input string to the top (the root with label S). For certain classes of grammars called weak precedence grammars we can construct a deterministic pda which acts as a bottom-up parser. We illustrate the method by constructing the parser for the grammar given in Example 6.12.

In bottom-up parsing we have to reverse the productions to get S finally. This suggests the following moves for a pda acting as bottom-up parser.

   (i) $\delta(p, \Lambda, \alpha^T) = \{(p, A)|$ there exists a production $A \to \alpha\}$
   (ii) $\delta(p, \sigma, \Lambda) = \{(p, \sigma)\}$ for all σ in Σ. Using (i) we replace α^T on the basis by A when $A \to \alpha$ is a production. The input symbol σ is moved onto the stack using (ii). For acceptability we require some moves when the PDS has S or Z_0 on the top.

As in top-down parsing we construct the pda accepting $L(G)\$$. Here we will have two types of operations, viz., shifting and reducing. By shifting we mean pushing the input symbol onto the stack (moves given by (ii)). By reducing we mean replacing α^T by A when $A \to \alpha$ is a production in G (moves given by (i)).

At every step we have (i) to decide whether to shift or to reduce (ii) to choose the prefix of the string on PDS for reducing, once we have decided to reduce. For (i) we use a relation P called a precedence relation. If $(a, b) \in P$ where a is the topmost symbol on PDS and b is the input symbol then we reduce. Otherwise we shift b onto the stack. Regarding (ii), we choose the longest prefix of the string on the PDS of the form α^T to be reduced to A (when $A \to \alpha$ is a production).

We illustrate the method using the grammar given in Example 6.12.

EXAMPLE 6.14 Construct a bottom-up parser for the language $L(G)\$$, where G is the grammar given in Example 6.12.

Here the productions are $E \to E + T$, $E \to T$, $T \to T*F$, $T \to F$, $F \to (E)$, $F \to x1$ and $F \to x2$. Using these productions, we can construct the precedence relation P. It is given in Table 6.5. If (a, b) is in P, then we have a tick mark '√' in the (a, b) cell of the table. Using Table 6.5 we can decide the moves. For example, if the stack symobl is F and the next input symbol is *, then we apply reduction. If the stack symbol is E, then any input symbol is pushed onto the stack.

Table 6.5 The Precedence Relation for Example 6.14

Stack symbol/ Input symbol	x	(	)	1	2	+	*	$
Z_0								
x								
(								
)				√		√	√	√
1				√		√	√	√
2				√		√	√	√
+								
*								
E								
T				√		√		√
F				√		√	√	√

Using the precedence relation and the moves given at the beginning of this section we can construct a deterministic pda. As in the construction of top-down parser, when we look ahead for one symbol we 'remember' it by changing state.

The deterministic pda which acts as a bottom-up parser is

$$A = (Q, \Sigma', \Gamma, \delta, p, Z_0, \varnothing)$$

where

$$\Sigma' = \Sigma \cup \{\$\}, \quad Q = \{p\} \cup \{p_\sigma : \sigma \in \Sigma'\}$$
$$\Gamma = \{E, T, F\} \cup \Sigma \cup \{Z_0, \$\}$$

δ is given by the following rules:

$R_1 : \delta(p, \sigma, \Lambda) = (p, \Lambda)$

$R_2 : \delta(p_\sigma, \Lambda, a) = (p, \sigma a)$ for all $(a, \sigma) \notin P$

$R_3 : \delta(p_\sigma, \Lambda, T + E) = (p_\sigma, E)$ when $(T, \sigma) \in P$

$R_4 : \delta(p_\sigma, \Lambda, Ta) = (p_\sigma, Ea)$ when $(T, \sigma) \in P$ and $a \in \Gamma - \{+\}$

$R_5 : \delta(p_\sigma, \Lambda, F*T) = (p_\sigma, T)$ when $(F, \sigma) \in P$

$R_6 : \delta(p_\sigma, \Lambda, Fa) = (p_\sigma, Ta)$ when $(F, \sigma) \in P$ and $a \in \Gamma - \{*\}$

$R_7 : \delta(p_\sigma, \Lambda, EC) = (p_\sigma, F)$ when $(\ ), \sigma) \in P$

$R_8 : \delta(p_\sigma, \Lambda, 1x) = (p_\sigma, F)$ when $(1, \sigma) \in P$

$R_9 : \delta(p_\sigma, \Lambda, 2x) = (p_\sigma, F)$ when $(2, \sigma) \in P$

$R_{10} : \delta(p_\$, \Lambda, E) = (p_\$, \Lambda)$

$R_{11} : \delta(p_\$, \Lambda, Z_0) = (p_\$, \Lambda)$

As A is deterministic, we have dropped parentheses on the RHS of $R_1 - R_{11}$. Using the pda A, we can get a bottom-up parsing for any input string w. The bottom-up parsing for $x1 + (x2)$ is given in Table 6.6.

Table 6.6 Bottom-up Parsing for $(x1) + (x2)$

Step	State	Unread input	Pushdown stack	Rule used	Production applied
1	p	$x1 + (x2)$	Z_0	—	
2	p_x	$1 + (x2)$	Z_0	R_1	
3	p	$1 + (x2)$	xZ_0	R_2	
4	p_1	$+ (x2)$	xZ_0	R_1	
5	p	$+ (x2)$	$1xZ_0$	R_2	
6	p_+	$(x2)$	$1xZ_0$	R_1	
7	p_+	$(x2)$	FZ_0	R_8	$F \to x1$
8	p_+	$(x2)$	TZ_0	R_6	$T \to F$
9	p_+	$(x2)$	EZ_0	R_4	$E \to T$
10	p	$(x2)$	$+EZ_0$	R_2	
11	$p_($	$x2)$	$+EZ_0$	R_1	
12	p	$x2)$	$(+EZ_0$	R_2	
13	p_x	$2)$	$(+EZ_0$	R_1	
14	p	$2)$	$x(+EZ_0$	R_2	
15	p_2	$)$	$x(+EZ_0$	R_1	
16	p	$)$	$2x(+EZ_0$	R_2	

Step	State	Unread input	Pushdown stack	Rule used	Production applied
17	$p_)$	S	$2x(+EZ_0$	R_1	
18	$p_)$	S	$F(+EZ_0$	R_9	$F \to x2$
19	$p_)$	S	$T(+EZ_0$	R_6	$T \to F$
20	$p_)$	S	$E(+EZ_0$	R_4	$E \to T$
21	p	S	$)E(+EZ_0$	R_2	
22	$p_\$$	Λ	$)E(+EZ_0$	R_1	
23	$p_\$$	Λ	$F+EZ_0$	R_7	$F \to (E)$
24	$p_\$$	Λ	$T+EZ_0$	R_6	$T \to F$
25	$p_\$$	Λ	EZ_0	R_3	$E \to E+T$
26	$p_\$$	Λ	Z_0	R_{10}	
27	$p_\$$	Λ	Λ	R_{11}	

By backtracking the productions we have applied, we get a rightmost derivation
$E \Rightarrow E + T \Rightarrow E + F \Rightarrow E + (E) \Rightarrow E + (T) \Rightarrow E + (F) \Rightarrow E + (x2) \Rightarrow T + (x2)$
$\Rightarrow F + (x2) \Rightarrow x1 + (x2)$.

In Chapter 8 we discuss how LR(k) grammars are amenable for parsing.

EXERCISES

1. If an initial ID of the pda A in Example 6.2 is $(q_0, aacaa, Z_0)$, what is the ID after the processing of $aacaa$? If the input string is (i) $abcba$, (ii) $abcb$, (iii) $acba$, (iv) $abac$, (v) $abab$, will A process the entire string? If so, what will be the final ID?

2. What is the ID that the pda A given in Example 6.5 reaches after processing (i) a^3b^2, (ii) a^2b^3, (iii) a^5, (iv) b^5, (v) b^3a^2, (vi) $ababab$ if A starts with the initial ID.

3. Construct a pda accepting by empty store each of the languages.
   (a) $\{a^n b^m a^n \mid m, n \geq 1\}$.
   (b) $\{a^n b^{2n} \mid n \geq 1\}$.
   (c) $\{a^m b^m c^n \mid m, n \geq 1\}$.
   (d) $\{a^m b^n \mid m > n \geq 1\}$.

4. Construct a pda accepting by final state each of the languages given in Exercise 3.

5. Construct a context-free grammar generating each of the following languages, and hence a pda accepting each of them by empty store.
   (a) $\{a^n b^n \mid n \geq 1\} \cup \{a^m b^{2m} \mid m \geq 1\}$.
   (b) $\{a^n b^m a^n \mid m, n \geq 1\} \cup \{a^n c^n \mid n \geq 1\}$.
   (c) $\{a^n b^m c^m d^n \mid m, n \geq 1\}$.

6. Let $L = \{a^m b^n \mid n < m\}$. Construct (i) a context-free grammar accepting L, (ii) a pda accepting L by empty store, (iii) a pda accepting L by final state.

7. Do Exercise 6 by taking L to be the set of all strings over $\{a, b\}$ consisting of twice as many a's as b's.

8. Construct a pda accepting the set of all even-length palindromes over $\{a, b\}$ by empty store.

9. Show that the set of all strings over $\{a, b\}$ consisting of equal number of a's and b's is accepted by a deterministic pda.

10. Apply the construction given in Theorem 6.4 to the pda M given in Example 6.1 to get a context-free grammar G accepting $N(M)$.

11. Apply the construction given in Theorem 6.4 to the pda obtained by solving Exercise 4.

12. Show that $\{a^n b^n | n \geq 1\} \cup \{a^m b^{2m} | m \geq 1\}$ cannot be accepted by a deterministic pda.

13. Show that a regular set accepted by a deterministic finite automaton with n states is accepted to final state by a deterministic pda with n states and one pushdown symbol. Deduce that every regular set is a deterministic context-free language. (A context-free language is deterministic if it is accepted by a deterministic pda.)

14. Show that every regular set accepted by a finite automaton with n states is accepted by a deterministic pda with one state and n pushdown symbols.

15. If L is accepted by a deterministic pda A, then show that L is accepted by deterministic pda A which never adds more than one symbol at a time (i.e. if δ $(q, a, z) = (q', \gamma)$, then $| \gamma | \leq 2$).

16. If L is accepted by a deterministic pda A, then show that L is accepted by a deterministic pda A which always (i) removes the topmost symbol, or (ii) does not change the topmost symbol, or (iii) pushes a single symbol above the topmost symbol.

7

Turing Machines and Linear Bounded Automata

In this chapter we introduce Turing machines. We construct Turing machines to accept a given language or to carry out some algorithm. Linear bounded automaton is introduced, and constructions for getting the grammar corresponding to a Turing machine and linear bounded automaton are given.

The Turing machine (TM) is a simple mathematical model of a general-purpose computer. In other words, Turing machine models the computing power of a computer, i.e. the Turing machine is capable of performing any calculation which can be performed by any computing machine.

7.1 TURING MACHINE MODEL

The Turing machine can be thought of as a finite-state automaton connected to a R/W (read/write) head. It has one tape which is divided into a number of cells. The block diagram of the basic model for Turing machine is given in Fig. 7.1.

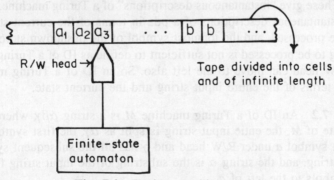

Fig. 7.1 Turing machine model.

Each cell can store only one symbol. The input to and the output from the finite state automaton are effected by the R/W head which can examine one cell at a time. In one move, the machine examines the present symbol under the R/W head on the tape and the present state of an automaton to determine

(i) a new symbol to be written on the tape in the cell under the R/W head,

185

(ii) a motion of the R/W head along the tape: either the head moves one cell left (L), or one cell right (R),

(iii) the next state of the automaton,

(iv) whether to halt or not.

The above model can be rigorously defined as follows:

Definition 7.1 A Turing machine M is a 7-tuple, viz. $(Q, \Sigma, \Gamma, \delta, q_0, b, F)$, where

1. Q is a finite nonempty set of states,
2. Γ is a finite nonempty set of tape symbols,
3. $b \in \Gamma$ is the blank,
4. Σ is a nonempty set of input symbols and is a subset of Γ and $b \notin \Sigma$,
5. δ is the transition function mapping the states of finite automaton and tape symbols to states, tape symbols and movement of the head, i.e. $Q \times \Gamma \rightarrow Q \times \Gamma \times \{L, R\}$,
6. $q_0 \in Q$ is the initial state, and
7. $F \subseteq Q$ is the set of final states.

NOTE: (a) The acceptability of a string is decided by the reachability from the initial state to some final state. So final states are also called accepting states.

(b) δ may not be defined for some elements of $Q \times \Gamma$.

7.2 REPRESENTATION OF TURING MACHINES

We can describe a Turing machine using (i) instantaneous descriptions using move-relations, (ii) transition table, and (iii) transition diagram (transition graph).

7.2.1 REPRESENTATION BY INSTANTANEOUS DESCRIPTIONS

'Snapshots' of a Turing machine in action can be used to describe a Turing machine. These give "instantaneous descriptions" of a Turing machine. We have defined instantaneous descriptions of a pda in terms of the current state, input string to be processed, and the topmost symbol of the pushdown store. But, the input string to be processed is not sufficient to define as ID of a Turing machine for the R/W head can move to the left also. So an ID of a Turing machine is defined in terms of the entire input string and the current state.

Definition 7.2 An ID of a Turing machine M is a string $\alpha\beta\gamma$, where β is the present state of M, the entie input string is split as $\alpha\gamma$, the first symbol of γ is the current symbol a under R/W head and γ has all the subsequent symbols of the input string, and the string α is the substring of the input string formed by all the symbols to the left of a.

EXAMPLE 7.1 A snapshot of Turing machine is shown in Fig. 7.2. Obtain the instantaneous description.

SOLUTION The present symbol under R/W head is a_1. The present state is q_3. So a_1 is written to the right of q_3. The nonblank symbols to the left of a_1 form

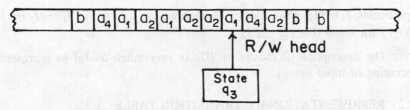

Fig. 7.2   A snapshot of Turing machine.

the string $a_4a_1a_2a_1a_2a_2$, which is written to the left of q_3. The sequence of nonblank symbols to the right of a_1 is a_4a_2. Thus the ID is as given in Fig. 7.3.

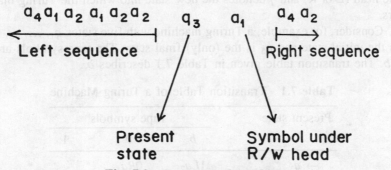

Fig. 7.3   Representation of ID.

NOTE: (a) For constructing the ID, we simply insert the current state in the input string to the left of the symbol under R/W head.

(b) We observe that the blank symbol may occur as part of the left or right substring.

Moves in a TM

As in the case of pushdown automata, $\delta(q, x)$ induces a change in ID of the Turing machine. We call this change in ID a move.

Suppose $\delta(q, x_i) = (p, y, L)$. The input string to be processed is $x_1x_2 \ldots x_n$, and the present symbol under R/W head is x_i. So the ID before processing x_i is $x_1x_2 \ldots x_{i-1}qx_i \ldots x_n$. After processing of x_i, the resulting ID is

$$x_1 \ldots x_{i-2} \, px_{i-1} \, yx_{i+1} \ldots x_n$$

This change of ID is represented by

$$x_1x_2 \ldots x_{i-1}qx_i \ldots x_n \vdash x_i \ldots x_{i-2} \, px_{i-1} \, yx_{i+1} \ldots x_n$$

If $\delta(q, x_i) = (p, y, R)$, then the change of ID is represented by

$$x_1x_2 \ldots x_{i-1}qx_i \ldots x_n \vdash x_1x_2 \ldots x_{i-1} \, ypx_{i+1} \ldots x_n$$

We can denote an ID by I_j for some j. $I_j \vdash I_k$ defines a relation among IDs. So the symbol $\vdash^*$ denotes the reflexive-transitive closure of the relation $\vdash$.

In particular, $I_j \vdash^* I_j$. Also, if $I_1 \vdash^* I_n$, then we can split this as $I_1 \vdash I_2 \vdash I_3 \vdash$ $\ldots \vdash I_n$ for some IDs, $I_2, \ldots, I_{n-1}$.

NOTE: The description of moves by IDs is very much useful to represent the processing of input strings.

7.2.2   REPRESENTATION BY TRANSITION TABLE

We give the definition of δ in the form of a table called the transition table. If $\delta(q, a) = (\gamma, \alpha, \beta)$, we write $\alpha\beta\gamma$ under a-column and q-row. So if we get $\alpha\beta\gamma$ in the table, it means that α is written in the current cell, β gives the movement of the head (L or R) and γ denotes the new state into which the Turing machine enters.

Consider, for example, a Turing machine with five states $q_1, \ldots, q_5$, where q_1 is the initial state and q_5 is the (only) final state. The tape symbols are 0, 1 and b. The transition table given in Table 7.1 describes δ.

Table 7.1   Transition Table of a Turing Machine

Present state	Tape symbols		
	b	0	1
$\rightarrow q_1$	$1Lq_2$	$0Rq_1$	
q_2	bRq_3	$0Lq_2$	$1Lq_2$
q_3		bRq_4	bRq_5
q_4	$0Rq_5$	$0Rq_4$	$1Rq_4$
Ⓠ_5	$0Lq_2$		

As in Chapter 2, the initial state is marked with $\rightarrow$ and final state with O.

EXAMPLE 7.2   Consider the TM description given in Table 7.1. Draw the computation sequence of the input string 00.

SOLUTION   We describe the computation sequence in terms of the contents of the tape and the current state. If the string in the tape is $a_1 a_2 \ldots a_j a_{j+1} \ldots a_m$ and the TM in state q is to read a_{j+1}, then we write $a_1 a_2 \ldots a_j q a_{j+1} \ldots a_m$.

For the input string $00b$, we get the following sequence:

$$q_1 00b \vdash 0q_1 0b \vdash 00q_1 b \vdash 0q_2 01 \vdash q_2 001$$

$$\vdash q_2 b001 \vdash bq_3 001 \vdash bbq_4 01 \vdash bb0q_4 1 \vdash bb01q_4 b$$

$$\vdash bb010q_5 \vdash bb01q_2 00 \vdash bb0q_2 100 \vdash bbq_2 0100$$

$$\vdash bq_2 b0100 \vdash bbq_3 0100 \vdash bbbq_4 100 \vdash bbb1q_4 00$$

$$\vdash bbb10q_4 0 \vdash bbb100q_4 b \vdash bbb1000q_5 b$$

$$\vdash bbb100q_2 00 \vdash bbb10q_2 000 \vdash bbb1q_2 0000$$

$$\vdash bbbq_2 10000 \vdash bbq_2 b10000 \vdash bbbq_3 10000 \vdash bbbbq_5 0000$$

7.2.3   REPRESENTATION BY TRANSITION DIAGRAM

We can use transition systems introduced in Chapter 2 to represent Turing machines. The states are represented by vertices. Directed edges are used to represent transition of states. The labels are triples of the form (α, β, γ), where $\alpha, \beta, \in \Gamma$ and $\gamma \in \{L, R\}$. When there is a directed edge from q_i to q_j with label (α, β, γ), it means that

$$\delta(q_i, \alpha) = (q_j, \beta, \gamma)$$

During the processing of an input string, suppose the Turing machine enters q_i and R/W head scans the (present) symbol α. As a result, the symbol β is written in the cell under R/W head. The R/W head moves to the left or to the right, depending on γ, and the new state is q_j.

Every edge in the transition system can be represented by a 5-tuple $(q_i, \alpha, \beta, \gamma, q_j)$. So each Turing machine can be described by the sequence of 5-tuples representing all the directed edges. The initial state is indicated by $\rightarrow$ and any final state is marked with O.

EXAMPLE 7.3 M is a Turing machine represented by the transition system in Fig. 7.4. Obtain the computation sequence of M for processing the input string 0011.

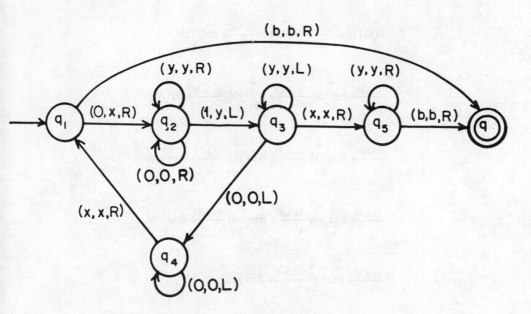

Fig. 7.4   Transition system for M.

SOLUTION   The initial tape input is $b0011b$. Let us assume that M is in state q_1 and the R/W head scans 0 (the first 0). We can represent this as in Fig. 7.5.
$$\downarrow$$
The figure can be represented by $b0011b$. From Fig. 7.4 we see that there is
$$q_1$$

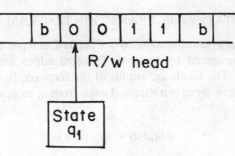

Fig. 7.5 TM processing 0011.

a directed edge from q_1 to q_2 with label $(0, x, R)$. So the current symbol 0 is replaced by x and the head moves right. The new state is q_2. Thus we get $bx011b$.

The change brought about by processing the symbol 0 can be represented as

$$\underset{q_1}{\overset{\downarrow}{b}}0011b \xrightarrow{(0,x,R)} bx\underset{q_2}{\overset{\downarrow}{0}}11b$$

The entire computation sequence reads as follows:

$$\underset{q_1}{\overset{\downarrow}{b}}0011b \xrightarrow{(0,x,R)} bx\underset{q_2}{\overset{\downarrow}{0}}11b \xrightarrow{(0,0,R)} bx0\underset{q_2}{\overset{\downarrow}{1}}1b$$

$$\xrightarrow{(1,y,L)} bx\underset{q_3}{\overset{\downarrow}{0}}y1b \xrightarrow{(0,0,L)} b\underset{q_4}{\overset{\downarrow}{x}}0y1b \xrightarrow{(x,x,R)} bx\underset{q_1}{\overset{\downarrow}{0}}y1b$$

$$\xrightarrow{(0,x,R)} bxx\underset{q_2}{\overset{\downarrow}{y}}1b \xrightarrow{(y,y,R)} bxxy\underset{q_2}{\overset{\downarrow}{1}}b \xrightarrow{(1,y,L)} bxx\underset{q_3}{\overset{\downarrow}{y}}yb$$

$$\xrightarrow{(y,y,L)} bx\underset{q_3}{\overset{\downarrow}{x}}yyb \xrightarrow{(x,x,R)} bx\underset{q_5}{\overset{\downarrow}{x}}yyb \xrightarrow{(y,y,R)} bxx\underset{q_5}{\overset{\downarrow}{y}}yb$$

$$\xrightarrow{(y,y,R)} bxxy\underset{q_5}{\overset{\downarrow}{y}}b \xrightarrow{(b,b,R)} bxxyy\underset{q_6}{\overset{\downarrow}{b}}b$$

7.3 LANGUAGE ACCEPTABILITY BY TURING MACHINES

Let us consider the Turing machine $M = (Q, \Sigma, \Gamma, \delta, q_0, b, F)$. A string w in Σ^* is said to be accepted by M if $q_0w \vdash^* \alpha_1 p \alpha_2$ for some $p \in F$ and $\alpha_1, \alpha_2 \in \Gamma^*$.

M does not accept w if the machine M either halts in a nonaccepting state or does not halt.

It should be noted that there are other equivalent definitions of acceptance by the Turing machine. We are not discussing them in this text.

EXAMPLE 7.4   Consider the Turing machine M described by the transition table given in Table 7.2. Describe the processing of (a) 011, (b) 0011, (c) 001 using IDs. Which of the above strings are accepted by M?

Table 7.2   Transition Table for Example 7.4

Present state	Tape symbol				
	0	1	x	y	b
→ q_1	xRq_2				bRq_5
q_2	$0Rq_2$	yLq_3		yRq_2	
q_3	$0Lq_4$		xRq_5	yLq_3	
q_4	$0Lq_4$		xRq_1		
q_5				yRq_5	bRq_6
q_6					

SOLUTION

(a) $q_1 011 \vdash xq_2 11 \vdash q_3 xy1 \vdash xq_5 y1 \vdash xyq_5 1$.

As $\delta(q_5, 1)$ is not defined, M halts; so the input string 011 is not accepted.

(b) $q_1 0011 \vdash xq_2 011 \vdash x0q_2 11 \vdash xq_3 0y1 \vdash q_4 x0y1 \vdash xq_1 0y1$

$\vdash xxq_2 y1 \vdash xxyq_2 1 \vdash xxq_3 yy \vdash xq_3 xyy \vdash xxq_5 yy$

$\vdash xxyq_5 y \vdash xxyyq_5 b \vdash xxyybq_6$

M halts. As q_6 is an accepting state, the input string 0011 is accepted by M.

(c) $q_1 001 \vdash xq_2 01 \vdash x0q_2 1 \vdash xq_3 0y \vdash q_4 x0y$

$\vdash xq_1 0y \vdash xxq_2 y \vdash xxyq_2$

M halts. As q_2 is not an accepting state, 001 is not accepted by M.

7.4 DESIGN OF TURING MACHINES

We now give the basic guidelines for designing a Turing machine.

(i) The fundamental objective in scanning a symbol by R/W head is to 'know' what to do in the future. The machine must remember the past symbols scanned. The Turing machine can remember this by going to the next unique state.

(ii) The number of states must be minimised. This can be achieved by changing the states only when there is a change in the written symbol or when there is a change in the movement of R/W head. We shall explain the design by a simple example.

EXAMPLE 7.5   Design a Turing machine to recognise all strings consisting of even number of 1's.

SOLUTION　The construction is made by defining moves in the following manner:

(i) q_1 is the initial state. M enters state q_2 on scanning 1 and writes b.

(ii) If M is in state q_2 and scans 1, it enters q_1 and writes b.

(iii) q_1 is the only accepting state.

So M accepts a string if it exhausts all input symbols and finally in state q_1. Symbolically,

$$M = (\{q_1, q_2\}, \{1, b\}, \{1, b\}, \delta, q_1, b, \{q_1\})$$

where δ is defined by Table 7.3.

Table 7.3　Transition Table for
Example 7.5

Present state	1
$\rightarrow \enclose{circle}{q_1}$	bq_2R
q_2	bq_1R

Let us obtain the computation sequence of 11. Thus, $q_1 11 \vdash bq_2 1 \vdash bbq_1$. As q_1 is an accepting state, 11 is accepted. $q_1 111 \vdash bq_2 11 \vdash bbq_1 1 \vdash bbbq_2$. M halts and as q_2 is not an accepting state, 111 is not accepted by M.

EXAMPLE 7.6　Design a Turing machine over $\{1, b\}$ which can compute concatenation function over $\Sigma = \{1\}$. If a pair of words (w_1, w_2) is the input, the output has to be $w_1 w_2$.

SOLUTION　Let us assume that the two words w_1 and w_2 are written initially on the input tape separated by symbol b. For example, if $w_1 = 11$, $w_2 = 111$, then the input and output tapes are as shown in Fig. 7.6.

Fig. 7.6　Input and output tapes.

We observe that the main task is to remove the symbol b. This can be done in the following manner:

(i) The separating symbol b is found and replaced by 1.

(ii) The rightmost 1 is found and replaced by a blank b.

(iii) The R/W head returns to the starting position.

A computation is illustrated in Table 7.4.

From the above computation sequence for the input string $11b111$, we can construct the transition table given in Table 7.5.

For the input string $1b1$, the computation sequence is given as

$$q_0 1b1 \vdash 1q_0 b1 \vdash 11q_1 1 \vdash 111q_1 b \vdash 11q_2 1b \vdash 1q_3 1bb$$

$$\vdash q_3 11bb \vdash q_3 b11bb \vdash bq_F 11bb.$$

Table 7.4   Computation for $11b111$

$$q_011b111 \vdash 1q_01b111 \vdash 11q_0b111 \vdash 111q_1111$$
$$\vdash 1111q_111 \vdash 11111q_11 \vdash 111111q_1b \vdash 11111q_21b$$
$$\vdash 1111q_31bb \vdash 111q_311bb \vdash 11q_3111bb \vdash 1q_31111bb$$
$$\vdash q_311111bb \vdash q_3b11111bb \vdash bq_F11111bb$$

Table 7.5   Transition Table for Example 7.6

Present state	Tape-symbols	
	1	b
→ q_0	$1Rq_0$	$1Rq_1$
q_1	$1Rq_1$	bLq_2
q_2	bLq_3	—
q_3	$1Lq_3$	bRq_F
q_F	—	—

EXAMPLE 7.7   Design a Turing machine M to recognise the language

$$\{1^n2^n3^n \mid n \geq 1\}.$$

SOLUTION   Before designing the required Turing machine M, let us evolve a procedure for processing the input string 112233. After processing, we require the ID to be of the form $bbbbbbq_7$. The processing is done by using five steps:

Step 1 q_1 is the initial state. The R/W head scans the leftmost 1, replaces 1 by b, and moves to the right. M enters q_2.

Step 2   On scanning the leftmost 2, the R/W head replaces 2 by b and moves to the right. M enters q_3.

Step 3   On scanning the leftmost 3, the R/W head replaces 3 by b, and moves to the right. M enters q_4.

Step 4   After scanning the rightmost 3, the R/W heads moves to the left until it finds the leftmost 1. As a result, the leftmost 1, 2 and 3 are replaced by b.

Step 5   Steps 1–4 are repeated until all 1's, 2's and 3's are replaced by blanks.
   The change of IDs due to processing of 112233 is given as

$$q_1112233 \vdash bq_212233 \vdash b1q_22233 \vdash b1bq_3233 \vdash b1b2q_333$$
$$\vdash b1b2bq_43 \vdash b1b2q_5b3 \vdash b1bq_5b2b3 \vdash b1q_5b2b3 \vdash bq_51b2b3$$
$$\vdash q_6b1b2b3 \vdash bq_1b2b3 \vdash bbq_2b2b3 \vdash bbbq_22b3$$
$$\vdash bbbq_3b3 \vdash bbbbq_33 \vdash bbbbbbq_4b \vdash bbbbbq_7bb$$

Thus,

$$q_1112233 \overset{*}{\vdash} q_7bbbbbb$$

As q_7 is an accepting state, the input string 112233 is accepted.

Now we can construct the transition table for M. It is given in Table 7.6.

Table 7.6 Transition Table for Example 7.7

Present state	Input tape symbol			
	1	2	3	b
$\rightarrow q_1$	bRq_2			bRq_1
q_2	$1Rq_2$	bRq_3		bRq_2
q_3		$2Rq_3$	bRq_4	bRq_3
q_4			$3Lq_5$	bLq_7
q_5	$1Lq_6$	$2Lq_5$		bLq_5
q_6	$1Lq_6$			bRq_1
$\widehat{q_7}$				

It can be seen from the table that strings other than those of the form $0^n1^n2^n$ are not accepted. It is advisable to compute the computation sequence for strings like 1223, 1123, 1233 and then see that these strings are rejected by M.

7.5 UNIVERSAL TURING MACHINES AND OTHER MODIFICATIONS

7.5.1 UNIVERSAL TURING MACHINE

The Turing machines that were considered for the design in the earlier examples are special-purpose computers. Designing general-purpose Turing machine is a more complex task. We must design a machine that can accept two inputs, i.e. (i) the input data and (ii) a description of computation (algorithm). This is precisely what a general-purpose computer does. It accepts data and a program (i.e. a description of the computation to be done). A general-purpose Turing machine is usually called universal Turing machine which is powerful enough to simulate the behaviour of any computer, including any Turing machine itself. More precisely, universal Turing machines can simulate the behaviour of an arbitrary Turing machine over any Σ.

7.5.2 MODIFICATIONS OF BASIC MODEL OF TURING MACHINES

The simple machines which we have designed are not necessarily the most efficient, but it is evident that even with very well-designed Turing machines, it will take a large number of states for simulating even a simple behaviour. Thus we can modify our basic model by (a) increasing the number of R/W heads, (b) making the tape two or three dimensional, and (c) adding special purpose memory, such as stacks or special purpose registers. All the above modifications in the Turing machine will almost speed up the operation of the machine, but do not increase the computing power/capability of doing something more than what the basic Turing machine model can do.

7.5.3   NONDETERMINISTIC TURING MACHINES

In the case of a basic model of Turing machine we have discussed till now, the processing of an input symbol results in the transition to a unique ID. So the processing of an input string results in a chain of IDs such as

$$ID \vdash ID_1 \vdash ID_2 \vdash \ldots \vdash ID_n$$

For the sake of convenience, let us write this chain as

$$ID \rightarrow ID_1 \rightarrow ID_2 \rightarrow \ldots \rightarrow ID_n$$

A natural generalisation can be obtained by allowing transition to several IDs as a result of the processing of an input symbol. This can be represented by using tree structures, as shown in Fig. 7.7. The generalised model is called a nondeterministic Turing machine.

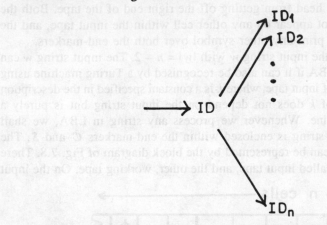

Fig. 7.7   Transition in nondeterministic TM.

A string w in Σ^* is said to be accepted by a nondeterministic TM if there exists a sequence of moves starting from the initial ID to an accepting condition.

It can be shown that the set of languages accepted by nondeterministic TM is a subset of the set of languages accepted by deterministic TMs. Actually these two sets of languages are equal.

The concept of nondeterministic model makes equivalence proofs easier.

7.6   THE MODEL OF LINEAR BOUNDED AUTOMATON

This model is important because (a) the set of context-sensitive languages is accepted by the model, and (b) the infinite storage is restricted in size but not in accessibility to the storage in comparison with the Turing machine model. It is called *linear bounded automaton (LBA)* because a linear function is used to restrict (to bound) the length of the tape.

In this section we define the model of linear bounded automaton and develop the relation between linear bounded automata and context-sensitive languages. It should be noted that the study of context-sensitive languages is important from practical point of view because many compiler languages lie between context-sensitive and context-free languages.

A linear bounded automaton is a nondeterministic Turing machine which has a single tape whose length is not infinite but bounded by a linear function of the length of the input string. The models can be described formally by the following set format:

$$M = (Q, \Sigma, \Gamma, \delta, q_0, b, \mathcal{C}, \mathcal{S}, F)$$

All the symbols have the same meaning as in the basic model of Turing machines with the difference that the input alphabet Σ contains two special symbols $\mathcal{C}$ and $\mathcal{S}$. $\mathcal{C}$ is called left-end marker which is entered in the left-most cell of the input tape and prevents the R/W head from getting off the left end of the tape. $\mathcal{S}$ is called right-end marker which is entered in the right-most cell of the input tape and prevents the R/W head from getting off the right end of the tape. Both the end-markers should not appear on any other cell within the input tape, and the R/W head should not print any other symbol over both the end-markers.

Let us consider the input string w with $|w| = n - 2$. The input string w can be recognised by an LBA if it can also be recognised by a Turing machine using no more than kn cells of input tape, where k is a constant specified in the description of LBA. The value of k does not depend on the input string but is purely a property of the machine. Whenever we process any string in LBA, we shall assume that the input string is enclosed within the end-markers $\mathcal{C}$ and $\mathcal{S}$. The above model of LBA can be represented by the block diagram of Fig. 7.8. There are two tapes: one is called input tape, and the other, working tape. On the input

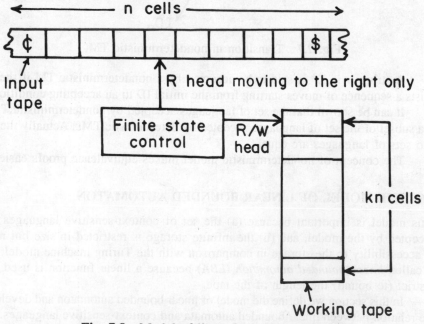

Fig. 7.8   Model of linear bounded automaton.

tape the head never prints and never moves left. On the working tape the head can modify the contents in any way, without any restriction.

In the case of LBA, an ID is denoted by (q, w, k), where $q \in Q$, $w \in \Gamma$ and k is some integer between 1 and n. The transition of IDs is similar except that k changes to $k - 1$ if the R/W head moves to the left and to $k + 1$ if the head moves to the right.

The language accepted by LBA is defined as the set

$$\{w \in (\Sigma - \{C, S\})^* | (q_0, Cw S, 1) \vdash^* (q, \alpha, i)$$

for some $q \in F$ and for some integer i between 1 and $n\}$.

NOTE: As a null string can be represented either by the absence of input string or by a completely blank tape, an LBA may accept the null string.

7.6.1 RELATION BETWEEN LBA AND CONTEXT-SENSITIVE LANGUAGES

The set of strings accepted by nondeterministic LBA is the set of strings generated by the context-sensitive grammars, excluding null strings. Now we give an important result:

If L is a context-sensitive language, then L is accepted by a linear bounded automaton. The converse is also true.

The construction and the proof are similar to those for Turing machines with some modifications.

7.7 TURING MACHINES AND TYPE 0 GRAMMARS

In this section we construct a type 0 grammar generating the set accepted by a given Turing machine M. The productions are constructed in two steps. In step 1 we construct productions which transform the string $[q_1 C w S]$ into the string $[q_2 b]$, where q_1 is the initial state, q_2 is an accepting state, C is the left-end-marker, and S is the right-end-marker. The grammar obtained by applying step 1 is called the *transformational grammar*. In step 2 we obtain inverse production rules by reversing the productions of the transformational grammar to get the required type 0 grammar G. The construction is in such a way that w is accepted by M if and only if w is in $L(G)$.

7.7.1 CONSTRUCTION OF A GRAMMAR CORRESPONDING TO TM

For understanding the construction, we have to note that a transition of ID corresponds to a production. We enclose IDs within brackets. So acceptance of w by M corresponds to the transformation of initial ID $[q_1 C w S]$ into $[q_2 b]$. Also, the 'length' of ID may change if R/W head reaches the left-end or right-end, i.e. when the left-hand side or right-hand side bracket is reached. So we get productions corresponding to transition of IDs with (a) no change in length, and (b) change in length. We assume that the transition table is given.

We now describe the construction which involves two steps:

Step 1 (i) *No change in length of* IDs: (a) *Right move.* $a_k R q_l$ corresponding to q_i-row and a_j-column leads to the production

$$q_i a_j \rightarrow a_k q_l$$

(b) *Left move.* $a_k L q_l$ corresponding to q_i-row and a_j-column yields several productions

$$a_m q_i a_j \rightarrow q_l a_m a_k \quad \text{for all } a_m \in \Gamma$$

(ii) *Change in length of* IDs: (a) *Left-end.* $a_k L q_l$ corresponding to q_i-row and a_j-column gives

$$[q_i a_j \rightarrow [q_l b a_k$$

When b occurs next to the left-bracket, it can be deleted. This is achieved by including the production $[b \rightarrow [$.

(b) *Right-end.* When b occurs to the left of], it can be deleted. This is achieved by the production

$$a_j b] \rightarrow a_j] \quad \text{for all } a_j \in \Gamma$$

When R/W head moves to the right of], the length increases. Corresponding to this we have a production

$$q_i] \rightarrow q_i b] \quad \text{for all } q_i \in Q$$

(iii) *Introduction of end-markers.* For introducing end-markers for the input string, the following productions are included:

$$a_i \rightarrow [q_1 \mathcal{C} a_i \quad \text{for } a_i \in \Gamma, a_i \neq b$$

$$a_i \rightarrow a_i \$] \quad \text{for all } a_i \in \Gamma, a_i \neq b$$

For removing the brackets from $[q_2 b]$, we include the production

$$[q_2 b] \rightarrow S$$

Recall that q_1 and q_2 are initial and final states, respectively.

Step 2 To get the required grammar, reverse the arrows of the productions obtained in step 1. The productions we get can be called *inverse productions*. The new grammar is called *generative grammar*. We illustrate the construction with an example.

EXAMPLE 7.8 Consider the TM described by the transition table given in Table 7.7. Obtain the inverse production rules.

SOLUTION In this example, q_1 is both initial and final.

Step 1: (i) *Productions corresponding to right moves*

$$q_1 \mathcal{C} \rightarrow \mathcal{C} q_1, \qquad q_1 1 \rightarrow b q_2, \qquad q_2 1 \rightarrow b q_1 \qquad (7.1)$$

(ii) (a) *Productions corresponding to left-end*

$$[b \rightarrow [\tag{7.2}$$

(b) *Productions corresponding to right-end*

$$bb] \rightarrow b], \qquad 1b] \rightarrow 1], \qquad q_1] \rightarrow q_1 b], \qquad q_2] \rightarrow q_2 b] \tag{7.3}$$

(iii)
$$1 \rightarrow [q_1 \mathbb{C} 1, \qquad 1 \rightarrow 1\mathcal{S}], \qquad [q_1 b] \rightarrow S \tag{7.4}$$

Table 7.7 Transition Table for Example 7.8

Present state	$\mathbb{C}$	b	1
$\rightarrow \textcircled{q_1}$	$\mathbb{C}Rq_1$		bRq_2
q_2			bRq_1

Step 2 The inverse productions are obtained by reversing the arrows of the productions (7.1)–(7.4).

$$\mathbb{C}q_1 \rightarrow q_1\mathbb{C}, \qquad bq_2 \rightarrow q_1 1, \qquad bq_1 \rightarrow q_2 1$$

$$[\rightarrow [b, \qquad b] \rightarrow bb], \qquad 1] \rightarrow 1b]$$

$$q_1 b \rightarrow q_1], \qquad q_2 b \rightarrow q_2], \qquad [q_1 \mathbb{C} 1 \rightarrow 1$$

$$1\mathcal{S}] \rightarrow 1, \qquad S \rightarrow [q_1 b]$$

Thus we have shown that there exists a type 0 grammar corresponding to a Turing machine. The converse is also true (we are not proving this), i.e. given a type 0 grammar G, there exists a Turing machine accepting $L(G)$. Actually, the class of recursively enumerable sets, type 0 languages, and the class of sets accepted by TM are one and the same. We have shown that there exists a recursively enumerable set which is not a context-sensitive language (see Theorem 3.4). As a recursive set is recursively enumerable, Theorem 3.4 gives a type 0 language which is not type 1. Hence, $\mathcal{L}_{csl} \subset \mathcal{L}_0$ (cf. Property 4, Section 3.3) is established.

7.8 LINEAR BOUNDED AUTOMATA AND LANGUAGES

A linear bounded automaton M accepts a string w if, after starting at the initial state with R/W head reading the left-end-marker, M halts over the right-end-marker in a final state. Otherwise, w is rejected.

The production rules for the generative grammar are constructed as in the case of Turing machines. The following additional productions are needed in the case of LBA.

$$a_i q_f \mathcal{S} \rightarrow q_f \mathcal{S} \quad \text{for all } a_i \in \Gamma$$

$$\mathbb{C}q_f \mathcal{S} \rightarrow \mathbb{C}q_f, \qquad \mathbb{C}q_f \rightarrow q_f$$

EXAMPLE 7.9   Find the grammar generating the set accepted by a linear bounded automaton M whose transition table is given in Table 7.8.

Table 7.8   Transition Table for Example 7.9

Present state	Tape input symbols			
	C	S	0	1
$\rightarrow q_1$	CRq_1		$1Lq_2$	$0Rq_2$
q_2	CRq_4		$1Rq_3$	$1Lq_1$
q_3		SLq_1	$1Rq_3$	$1Rq_3$
$\textcircled{q_4}$		Halt	$0Lq_4$	$0Rq_4$

SOLUTION

Step 1:   (A) (i) *Productions corresponding to right moves.* The seven right moves in Table 7.8 give the following productions:

$$q_1C \rightarrow Cq_1, \qquad q_30 \rightarrow 1q_3$$
$$q_11 \rightarrow 0q_2, \qquad q_31 \rightarrow 1q_3 \qquad\qquad (7.5)$$
$$q_2C \rightarrow Cq_4, \qquad q_41 \rightarrow 0q_4$$
$$q_20 \rightarrow 1q_3$$

(ii) *Productions corresponding to left moves.* There are four left moves in Table 7.8. Each left move yields four productions (corresponding to the four tape symbols). These are:

(a) $1Lq_2$ corresponding to q_1-row and 0-column gives

$$Cq_10 \rightarrow q_2C1, \qquad Sq_10 \rightarrow q_2S1, \qquad 0q_10 \rightarrow q_201, \qquad 1q_10 \rightarrow q_211 \quad (7.6)$$

(b) $1Lq_1$ corresponding to q_2-row and 1-column yields

$$Cq_21 \rightarrow q_1C1, \qquad Sq_21 \rightarrow q_1S1, \qquad 0q_21 \rightarrow q_101, \qquad 1q_21 \rightarrow q_111 \quad (7.7)$$

(c) SLq_1 corresponding to q_3-row and S-column gives

$$Cq_3S \rightarrow q_1CS, \qquad Sq_3S \rightarrow q_1SS, \qquad 0q_3S \rightarrow q_10S, \qquad 1q_3S \rightarrow q_11S \quad (7.8)$$

(d) $0Lq_4$ corresponding to q_4-row and 0-column yields

$$Cq_40 \rightarrow q_4C0, \qquad Sq_40 \rightarrow q_4S0, \qquad 0q_40 \rightarrow q_400, \qquad 1q_40 \rightarrow q_410 \quad (7.9)$$

(B) There are no productions corresponding to change in length.

(C) The productions for introducing end-markers are

$$C \rightarrow [q_1CC, \qquad C \rightarrow CS]$$
$$S \rightarrow [q_1CS, \qquad S \rightarrow SS] \qquad\qquad (7.10)$$

$$0 \to [q_1 \mathcal{C} 0, \quad 0 \to 0\mathcal{S}]$$

$$1 \to [q_1 \mathcal{C} 1, \quad 1 \to 1\mathcal{S}]$$

$$[q_4] \to S \quad\quad\quad\quad (7.11)$$

(D) LBA productions

$$\mathcal{C} q_4 \mathcal{S} \to q_4 \mathcal{S}, \quad\quad \mathcal{C} q_4 \mathcal{S} \to \mathcal{C} q_4$$

$$\mathcal{S} q_4 \mathcal{S} \to q_4 \mathcal{S}, \quad\quad \mathcal{C} q_4 \to q_4 \quad\quad\quad (7.12)$$

$$0 q_4 \mathcal{S} \to q_4 \mathcal{S},$$

$$1 q_4 \mathcal{S} \to q_4 \mathcal{S}$$

Step 2 The productions of the generative grammar are obtained by reversing the arrows of productions given by (7.5) – (7.12).

7.9   HALTING PROBLEM OF TURING MACHINES

In this section we study unsolvable problems. We prove that the halting problem of Turing machines is unsolvable. We also discuss some more unsolvable problems and Post correspondence problem.

7.9.1   UNSOLVABLE PROBLEMS

In the theory of Computer Science, we often come across a set of problems in which yes/no answers (two outputs) are required. Some examples are:

(i) It is easy to write a program that will search through all positive integers x, y, z and number $n > 2$ for a solution to the equation $x^n + y^n = z^n$. The problem is to determine whether or not the program will halt if and when a solution is found (Fermat's last 'theorem').

(ii) For any programming language, to determine whether or not: (a) a given program can loop for ever on some input, (b) a given program ever produces an output, (c) a given program eventually halts on the given input.

(iii) For formal languages to determine whether or not: (a) two context-free grammars are equivalent (equivalence problem of context-free grammars), (b) the language generated by a context-sensitive language is empty—this is the emptiness problem of context-sensitive grammars—, (c) a given string belongs to a type 0 language (membership-test problem of type 0 grammars).

(iv) The halting problem of Turing machines.

Definition 7.3   A class of problems with two outputs (yes/no) is said to be solvable (decidable) if there exists some definite algorithm which always terminates (halts) with two outputs (yes/no). Otherwise, the class of problems is said to be unsolvable (undecidable).

All the problems stated above (examples (i)–(iv)) are unsolvable. In this section we prove that the halting problem of Turing machine is unsolvable.

According to Church's thesis, a Turing machine can be treated as the most general computing system. So, finding an algorithm for an yes/no problem is equivalent to constructing a TM which can execute the algorithm.

Before proceeding to prove the theorem regarding the halting problem of TM, we make a few remarks regarding the encoding mechanism of a Turing machine. (We have already introduced some of them in Section 7.2.) The transition function of a Turing machine can be described by a set of quintuples (5-tuples). For example, $\delta(q, a) = (\gamma, \alpha, \beta)$ can be represented by a quintuple (q, a, α, β, r). By encoding the states, the tape symbols and these quintuples as strings over some alphabet Σ, the Turing machine can be encoded as a string over Σ. (Mostly, Σ is taken as $\{0, 1\}$ so that TM is represented by a binary string.) Such an encoded string representing M is denoted by $d(M)$. A pair (M, x), where M is a TM and x is an input string, is encoded as $d(M) * x$.

Theorem 7.1 (Turing Theorem)   The halting problem (HP) of Turing machine over $\Sigma = \{0, 1\}$ is unsolvable (i.e. the problem of determining whether or not an arbitrary Turing machine M over $\{0, 1\}$ halts for an arbitrary input x in Σ^* is unsolvable).

PROOF   We prove the theorem by contradiction. Let M be an arbitrary Turing machine. Let $d(M)$ be the encoded binary string representing M. Then the machine-string pair (M, x) will have $d(M) * x$ as its encoded description. According to our assumption, HP is solvable. Hence there exists an algorithm P which decides the HP, i.e. (a) if M halts for input x, then P reaches an accept halt; (b) if M does not halt for input x, then P reaches a reject halt.

Let us construct a new algorithm Q based on P as follows: (c) It takes $d(M)$ as input and copies it to obtain $d(M) * d(M)$ and then applies algorithm P to this input (i.e. $d(M) * d(M)$), (d) Q loops for ever if P reaches an accept halt and Q halts if P reaches a reject halt.

By Church's thesis, there exists a Turing machine, say M', which can execute the algorithm Q. Since the algorithm P, as also Q, works for an arbitrary machine M, Q also works for the Turing machine M'. So we take $M = M'$. From (d) and (a) we can conclude that M' loops for ever if M' halts. From (d) and (b) we conclude that M' halts if M' loops for ever. Thus, we obtain the conclusion "M' halts if and only if M' loops". This is a contradiction and, therefore, HP is unsolvable. ∎

Even if the halting problem is unsolvable, we can run the machine with a given input. If it halts, then a specific case is answered. If it does not halt, it may be possible to conclude that it will never halt by detecting some pattern within the operation. The unsolvability of HP asserts that it is not possible to detect such patterns for all the cases. It may be possible to develop a heuristic procedure, but it is also possible to give an instance where the procedure fails.

The reduction technique we are going to introduce is very useful in establishing the unsolvability of some problem as compared to a known unsolvable problem.

7.9.2   REDUCTION TECHNIQUE

A class $\mathscr{S}$ of yes/no problems is reducible to another class $\mathscr{S}'$ of yes/no problems if there is a Turing machine that takes any problem P from $\mathscr{P}$ as input and gives some problem P' from $\mathscr{P}'$ as output such that the answer to P is 'yes' if and only if the answer to the corresponding problem P' is 'yes'.

When $\mathscr{P}$ is reducible to $\mathscr{P}'$ and $\mathscr{P}$ is unsolvable, $\mathscr{P}'$ is also unsolvable. We have proved that the HP of Turing machines is unsolvable. So, if the HP of Turing machines is reducible to a class $\mathscr{P}'$ of yes/no problems, then $\mathscr{P}'$ is unsolvable. We illustrate the reduction technique by the following examples.

EXAMPLE 7.10   Prove that the empty-word HP of TM is unsolvable.

SOLUTION   We shall prove this by the above reduction technique. Let M be an arbitrary Turing machine over $\Sigma = \{0, 1\}$. Let us construct another Turing machine M' over $\{0, 1\}$ which generates any word $x \in \Sigma^*$ onto the tape and then applies Turing machine M to it. Then M halts for input x if and only if M' halts for input Λ (the empty string). Thus the empty-word HP of Turing machines is unsolvable.

The following example is an assertion stronger than the HP of Turing machine. The HP we have discussed earlier is concerned with an arbitrary Turing machine and arbitrary input string x. The question there relates to a particular TM and arbitrary x.

EXAMPLE 7.11   Prove that there exists a Turing machine M for which the halting problem is unsolvable (i.e. the problem of determining whether or not M halts when it operates on an arbitrary input string).

SOLUTION   As we have the Universal Turing machine U which simulates every Turing machine, the present problem is equivalent to the HP of Turing machines and is therefore unsolvable.

EXAMPLE 7.12   Show that there exists a Turing machine M over $\{0, 1\}$ and a state q_m such that there is no algorithm to determine whether or not M will enter the state q_m when it begins with a given ID.

SOLUTION   We prove this by reduction technique. There exists a Turing machine M' for which the halting problem is unsolvable (see Example 7.11). We construct a Turing machine M with q_m as the accepting state which copies any string x onto the tape and then simulates M'. Thus, M' halts if and only if M enters q_m once it starts with a given ID. As the halting problem for M' is unsolvable, the given problem is also unsolvable.

7.9.3   THE POST CORRESPONDENCE PROBLEM

The Post Correspondence Problem (PCP) was first introduced by Emil Post in 1946. Later, the problem was found to have many applications in the theory of formal languages. The problem over an alphabet Σ belongs to a class of yes/no problems and is stated as follows: Consider the two lists $x = (x_1 \dots x_n)$, $y = (y_1 \dots y_n)$ of nonempty strings over an alphabet $\Sigma = \{0, 1\}$. The PCP is to determine whether or not there exist $i_1, \dots, i_m$, where $1 \le i_j \le n$, such that

$$x_{i_1} \dots x_{i_m} = y_{i_1} \dots y_{i_m}$$

NOTE: The indices i_j's need not be distinct and m may be greater than n. Also, if there exists a solution to PCP, there exists infinitely many solutions.

EXAMPLE 7.13   Does PCP with two lists $x = (b, bab^3, ba)$ and $y = (b^3, ba, a)$ have a solution?

SOLUTION   We have to determine whether or not there exists a sequence of substrings of x such that the string formed by this sequence and the string formed by the sequence of corresponding substrings of y are identical. The required sequence is given by $i_1 = 2, i_2 = 1, i_3 = 1, i_4 = 3$, i.e. $(2, 1, 1, 3)$, and $m = 4$. The corresponding strings are

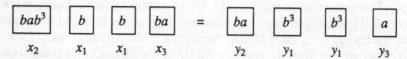

Thus, PCP has a solution.

EXAMPLE 7.14   Prove that PCP with two lists $x = (01, 1, 1), y = (01^2, 10, 1^2)$ has no solution.

SOLUTION   For each substring $x_i \in x$ and $y_i \in y$, we have $|x_i| < |y_i|$ for all i. Hence the string generated by a sequence of substrings of x is shorter than the string generated by the sequence of corresponding substrings of y. Therefore, the PCP has no solution.

NOTE: If the first substring used in PCP is always x_1 and y_1, then the PCP is known as *Modified Post Correspondence Problem*.

EXAMPLE 7.15   Explain how a Post Correspondence Problem can be treated as a game of dominoes.

SOLUTION   The PCP may be thought of as a game of dominoes in the following way: Let each domino contain some x_i in the upper half, and the corresponding substring of y in the lower half. A typical domino is as shown as

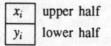

The PCP is equivalent to placing the dominoes one after another as a sequence (of course repetitions are allowed). To win the game, the same string should appear in the upper half and the lower half. So winning the game is equivalent to a solution of PCP.

We state the following theorem by Emil Post without proof.

Theorem 7.2   The PCP over Σ for $|\Sigma| \geq 2$ is unsolvable.

It is possible to reduce the PCP to many classes of two outputs (yes/no) problems in formal language theory. The following results can be proved by the reduction technique applied to PCP.

(i) If L_1 and L_2 are any two context-free languages (type 2) over an alphabet Σ and $|\Sigma| \geq 2$, there is no algorithm to determine whether or not
   (a) $L_1 \cap L_2 = \emptyset$,
   (b) $L_1 \cap L_2$ is a context-free language,
   (c) $L_1 \subseteq L_2$,
   (d) $L_1 = L_2$.
(ii) If G is a context-sensitive grammar (type 1), there is no algorithm to determine whether or not
   (a) $L(G) = \emptyset$,
   (b) $L(G)$ is infinite,
   (c) $x_0 \in L(G)$ for a fixed string x_0.
(iii) If G is a type 0 grammar, there is no algorithm to determine whether or not any string $x \in \Sigma^*$ is in $L(G)$.

7.10   NP–COMPLETENESS

7.10.1   THE CLASSES P AND NP

We have seen that a solvable problem is one that admits an algorithm. In this case a problem is solvable 'in principle'. But, in practice, the algorithm may require a lot of space (memory) and time (time to apply the steps of the algorithm). When the space and time required for implementing the algorithm are reasonable, we can say that the problem is tractable (i.e. solvable in practice).

In our discussion we restrict our attention only to the time required for performing the algorithm and that too to decision problems. Usually the time required is expressed as a function of the size of the input. (In the case of decision problem it is the length of the input string.)

A decision problem is tractable if there is an algorithm to solve the given problem and the time required is expressed as a polynomial $p(n)$, n being the length of the input string. Usually problems are intractable if the time required for any of the algorithm is at least $f(n)$, where f is an exponential function of n.

For defining **P** we require the time complexity of a Turing machine. As the time required depends on the number of moves, the definition is given in terms of the number of moves.

Definition 7.4   The time complexity of a (deterministic) Turing machine $T(n)$ is the maximum number of moves made by M in processing any input string of length n, taken over all inputs of length n.

Now we can define class **P** among the class of all languages.

Definition 7.5   A language L is said to be in class **P** if there exists a (deterministic) Turing machine M such that M is of time complexity $p(n)$ for some polynomial p and M accepts L.

We have defined non-deterministic TM in section 7.5.3. On reading an input symbol, a non-deterministic TM moves from one ID to one of several possible ID's. So for any input string w there are several sequences of moves and w is accepted by the machine if one of the sequences leads to an accepting condition.

Now we can define the time complexity of a non-deterministic TM.

Definition 7.6 A nondeterministic Turing machine M is of time complexity $T(n)$ if for every accepted input string of length n there is some sequence of atmost $T(n)$ moves leading to an accepting condition.

Now we are in a position to define class **NP**.

Definition 7.7 A language L is in class **NP** if there is a nondeterministic Turing machine M such that M is of time complexity $p(n)$ for some polynomial p and M accepts L.

Although the definitions of **P** and **NP** are worded similarly, there is a vast difference between them. When L is in **P**, the number of moves to test whether any input string of length n is less than or equal to $p(n)$. When L is in **NP**, the number of moves for testing is less than or equal to n only for strings accepted by M. Thus in the case of **NP**, the bound $p(n)$ for the number of moves is useful only when we are able to find a string w in L. But it may be very difficult to find a string w in L. In short, members of **P** admit 'easy' solutions whereas members of **NP** admit 'easy' solutions to verify that some string is a solution. To appreciate the usefulness of the class **NP** consider the case of Four colour problem or Fermat's last theorem. Now there is a proof for both of them. But to check the proof itself is an extremely time-consuming task. On the other hand, there are some problems which are not even known to belong to **NP**.

One of the open problems in theoretical computer science is whether $\mathbf{P} = \mathbf{NP}$. It is obvious that $\mathbf{P} \subseteq \mathbf{NP}$. It is not known whether there exists some language L in **NP**, which does not have a deterministic TM accepting it. Many practical and important problems are known to be in **NP**. So far none of them admit a deterministic Turing machine accepting it.

Definition 7.8 Let L_1 and L_2 be two languages over Σ_1 and Σ_2 respectively, then there is a polynomial-time transformation from L_1 to L_2 if

    (i) There exists a function $f: \Sigma_1^* \to \Sigma_2^*$ such that $w \in L_1$ if and only if $w \in L_2$.

    (ii) f can be computed by a deterministic TM of polynomial time complexity.

Definition 7.9 A language $L \subseteq \Sigma *$ is NP-complete if

    (i) L is in **NP**.

    (ii) for every language L_1 in **NP** there is a polynomial time transformation from L to L_1.

So the problem "$\mathbf{P} = \mathbf{NP}$" is indeed difficult.

7.10.2 NP-COMPLETENESS

S. A. Cook introduced the concept of NP-completeness as a step towards solving "$\mathbf{P} = \mathbf{NP}$". Now a number of NP-complete problems exist in several areas. For defining an NP-complete problem, we require the notion of a polynomial-time transformation (Definition 7.8) and the construction of a function by a Turing machine (Chapter 9).

The definition of **P** and **NP** etc. can be extended to the class of all problems. There are several NP-complete problems in various fields like propositional calculus, graph theory, operations research etc. Actually, hundreds of such problems are known so far. We give four NP-complete problems at the end of this section.

The significance of NP-completeness lies in the following theorem (which is stated without proof).

Theorem 7.3   Let L be an NP-complete language. Then **P = NP** if and only if L is in **P**.

Using the definition of NP-completeness and Theorem 7.3, we can have the following properties of the class of NP-complete problems:

Property 1   No polynomial time algorithm has been found for any one of them.

Property 2   It is not established that polynomial time algorithm for these problems do not exist.

Property 3   If a polynomial-time algorithm is found for one of them, there will be polynomial-time algorithm for all of them.

Property 4   If it can be proved that no polynomial time algorithm exists for any one of them, then it will not exist for every one of them.

Thus we can answer the question "**P = NP**" by knowing the full information about any one NP-complete problem.

We end this section by listing some NP-complete problems from several areas.

1. Travelling Salesman Problem.   Given n cities, the distance between them and a number D, does there exist a tour programme for a salesman to visit all the cities so that the total distance travelled is atmost D?

2. Zero-one Programming Problem.   Given m simultaneous equations

$$\sum_{j=1}^{m} a_{ij}x_j = b_i, \qquad i = 1, 2, ..., n$$

does there exist values, zero or one, for x_j so that the above equations are satisfied?

3. Satisfiability Problem.   Given a formula involving propositional variables and logical connectives (Refer section 10.2), does there exist a choice of truth values for the variables for which the given formula assumes the truth value **T**?

4. Vertex Cover Problem.   Given a graph G and a natural number k, does there exist a vertex cover for G with k vertices? (A subset C of vertices of G is a vertex cover for G if each edge of G has an end vertex in C.)

It is interesting to note that existence of a polynomial time algorithm for a problem in one area like problem 4 in graph theory leads to the existence of a polynomial time algorithm for a problem in operations research like problem 2.

EXERCISES

1. Draw the transition diagram of the Turing machine given in Table 7.1.

2. Represent the transition function of the Turing machine given in Example 7.2 as a set of quintuples.

3. Construct the computation sequence for the input $1b11$ for the Turing machine given in Example 7.5.

4. Construct the computation sequence for strings 1213, 2133, 312 for the Turing machine given in Example 7.7.

5. Explain how a Turing machine can be considered as a computer of integer functions (i.e. as one that can compute integer functions; we shall discuss more about this in Chapter 9).

6. Design a Turing machine that converts a binary string into its equivalent unary string.

7. Construct a Turing machine that enumerates $\{0^n1^n \mid n \geq 1\}$.

8. Construct a Turing machine that can accept the set of all even palindromes over $\{0, 1\}$.

9. Construct a Turing machine that can accept the strings over $\{0, 1\}$ containing even number of 1's.

10. Design a Turing machine to recognise the language $\{a^nb^nc^m \mid n, m \geq 1\}$.

11. Design a Turing machine that can compute proper subtraction, i.e. $m \dot- n$, where m and n are positive integers. $m \dot- n$ is defined as $m - n$ if $m > n$ and 0 if $m \leq n$.

12. Prove that the recursiveness problem of type 0 grammars is unsolvable.

13. Prove that there is no algorithm that can determine whether or not a given TM eventually halts with complete blank tape when it starts with a given tape configuration.

14. Prove that the problem of determining whether or not a TM over $\{0, 1\}$ will ever print the symbol 1, with a given tape configuration is unsolvable.

15. Prove that the problem of determining whether or not a given context-sensitive language is context-free is unsolvable.

16. (a) Show that $\{x \mid x$ is a set and $x \notin x\}$ is not a set. (Note that this seems to be well-defined. This is one version of Russell's paradox.)

    (b) A village barber shaves those who do not shave themselves but no others. Can he achieve his goal? For example, who is to shave the barber? (This is a popular version of Russell's paradox.)

    [Hint: (a)   Let $S = \{x \mid x$ be a set and $x \notin x\}$. If S were a set, then $S \in S$ or $S \notin S$. If $S \notin S$ by the "definition" of S, then $S \in S$. On the other hand, if $S \in S$ by the "definition" of S, then $S \notin S$. Thus we can neither assert that $S \notin S$ nor $S \in S$. (This is Russell's paradox.) Therefore, S is not a set.

    (b)   Let $S = \{x \mid x$ be a person and x does not shave himself$\}$. Let b denote the barber. Examine whether $b \in S$. (The argument is similar to that given for (a).) It is instructive to read the proof of HP of Turing machines and this example, and grasp the similarity.]

17. Comment on the following: "We have developed an algorithm so complicated that no Turing machine can be constructed to execute the algorithm no matter how much (tape) space and time is allowed".

18. Prove that PCP is solvable if $|\Sigma| = 1$.

19. Let $x = (x_1 \ldots x_n)$ and $y = (y_1 \ldots y_n)$ be two lists of nonempty strings over Σ and $|\Sigma| \geq 2$. (i) Is PCP solvable for $n = 1$? (ii) Is PCP solvable for $n = 2$?

20. Prove that PCP with $\{(01, 011), (1, 10), (1, 11)\}$ has no solution. (Here, $x_1 = 01$, $x_2 = 1$, $x_3 = 1$, $y_1 = 011$, $y_2 = 10$, $y_3 = 11$.)

21. Show that the PCP with $S = \{(0, 10), (1^2 0, 0^3), (0^2 1, 10)\}$ has no solution. [*Hint*: No pair has common nonempty initial substring.]

22. Does the PCP with $x = (b^3, ab^2)$ and $y = (b^3, bab^3)$ have a solution?

23. Find at least three solutions to PCP defined by the dominoes:

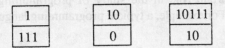

24. (a) Can you simulate a Turing machine on a general-purpose computer? Explain.
(b) Can you simulate a general-purpose computer on a Turing machine? Explain.

8

LR(k) grammars

In this chapter we study LR(k) grammars (a subclass of context-free grammars) which play an important role in the study of programming languages and the design of compilers. For example, a typical programming language such as ALGOL has LR(1) parser.

8.1 LR(k) GRAMMARS

In Chapters 3 and 5 we were mainly interested in generating strings using productions and performing the membership test. In the design of programming languages and compilers, it is essential to develop the parsing techniques, i.e. techniques for obtaining the 'reverse derivation' of a given string in a context-free language. In other words, we require techniques to find a derivation tree for a given sentence w in a context-free language.

To find a derivation tree for a given sentence w, we can start with w and replace a substring, say w_1 of w, by a variable A if $A \to w_1$ is a production. We repeat the process until we get S. But this is more easily said than done, for at every stage there may be several choices and we have to choose one among them. If we make a wrong choice, we will not get S, and in this case we have to backtrack and try some other substring. However, for certain subclass of context-free grammars, it is possible to carry out the process, i.e. getting the derivation in the reverse order for a given string w in a deterministic way. LR(k) grammars form one such subclass. Here, LR(k) stands for left-to-right scan of the input string producing a right-most derivation using k symbol lookahead on the input string.

Before discussing LR(k) grammars, we should note that although parsing gives only the syntactical structure of a string, it is the first step in understanding the 'meaning' of the sentence.

Consider some sentential form $\alpha\beta w$ of a context-free grammar G, where α, $\beta \in (V_N \cup \Sigma)^*$ and $w \in \Sigma^*$. Suppose we are interested in finding the production applied in the last step of the derivation for $\alpha\beta w$. If $A \to \beta$ is a production, it is likely that $A \to \beta$ is the production applied in the last step, but we cannot definitely say that this is the case. If it is possible to assert that $A \to \beta$ is the production applied in the last step by looking ahead for k symbols (i.e. k symbols to the right of β in $\alpha\beta w$), then G is called an LR(k) grammar. The production $A \to \beta$ is called a handle production and β is called a handle.

We write $\alpha \overset{*}{\underset{R}{\Rightarrow}} \beta$ if β is derived from α by a right-most derivation. Before giving the rigorous definition of an LR(k) grammar, let us consider a grammar for which parsing is possible by looking ahead for one symbol.

EXAMPLE 8.1 Let G be $S \to AB, A \to aAb, A \to \Lambda, B \to Bb, B \to b$. It is easy to see that $L(G) = \{a^m b^n \mid n > m \geq 1\}$. Some sentential forms of G obtained by right-most derivations are $AB, ABb^k, a^m Ab^m b^k, a^m b^{m+k}$, where $k \geq 1$. AB appears as the R.H.S. of $S \to AB$. So AB may be a handle for AB or ABb^k. If we apply the handle to AB, we get $S \underset{R}{\Rightarrow} AB$. If apply the handle to ABb^k, we get $Sb^k \Rightarrow ABb^k$. But Sb^k is not a sentential form. So to decide whether AB can be a handle, we have to scan the symbol to the right of AB. If it is Λ, then AB serves as a handle. If the next symbol is b, AB cannot be a handle. So only by looking ahead for one symbol we are able to decide whether AB is a handle. Let us consider $a^2 b^3$. As we scan from left to right, we see that the handle production $A \to \Lambda$ may be applied. Λ can serve as a handle only when it is taken between the right-most a and left-most b. In this case we get $a^2 Ab^3 \underset{R}{\Rightarrow} a^2 b^3$, and we are able to decide that $A \to \Lambda$ is a handle production only by looking ahead of one symbol (to the right of Λ). If Λ is taken between two a's, we get $aAab^3 \underset{R}{\Rightarrow} a^2 b^3$. But $aAab^3$ is not a sentential form. Similarly, we can see that the correct handle production can be determined by looking ahead of one symbol for various sentential forms.

A rigorous definition of an LR(k) grammar is now given.

Definition 8.1 Let $G = (V_N, \Sigma, P, S)$ be a context-free grammar in which $S \overset{n}{\Rightarrow} S$ only when $n = 0$. G is an LR(k) grammar ($k \geq 0$) if

(i) $S \overset{*}{\underset{R}{\Rightarrow}} \alpha Aw \underset{R}{\Rightarrow} \alpha \beta w$, where $\alpha, \beta \in V_N^*, w \in \Sigma^*$,

(ii) $S \overset{*}{\underset{R}{\Rightarrow}} \alpha' A' w' \underset{R}{\Rightarrow} \alpha' \beta' w'$, where $\alpha', \beta' \in V^*, w' \in \Sigma^*$, and

(iii) the first $|\alpha\beta| + k$ symbols of $\alpha\beta w$ and $\alpha' \beta' w'$ coincide. Then $\alpha = \alpha'$, $A = A', \beta = \beta'$.

Remarks 1. If $\alpha\beta w$ or $\alpha' \beta' w'$ have less than $|\alpha\beta| + k$ symbols, we add some 'blank symbols', say $\mathcal{S}$, on the right and compare.

2. It is easy to see how we can get the derivation tree for a given terminal string. For getting the derivation tree, we want to get the derivation "in the reverse order". Suppose a sentential form $\alpha\beta w$ is encountered. We can get a right-most derivation of βw in the following way: If $A \to \beta$ is a production, then we have to decide whether $A \to \beta$ is used in the last step of a right-most derivative of $\alpha\beta w$. On seeing k symbols beyond β in $\alpha\beta w$, we are able to decide that $A \to \beta$ is the required production in the last step. For, if $\alpha' \beta' w'$ is another sentential form satisfying condition (iii), then we can apply $A' \to \beta'$ in the last step of a right-most derivation of $\alpha' \beta' w'$. But by definition it follows that $A = A'$, $\beta = \beta'$ and $\alpha = \alpha'$. So $A \to \beta$ is the only possible production we can apply and we are able to decide this after 'seeing' the k symbols beyond β. We repeat the process until we get S.

3. If G is an LR(k) grammar it is an LR(k') grammar for all $k' > k$.

EXAMPLE 8.2   Let G be the grammar $S \to aA$, $A \to Abb \mid b$. Show that G is an LR(0) grammar.

SOLUTION   It is easy to see that any element in $L(G)$ is of the form ab^{2n+1}. The sentential forms of G are aA, aAb^{2n}, ab^{2n+1}. Let us find out the last production applied in the derivation of ab^{2n+1}. As aA, Abb, b are the possible right-hand sides of productions, only $A \to b$ can be the last production; we are able to decide this without looking at any symbol to the right of b. Similarly, the last productions for aAb^{2n} and aA are $A \to Abb$ and $S \to aA$, respectively. (We are able to say that $A \to Abb$ is the last production for any sentential form aAb^{2n} for all $n \geq 1$.) Thus, G is an LR(0) grammar.

EXAMPLE 8.3   Consider the grammar G given in Example 8.1. Show that G is an LR(1) grammar, but not an LR(0) grammar. Also, find the derivation tree for a^2b^4.

SOLUTION   In Example 8.1 we have shown that for sentential forms of G we can determine the last step of a right-most derivation by looking ahead of one symbol. So G is LR(1). We have also seen that $S \to AB$ is a handle production for the sentential form AB, but not for ABb^k. In other words, the handle production cannot be determined without looking ahead. So G is not LR(0).

To get the derivation tree for a^2b^4, we scan a^2b^4 from left to right. After scanning a, we look ahead. If the next symbol is a, we continue to scan. If the next symbol is b, we decide that $A \to \Lambda$ is the required handle production. Thus the last step of the right-most derivation of a^2b^4 is

$$a^2Ab^4 \underset{R}{\Rightarrow} a^2\Lambda b^4$$

To get the last step of a^2Ab^4, we scan a^2Ab^4 from left to right. aAb is a possible handle. We are able to decide that this is the right handle without looking ahead and so we get

$$aAbb^2 \underset{R}{\Rightarrow} a^2Ab^4$$

Once again using the handle aAb, we obtain

$$Ab^2 \underset{R}{\Rightarrow} aAbb^2$$

To get the last step of the right-most derivation of Ab^2, we scan Ab^2. A possible handle production is $B \to b$. We also note that this handle production can be applied to the first b we encounter, but not to last b. So we get $ABb \underset{R}{\Rightarrow} Ab^2$.

For ABb, a possible a-handle is Bb. Hence we get $AB \underset{R}{\Rightarrow} ABb$. Finally, we obtain $S \underset{R}{\Rightarrow} AB$. Thus we have the following derivations:

$$a^2Ab^4 \underset{R}{\Rightarrow} a^2\Lambda b^4 \qquad \text{by looking ahead of one symbol}$$

$$aAbb^2 \underset{R}{\Rightarrow} a^2Ab^4 \qquad \text{by not looking ahead of any symbol}$$

$$Ab^2 \underset{R}{\Rrightarrow} aAbb^2 \quad \text{by not looking ahead of any symbol}$$

$$ABb \underset{R}{\Rrightarrow} Ab^2 \quad \text{by not looking ahead of any symbol}$$

$$AB \underset{R}{\Rrightarrow} ABb \quad \text{by not looking ahead of any symbol}$$

$$S \underset{R}{\Rrightarrow} AB \quad \text{by looking ahead of one symbol}$$

The derivation tree for a^2b^4 is as shown in Fig. 8.1.

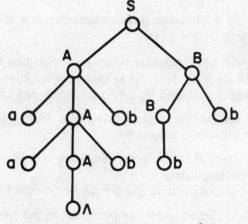

Fig. 8.1 Derivation tree for a^2b^4.

8.2 PROPERTIES OF LR(k) GRAMMARS

In this section we give some important properties of LR(k) grammars which are useful for parsing and other applications.

Recall the definition of an ambiguous grammar. A grammar G is ambiguous if there exists $w \in L(G)$ which has two derivation trees. The next theorem gives the relation between LR(k) grammars and unambiguous grammars.

Property 1 Every LR(k) grammar G is unambiguous.

PROOF   We have to show that for any $x \in \Sigma^*$, there exists a unique right-most derivation. Suppose we have two right-most derivations for x, viz.

$$S \underset{R}{\Rightarrow} \alpha Aw \underset{R}{\Rightarrow} \alpha\beta w = x \tag{8.1}$$

$$S \underset{R}{\overset{*}{\Rightarrow}} \alpha'A'w' \underset{R}{\Rightarrow} \alpha'\beta'w' = x \tag{8.2}$$

As $\alpha\beta w = \alpha'\beta'w'$, from the definition it follows that $\alpha = \alpha'$, $A = A'$ and $\beta = \beta'$. As $\alpha\beta w = \alpha'\beta'w'$, we get $w = w'$, and so $\alpha Aw = \alpha'A'w'$. Hence the last step in the derivations (8.1) and (8.2) is the same. Repeating the arguments for the other sentential forms derived in the course of (8.1) and (8.2), we can show that (8.1) is the same as (8.2). Therefore, G is unambiguous. ∎

We have seen that the deterministic and nondeterministic finite automata behave in the same way in so far as acceptability of languages is concerned. The same is the case with Turing machines. But the behaviour of deterministic and nondeterministic pushdown automata is different. In Chapter 6 we have proved that any pushdown automaton accepts a context-free language and for any context-free language L, we can construct a pushdown automaton accepting L. The following property gives the relation between LR(k) grammars and pushdown automata.

Property 2   If G is an LR(k) grammar, there exists a deterministic pushdown automaton A accepting $L(G)$.

Property 3   If A is a deterministic pushdown automaton A, there exists an LR(1) grammar G such that $L(G) = N(A)$.

Property 4   If G is an LR(k) grammar, where $k > 1$, then there exists an equivalent grammar G_1 which is LR(1). In so far as languages are concerned, it is enough to study the languages generated by LR(0) grammars and LR(1) grammars.

Definition 8.2   A context-free language is said to be deterministic if it is accepted by a deterministic pushdown automaton.

Property 5   The class of deterministic languages is a proper subclass of the class of context-free languages.
The class of deterministic languages can be denoted by $\mathscr{L}_{dcfl}$

Property 6 $\mathscr{L}_{dcfl}$ is closed under complementation but not under union and intersection.
The following definition is useful in characterising the languages accepted by an LR(0) grammar.

Definition 8.3   A context-free language has prefix property if no proper prefix of strings of L belongs to L.

Property 7   A context-free language is generated by an LR(0) grammar if and only if it is accepted by a deterministic pushdown automaton and has prefix property.

Property 8   There is an algorithm to decide whether a given context-free grammar is LR(k) for a given natural number k.

8.3   CLOSURE PROPERTIES OF LANGUAGES

We have discussed closure properties under union, concatenation, and so on in Chapter 3. In this section we discuss closure properties under intersection, complementation, etc. Recall that $\mathscr{L}_0$, $\mathscr{L}_{csl}$, $\mathscr{L}_{cfl}$, $\mathscr{L}_{rl}$ are the families of type 0 languages, context-sensitive languages, context-free languages and regular languages, respectively.

Property 1   Each of the classes $\mathscr{L}_0$, $\mathscr{L}_{csl}$, $\mathscr{L}_{cfl}$, $\mathscr{L}_{rl}$ is closed under union, concatenation, closure and transpose operation (Theorems 3.5–3.7).

Property 2 $\mathscr{L}_{rl}$ is closed under intersection and complementation (Theorems 4.7 and 4.8).

Property 3 $\mathscr{L}_{cn}$ is not closed under intersection and complementation.

We establish property 3 by a counter-example. We have already seen that $L_1 = \{a^n b^n c^i \mid n \geq 1, i \geq 0\}$ and $L_2 = \{a^i b^n c^n \mid n \geq 1, j \geq 0\}$ are context-free languages (Examples 3.8 and 3.9). $L_1 \cap L_2 = \{a^n b^n c^n \mid n \geq 1\}$. In Example 5.18, we have shown that $\{a^n b^n c^n \mid n \geq 1\}$ is not context-free. Thus, $\mathscr{L}_{cn}$ is not closed under intersection.

Using De Morgan's law, we can write $L_1 \cap L_2 = (L_1^c \cup L_2^c)^c$. We have proved in Chapter 3 that $\mathscr{L}_{cn}$ is closed under union. If $\mathscr{L}_{cn}$ were closed under complementation, then $L_1 \cap L_2$ turns out to be context-free which is not true. Hence, $\mathscr{L}_{cn}$ is not closed under complementation.

EXERCISES

1. Show that the grammar $S \to aAb$, $A \to aAb \mid a$ is LR(1). Is it LR(0)?

2. Show that the grammar $S \to 0A2$, $A \to 1A1$, $A \to 1$ is not LR(0).

3. Is $S \to AB$, $S \to aA$, $A \to aA$, $A \to a$, $B \to a$ LR(k) for some k?

4. Show that $\{a^m b^m c^n \mid m, n \geq 1\} \cup \{a^m b^n c^n \mid m, n \geq 1\}$ cannot be generated by an LR(k) grammar for any k.

5. Are the following statements true? (a) If G is unambiguous, it is LR(k) for some k. (b) If G is unambiguous, it is LR(k) for every k. Justify your answer.

6. Is $S \to C \mid D$, $C \to aC \mid b$, $D \to aD \mid C$ LR(0)?

7. For a production $A \to \beta$ of a context-free grammar G and w in $\Sigma^* \mathcal{S}^k$ ($\mathcal{S}$ is a symbol not in $V_N \cup \Sigma$), define $R_k(w)$ to be the set of all strings of the form $\alpha\beta w$ such that $A \to \beta$ is a handle for $\alpha\beta ww'$ for some w' in $\Sigma^* \mathcal{S}^*$ and $S\mathcal{S} \xrightarrow[R]{*} \alpha A ww' \xrightarrow[R]{} \alpha\beta ww'$. (In other words, a string $\alpha\beta w$ is in $R_k(w)$ if we get a penultimate step of a right-most derivation of $\alpha\beta ww'$ for some w'.) Show that $R_k(w)$ is a regular set.

[*Hint*: Define $G' = (V_N', V_N \cup \Sigma, P', S')$, where

$$V_N' = \{[A, w] \mid A \in V_N, w \in \Sigma^* \mathcal{S}^k \text{ and } |w| = k\}$$

$$S' = [S, \mathcal{S}^k]$$

and each production in P induces a production in P' in the following manner:

   (a) If $A \to x$ is in P, where $x \in \Sigma^*$, then $[A, w] \to xw$ is included in P'.

   (b) If $A \to X_1 X_2 \ldots X_m$ is in P, $X_j \in V_N$, $X_{j+1} \ldots X_m w \xrightarrow[G]{*} w'w''$ for some w', w'' in $\Sigma^* \mathcal{S}^*$ with $|w'| = k$, then $[A, w] \to B_1 \ldots B_{j-1}[B_j, w']$ is included in P'.

As the productions in P' have either a terminal string or a terminal string followed by a variable on R.H.S., G' can be reduced to an equivalent regular grammar. Use the principle of induction to show that

$$[S, \mathcal{S}^k] \underset{G'}{\overset{*}{\Rightarrow}} [A, w] \quad \text{if and only if for some } w' \, S\mathcal{S}^k \underset{R}{\overset{*}{\Rightarrow}} \alpha \, Aww'.$$

This will establish $L(G') = R_k(w)$.]

8. Prove that a context-free grammar G is LR(k) if and only if the following holds: A string γ in $R_k(w)$ corresponding to a production $A_1 \rightarrow \beta_1$ is a substring of some element δ in $R_k(w')$ corresponding to a production $A_2 \rightarrow \beta_2$ implies $\gamma = \delta$, $A_1 = A_2$, $\beta_1 = \beta_2$.

[*Hint*: The proof follows from the definition of LR(k) grammars.]

9. Prove property 2 of section 8.2.

SOLUTION   We give an outline of the construction of the required dpda A. A accepts a string w if $S\mathcal{S}^k$ remains in the stack after the processing of w. For this purpose, A has to simulate the reverse derivation of w. This is achieved by finding suitable handles. $R_k(w)$'s are defined precisely for this purpose (refer Exercise 8.7). As $R_k(w)$'s are regular, there exist deterministic finite automata $M_k(w)$ corresponding to $R_k(w)$.

For our deterministic pda A to contain the information regarding the finite automata, the pushdown store of A is required to have an additional track. In the first track, symbols from $V_N \cup \Sigma$ are written or erased. In the additional track, the information regarding $M_k(w)$'s is stored in the form of maps. The map N_α gives the states of finite automata $M_k(w)$ after the processing of a string α for all productions in G and strings w in $\Sigma^*\mathcal{S}^*$ of length k. The existence of a suitable handle is indicated by a final state of $M_k(w)$ (in the second track).

We can describe the way A acts as follows: A is capable of reading $k + 1$ symbols on PDS, where l is the length of the longest R.H.S. of productions of G. (This can be achieved by modifying the finite control.) A reads the top m symbols on track 1 for some $m \le k + l$. The second track is suitably manipulated. For example, if $X_1 \ldots X_m$ is in track 1, then track 2 stores the maps $N_{X_1} N_{X_1 X_2} \ldots N_{X_1 \ldots X_m}$. If a suitable handle is found, then a sentential form is obtained by replacing the R.H.S. of the handle of its L.H.S. in the given string on track 1. As G is LR(k), this can be done in atmost one way.

The above process is repeated until it is no longer possible. If m symbols are not sufficient to carry out the process, more symbols are read and placed on the stack (track 1).

If stack 1 has $S\mathcal{S}^k$ at a particular stage, A accepts the corresponding string. A is the required dpda accepting $L(G)$.

9

Computability

In this chapter we shall discuss the class of primitive recursive functions—a subclass of partial recursive functions. Turing machine is viewed as a mathematical model of partial recursive function.

9.1 INTRODUCTION AND BASIC CONCEPTS

In Chapters 4, 6 and 7, we considered automata as accepting devices. In this chapter we shall study automata as computing machines. The problem of finding out whether a given problem is 'solvable' by automata reduces to the evaluation of functions on the set of natural numbers or a given alphabet by mechanical means.

We start with the definition of partial and total functions.

A partial function f from X to Y is a rule which assigns to every element of X atmost one element of Y.

A total function from X to Y is a rule which assigns to every element of X a unique element of Y. For example, if R denotes the set of all real numbers, the rule f from R to itself given by $f(r) = + \sqrt{r}$ is a partial function since $f(r)$ is not defined as a real number when r is negative. But $g(r) = 2r$ is a total function from R to itself. (Note that all the functions considered in the earlier chapters were total functions.)

In this chapter we consider total functions from X^k to X, where $X = \{0, 1, 2, 3, \ldots\}$ or $X = \{a, b\}^*$. Throughout this chapter we denote $\{0, 1, 2, \ldots\}$ by N and $\{a, b\}$ by Σ. (Recall that X^k is the set of all k-tuples of elements of X.) For example, $f(m, n) = m - n$ defines a partial function from N to itself as $f(m, n)$ is not defined when $m - n < 0$; $g(m, n) = m + n$ defines a total function from N to itself.

Remark   A partial or total function f from X^k to X is also called a function of k variables and denoted by $f(x_1, x_2, \ldots, x_k)$. For example, $f(x_1, x_2) = 2x_1 + x_2$ is a function of two variables; $f(1, 2) = 4$, 1 and 2 are called arguments and 4 is called a value. $g(w_1, w_2) = w_1 w_2$ is a function of two variables ($w_1 w_2 \in \Sigma^*$); $g(ab, aa) = abaa$, ab, aa are called arguments and $abaa$ is a value.

9.2 PRIMITIVE RECURSIVE FUNCTIONS

In this section we construct primitive recursive functions over N and Σ. We define some initial functions and declare them as primitive recursive functions. By applying certain operations on the primitive recursive functions obtained so far, we get the class of primitive recursive functions.

9.2.1   INITIAL FUNCTIONS

The initial functions over N are given in Table 9.1. In particular,

$$S(4) = 5, \qquad Z(7) = 0$$

$$U_2^3(2, 4, 7) = 4, \qquad U_1^3(2, 4, 7) = 2, \qquad U_3^3(2, 4, 7) = 7$$

Table 9.1   Initial Functions over N

Zero function Z defined by $Z(x) = 0$.
Successor function S defined by $S(x) = x + 1$.
Projection function U_i^n defined by $U_i^n(x_1 ,..., x_n) = x_i$.

NOTE: As $U_1^1(x) = x$ for every x in N, U_1^1 is simply the identity function. So U_i^n is also termed as a generalised identity function.

The initial functions over Σ are given in Table 9.2. In particular,

$$\text{nil }(abab) = \Lambda$$

$$\text{cons } a(abab) = aabab$$

$$\text{cons } b(abab) = babab$$

NOTE: We note that cons $a(x)$ and cons $b(x)$ simply denote the concatenation of the 'constant' string a and x and the concatenation of the constant string b and x.

Table 9.2   Initial Functions over $\{a, b\}$

---

nil $(x) = \Lambda$
cons $a(x) = ax$
cons $b(x) = bx$

In the following definition, we introduce an operation on functions over X.

Definition 9.1   If $f_1, f_2, ..., f_k$ are partial functions of n variables and g is a partial function of k variables, then the composition of g with $f_1, f_2, ..., f_k$ is a partial function of n variables defined by

$$g\left(f(x_1, x_2, ..., x_n), f_2(x_1, x_2, ..., x_n), ..., f_k(x_1, x_2, ..., x_n)\right)$$

If, for example, f_1, f_2 and f_3 are partial functions of two variables and g is a partial function of 3 variables, then the composition of g with f_1, f_2, f_3 is given by $g(f_1(x_1, x_2), f_2(x_1, x_2), f_3(x_1, x_2))$.

EXAMPLE 9.1   Let $f_1(x, y) = x + y, f_2(x, y) = 2x, f_3(x, y) = xy$ and $g(x, y, z) = x + y + z$ be functions over N. Then

$$g(f_1(x, y), f_2(x, y), f_3(x, y)) = g(x + y, 2x, xy)$$

$$= x + y + 2x + xy$$

Thus the composition of g with f_1, f_2, f_3 is given by a function h:

$$h(x, y) = x + y + 2x + xy$$

NOTE: Definition 9.1 generalises the composition of two functions. The concept is useful where a number of outputs become the inputs for a subsequent step of a program.

The composition of g with $f_1, ..., f_n$ is total when $g, f_1, f_2, ..., f_n$ are total. The function given in Example 9.1 is total as f_1, f_2, f_3 and g are total.

EXAMPLE 9.2   Let $f_1(x, y) = x - y$, $f_2(x, y) = y - x$ and $g(x, y) = x + y$ be functions over N. f_1 is defined only when $x \geq y$ and f_2 is defined only when $y \geq x$. So f_1 and f_2 are defined only when $x = y$. Hence when $x = y$,

$$g(f_1(x, y), f_2(x, y)) = g(x - x, x - x) = g(0, 0) = 0$$

Thus the composition of g with f_1 and f_2 is defined only for (x, x), where $x \in N$.

EXAMPLE 9.3 Let

$$f_1(x_1, x_2) = x_1 x_2, \qquad f_2(x_1, x_2) = \Lambda, \qquad f_3(x_1, x_2) = x_1$$

$$g(x_1, x_2, x_3) = x_2 x_3$$

be functions over Σ. Then

$$g(f_1(x_1, x_2), f_2(x_1, x_2), f_3(x_1, x_2)) = g(x_1 x_2, \Lambda, x_1) = \Lambda x_1 = x_1$$

So the composition of g with f_1, f_2, f_3 is given by a function h, where $h(x_1, x_2) = x_1$.

The next definition gives a mechanical process of computing a function.

Definition 9.2   A function $f(x)$ over N is defined by recursion if there exists a constant k (a natural number) and a function $h(x, y)$ such that

$$f(0) = k, \qquad f(n + 1) = h(n, f(n)) \tag{9.1}$$

By induction on n, we can define $f(n)$ for all n. As $f(0) = k$, there is basis for induction. Once $f(n)$ is known, $f(n + 1)$ can be evaluated by using (9.1).

EXAMPLE 9.4   Define $n!$ by recursion.

SOLUTION $f(0) = 1$ and $f(n + 1) = h(n, f(n))$, where $h(x, y) = S(x) * y$.

The above definition can be generalised for $f(x_1, x_2, ..., x_n, x_{n+1})$. We fix n variables in $f(x_1, x_2, ..., x_{n+1})$, say $x_1, x_2, ..., x_n$. We apply Definition 9.2 to $f(x_1, x_2, ..., x_n, y)$. In place of k we get a function $g(x_1, x_2, ..., x_n)$ and in place of $h(x, y)$, we obtain $h(x_1, x_2, ..., x_n, y, f(x_1, ..., x_n, y))$.

Definition 9.3 A function f of $n + 1$ variables is defined by recursion if there exists a function g of n variables, and a function h of $n + 2$ variables, and f is defined as follows:

$$f(x_1, x_2, ..., x_n, 0) = g(x_1, x_2, ..., x_n) \qquad (9.2)$$

$$f(x_1 ... x_n, y + 1) = h(x_1, x_2, ..., x_n, y, f(x_1, x_2, ..., x_n, y)) \qquad (9.3)$$

We may note that f can be evaluated for all arguments $(x_1, x_2, ..., x_n, y)$ by induction on y for fixed $x_1, x_2, ..., x_n$. The process is repeated for every $x_1, x_2, ..., x_n$.

Now we can define primitive recursive functions over N.

9.2.2 PRIMITIVE RECURSIVE FUNCTIONS OVER N

Definition 9.4 A total function f over N is called primitive recursive if (a) it is any one of the three initial functions, or (b) it can be obtained by applying composition and recursion finite number of times to the set of initial functions.

EXAMPLE 9.5 Show that the function $f_1(x, y) = x + y$ is primitive recursive.

SOLUTION f_1 is a function of two variables. If we want f_1 to be defined by recursion, we need a function g of a single variable and a function h of three variables.

$$f_1(x, 0) = x + 0 = x$$

By comparing $f_1(x, 0)$ with L.H.S. of (9.2), we see that g can be defined by

$$g(x) = x = U_1^1(x)$$

Also, $f_1(x, y + 1) = x + (y + 1) = (x + y) + 1 = f_1(x, y) + 1$
By comparing $f_1(x, y + 1)$ with L.H.S. of (9.3), we have

$$h(x, y, f_1(x, y)) = f_1(x, y) + 1 = S(f_1(x, y)) = S(U_3^3(x, y, f_1(x, y)))$$

Define $h(x, y, z) = S(U_3^3(x, y, z))$. As $g = U_1^1$, it is an initial function. h is obtained from the initial functions U_3^3 and S by composition, and f_1 by recursion using g and h. Thus f_1 is obtained by applying composition and recursion finite number of times to initial functions U_1^1, U_3^3 and S. So f_1 is primitive recursive.

NOTE: A total function is primitive recursive if it can be obtained by applying composition and recursion a finite number of times to primitive recursive functions $f_1, f_2, ..., f_m$. This is clear as each f_i is obtained by applying composition and recursion a finite number of times to initial functions.

EXAMPLE 9.6 The function $f_2(x, y) = x * y$ is primitive recursive.

SOLUTION As multiplication of two natural numbers is simply repeated addition, f_2 has to be primitive recursive. We prove this as follows:

$$f_2(x, 0) = 0, \qquad f_2(x, y + 1) = x * (y + 1) = f_2(x, y) + x$$

i.e. $f_2(x, y + 1) = f_1(f_2(x, y), x)$. Comparing these with (9.2) and (9.3), we can write $f_2(x, 0) = Z(x)$ and $f_2(x, y + 1) = f_1(U_3^3(x, y, f_2(x, y)), U_1^3(x, y, f_2(x, y))))$. By taking $g = Z$ and h defined by $h(x, y, z) = f_1(U_3^3(x, y, z), U_1^3(x, y, z))$, we see that f_2 is defined by recursion. As g and h are primitive recursive, f_2 is primitive recursive (by the above note).

EXAMPLE 9.7 Show that $f(x, y) = x^y$ is a primitive recursive function.

SOLUTION We define

$$f(x, 0) = 1$$

$$f(x, y + 1) = x * f(x, y)$$

$$= U_1^3(x, y, f(x, y)) * U_3^3(x, y, f(x, y))$$

Therefore, $f(x, y)$ is primitive recursive.

EXAMPLE 9.8 Show that the following functions are primitive recursive:

   (a) The predecessor function $p(x)$ defined by

$$p(x) = x - 1 \quad \text{if } x \neq 0, \quad p(x) = 0 \quad \text{if } x = 0.$$

   (b) Proper subtraction function $\dot-$ defined by

$$x \dot- y = x - y \quad \text{if } x \geq y \text{ and } x \dot- y = 0 \quad \text{if } x < y.$$

   (c) Absolute value function $|\ |$ given by

$$|x| = x \quad \text{if } x \geq 0, \quad |x| = -x \quad \text{if } x < 0.$$

   (d) min (x, y), i.e. minimum of x and y.

SOLUTION

   (a) $p(0) = 0$ and $p(y + 1) = U_1^2(y, p(y))$.

   (b) $x \dot- 0 = x$ and $x \dot- (y + 1) = p(x \dot- y)$.

   (c) $|x - y| = (x \dot- y) + (y \dot- x)$.

   (d) $\min(x, y) = x \dot- (x \dot- y)$.

The first function is defined by recursion using an initial function. So it is primitive recursive.

The second function is defined by recursion using the primitive recursive function p and so is primitive recursive. Similarly, the last two functions are primitive recursive.

9.2.3 PRIMITIVE RECURSIVE FUNCTIONS OVER $\{a, b\}$

For constructing the primitive recursive function over $\{a, b\}$, the process is similar to that of function over N except for some minor modifications. It should be noted that Λ plays the role of 0 in (9.2) and ax or bx plays the role of $y + 1$ in (9.3). Recall that Σ denotes $\{a, b\}$.

Definition 9.5   A function $f(x)$ over Σ is defined by recursion if there exists a 'constant' string $w \in \Sigma^*$ and functions $h_1(x, y)$ and $h_2(x, y)$ such that

$$f(\Lambda) = w \tag{9.4}$$

$$f(ax) = h_1(x, f(x))$$

$$f(bx) = h_2(x, f(x)) \tag{9.5}$$

(h_1 and h_2 may be functions in one variable)

Definition 9.6   A function $f(x_1, x_2, ..., x_n)$ over Σ is defined by recursion if there exist functions $g(x_1, ..., x_{n-1})$, $h_1(x_1, ..., x_{n+1})$, $h_2(x_1, ..., x_{n+1})$ such that

$$f(\Lambda, x_2, ..., x_n) = g(x_2, ..., x_n) \tag{9.6}$$

$$f(ax_1, x_2, ..., x_n) = h_1(x_1, x_2, ..., x_n, f(x_1, x_2, ..., x_n))$$

$$f(bx_1, x_2, ..., x_n) = h_2(x_1, x_2, ..., x_n, f(x_1, x_2, ..., x_n)) \tag{9.7}$$

(h_1 and h_2 may be functions of m variables, where $m < n + 1$).

Now we can define the class of primitive recursive functions over Σ.

Definition 9.7   A total function f is primitive recursive if (a) it is any one of the three initial functions (given in Table 9.2), or (b) it can be obtained by applying composition and recursion finite number of times to the initial functions.

In Example 9.9 we give some primitive recursive functions over Σ.

NOTE: As in the case of functions over N, a total function over Σ is primitive recursive if it is obtained by applying composition and recursion a finite number of times to primitive recursive functions $f_1, f_2, ..., f_m$.

EXAMPLE 9.9   Show that the following functions are primitive recursive:

   (a) Constant functions a and b (i.e. $a(x) = a$, $b(x) = b$)
   (b) Identity function
   (c) Concatenation
   (d) Transpose
   (e) Head function (i.e. head $(a_1a_2 ... a_n) = a_1$)
   (f) Tail function (i.e. tail $(a_1a_2 ... a_n) = a_2 ... a_n$)
   (g) The conditional function "if $x_1 \neq \Lambda$ then x_2 else x_3".

SOLUTION   (a) As $a(x) = $ cons a (nil (x)), the function $a(x)$ is the composition of the initial function cons a with the initial function nil and is hence primitive recursive.

   (b) Let us denote the function by id. Then,

$$\text{id } (\Lambda) = \Lambda$$

$$\text{id } (ax) = \text{cons } a(x)$$

$$\text{id } (bx) = \text{cons } b(x)$$

So id is defined by recursion using cons a and cons b. Therefore, the identity function is primitive recursive.

(c) The concatenation function can be defined by

$$\text{concat } (x_1, x_2) = x_1 x_2$$

$$\text{concat } (\Lambda, x_2) = \text{id } (x_2)$$

$$\text{concat } (ax_1, x_2) = \text{cons } a \text{ (concat } (x_1, x_2))$$

$$\text{concat } (bx_1, x_2) = \text{cons } b \text{ (concat } (x_1, x_2))$$

So concat is defined by recursion using id, cons a and cons b. Therefore, concat is primitive recursive.

(d) The transpose function can be defined by trans $(x) = x^T$. Then

$$\text{trans } (\Lambda) = \Lambda$$

$$\text{trans } (ax) = \text{concat } (\text{trans } (x), a(x))$$

$$\text{trans } (bx) = \text{concat } (\text{trans } (x), b(x))$$

Thus, trans (x) is primitive recursive.

(e) The head function head (x) satisfies

$$\text{head } (\Lambda) = \Lambda$$

$$\text{head } (ax) = a(x)$$

$$\text{head } (bx) = b(x)$$

Therefore, head (x) is primitive recursive.

(f) The tail function tail (x) satisfies

$$\text{tail } (\Lambda) = \Lambda$$

$$\text{tail } (ax) = \text{id } (x)$$

$$\text{tail } (bx) = \text{id } (x)$$

Therefore, tail (x) is primitive recursive.

(g) The conditional function can be defined by

$$\text{cond } (x_1, x_2, x_3) = \text{``if } x_1 \neq \Lambda \text{ then } x_2 \text{ else } x_3\text{''}$$

Then,

$$\text{cond } (\Lambda, x_2, x_3) = \text{id } (x_3)$$

$$\text{cond } (ax_1, x_2, x_3) = \text{id } (x_2)$$

$$\text{cond } (bx_1, x_2, x_3) = \text{id } (x_2)$$

Thus, id (x_1, x_2, x_3) is primitive recursive.

9.3   RECURSIVE FUNCTIONS

By introducing one more operation on functions, we define the class of recursive functions, which includes the class of primitive recursive functions.

Definition 9.8   Let $g(x_1, x_2, ..., x_n, y)$ be a total function over N. g is a regular function if there exists some natural number y_0 such that $g(x_1, x_2, ..., x_n, y_0) = 0$ for all values $x_1, x_2, ..., x_n$ in N.

For instance, $g(x, y) = \min(x, y)$ is a regular function since $g(x, 0) = 0$ for all x in N. But, $f(x, y) = |x - y|$ is not regular since $f(x, y) = 0$ only when $x = y$, and so we cannot find a fixed y such that $f(x, y) = 0$ for all x in N.

Definition 9.9   A function $f(x_1, x_2, ..., x_n)$ over N is defined from a total function $g(x_1, x_2, ..., x_n, y)$ by minimisation if (a) $f(x_1, x_2, ..., x_n)$ is the least value of all y's such that $g(x_1, x_2, ..., x_n, y) = 0$ if it exists. The least value is denoted by μ_y $(g(x_1, x_2, ..., x_n, y) = 0)$, (b) $f(x_1, x_2, ..., x_n)$ is undefined if there is no y such that $g(x_1, x_2 ... x_n, y) = 0$.

NOTE: In general, f is partial. But, if g is regular then f is total.

Definition 9.10   A function is recursive if it can be obtained from the initial functions by a finite number of applications of composition, recursion and minimisation over regular functions.

Definition 9.11   A function is partial recursive if it can be obtained from the initial functions by a finite number of applications of composition, recursion and minimisation.

EXAMPLE 9.10 $f(x) = x/2$ is partial recursive function over N.

SOLUTION   Let $g(x, y) = |2y - x|$. $2y - x = 0$ for some y only when x is even. Let $f_1(x) = \mu_y (|2y - x| = 0)$. Then $f_1(x)$ is defined only for even values of x and is equal to $x/2$. When x is odd, $f_1(x)$ is not defined. f_1 is partial recursive. As $f(x) = x/2 = f_1(x)$, f is a partial recursive function.

The following example gives a recursive function which is not primitive recursive.

EXAMPLE 9.11   Ackermann's function is defined by

$$A(0, y) = y + 1 \tag{9.8}$$

$$A(x + 1, 0) = A(x, 1) \tag{9.9}$$

$$A(x + 1, y + 1) = A(x, A(x + 1, y)) \tag{9.10}$$

$A(x, y)$ can be computed for every (x, y), and hence $A(x, y)$ is total. Ackermann's function is not primitive recursive but recursive.

EXAMPLE 9.12   Compute $A(1, 1)$, $A(2, 1)$, $A(1, 2)$, $A(2, 2)$.

SOLUTION

$$A(1, 1) = A(0 + 1, 0 + 1)$$

$$= A(0, A(1, 0)) \quad \text{by (9.10)}$$

$$= A(0, A(0, 1)) \quad \text{by (9.9)}$$

$$= A(0, 2) \quad\quad \text{by (9.8)}$$

$$= 3 \quad\quad\quad \text{by (9.8)}$$

$$A(1, 2) = A(0 + 1, 1 + 1)$$

$$= A(0, A(1, 1)) \quad \text{by (9.10)}$$

$$= A(0, 3)$$

$$= 4 \quad\quad\quad\quad\quad \text{by (9.8)}$$

$$A(2, 1) = A(1 + 1, 0 + 1)$$

$$= A(1, A(2, 0)) \quad \text{by (9.10)}$$

$$= A(1, A(1, 1)) \quad \text{by (9.9)}$$

$$= A(1, 3)$$

$$= A(0 + 1, 2 + 1)$$

$$= A(0, A(1, 2)) \quad \text{by (9.10)}$$

$$= A(0, 4)$$

$$= 5$$

$$A(2, 2) = A(1 + 1, 1 + 1)$$

$$= A(1, A(2, 1)) \quad \text{by (9.10)}$$

$$= A(1, 5)$$

$$A(1, 5) = A(0 + 1, 4 + 1)$$

$$= A(0, A(1, 4)) \quad \text{by (9.10)}$$

$$= 1 + A(1, 4) \quad \text{by (9.8)}$$

$$= 1 + A(0 + 1, 3 + 1)$$

$$= 1 + A(0, A(1, 3))$$

$$= 1 + 1 + A(1, 3)$$

$$= 1 + 1 + 1 + A(1, 2)$$

$$= 1 + 1 + 1 + 4$$

$$= 7$$

As $A(2, 2) = A(1, 5), \ A(2, 2) = 7$

Till now we have dealt with recursive and partial recursive functions over N. We can define partial recursive functions over Σ using primitive recursive predicates and minimisation process. As the process is similar, we do not discuss it here.

The concept of recursion occurs in some programming languages when a procedure has a call to the same procedure for a different parameter. Such a procedure is called a recursive procedure. Certain programming languages like Pascal, PL/I, SNOBOL 4 allow recursive procedures.

9.4 PARTIAL RECURSIVE FUNCTIONS AND TURING MACHINES

In this section we prove that partial recursive functions introduced in the earlier sections are Turing-computable.

9.4.1 COMPUTABILITY

In mid 1930's, mathematicians and logicians were trying to rigorously define computability and algorithms. In 1934 Kurt Gödel pointed out that primitive recursive functions can be computed by a finite procedure (i.e. an algorithm). He also hypothesized that any function computable by a finite procedure can be specified by a recursive function. Around 1936, Turing and Church independently designed a 'computing machine' (later termed as *Turing machine*) which can carry out a finite procedure.

For formalising computability, Turing assumed that, while computing, a person writes symbols on a one-dimensional paper (instead of a two-dimensional paper as is usually done) which can be viewed as a tape divided into cells. He scans the cells one at a time and usually performs one of the three simple operations, viz. (i) writing a new symbol in the cell he is scanning, (ii) moving to the cell left of the present cell, and (iii) moving to the cell right of the present cell. These observations led Turing to propose a computing machine. The Turing machine model we have introduced in Chapter 7 is based on these three simple operations but with slight variations. In order to introduce computability, we consider the Turing machine model due to Post. In the present model the transition function is represented by a set of quadruples (i.e. 4-tuples), whereas the transition function of the model we have introduced in Chapter 7 can be represented by a set of quintuples (5-tuples). For example, $\delta (q_i, a) = (q_j, \alpha, \beta)$ is represented by the quintuple $q_i a \alpha \beta q_j$. Using the model specifying the transition function in terms of quadruples, we define Turing-computable functions and prove that partially recursive functions are Turing-computable.

9.4.2 A TURING MODEL FOR COMPUTATION

As in the model introduced in Chapter 7, Q, q_0 and Γ denote the set of states, the initial state, and the set of tape symbols, respectively. The blank symbol b is in Γ. The only difference is regarding the transition function. In the present model the transition function represents only one of the three basic operations

(i) writing a new symbol in the cell scanned,
(ii) moving to the left cell, and
(iii) moving to the right cell.

Each operation is followed by a change of state. Suppose the Turing machine M is in state q and scans a_i. If a_j is written and M enters q', then this basic operation is represented by the quadruple qa_ia_jq'. Similarly, the other two operations are represented by the quadruples qa_iLq' and qa_iRq'. Thus the transition function can be specified by a set P of quadruples. As in Chapter 7, we can define instantaneous descriptions, i.e. IDs.

Each quadruple induces a change of IDs. For example, qa_ia_jq' induces

$$\alpha q a_i \beta \vdash \alpha q' a_j \beta$$

qa_iLq' induces

$$a_1 a_2 \ldots a_{i-1} q a_i \ldots a_n \vdash a_1 a_2 \ldots a_{i-2} q' a_{i-1} a_i \ldots a_n$$

and qa_iRq' induces

$$a_1 \ldots a_{i-1} q a_i \ldots a_n \vdash a_1 \ldots a_i q' a_{i+1} \ldots a_n$$

When we require M to perform some computation, we 'feed' the input by initial tape expression denoted by X. So $q_0 X$ is the initial ID for the given input. For computing with the given input X, the Turing machine processes X using appropriate quadruples in P. As a result, we have $q_0 X = \text{ID}_1 \vdash \text{ID}_2 \vdash \ldots$. When an ID, say ID_n, is reached, which cannot be changed using any quadruple in P, M halts. In this case, ID_n is called a terminal ID. Actually, $\alpha q_i a \beta$ is a terminal ID if there is no quadruple starting with $q_i a$. The terminal ID is called the result of X and denoted by Res (X). The computed value corresponding to input X can be obtained by deleting the state appearing in it as also some more symbols from Res (X).

9.4.3 TURING-COMPUTABLE FUNCTIONS

Before developing the concept of Turing-computable functions, let us recall Example 7.6. The TM developed in Example 7.6 concatenates two strings α and β. Initially, α and β appear on the input tape separated by a blank b. Finally, the concatenated string $\alpha\beta$ appears on the input tape. The same method can be adopted with slight modifications for computing $f(x_1, \ldots, x_m)$. Suppose we want to construct a TM which can compute $f(x_1, \ldots, x_m)$ over N for given arguments $a_1, \ldots, a_m$. Initially, the input $a_1, a_2, \ldots, a_m$ appears on the input tape separated by markers $x_1, \ldots, x_m$. The computed value $f(a_1, \ldots, a_m)$, say c, appears on the input tape once the computation is over. To locate c, we need another marker, say y. The value c appears to the right of x_m and to the left of y. To make the construction simpler, we use tally notation to represent elements of N. In tally notation, 0 is represented by a string of b's. A positive integer n is represented by a string consisting of n 1's. So the initial tape expression takes the form $1^{a_1} x_1 1^{a_2} x_2 \ldots 1^{a_m} x_m$ by. As a result of computation, the initial ID $q_0 1^{a_1} x_1 1^{a_2} x_2 \ldots 1^{a_m} x_m$ by is changed to a terminal ID of the form $1^{a_1}x_11^{a_2}x_2 \ldots 1^{a_m}x_m1^cq'y$ for some $q' \in Q$. In fact, the position of q' in a terminal ID is immaterial and it can appear anywhere in Res (X). The computed value is found between x_m and y. Sometimes we may have to omit leading b's.

We say a function $f(x_1, \ldots, x_m)$ is Turing-computable for arguments $a_1, \ldots, a_m$ if there exists a Turing machine for which

$$q_01^{a_1}x_11^{a_2}x_2 \ldots 1^{a_m}x_m \text{ by} \overset{*}{\vdash} \text{ID}_n$$

where ID_n is a terminal ID containing $f(a_1, \ldots, a_m)$ to the left of y.

Our ultimate aim is to prove that partial recursive functions are Turing-computable. For this purpose, first of all we prove that the three initial primitive recursive functions are Turing-computable.

9.4.4   CONSTRUCTION OF TURING MACHINE THAT CAN COMPUTE THE ZERO FUNCTION Z

The zero function Z is defined as $Z(a_1) = 0$ for all $a_1 \geq 0$. So the initial tape expression can be taken as $X = 1^{a_1}x_1 \, by$. As we require the computed value $Z(a_1)$, viz., 0, to appear to the left of y, we require the machine to halt without changing the input. (Note that 0 is represented by b in tally notation.)

Thus we define a TM by taking $Q = \{q_0, q_1\}$, $\Gamma = \{b, 1, x_1, y\}$, $X = 1^a x_1 \, by$. P consists of q_0bRq_0, q_01Rq_0, $q_0x_1x_1q_1$. q_0bRq_0 and q_01Rq_0 are used to move to the right until x_1 is encountered. $q_0x_1x_1q_1$ enables the TM to enter state q_1. M enters q_1 without altering the tape symbol. In terms of change of IDs, we have

$$q_01^{a_1}x_1 \, by \overset{*}{\vdash} 1^{a_1}q_0x_1 \, by \vdash 1^{a_1}q_1x_1 \, by$$

As there is no quadruple starting with q_1, M halts and Res $(X) = 1^{a_1}q_1x_1 \, by$. By deleting q_1 in Res (X), we get $1^{a_1}x_1 by$ (which is the same as X) yielding 0 (given by b).

NOTE: We can also represent the quadruples in a tabular form which is similar to the transition table obtained in Chapter 7. In this case we have to specify (a) the new symbol written, or (b) movement to the left (denoted by L), or (c) movement to the right (denoted by R). So we get Table 9.3.

Table 9.3   Representation of Quadruples

States	b	1	x_1	y
q_0	(R, q_0)	(R, q_0)	(x_1, q_1)	
q_1				

9.4.5   CONSTRUCTION OF TURING MACHINE FOR COMPUTING THE SUCCESSOR FUNCTION

The successor function S is defined by $S(a_1) = a_1 + 1$ for all $a_1 \geq 0$. So the initial tape expression can be taken as $X = 1^{a_1} x_1 by$ (as in the case of the zero function). At the end of the computation, we require 1^{a_1+1} to appear to the left of y. Hence we define a TM by taking

$$Q = \{q_0, \ldots, q_9\}, \qquad \Gamma = \{b, 1, x_1, y\}, \qquad X = 1^{a_1} x_1\, by$$

P consists of

(i) $q_0 bRq_0,\ q_0 1bq_1,\ q_0 x_1 Rq_6$

(ii) $q_1 bRq_1,\ q_1 1Rq_1,\ q_1 x_1 Rq_1,\ q_1 y1 q_2$

(iii) $q_2 1Rq_2,\ q_2 byq_3,$

(iv) $q_3 bLq_3,\ q_3 1Lq_3,\ q_3 yLq_3,\ q_3 x_1 Lq_4$

(v) $q_4 1Lq_4,\ q_4 b1q_5,$

(vi) $q_5 1Rq_0,$

(vii) $q_6 bRq_6,\ q_6 1Rq_6,\ q_6 x_1 Rq_6,\ q_6 yLq_7$

(viii) $q_7 1Lq_7,\ q_7 b1q_8,$

(ix) $q_8 bLq_8,\ q_8 1Lq_8,\ q_8 yLq_8,\ q_8 x_1 x_1 q_9.$

The corresponding operations can be explained as follows:

(i) If M starts from initial ID, the head replaces the first 1 it encounters by b. Afterwards the head moves to the right until it encounters y (as a result of $q_0 1bq_1,\ q_1 bRq_1,\ q_1 1Rq_1,\ q_1 x_1 Rq_1$).

(ii) y is replaced by 1 and M enters q_2. Once the end of the input tape is reached, y is added to the next cell. M enters q_3 ($q_1 y1 q_2,\ q_2 1Rq_2,\ q_2 byq_3$)

(iii) Then the head moves to the left and the state is not changed until x_1 is encountered ($q_3 yLq_3,\ q_3 yLq_3,\ q_3 bLq_3$).

(iv) On encountering x_1, the head moves to the left and M enters q_4. Once again the head moves to the left till the left end of the input string is reached ($q_3 x_1 Lq_4,\ q_1 1Lq_4$).

(v) The leftmost blank (written in point (i)) is replaced by 1 and M enters q_5 ($q_4 b1q_5$).

   Thus at the end of operations (i)–(v), the input part remains unaffected but the first 1 is added to the left of y.

(vi) Then the head scans the second 1 of the input string and moves right, and M enters q_0 ($q_5 1Rq_0$).

   Operations (i)–(vi) are repeated until all the 1's of the input part (i.e. in 1^{a_1}) are exhausted and 11 ... 1 (a_1 times) appear to the left of y. Now the present state is q_0, and the current symbol is x_1.

(vii) M in state q_0 scans x_1, moves right, and enters q_6. It continues to move to the right until it encounters y ($q_0 x_1 Rq_6,\ q_6 bRq_6,\ q_6 1Rq_6,\ q_6 x_1 Rq_6$).

(viii) On encountering y, the head moves to the left and M enters q_7, after which the head moves to the left until it encounters b appearing to the left of 1^{a_1} of the output part. This b is changed to 1 and M enters q_8 ($q_6 yLq_7,\ q_7 1Lq_7,\ q_7 b1q_8$).

(ix) Once M is in q_8, the head continues to move to the left and on scanning x_1, M enters q_9. As there is no quadruple starting with q_9, M halts ($q_8 bLq_8,\ q_8 1Lq_8,\ q_8 x_1 x_1 q_9$).

The machine halts, and the terminal ID is $1^{a_1}q_9x_11^{a_1+1}y$. For example, let us compute $S(1)$. In this case the initial ID is q_01x_1by. As a result of the computation, we have the following moves:

$$q_01x_1by \vdash q_1bx_1by \vdash bq_1x_1by$$

$$\vdash bx_1q_1by \vdash bx_1bq_1y \vdash bx_1bq_21$$

$$\vdash bx_1b1q_2b \vdash bx_1b1q_3y \vdash bx_1bq_31y$$

$$\overset{*}{\vdash} bq_3x_1b1y \vdash q_4bx_1b1y \vdash q_51x_1b1y$$

$$\overset{*}{\vdash} 1q_6x_1b1y \overset{*}{\vdash} 1x_1b1q_6y \vdash 1x_1bq_71y$$

$$\vdash 1x_1q_7b1y \vdash 1x_1q_811y \vdash 1q_8x_111y$$

$$\vdash 1q_9x_111y$$

Thus, M halts and $S(1) = 2$ (given by 11 to the left of y).

9.4.6   CONSTRUCTION OF TURING MACHINE FOR COMPUTING THE PROJECTION U_i^m

Recall $U_i^m(a_1, ..., a_m) = a_i$. The initial tape expression can be taken as

$$X = 1^{a_1}x_11^{a_2}x_2 ... 1^{a_m}x_m \ by$$

We define a Turing machine by taking $Q = \{q_0, ..., q_8\}$

$\Gamma = \{b, 1, x_1, ..., x_m, y\}$. P consists of

$$q_0zRq_0 \quad \text{for all } z \in \Gamma - \{x_i\}$$

$$q_0x_iLq_1, \qquad q_1bbq_8, \qquad q_1bq_2$$

$$q_2zRq_2 \quad \text{for all } z \in \Gamma - \{y\}$$

$$q_2y1q_3, \qquad q_31Rq_3, \qquad q_3byq_4$$

$$q_4zLq_4 \quad \text{for all } z \in \Gamma - \{x_i\}$$

$$q_4x_iLq_5, \qquad q_51Lq_5, \qquad q_5b1q_6, \qquad q_61Lq_7, \qquad q_71bq_2$$

$$q_7zRq_8 \quad \text{for all } z \in \Gamma - \{1\}$$

The operations of M are as follows:

(i) M starts from initial ID and the head moves to the right until it encounters x_i (q_0zRq_0).

(ii) On seeing x_i, the head moves to the left ($q_0x_iLq_1$).

(iii) The head replaces 1 (the right-most 1 in 1^{a_i}) by b (q_1bq_2).

(iv) The head moves to the right until it encounters y and replaces y by 1 (q_2zRq_2, $z \in \Gamma - \{y\}$ and q_2y1q_3).

(v)   On reaching the right end, the head scans 'b' and replaces this b by y (q_3byq_4).

(vi)   The head moves to the left until it scans the symbol b. This b is replaced by 1 (q_4zLq_4, $z \in \Gamma - \{x_i\}$, $q_4x_iLq_5$, q_5b1q_6).

(vii)   The head moves to the left and one of the 1's in 1^{a_i} is replaced by b. M reaches q_2 (q_61Lq_7, q_71bq_2).

As a result of (i)–(vii), one of the 1's in 1^{a_i} is replaced by b and 1 is added to the left of y. Steps (iv)–(vii) are repeated for all 1's in 1^{a_i}.

(viii)   On scanning x_{i-1}, the head moves to the right and M enters q_8 ($q_7 x_{i-1}Rq_8$).

As there are no quadruples starting with q_8, the Turing machine M halts. When $i \neq 1$ and $a_i \neq 0$, the terminal ID is $1^{a_1}x_1 \ldots x_{i-1}q_81^{a_i}x_i \ldots x_nb1^{a_i}y$. For example, let us compute U_2^3 (1, 2, 1):

$$q_01x_11 1x_21x_3by \vdash^* 1x_11 1q_0x_21x_3by$$

$$\vdash 1x_11q_11x_21x_3by \vdash 1x_11q_2bx_21x_3by$$

$$\vdash^* 1x_11bx_21x_3bq_2y \vdash 1x_11bx_21x_3bq_31$$

$$\vdash 1x_11bx_21x_3b1q_3b \vdash 1x_11bx_21x_3b1q_4y$$

$$\vdash^* 1x_11bq_4x_21x_3b1y \vdash 1x_11q_5bx_21x_3b1y$$

$$\vdash 1x_11q_61x_21x_3b1y \vdash 1x_1q_71 1x_21x_3b1y$$

$$\vdash 1x_1q_2b1x_21x_3b1y$$

From the above derivation we see that

$$1x_11q_2bx_21x_3by \vdash^* 1x_1q_2b1x_21x_3b1y$$

Repeating the above steps, we get

$$1x_1q_2b1x_21x_3b1y \vdash^* 1x_1q_811x_21x_3b1 1y$$

It should be noted that this construction is similar to that for the successor function. While computing U_i^m, the head skips the portion of the input corresponding to a_j, $j \neq i$. For every 1 in 1^{a_i}, 1 is added to the left of y.

Thus we have shown that the three initial primitive recursive functions are Turing-computable. Next we construct Turing machines that can perform composition, recursion, and minimisation.

9.4.7   CONSTRUCTION OF TURING MACHINE THAT CAN PERFORM COMPOSITION

Let $f_1(x_1, x_2, \ldots, x_m)$, $\ldots f_k(x_1, \ldots, x_m)$ be Turing-computable functions. Let $g(y_1, \ldots, y_k)$ be Turing-computable. Let $h(x_1, \ldots, x_m) = g(f_1(x_1, \ldots, x_m) \ldots,$

$f_k(x_1, \ldots, x_m))$. We construct a Turing machine that can compute $h(a_1, \ldots, a_m)$ for given arguments $a_1, \ldots, a_m$. This involves the following steps:

Step 1   Construct Turing machines $M_1, \ldots, M_k$ which can compute $f_1, \ldots, f_k$, respectively. For the TMs $M_1, \ldots, M_k$, let $\Gamma = \{1, b, x_1, x_2, \ldots, x_m, y\}$ and $X = 1^{a_1} x_1 \ldots 1^{a_m} x_m by$. But the number of states for these TMs will vary. Let $n_1 + 1, \ldots, n_k + 1$ be the number of states for $M_1, \ldots, M_k$, respectively. As usual, the initial state is q_0 and the states for M_i are $q_0, \ldots, q_{n_i}$. As in the earlier constructions, the set P_i of quadruples for M_i is constructed in such a way that there is no quadruple starting with q_{n_i}.

Step 2   Let $f_i(a_1, \ldots, a_m) = b_i$ for $i = 1, 2, \ldots, k$. At the end of Step 1, we have M_i's and the computed values b_i's. As g is Turing-computable, we can construct a TM M_{k+1} which can compute $g(b_1, \ldots, b_k)$. For M_{k+1},

$$\Gamma = \{1, b, x_1', \ldots, x_m', y\}, \qquad X' = 1^{b_1} x_1' \ldots 1^{b_m} x_m' by$$

(We use different markers for M_{k+1} so that the TM computing h to be constructed need not scan the inputs $a_1, \ldots, a_m$.) Let $n_{k+1} + 1$ be the number of states of M_{k+1}. As in the earlier constructions, M_{k+1} has no quadruples starting with $q_{n_{k+1}}$.

Step 3   At the end of step 2, we have TM's $M_1, \ldots, M_k, M_{k+1}$ which give $b_1, \ldots, b_m$ and $g(b_1, \ldots, b_k) = c$ (say), respectively. So we are able to compute $h(a_1, \ldots, a_m)$ using $k + 1$ Turing machines. Our objective is to construct a single TM M_{k+2} which can compute $h(a_1, \ldots, a_m)$. We outline the construction of M without giving the complete details of the encoding mechanism. For M, let

$$\Gamma = \{1, b, x_1, \ldots, x_m, x_1', \ldots, x_m', y\}$$

$$X = 1^{a_1} x_1 1^{a_2} x_2 \ldots 1^{a_m} x_m by$$

(i)   In the beginning, M simulates M_1. As a result, the value $b_1 = f_1(a_1, \ldots, a_m)$ is obtained as output. Thus we get the tape expression $1^{a_1} x_1 1^{a_2} x_2 \ldots 1^{a_m} x_m 1^{b_1} y$ which is the same as that obtained by M_1 while halting. M does not halt but changes y to x_1' and adds by to the right of x_1'. The head moves to the left to reach the beginning of X.

(ii)   The tape expression obtained at the end of (i) is

$$1^{a_1} x_1 1^{a_2} x_2 \ldots 1^{a_m} x_m 1^{b_1} x_1' by$$

The construction given in (i) is repeated, i.e. M simulates $M_2, \ldots, M_k$, changes y to x_i', and adds by to the right of x_i'. After simulating M_k, the tape expression is

$$X' = 1^{a_1} x_1 \ldots 1^{a_m} x_m 1^{b_1} x_1' \ldots 1^{b_{k-1}} x_{k-1} 1^{b_k} x_k' by$$

Then the head moves to the left until it is positioned at the cell having 1 just to the right of x_m.

(iii) M simulates M_{k+1}. M_{k+1} with initial tape expression X' halts with the tape expression $1^{b_1}x_1' \ldots 1^{b_k}x_k'1^c y$. As a result, the corresponding tape expression for M is obtained as

$$1^{a_1}x_1 1^{a_2}x_2 \ldots 1^{a_m}x_m 1^{b_1}x_1' \ldots 1^{b_k}x_k'1^c y$$

(iv) The required value is obtained to the left of y, but $1^{b_1}x_1' \ldots 1^{b_k}x_k'$ also appears to the left of c. M erases all these symbols and moves $1^c y$ just to the right of x_m. The head moves to the cell having x_m and M halts. The final tape expression is $1^{a_1}x_1 1^{a_2}x_2 \ldots 1^{a_m}x_m 1^c y$.

9.4.8 CONSTRUCTION OF TURING MACHINE THAT CAN PERFORM RECURSION

Let $g(x_1, \ldots, x_m)$, $h(y_1, y_2, \ldots, y_{m+2})$ be Turing-computable. Let $f(x_1 \ldots x_{m+1})$ be defined by recursion as follows:

$$f(x_1, \ldots, x_m, 0) = g(x_1 \ldots x_m)$$

$$f(x_1, \ldots, x_m, y + 1) = h(x_1, \ldots, x_m, y, f(x_1, \ldots, x_m, y))$$

For the Turing machine M, computing $f(a_1, \ldots, a_m, c)$, (say k), X is taken as

$$1^{a_1}x_1 \ldots 1^{a_m}x_m 1^c x_{m+1}by$$

As the construction is similar to the construction for computing composition, we outline the steps of the construction.

Step 1 Let M simulate the Turing machine M' which computes $g(a_1, \ldots, a_m)$. The computed value, viz. $g(a_1, \ldots, a_m)$, is placed to the left of y. If $c = 0$, then the computed value $g(a_1, \ldots, a_m)$ is $f(a_1, \ldots, a_m, 0)$. The head is placed to the right of x_m and M halts.

Step 2 If c is not equal to zero, 1^c to the left of x_{m+1} is replaced by b^c. The marker y is changed to x_{m+2} and by is added to the right of x_{m+2}. The head moves to the left of 1^{a_1}.

Step 3 h is computable. M is allowed to compute h for the arguments $a_1, \ldots, a_m$, $0, g(a_1, \ldots, a_m)$ which appear to the left of $x_1, \ldots, x_m, x_{m+1}, x_{m+2}$, respectively. The computed value is $f(a_1, \ldots, a_m, 1) . f(a_1, \ldots, a_m, 2) \ldots f(a_1, \ldots, a_m, c)$ are computed successively by replacing the right-most b and computing h for respective arguments.

The computation stops with a terminal ID, viz.

$$b1^{a_1}x_1 1^{a_2} \ldots q_f 1^c x_{n+1}1^k y, \qquad k = f(a_1, \ldots, a_m, c)$$

9.4.9 CONSTRUCTION OF TURING MACHINE THAT CAN PERFORM MINIMISATION

When $f(x_1, \ldots, x_m)$ is defined from $g(x_1, \ldots, x_m, y)$ by minimisation, $f(x_1, \ldots, x_m)$ is the least of all k's such that $g(x_1, \ldots, x_m, k) = 0$. So the problem reduces to computing $g(a_1, \ldots, a_m, k)$ for given arguments $a_1, \ldots, a_m$ and for values of k

starting from 0. $f(a_1, ..., a_m)$ is the first k for which $g(a_1, ..., a_m, k) = 0$. Hence, as soon as the computed value of $g(a_1, ..., a_m, y)$ is zero, the required Turing machine M has to halt. Of course, when no such y exists, M never halts, and $f(a_1, ..., a_m)$ is not defined.

Thus the construction of M is in such a way that it simulates the TM that computes $g(a_1, ..., a_m, k)$ for successive values of k. Once the computed value $g(a_1, ..., a_m, k) = 0$ for the first time, M erases by and changes x_{m+1} to y. The head moves to the left of x_m and M halts.

As partial recursive functions are obtained from the initial functions by a finite number of applications of composition, recursion and minimisation (Definition 9.11) by the various constructions we have made in this section, partial recursive functions become Turing-computable.

Using Godel numbering which converts operations of Turing machines into numeric quantities, it can be proved that Turing-computable functions are partial recursive. (For proof, refer Mendelson (1964).)

EXERCISES

1. Test which of the following functions are total. If a function is not total, specify the arguments for which the function is defined.
  (a) $f(x) = x/3$ over N.
  (b) $f(x) = 1/(x - 1)$ over N.
  (c) $f(x) = x^2 - 4$ over N.
  (d) $f(x) = x + 1$ over N.
  (e) $f(x) = x^2$ over N.

2. Show that the following functions are primitive recursive:

  (a) $\chi_{\{0\}}(x) = \begin{cases} 1 & \text{if } x = 0 \\ 0 & \text{if } x \neq 0 \end{cases}$

  (b) $f(x) = x^2$.

  (c) $f(x, y) = $ maximum of x and y.

  (d) $f(x) = \begin{cases} x/2 & \text{when } x \text{ is even} \\ (x - 1)/2 & \text{when } x \text{ is odd} \end{cases}$

  (e) The sign function defined by
     $\text{sgn}(0) = 0, \qquad \text{sgn}(x) = 1 \quad \text{if } x > 0$.

  (f) $L(x, y) = \begin{cases} 1 & \text{if } x > y \\ 0 & \text{if } x \leq y \end{cases}$

  (g) $E(x, y) = \begin{cases} 1 & \text{if } x = y \\ 0 & \text{if } x \neq y \end{cases}$

3. Compute $A(3, 2)$, $A(2, 3)$, $A(3, 3)$.

4. Show that the following functions are primitive recursive:
  (a) $q(x, y) = $ the quotient obtained when x is divided by y

(b) $r(x, y)$ = the remainder obtained when x is divided by y

(c) $f(x) = \begin{cases} 2x & \text{if } x \text{ is a perfect square} \\ 2x + 1 & \text{otherwise} \end{cases}$

5. Show that $f(x)$ = integral part of $\sqrt{x}$ is partial recursive.

6. Show that the Fibonacci numbers are generated by a primitive recursive function.

7. Let $f(0) = 1, f(1) = 2, f(2) = 3$ and $f(x + 3) = f(x) + f(x + 1)^2 + f(x + 2)^3$. Show that $f(x)$ is primitive recursive.

8. The characteristic function χ_A of a given set A is defined as

$$\chi_A(a) = \begin{cases} 0 & \text{if } a \notin A \\ 1 & \text{if } a \in A \end{cases}$$

If A, B are subsets of N and χ_A, χ_B are recursive, show that $\chi_{A^c}, \chi_{A \cup B}, \chi_{A \cap B}$ are also recursive.

9. Show that the characteristic function of the set of all even numbers is recursive. Prove that the characteristic function of the set of all odd integers is recursive.

10. Show that the function $f(x, y) = x - y$ is partial recursive.

11. Show that a constant function over N, i.e. $f(n) = k$ for all n in N, where k is a fixed number, is primitive recursive.

12. Show that the characteristic function of a finite subset of N is primitive recursive.

13. Show that the addition function $f_1(x, y)$ is Turing-computable. (Represent x and y in tally notation and use concatenation.)

14. Show that the Turing machine M in the Post notation (i.e. the transition function specified by quadruples) can be simulated by a Turing machine M (as defined in Chapter 7).

[*Hint*: The transition given by a quadruple can be simulated by two quintuples of M' by adding new states to M'.]

15. Compute $Z(4)$ using the Turing machine constructed for computing the zero function.

16. Compute $S(3)$ using the Turing machine which computes S.

17. Compute $U_1^3(2, 1, 1), U_2^3(1, 2, 1), U_3^3(1, 2, 1)$ using the Turing machines which can compute the projection functions.

18. Construct a Turing machine which can compute $f(x) = x + 2$.

19. Construct a Turing machine which can compute $f(x_1, x_2) = x_1 + 2$ for the arguments 1, 2 (i.e. $x_1 = 1, x_2 = 2$).

20. Construct a Turing machine which can compute $f(x_1, x_2) = x_1 + x_2$ for the arguments 2, 3 (i.e. $x_1 = 2, x_2 = 3$).

10

Propositions and Predicates

In this chapter we introduce propositions and logical connectives. Normal forms for well-formed formulas are given. Predicates are introduced. Finally we discuss rules of inference for propositional calculus and predicate calculus.

10.1 PROPOSITIONS (OR STATEMENTS)

A proposition (or a statement) is a declarative sentence that is either true or false, but not both. When it is true we say that its truth value is T. When it is false we say that its truth value is F.

Consider, for example, the following sentences in English:

1. New Delhi is the capital of India.
2. The square of 4 is 16.
3. The square of 5 is 27.
4. Every college will have a computer by 2000 A.D.
5. Mathematical logic is a difficult subject.
6. Madras is a beautiful city.
7. Bring me coffee.
8. No, thank you.
9. This statement is false.

The sentences 1–3 are propositions. Sentences 1 and 2 have truth value T. Sentence 3 has truth value F. Although we cannot *know* the truth value of 4 at present, we definitely know that it is true or false, but not both. So 4 is a proposition. For the same reason, 5 and 6 are propositions; for any person, mathematical logic is either difficult or not difficult, but not both. For 7 and 8, we cannot assign truth values as they are not declarative sentences. Sentence 9 looks like a proposition. However, if we assign the truth value T for sentence 9, then the sentence asserts that it is false. If we assign the truth value F for sentence 9, then the sentence asserts that it is true. Thus in any case, 9 has both truth values (or no truth value). Therefore, 9 is not a proposition.

We use capital letters to denote propositions.

10.1.1 CONNECTIVES (PROPOSITIONAL CONNECTIVES OR LOGICAL CONNECTIVES)

Just as we form new sentences from given sentences using 'and', 'but', 'if', etc., we can get new propositions from given propositions using 'connectives'. But the new sentence obtained from the given propositions using connectives will be a proposition only when the new sentence has a truth value T or F (but not both). The truth value of the new sentence depends on the (logical) connectives and the truth value of the given propositions.

Let us define the following connectives:

(i) Negation (NOT)
(ii) Conjunction (AND)
(iii) Disjunction (OR)
(iv) Implication (IF ... THEN ...)
(v) If and only if.

(i) Negation (NOT)

If P is a proposition then negation P or NOT P (denoted by $\neg P$) is a proposition whose truth value is T if P has truth value F, and F if P has truth value T. Usually, the truth values of the proposition defined using a connective is given by a table called truth table for that connective (Table 10.1).

Table 10.1   Truth Table for Negation

P	$\neg P$
T	F
F	T

(ii) Conjunction (AND)

If P and Q are two propositions, then the conjunction of P and Q (read as "P and Q") is a proposition whose truth values are given in the Truth Table 10.2 and denoted by $P \wedge Q$.

Table 10.2   Truth Table for Conjunction

P	Q	$P \wedge Q$
T	T	T
T	F	F
F	T	F
F	F	F

(iii) Disjunction (OR)

If P and Q are two propositions, then the disjunction of P and Q (read as P or Q) is a proposition whose truth values are given in the truth table (Table 10.3), and denoted by $P \vee Q$.

It should be noted that $P \vee Q$ is true if P is true or Q is true or both are true. We define another connective Exclusive OR in Exercises where "OR" is used in the exclusive sense.

Table 10.3 Truth Table for Disjunction

P	Q	$P \vee Q$
T	T	T
T	F	T
F	T	T
F	F	F

EXAMPLE 10.1 If P represents "This book is nice" and Q represents "This book is cheap", write the following sentences in symbolic form:

    (a) This book is good and cheap.
    (b) This book is not good but cheap.
    (c) This book is costly but good.
    (d) This book is neither good nor cheap.
    (e) This book is good or cheap.

SOLUTION

    (a) is $P \wedge Q$.
    (b) is $(\neg P) \wedge Q$.
    (c) is $(\neg Q) \wedge P$.
    (d) is $(\neg P) \wedge (\neg Q)$.
    (e) is $P \vee Q$.

NOTE: The truth tables for $P \wedge Q$ and $Q \wedge P$ coincide. So $P \wedge Q$ and $Q \wedge P$ are equivalent (for the definition, see Section 10.1.4). But in natural languages this need not happen. For example, the two sentences, viz. I went to the Railway station and boarded the train, and I boarded the train and went to the Railway station, have different meanings. Obviously, we cannot write the second sentence in place of the first sentence.

(iv) Implication (IF ... THEN ...)

If P and Q are two propositions, then "IF P THEN Q" is a proposition whose truth values are given in the truth table (Table 10.4), and is denoted by $P \Rightarrow Q$. We also read $P \Rightarrow Q$ as "P implies Q".

Table 10.4 Truth Table for Implication

P	Q	$P \Rightarrow Q$
T	T	T
T	F	F
F	T	T
F	F	T

We can note that $P \Rightarrow Q$ assumes the truth value F only if P has truth value T and Q has truth value F. In all the other cases, $P \Rightarrow Q$ assumes the truth value T. In the case of natural languages, we are concerned about the truth values of the sentence "IF P THEN Q" only when P is true. When P is false, we are not concerned about the truth value of "IF P THEN Q". But in the case of mathematical logic, we have to definitely specify the truth value of $P \Rightarrow Q$ in all cases. So the truth value of $P \Rightarrow Q$ is defined as T when P has truth value F (irrespective of the truth value of Q).

EXAMPLE 10.2 Find the truth values of the following propositions:

1. If 2 is not an integer, then 1/2 is an integer.
2. If 2 is an integer then 1/2 is an integer.

SOLUTION Let P and Q be "2 is an integer", "1/2 is an integer", respectively. Then proposition 1 is true (as P is false and Q is false) and proposition 2 is false (as P is true and Q is false).

The above example illustrates the following: "We can prove anything if we start with a false assumption." $P \Rightarrow Q$ whenever we want to 'translate' any one of the following: "P only if Q", "P is a sufficient condition for Q", "Q is a necessary condition for P", "Q follows from P", "Q whenever P", "Q provided P".

(v) If and Only If

If P and Q are two statements, then P if and only if Q (denoted by $P \Leftrightarrow Q$) is a statement whose truth value is T when the truth values of P and Q are the same and whose truth value is F when the statements differ. The truth table is given in Table 10.5.

Table 10.5 Truth Table for If and Only If

P	Q	$P \Leftrightarrow Q$
T	T	T
T	F	F
F	T	F
F	F	T

Table 10.6 summarises the representation and meaning of logical connectives:

Table 10.6 Logical Connectives

Connective	Resulting proposition	Read as
Negation $\neg$	$\neg P$	NOT P
Conjunction $\wedge$	$P \wedge Q$	P AND Q
Disjunction $\vee$	$P \vee Q$	P OR Q (or both)
Implication $\Rightarrow$	$P \Rightarrow Q$	IF P THEN Q (P IMPLIES Q)
IF AND ONLY IF $\Leftrightarrow$	$P \Leftrightarrow Q$	P IF AND ONLY IF Q

EXAMPLE 10.3 Translate the following sentences into propositional forms:

(a) If it is not raining and I have time then I will go to a movie.
(b) It is raining and I will not go to a movie.
(c) It is not raining.
(d) I will not go to a movie.
(e) I will go to a movie only if it is not raining.

SOLUTION Let P be the proposition "It is raining".
Let Q be the proposition "I have time".
Let R be the proposition "I will go to a movie".

Then

(a) is $(\neg P \wedge Q) \Rightarrow R$.
(b) is $P \wedge \neg R$.
(c) is $\neg P$.
(d) is $\neg R$.
(e) $R \Rightarrow \neg P$.

EXAMPLE 10.4 If P, Q, R are propositions given in Example 10.3, write the sentences in English corresponding to (a) $(\neg P \wedge Q) \Leftrightarrow R$, (b) $(Q \Rightarrow R) \wedge (R \Rightarrow Q)$, (c) $\neg (Q \vee R)$, and (d) $R \Rightarrow \neg P \wedge Q$.

SOLUTION Proposition (a) can be expressed as "I will go to a movie if and only if it is not raining and I have time"; proposition (b) can be expressed as "I will go to a movie if and only if I have time", and propositions (c) and (d) can be expressed as "It is not the case that I have time or I will go to a movie" and "I will go to a movie, only if it is not raining or I have time", respectively.

10.1.2 WELL-FORMED FORMULAS

Consider $P \wedge Q$ and $Q \wedge P$, where P and Q are any two propositions. The truth tables of these two propositions are identical. This happens when we have any proposition in place of P and any proposition in place of Q. So we can develop the concept of a propositional variable (corresponding to propositions) and well-formed formulas (corresponding to propositions involving connectives).

Definition 10.1 A propositional variable is a symbol representing any proposition. We note that usually a real variable is represented by the symbol x. This means that x is not a real number but can take a real value. Similarly, a propositional variable is not a proposition but can be replaced by a proposition.

Definition 10.2 A well-formed formula (wff) is defined recursively as follows:

(i) If P is a propositional variable then it is a wff.
(ii) If α is a wff, then $\neg \alpha$ is a wff.
(iii) If α and β are well-formed formulas, then $(\alpha \vee \beta)$, $(\alpha \wedge \beta)$, $(\alpha \Rightarrow \beta)$, $(\alpha \Leftrightarrow \beta)$ are well-formed formulas.
(iv) A string of symbols is a wff if and only if it is obtained by finitely many applications of (i)–(iii).

NOTE: A wff is not a proposition, but if we substitute the proposition in place of propositional variable, we get a proposition. For example,

   (i) $(\neg (P \vee Q) \wedge (\neg Q \wedge R)) \Rightarrow Q)$ is a wff.
   (ii) $(\neg P \wedge Q) \Leftrightarrow Q$ is a wff.

NOTE: We can drop parentheses when there is no ambiguity. For example, in propositions we can remove the outermost parentheses. We can also specify the hierarchy of connectives and avoid parentheses.

For the sake of convenience, we can refer to a wff as a formula.

10.1.3   TRUTH-TABLE FOR A WELL-FORMED FORMULA

If we replace the propositional variables in a formula α by propositions, we get a proposition involving connectives. The table giving the truth value of such proposition obtained by replacing the propositional variables by arbitrary propositions is called the truth table of α.

If α involves n propositional constants, we have 2^n possible combinations of truth values of propositions replacing the variables.

EXAMPLE 10.5   Obtain the truth table for $\alpha = (P \vee Q) \wedge (P \Rightarrow Q) \wedge (Q \Rightarrow P)$.

SOLUTION   The truth table of the given wff is given in Table 10.7.

Table 10.7   Truth Table of Example 10.5

P	Q	$P \vee Q$	$P \Rightarrow Q$	$(P \vee Q) \wedge (P \Rightarrow Q)$	$(Q \Rightarrow P)$	α
T	T	T	T	T	T	T
T	F	T	F	F	T	F
F	T	T	T	T	F	F
F	F	F	T	F	T	F

EXAMPLE 10.6   Construct the truth table for $\alpha = (P \vee Q) \Rightarrow ((P \vee R) \Rightarrow (R \vee Q))$.

SOLUTION   The truth table is given in Table 10.8.

Some formulas have the truth value T for all possible assignments of truth values to the propositional variables. For example, $P \vee \neg P$ has the truth value T irrespective of the truth value of P. Such formulas are called tautologies.

Definition 10.3   A tautology or a universally true formula is a well-formed formula whose truth value is T for all possible assignments of truth values to the propositional variables.

For example, $P \vee \neg P$, $(P \wedge Q) \Rightarrow P$ and $((P \Rightarrow Q) \wedge (Q \Rightarrow R)) \Rightarrow (P \Rightarrow R)$ are tautologies.

NOTE: When it is not clear whether a given formula is a tautology, we can construct the truth table and verify that the truth value is T for all combinations of truth values of the propositional variables appearing in the given formula.

Table 10.8   Truth Table of Example 10.6

P	Q	R	$P \vee R$	$R \vee Q$	$(P \vee R) \Rightarrow (R \vee Q)$	$(P \vee Q)$	α
T	T	T	T	T	T	T	T
T	T	F	T	T	T	T	T
T	F	T	T	T	T	T	T
T	F	F	T		F	T	F
F	T	T	T	T	T	T	T
F	T	F	F		T	T	T
F	F	T	T	T	T	F	T
F	F	F	F	F	F	F	T

EXAMPLE 10.7   Show that $\alpha = (P \Rightarrow (Q \Rightarrow R)) \Rightarrow ((P \Rightarrow Q) \Rightarrow (P \Rightarrow R))$ is a tautology.

SOLUTION   We give the truth table for α in Table 10.9.

Table 10.9   Truth Table of Example 10.7

P	Q	R	$Q \Rightarrow R$	$P \Rightarrow (Q \Rightarrow R)$	$P \Rightarrow Q$	$P \Rightarrow R$	$(P \Rightarrow Q) \Rightarrow (P \Rightarrow R)$	α
T	T	T	T	T	T	T	T	T
T	T	F	F	F	T	F	F	T
T	F	T	T	T	F	T	T	T
T	F	F	T	T	F	F	T	T
F	T	T	T	T	T	T	T	T
F	T	F	F	T	T	T	T	T
F	F	T	T	T	T	T	T	T
F	F	F	T	T	T	T	T	T

Definition 10.4   A contradiction (or absurdity) is a wff whose truth value is F for all possible assignments of truth values to the propositional variables.

$P \wedge \neg P$ and $(P \wedge Q) \wedge \neg Q$ are, for example, contradictions.

NOTE: α is a contradiction if and only if $\neg \alpha$ is a tautology.

10.1.4   EQUIVALENCE OF WELL-FORMED FORMULAS

Definition 10.5   Two wffs α and β in propositional variables $P_1, P_2, \ldots, P_n$ are equivalent (or logically equivalent) if the formula $\alpha \Leftrightarrow \beta$ is a tautology. When α and β are equivalent, we write $\alpha \equiv \beta$.

NOTE: α and β are equivalent if the truth tables for α and β are the same.

For example, $P \wedge Q \equiv Q \wedge P$ and $P \wedge P \equiv P$.

NOTE: It is important to note the difference between $\alpha \Leftrightarrow \beta$ and $\alpha \equiv \beta$. $\alpha \Leftrightarrow \beta$ is a formula, whereas $\alpha \equiv \beta$ is not a formula, but it denotes the relation between α and β.

EXAMPLE 10.8   Show that $(P \Rightarrow (Q \vee R)) \equiv ((P \Rightarrow Q) \vee (P \Rightarrow R))$.

SOLUTION Let $\alpha = (P \Rightarrow Q \vee R)$ and $\beta = ((P \Rightarrow Q) \vee (P \Rightarrow R))$. We construct the truth values of α and β for all assignments of truth values to the variables P, Q and R. These are given in Table 10.10.

Table 10.10 Truth Table of Example 10.8

P	Q	R	$Q \vee R$	$P \Rightarrow Q \vee R$	$P \Rightarrow Q$	$P \Rightarrow R$	$(P \Rightarrow Q) \vee (P \Rightarrow R)$
T	T	T	T	T	T	T	T
T	T	F	T	T	T	F	T
T	F	T	T	T	F	T	T
T	F	F	F	F	F	F	F
F	T	T	T	T	T	T	T
F	T	F	T	T	T	T	T
F	F	T	T	T	T	T	T
F	F	F	F	T	T	T	T

As the columns corresponding to α and β coincide, $\alpha \equiv \beta$.

As the truth value of a tautology is T, irrespective of the truth values of propositional variables, we denote any tautology by **T**. Similarly, we denote any contradiction by **F**.

10.1.5 LOGICAL IDENTITIES

Some equivalences are useful for deducing other equivalences. We call them identities and give a list of such identities in Table 10.11.

The identities I_1–I_{12} can be used to simplify formulas. If a formula β is part of another formula α, and β is equivalent to β', then we can replace β by β' in α and the resulting wff is equivalent to α.

EXAMPLE 10.9 Show that $(P \wedge Q) \vee (P \wedge \neg Q) \equiv P$.

SOLUTION L.H.S. $= (P \wedge Q) \vee (P \wedge \neg Q)$

$\equiv P \wedge (Q \vee \neg Q)$ by using Distributive law (i.e. I_4)

$\equiv P \wedge \mathbf{T}$ by using I_8

$\equiv P$ by using I_8

EXAMPLE 10.10 Show that $(P \Rightarrow Q) \wedge (R \Rightarrow Q) \equiv (P \vee R) \Rightarrow Q$

SOLUTION L.H.S. $= (P \Rightarrow Q) \wedge (R \Rightarrow Q)$

$\equiv (\neg P \vee Q) \wedge (\neg R \vee Q)$ by using I_{12}

$\equiv (Q \vee \neg P) \wedge (Q \vee \neg R)$ by using Commutative law

$\equiv Q \vee (\neg P \wedge \neg R)$ by using Distributive law

$\equiv Q \vee (\neg (P \vee R))$ by using De Morgan's law

$\equiv (\neg (P \vee R)) \vee Q$ by using Commutative law

$$\equiv (P \vee R) \Rightarrow Q \quad \text{by using } I_{12}$$

$$= \text{R.H.S.}$$

Table 10.11   Logical Identities

I_1 Idempotent laws:

$$P \vee P \equiv P, \qquad P \wedge P \equiv P$$

I_2 Commutative laws:

$$P \vee Q \equiv Q \vee P, \qquad P \wedge Q \equiv Q \wedge P$$

I_3 Associative laws:

$$P \vee (Q \vee R) \equiv (P \vee Q) \vee R, \qquad P \wedge (Q \wedge R) \equiv (P \wedge Q) \wedge R$$

I_4 Distributive laws:

$$P \vee (Q \wedge R) \equiv (P \vee Q) \wedge (P \vee R), \qquad P(Q \vee R) \equiv (P \wedge Q) \vee (P \wedge R)$$

I_5 Absorption laws:

$$P \vee (P \wedge Q) \equiv P, \qquad P \wedge (P \vee Q) \equiv P$$

I_6 De Morgan's laws:

$$\neg(P \vee Q) \equiv \neg P \wedge \neg Q, \qquad \neg(P \wedge Q) \equiv \neg P \vee \neg Q$$

I_7 Double negation:

$$P \equiv \neg(\neg P)$$

I_8 $P \vee \neg P \equiv \mathbf{T}, \qquad P \wedge \neg P \equiv \mathbf{F}$

I_9 $P \vee \mathbf{T} \equiv \mathbf{T}, \qquad P \wedge \mathbf{T} \equiv P, \qquad P \vee \mathbf{F} \equiv P, \qquad P \wedge \mathbf{F} \equiv \mathbf{F}$

I_{10} $(P \Rightarrow Q) \wedge (P \Rightarrow \neg Q) \equiv \neg P$

I_{11} Contrapositive:

$$P \Rightarrow Q \equiv \neg Q \Rightarrow \neg P$$

I_{12} $P \Rightarrow Q \equiv (\neg P \vee Q)$

10.2   NORMAL FORMS OF WELL-FORMED FORMULAS

We have seen various well-formed formulas in terms of two propositional variables, say P and Q. We also know that two such formulas are equivalent if and only if they have the same truth table. The number of distinct truth tables for formulas in P and Q is 2^4 (As the possible combinations of truth values of P and Q are TT, TF, FT, FF, the truth table of any formula in P and Q has 4 rows. So the number of distinct truth tables is 2^4). Thus there are only 16 distinct (nonequivalent) formulas, and any formula in P and Q is equivalent to one of these 16 formulas.

In this section we give a method of reducing a given formula to an equivalent form called a 'normal form'. We also use 'sum' for disjunction, 'product' for conjunction, and 'literal' either for P or for $\neg P$, where P is any propositional variable.

Definition 10.6   An elementary product is a product of literals. An elementary sum is a sum of literals. For example, $P \wedge \neg Q, \neg P \wedge \neg Q, P \wedge Q, \neg P \wedge Q$ are elementary products. $P \vee \neg Q, P \vee \neg R$ are elementary sums.

Definition 10.7   A formula is in disjunctive normal form if it is a sum of elementary products. For example, $P \vee (Q \wedge R)$ and $P \vee (\neg Q \wedge R)$ are in disjunctive normal form. $P \wedge (Q \vee R)$ is not in disjunctive normal form.

10.2.1   CONSTRUCTION TO OBTAIN A DISJUNCTIVE NORMAL FORM OF A GIVEN FORMULA

Step 1   Eliminate $\Rightarrow$ and $\Leftrightarrow$ using logical identities. (We can use I_{12}, i.e., $P \Rightarrow Q \equiv (\neg P \vee Q)$.)

Step 2   Use De Morgan's laws (I_6) to eliminate $\neg$ before sums or products. The resulting formula has $\neg$ only before propositional variables, i.e. it involves sum, product and literals.

Step 3   Apply distributive laws (I_4) repeatedly to eliminate product of sums. The resulting formula will be a sum of products of literals i.e. sum of elementary products.

EXAMPLE 10.11   Obtain a disjunctive normal form of

$$P \vee (\neg P \Rightarrow (Q \vee (Q \Rightarrow \neg R)))$$

SOLUTION

$$P \vee (\neg P \Rightarrow (Q \vee (Q \Rightarrow \neg R)))$$

$\equiv P \vee (\neg P \Rightarrow (Q \vee (\neg Q \vee \neg R)))$ (step 1 using I_{12})

$\equiv P \vee (P \vee (Q \vee (\neg Q \vee \neg R)))$ (step 1 using I_{12} and I_7)

$\equiv P \vee P \vee Q \vee \neg Q \vee \neg R$ by using I_3

$\equiv P \vee Q \vee \neg Q \vee \neg R$ by using I_1

Thus, $P \vee Q \vee \neg Q \vee \neg R$ is a disjunctive normal form of the given formula.

EXAMPLE 10.12   Obtain the disjunctive normal form of

$$(P \wedge \neg (Q \wedge R)) \vee (P \Rightarrow Q).$$

SOLUTION

$$(P \wedge \neg (Q \wedge R)) \vee (P \Rightarrow Q)$$

$\equiv (P \wedge \neg (Q \wedge R)) \vee (\neg P \vee Q)$ (step 1 using I_{12})

$\equiv (P \wedge (\neg Q \vee \neg R)) \vee (\neg P \vee Q)$ (step 2 using I_7)

$\equiv (P \wedge \neg Q) \vee (P \wedge \neg R) \vee \neg P \vee Q$ (step 3 using I_4 and I_3)

Therefore, $(P \wedge \neg Q) \vee (P \wedge \neg R) \vee \neg P \vee Q$ is a disjunctive normal form of the given formula.

For the same formula, we may get different disjunctive normal forms. For example, $(P \wedge Q \wedge R) \vee (P \wedge Q \wedge \neg R)$ and $P \wedge Q$ are disjunctive normal forms of $P \wedge Q$. So, we introduce one more normal form, called *the principal disjunctive normal form* or *sum-of-products canonical form* in the next definition. The advantages of constructing principal disjunctive normal forms are:

(i) For a given formula, its principal disjunctive normal form is unique.

(ii) Two formulas are equivalent if and only if their principal disjunctive normal forms coincide.

Definition 10.8   A min term in n propositional variables $P_1, ..., P_n$ is $Q_1 \wedge Q_2 ... \wedge Q_n$, where each Q_i is either P_i or $\neg P_i$.

For example, the min terms in P_1 and P_2 are $P_1 \wedge P_2$, $\neg P_1 \wedge P_2$, $P_1 \wedge \neg P_2$, $\neg P_1 \wedge \neg P_2$. The number of min terms in n variables is 2^n.

Definition 10.9   A formula α is in principal disjunctive normal form if α is a sum of min terms.

10.2.2   CONSTRUCTION TO OBTAIN THE PRINCIPAL DISJUNCTIVE NORMAL FORM OF A GIVEN FORMULA

Step 1   Obtain a disjunctive normal form.

Step 2   Drop elementary products which are contradictions (such as $P \wedge \neg P$).

Step 3   If P_i and $\neg P_i$ are missing in an elementary product α, replace α by $(\alpha \wedge P_i) \vee (\alpha \wedge \neg P_i)$.

Step 4   Repeat step 3 until all elementary products are reduced to sum of min terms. Use idempotent laws to avoid repetition of min terms.

EXAMPLE 10.13   Obtain the canonical sum-of-products form (i.e. principal disjunctive normal form) of $\alpha = P \vee (\neg P \wedge \neg Q \wedge R)$.

SOLUTION α is already in disjunctive normal form. There are no contradictions. So we have to introduce missing variables (step 3). $\neg P \wedge \neg Q \wedge R$ in α is already a min term. Now,

$$P \equiv (P \wedge Q) \vee (P \wedge \neg Q)$$
$$\equiv ((P \wedge Q \wedge R) \vee (P \wedge Q \wedge \neg R)) \vee (P \wedge \neg Q \wedge R) \vee (P \wedge \neg Q \wedge \neg R)$$
$$\equiv ((P \wedge Q \wedge R) \vee (P \wedge Q \wedge \neg R)) \vee ((P \wedge \neg Q \wedge R) \vee (P \wedge \neg Q \wedge \neg R))$$

Therefore, the canonical sum-of-products form of α is

$$(P \wedge Q \wedge R) \vee (P \wedge Q \wedge \neg R) \vee (P \wedge \neg Q \wedge R)$$
$$\vee (P \wedge \neg Q \wedge \neg R) \vee (\neg P \wedge \neg Q \wedge R)$$

EXAMPLE 10.14   Obtain the principal disjunctive normal form of

$$\alpha = (\neg P \vee \neg Q) \Rightarrow (\neg P \wedge R)$$

SOLUTION

$\alpha = (\neg P \vee \neg Q) \Rightarrow (\neg P \wedge R)$

$\equiv (\neg(\neg P \vee \neg Q)) \vee (\neg P \wedge R)$ by using I_{12}

$\equiv (P \wedge Q) \vee (\neg P \wedge R)$ by using De Morgan's law

$\equiv ((P \wedge Q \wedge R) \vee (P \wedge Q \wedge \neg R)) \vee ((\neg P \wedge R \wedge Q) \vee (\neg P \wedge R \wedge \neg Q))$

$\equiv (P \wedge Q \wedge R) \vee (P \wedge Q \wedge \neg R) \vee (\neg P \wedge Q \wedge R) \vee (\neg P \wedge \neg Q \wedge R)$

So, the principal disjunctive normal form of α is

$$(P \wedge Q \wedge R) \vee (P \wedge Q \wedge \neg R) \vee (\neg P \wedge Q \wedge R) \vee (\neg P \wedge \neg Q \wedge R)$$

A min term of the form $Q_1 \wedge Q_2 \dots \wedge Q_n$ can be represented by $a_1 a_2 \dots a_n$, where $a_i = 0$ if $Q_i = \neg P_i$ and $a_i = 1$ if $Q_i = P_i$. So the principal disjunctive normal form can be represented by a 'sum' of binary strings. For example, $(P \wedge Q \wedge R) \vee (P \wedge Q \wedge \neg R) \vee (\neg P \wedge \neg Q \wedge R)$ is represented by $111 \vee 110 \vee 001$.

The min terms in two variables P and Q are 00, 01, 10, and 11. Each wff is equivalent to its principal disjunctive normal form. Every principal disjunctive normal form corresponds to the min terms in it, and hence to a subset of $\{00, 01, 10, 11\}$. As the number of subsets is 2^4, the number of distinct formulas is 16. (Refer to the remarks made at the beginning of this section.)

The truth table and the principal disjunctive normal form of α are closely related. Each min term corresponds to a particular assignment of truth values to the variables yielding truth value T to α. For example, $P \wedge Q \wedge \neg R$ corresponds to the assignment of T, T, F to P, Q and R, respectively. So, if the truth table of α is given, then the min terms are those corresponding to assignments yielding truth value T to α.

EXAMPLE 10.15 For a given formula α, the truth table is given in Table 10.12. Find the principal disjunctive normal form.

Table 10.12 Truth Table of Example 10.15

P	Q	R	α
T	T	T	T
T	T	F	F
T	F	T	F
T	F	F	T
F	T	T	T
F	T	F	F
F	F	T	F
F	F	F	F

SOLUTION We have T in the α-column corresponding to the rows 1, 4, 5 and 8. The min term corresponding to the first row is $P \wedge Q \wedge R$.

Similarly, the min terms corresponding to rows 4, 5 and 8 are $P \wedge \neg Q \wedge \neg R, \neg P \wedge Q \wedge R$ and $\neg P \wedge \neg Q \wedge \neg R$. Therefore, the principal disjunctive normal form of α is

$$(P \wedge Q \wedge R) \vee (P \wedge \neg Q \wedge \neg R) \vee (\neg P \wedge Q \wedge R) \vee (\neg P \wedge \neg Q \wedge \neg R)$$

We can form the 'dual' of disjunctive normal form which is termed as conjunctive normal form.

Definition 10.10   A formula is in conjunctive normal form if it is a product of elementary sums.

If α is in disjunctive normal form, then $\neg \alpha$ is in conjunctive normal form. (This can be seen by applying De Morgan's laws.) So to obtain the conjunctive normal form of α, we construct the disjunctive normal form of $\neg \alpha$ and use negation.

Definition 10.11   A max term in n propositional variables $P_1, P_2, ..., P_n$ is $Q_1 \vee Q_2 ... \vee Q_n$, where each Q_i is either P_i or $\neg P_i$.

Definition 10.12   A formula α is in principal conjunctive normal form if α is a product of max terms. For obtaining the principal conjunctive normal form of α, we can construct the principal disjunctive normal form of $\neg \alpha$ and apply negation ($\neg$).

EXAMPLE 10.16   Find the principal conjunctive normal form of $\alpha = P \vee (Q \Rightarrow R)$.

SOLUTION

$$\neg \alpha = \neg (P \vee (Q \Rightarrow R))$$

$$\equiv \neg (P \vee (\neg Q \vee R)) \qquad \text{by using } I_{12}$$

$$\equiv \neg P \wedge (\neg (\neg Q \vee R)) \quad \text{by using De Morgan's law}$$

$$\equiv \neg P \wedge (Q \wedge \neg R) \qquad \text{by using De Morgan's law and } I_7$$

$\neg P \wedge Q \wedge \neg R$ is the principal disjunctive normal form of $\neg \alpha$. Hence, the principal conjunctive normal form of α is

$$\neg (\neg P \wedge Q \wedge \neg R) = P \vee \neg Q \vee R$$

The logical identities given in Table 10.11 and the normal forms of well-formed formulas bear a close resemblance to identities in Boolean algebras and normal forms of Boolean functions. Actually, the propositions under $\vee$, $\wedge$ and $\neg$ form a Boolean algebra if equivalent propositions are identified. **T** and **F** act as bounds (i.e. 0 and 1 of a Boolean algebra). Also, the statement formulas form a Boolean algebra under $\vee$, $\wedge$ and $\neg$ if equivalent formulas are identified.

The normal forms of well-formed formulas correspond to normal forms of Boolean functions and we can 'minimise' a formula in a similar manner.

10.3   RULES OF INFERENCE FOR PROPOSITIONAL CALCULUS (STATEMENT CALCULUS)

In logical reasoning, a certain number of propositions are assumed to be true, and based on that assumption some other propositions are derived (deduced or inferred). In this section we give some important rules of logical reasoning or rules of inference. The propositions that are assumed to be true are called *hypotheses* or *premises*. The proposition derived by using the rules of inference is called a *conclusion*. The process of deriving conclusions based on the assumption of premises is called a *valid argument*. So in a valid argument we are concerned with the process of arriving at the conclusion rather than obtaining the conclusion.

The rules of inference are simply tautologies in the form of implication (i.e. $P \Rightarrow Q$). For example, $P \Rightarrow (P \vee Q)$ is such a tautology, and it is a rule of inference. We write this in the form $\dfrac{P}{\therefore P \vee Q}$. Here P denotes a premise. The proposition below the line, i.e. $P \vee Q$, is the conclusion.

We give in Table 10.13 some of the important rules of inference. Of course we can derive more rules of inference and use them in valid arguments.

For valid arguments, we can use the rules of inference given in Table 10.13. As logical identities given in Table 10.11 are two-way implications, we can also use them as rules of inference.

EXAMPLE 10.17   Can we conclude S from the following premises?

(i) $P \Rightarrow Q$
(ii) $P \Rightarrow R$
(iii) $\neg (Q \wedge R)$
(iv) $S \vee P$

SOLUTION   The valid argument for deducing S from the given four premises is given as a sequence. On the left, the well-formed formulas are given. On the right we indicate whether the proposition is a premise (hypothesis) or a conclusion. If it is a conclusion, we indicate the premises and the rules of inference or logical identities used for deriving the conclusion.

1. $P \Rightarrow Q$	Premise (i)
2. $P \Rightarrow R$	Premise (ii)
3. $(P \Rightarrow Q) \wedge (P \Rightarrow R)$	Lines 1, 2 and RI_2
4. $\neg (Q \wedge R)$	Premise (iii)
5. $\neg Q \vee \neg R$	Line 4 and De Morgan's law (I_6)
6. $\neg P \vee \neg P$	Lines 3, 5 and destructive dilemma (RI_9)
7. $\neg P$	Idempotent law I_1
8. $S \vee P$	Premise (iv)
9. S	Lines 7, 8 and disjunctive syllogism RI_6

Thus we can conclude S from the given premises.

EXAMPLE 10.18   Derive S from the following premises using a valid argument:

(i) $P \Rightarrow Q$
(ii) $Q \Rightarrow \neg R$
(iii) $P \vee S$
(iv) R

Table 10.13   Rules of Inference

Rules of Inference	Implication Form
RI_1: Addition	

$$\frac{P}{\therefore P \vee Q}$$

$$P \Rightarrow (P \vee Q)$$

RI_2: Conjunction

$$\frac{Q}{\therefore P \wedge Q}$$

$$P \wedge Q \Rightarrow P \wedge Q$$

RI_3: Simplification

$$\frac{P \wedge Q}{\therefore P}$$

$$(P \wedge Q) \Rightarrow P$$

RI_4: Modus ponens

$$\frac{\begin{array}{c} P \\ P \Rightarrow Q \end{array}}{\therefore Q}$$

$$(P \wedge (P \Rightarrow Q)) \Rightarrow Q$$

RI_5: Modus tollens

$$\frac{\begin{array}{c} \neg Q \\ P \Rightarrow Q \end{array}}{\therefore \neg P}$$

$$(\neg Q \wedge (P \Rightarrow Q)) \Rightarrow \neg P$$

RI_6: Disjunctive syllogism

$$\frac{\begin{array}{c} \neg P \\ P \vee Q \end{array}}{\therefore Q}$$

$$(\neg P \wedge (P \vee Q)) \Rightarrow Q$$

RI_7: Hypothetical syllogism

$$\frac{\begin{array}{c} P \Rightarrow Q \\ Q \Rightarrow R \end{array}}{\therefore P \Rightarrow R}$$

$$((P \Rightarrow Q) \wedge (Q \Rightarrow R)) \Rightarrow (P \Rightarrow R)$$

RI_8: Constructive dilemma

$$\frac{\begin{array}{c} (P \Rightarrow Q) \wedge (R \Rightarrow S) \\ P \vee R \end{array}}{\therefore Q \vee S}$$

$$(P \Rightarrow Q) \wedge (R \Rightarrow S) \wedge (P \vee R) \Rightarrow (Q \vee S)$$

RI_9: Destructive dilemma

$$\frac{\begin{array}{c} (P \Rightarrow Q) \wedge (R \Rightarrow S) \\ \neg Q \vee \neg S \end{array}}{\therefore P \vee R}$$

$$(P \Rightarrow Q) \wedge (R \Rightarrow S) \wedge (\neg Q \vee \neg S) \Rightarrow (\neg P \vee \neg R)$$

SOLUTION

1.	$P \Rightarrow Q$	Premise (i)
2.	$Q \Rightarrow \neg R$	Premise (ii)
3.	$P \Rightarrow \neg R$	Lines 1, 2 and hypothetical syllogism RI_7
4.	R	Premise (iv)
5.	$\neg(\neg R)$	Line 4 and double negation I_7

6. $\neg P$ Lines 3, 5 and modus tollens RI_5
7. $P \vee S$ Premise (iii)
8. S Lines 6, 7 and disjunctive syllogism RI_6

Thus we have derived S from the given premises.

EXAMPLE 10.19 Check the validity of the following argument:

If Ram has completed B.E. Computer Science or M.B.A., then he is assured of a good job. If Ram is assured of a good job, he is happy. Ram is not happy. So Ram has not completed M.B.A.

SOLUTION We can name the propositions in the following way:

P denotes "Ram has completed B.E. Computer Science".
Q denotes "Ram has completed M.B.A.".
R denotes "Ram is assured of a good job".
S denotes "Ram is happy".

The given premises are:

(i) $(P \vee Q) \Rightarrow R$.
(ii) $R \Rightarrow S$.
(iii) $\neg S$.

The conclusion is $\neg Q$.

1. $(P \vee Q) \Rightarrow R$ Premise (i)
2. $R \Rightarrow S$ Premise (ii)
3. $(P \vee Q) \Rightarrow S$ Lines 1, 2 and hypothetical syllogism RI_7
4. $\neg S$ Premise (iii)
5. $\neg(P \vee Q)$ Lines 3, 4 and modus tollens
6. $\neg P \wedge \neg Q$ De Morgan's law I_6
7. $\neg Q$ Line 6 and simplification RI_3

Thus the argument is valid.

EXAMPLE 10.20 Test the validity of the following argument:

If milk is black then every crow is white. If every crow is white then it has four legs. If every crow has four legs then every buffalo is white and brisk. The milk is black.

Therefore, the buffalo is white.

SOLUTION We name the propositions in the following way:

P denotes "The milk is black".
Q denotes "Every crow is white".
R denotes "Every crow has four legs".
S denotes "Every buffalo is white".
T denotes "Every buffalo is brisk".

The given premises are:

(i) $P \Rightarrow Q$.

    (ii) $Q \Rightarrow R$.

    (iii) $R \Rightarrow S \wedge T$.

    (iv) P.

The conclusion is S.

1. P	Premise (iv)
2. $P \Rightarrow Q$	Premise (i)
3. Q	Modus ponens RI_4
4. $Q \Rightarrow R$	Premise (ii)
5. R	Modus ponens RI_4
6. $R \Rightarrow S \wedge T$	Premise (iii)
7. $S \wedge T$	Modus ponens RI_4
8. S	Simplification RI_3

Thus the argument is valid.

10.4   PREDICATE CALCULUS

Consider two propositions "Ram is a student", and "Sam is a student". As propositions, there is no relation between them, but we know they have something in common. Both Ram and Sam share the property of being a student. We can replace the two propositions by a single statement "x is a student". By replacing x by Ram or Sam (or any other name), we get many propositions. The common feature expressed by "is a student" is called a predicate. In predicate calculus we deal with sentences involving predicates. Statements involving predicates occur in Mathematics and programming languages. For example, "$2x + 3y = 4z$", "IF (D. GE. 0.0) GO TO 20" are statements in Mathematics and FORTRAN, respectively involving predicates. Some logical deductions are possible only by 'separating' predicates.

10.4.1   PREDICATES

A part of a declarative sentence describing the properties of an object or relation among objects is called a predicate. For example, "is a student" is a predicate.

    Sentences involving predicates describing the property of objects are denoted by P(x), where P denotes the predicate and x is a variable denoting any object. For example, P(x) can denote "x is a student". In this sentence, x is a variable and P denotes the predicate "is a student".

    The sentence "x is the father of y" also involves a predicate "is the father of ". Here the predicate describes the relation between two persons. We can write this sentence as $F(x, y)$. Similarly, $2x + 3y = 4z$ can be described by $S(x, y, z)$.

NOTE: Although, P(x), involving a predicate looks like a proposition, it is not a proposition. As P(x) involves a variable x, we cannot assign a truth value to P(x). However, if we replace x by an individual object, we get a proposition. For example, if we replace x by Ram in P(x), we get the proposition "Ram is a student". (We can denote this proposition by P (Ram).) If we replace x by 'A cat', then also we get a proposition (whose truth value is F). $S(2, 0, 1)$ is the proposition

$2 \cdot 2 + 3 \cdot 0 = 4 \cdot 1$ (whose truth value is T). $S(1, 1, 1)$ is the proposition $2 \cdot 1 + 3 \cdot 1 = 4 \cdot 1$ (whose truth value is F).

The following definition is regarding possible 'values' which can be assigned to variables.

Definition 10.13 For a declarative sentence involving a predicate, the universe of discourse, or simply the universe, is the set of all possible values which can be assigned to variables.

For example, the universe of discourse for $P(x)$: "x is a student", can be taken as the set of all human names; the universe of discourse for $E(n)$: "n is an even integer", can be taken as the set of all integers (or the set of all real numbers).

NOTE: In most examples, the universe of discourse is not specified but can be easily given.

Remark We have seen that by giving values to variables, we can get propositions from declarative sentences involving predicates. Some sentences involving variables can also be assigned truth values. For example, consider "There exists x such that $x^2 = 5$", and "For all x, $x^2 = (-x)^2$". Both these sentences can be assigned truth values (T in both cases). "There exists" and "For all" quantify the variables.

Universal and Existential Quantifier

The phrase 'for all' (denoted by $\forall$) is called the universal quantifier. Using this symbol, we can write "For all x, $x^2 = (-x)^2$" as $\forall\, xQ(x)$, where $Q(x)$ is "$x^2 = (-x)^2$".

The phrase 'there exists' (denoted by $\exists$) is called the existential quantifier. The sentence "There exists x such that $x^2 = 5$" can be written as $\exists xR(x)$, where $R(x)$ is '$x^2 = 5$'.

$P(x)$ in $\forall\, xP(x)$ or in $\exists\, xP(x)$ is called the scope of the quantifier $\forall$ or $\exists$.

NOTE: The symbol $\forall$ can be read as 'for every', 'for any', 'for each', 'for arbitrary'. The symbol $\exists$ can be read as 'for some' for 'at least one'.

When we use quantifiers, we should specify the universe of discourse. If we change the universe of discourse, the truth value may change. For example, consider $\exists xR(x)$, where $R(x)$ is $x^2 = 5$. If the universe of discourse is the set of all integers, then $\exists xR(x)$ is false. If the universe of discourse is the set of all real numbers, then $\exists xR(x)$ is true (when $x = \pm \sqrt{5}, x^2 = 5$).

The logical connectives involving predicates can be used for declarative sentences involving predicates. The following example illustrates the use of connectives.

EXAMPLE 10.21 Express the following sentences involving predicates in symbolic form:

1. All students are clever.
2. Some students are not successful.
3. Every clever student is successful.

4. There are some successful students who are not clever.
5. Some students are clever and successful.

SOLUTION   As quantifiers are involved, we have to specify the universe of discourse. We can take the universe of discourse as the set of all students.

Let $C(x)$ denote "x is clever".
Let $S(x)$ denote "x is successful".

Then sentence 1 can be written as $\forall x C(x)$. Sentences 2–5 can be written as

$$\exists x(\neg S(x)), \qquad \forall x(C(x) \Rightarrow S(x)),$$

$$\exists x(S(x) \wedge \neg C(x)), \qquad \exists x(C(x) \wedge S(x))$$

10.4.2   WELL-FORMED FORMULAS OF PREDICATE CALCULUS

A well-formed formula (wff) of predicate calculus is a string of variables such as $x_1, x_2, ..., x_n$, connectives, parentheses and quantifiers defined recursively by the following rules:

(i) $P(x_1, ..., x_n)$ is a wff, where P is a predicate involving n variables $x_1, x_2, ..., x_n$.

(ii) If α is a wff, then $\neg\alpha$ is a wff.

(iii) If α and β are wffs, then $\alpha \vee \beta, \alpha \wedge \beta, \alpha \Rightarrow \beta, \alpha \Leftrightarrow \beta$ are also wffs.

(iv) If α is a wff and x is any variable, then $\forall x(\alpha), \exists x(\alpha)$ are wffs.

(v) A string is a wff if and only if it is obtained by finitely many applications of rules (i) – (iv).

NOTE: A proposition can be viewed as a sentence involving a predicate with 0 variables. So propositions are wffs of predicate calculus by rule (i).

We call wffs of predicate calculus as predicate formulas for convenience. The well-formed formulas introduced in Section 10.1 can be called proposition formulas (or statement formulas) to distinguish them from predicate formulas.

Definition 10.14   Let α and β be two predicate formulas in variables $x_1, ..., x_n$, and let U be a universe of discourse for α and β. Then α and β are equivalent to each other over U if for every possible assignment of values to each variable in α and β the resulting statements have the same truth values. We can write $\alpha \equiv \beta$ over U.

We say that α and β are equivalent to each other $(\alpha \equiv \beta)$ if $\alpha \equiv \beta$ over U for every universe of discourse U.

Remark   In predicate formulas the predicate variables may or may not be quantified. We can classify the predicate variables in a predicate formula, depending on whether they are quantified or not. This leads to the following definitions.

Definition 10.15   If a formula of the form $\exists x P(x)$ or $\forall x P(x)$ occurs as part of a predicate formula α, then such part is called an x-bound part of α, and the occurrence of x is called a bound occurrence of x. An occurrence of x is free if it is not a bound occurrence. A predicate variable in α is free if its occurrence is free in any part of α.

In $\alpha = (\exists x_1 P(x_1, x_2)) \wedge (\forall x_2 Q(x_2, x_3))$, for example, the occurrence of x_1 in $\exists x_1 P(x_1, x_2)$ is a bound occurrence and that of x_2 is free. In $\forall x_2 Q(x_2, x_3)$, the occurrence of x_2 is a bound occurrence. The occurrence of x_3 in α is free.

NOTE: Quantified parts of a predicate formula such as $\forall x P(x)$ or $\exists x P(x)$ are propositions. We can assign values from the universe of discourse only to free variables in a predicate formula α.

Definition 10.16 A predicate formula is valid if for all possible assignments of values from any universe of discourse to free variables, the resulting propositions have truth value T.

Definition 10.17 A predicate formula is satisfiable if for some assignment of values to predicate variables the resulting proposition has truth value T.

Definition 10.18 A predicate formula is unsatisfiable if for all possible assignments of values from any universe of discourse to predicate variables the resulting propositions have truth value F.

We note that valid predicate formulas correspond to tautologies among proposition formulas and unsatisfiable predicate formulas correspond to contradictions.

10.5 RULES OF INFERENCE FOR PREDICATE CALCULUS

Before discussing the rules of inference, we note that: (a) proposition formulas are also predicate formulas; (b) predicate formulas where all the variables are quantified are proposition formulas. Therefore, all the rules of inference for proposition formulas are also applicable for predicate calculus wherever necessary.

For predicate formulas not involving connectives such as $A(x)$, $P(x, y)$, we can get equivalences and rules of inference similar to those given in Tables 10.11 and 10.13. For Example, corresponding to I_6 in Table 10.11 we get $\neg(P(x) \vee Q(x)) \equiv \neg(P(x)) \wedge \neg(Q(x))$. Corresponding to RI_3 in Table 10.13 $P \wedge Q \Rightarrow P$, we get $P(x) \wedge Q(x) \Rightarrow P(x)$. Thus we can replace propositional variables by predicate variables in Tables 10.11 and 10.13.

Some necessary equivalences involving the two quantifiers and valid implications are given in Table 10.14.

Sometimes when we wish to derive some conclusion from a given set of premises involving quantifiers, we may have to eliminate the quantifiers before applying the rules of inference for proposition formulas. Also, when the conclusion involves quantifiers, we may have to introduce quantifiers. The necessary rules of inference for addition and deletion of quantifiers are given in Table 10.15.

EXAMPLE 10.22 Discuss the validity of the following argument:

(i) All graduates are educated.
(ii) Ram is a graduate. Therefore,
(iii) Ram is educated.

Table 10.14   Equivalences Involving Quantifiers

I_{13}	Distributivity of $\exists$ over $\vee$:
	$\exists x(P(x) \vee Q(x)) \equiv \exists xP(x) \vee \exists xQ(x)$
	$\exists x(P \vee Q(x)) \equiv P \vee (\exists xQ(x))$
I_{14}	Distributivity of $\forall$ over $\wedge$:
	$\forall x(P(x) \wedge Q(x)) \equiv \forall xP(x) \wedge \forall xQ(x)$
	$\forall x(P \wedge Q(x)) \equiv P \wedge (\forall xQ(x))$
I_{15}	$\neg(\exists xP(x)) \equiv \forall x \ \neg(P(x))$
I_{16}	$\neg(\forall xP(x)) \equiv \exists x \ \neg(P(x))$
I_{17}	$\exists x(P \wedge Q(x)) \equiv P \wedge (\exists xQ(x))$
I_{18}	$\forall x(P \vee Q(x)) \equiv P \vee (\forall xQ(x))$
RI_{10}	$\forall xP(x) \Rightarrow \exists xP(x)$
RI_{11}	$\forall xP(x) \vee \forall xQ(x) \Rightarrow \forall x(P(x) \vee Q(x))$
RI_{12}	$\exists x(P(x) \wedge Q(x)) \Rightarrow \exists xP(x) \wedge \exists xQ(x)$

Table 10.15   Rules of Inference for Addition and
Deletion of Quantifiers

RI_{13}: Universal instantiation

$$\frac{\forall xP(x)}{\therefore P(c)}$$

c is some element of the universe.

RI_{14}: Existential instantiation

$$\frac{\exists xP(x)}{\therefore P(c)}$$

c is some element for which $P(c)$ is true.

RI_{15}: Universal generalisation

$$\frac{P(x)}{\forall xP(x)}$$

x should not be free in any of the given premises.

RI_{16}: Existential generalisation

$$\frac{P(c)}{\therefore \exists xP(x)}$$

c is some element of the universe.

SOLUTION   Let $G(x)$ denote "x is a graduate".

Let $E(x)$ denote "x is educated".
Let R denote "Ram".

So the premises are $\forall x(G(x) \Rightarrow E(x))$ and $G(R)$. The conclusion is $E(R)$.

$\forall x(G(x) \Rightarrow E(x))$	Premise (i)
$G(R) \Rightarrow E(R)$	Universal instantiation RI_{13}

$G(R)$ Premise (ii)

$\therefore\ E(R)$ Modus ponens RI_4

Thus the conclusion, viz. (iii), is valid.

EXAMPLE 10.23 Discuss the validity of the following argument: All graduates
can read and write. Ram can read and write. Therefore, Ram is a graduate.

SOLUTION Let $G(x)$ denote "x is a graduate". Let $L(x)$ denote "x can read and
write". Let R denote "Ram".

The premises are: $\forall x(G(x) \Rightarrow L(x))$ and $L(R)$.

The conclusion is $G(R)$.

$((G(R) \Rightarrow L(R)) \wedge L(R)) \Rightarrow G(R)$ is not a tautology.

So we cannot derive $G(R)$. For example, a school boy can read and write
and he is not a graduate.

EXAMPLE 10.24 Discuss the validity of the following argument: All educated
persons are well behaved. Ram is educated. No well-behaved person is quarrelsome.
Therefore, Ram is not quarrelsome.

SOLUTION Let the universe of discourse be the set of all educated persons.

Let $P(x)$ denote "x is well-behaved".

Let y denote "Ram".

Let $Q(x)$ denote "x is quarrelsome".

So the premises are:

(i) $\forall x P(x)$.

(ii) y is a particular element of the universe of discourse.

(iii) $\forall x(P(x) \Rightarrow \neg Q(x))$.

To obtain the conclusion, we have the following arguments:

1. $\forall x P(x)$ Premise (i)
2. $P(y)$ Universal instantiation RI_{13}
3. $\forall x(P(x) \Rightarrow \neg Q(x))$ Premise (iii)
4. $P(y) \Rightarrow \neg Q(y)$ Universal instantiation RI_{13}
5. $P(y)$ Line 2
6. $\neg Q(y)$ Modus ponens RI_4

$\neg Q(y)$ means "Ram is not quarrelsome". Thus the argument is valid.

EXERCISES

1. Which of the following sentences are propositions?

(a) A triangle has three sides.

(b) 11111 is a prime number.

(c) Every dog is an animal.

(d) Ram ran home.

(e) A regular set is a context-free language.

(f) $\{a^n b^n \mid n \geq 1\}$ is a regular set.

(g) Go home and take rest.

2. Express the following sentence in symbolic form: For any two numbers a and b, only one of the following holds: $a < b$, $a = b$, and $a > b$.

3. The connective Exclusive OR (denoted by $\bar{\vee}$) is defined by Table 10.16.

Table 10.16   Truth Table for Exclusive OR

P	Q	$P \bar{\vee} Q$
T	T	F
T	F	T
F	T	T
F	F	F

Give an example of a sentence in English (i) in which Exclusive OR is used, (ii) in which OR is used. Show that $\bar{\vee}$ is associative, commutative and distributive over $\wedge$.

4. Find two connectives, using which any other connective can be described.

5. The connective NAND denoted by $\uparrow$ (also called Sheffer stroke) is defined as follows: $P \uparrow Q = \neg(P \wedge Q)$. Show that every connective can be expressed in terms of $\uparrow$.

6. The connective NOR denoted by $\downarrow$ (also called Peirce arrow) is defined as follows: $P \downarrow Q = \neg(P \vee Q)$. Show that all the connectives can be expressed in terms of NOR.

7. Construct the truth table for

(a) $(P \vee Q) \Rightarrow ((P \vee R) \Rightarrow (R \vee Q))$; and

(b) $(P \vee (Q \Rightarrow R)) \Leftrightarrow ((P \vee \neg R) \Rightarrow Q)$.

8. Prove the following equivalences:

(a) $(\neg P \Rightarrow (\neg P \Rightarrow (\neg P \wedge Q))) \equiv P \vee Q$.

(b) $P \equiv (P \vee Q) \wedge (P \vee \neg Q)$.

(c) $\neg(P \Leftrightarrow Q) \equiv (P \wedge \neg Q) \vee (\neg P \wedge Q)$.

9. Prove the logical identities given in Table 10.11 using truth tables.

10. Show that $P \Rightarrow (Q \Rightarrow (R \Rightarrow (\neg P \Rightarrow (\neg Q \Rightarrow \neg R))))$ is a tautology.

11. Is $(P \Rightarrow \neg P) \Rightarrow \neg P$ (i) a tautology, (ii) a contradiction, (iii) neither a tautology nor a contradiction?

12. Is the implication $(P \wedge (P \Rightarrow \neg Q)) \vee (Q \Rightarrow \neg Q) \Rightarrow \neg Q$ a tautology?

13. Obtain the principal disjunctive normal form of

(a) $P \Rightarrow (P \Rightarrow Q \wedge (\neg(\neg Q \vee \neg P)))$, and

(b) $(Q \wedge \neg R \wedge \neg S) \vee (R \wedge S)$.

14. Simplify the formula whose principal disjunctive normal form is $110 \vee 100 \vee 010 \vee 000$.

15. Test the validity of the following argument:

(a) $P \Rightarrow Q$

$\dfrac{R \Rightarrow \neg Q}{\therefore P \Rightarrow \neg R}$

(b) $R \Rightarrow \neg Q$

$P \Rightarrow Q$

$\dfrac{\neg R \Rightarrow S}{\therefore P \Rightarrow S}$

(c) P

Q

$\neg Q \Rightarrow R$

$\dfrac{Q \Rightarrow \neg R}{\therefore R}$

(d) $P \Rightarrow Q \wedge R$

$Q \vee S \Rightarrow T$

$\dfrac{S \vee P}{\therefore T}$

16. Test the validity of the following argument: If Ram is clever then Prem is well-behaved. If Joe is good then Sam is bad and Prem is not well-behaved. If Lal is educated then Joe is good or Ram is clever. Hence if Lal is educated and Prem is not well-behaved then Sam is bad.

17. A company called for applications from candidates, and stipulated the following conditions:

(a) The applicant should be a graduate.

(b) If he knows COBOL he should know FORTRAN.

(c) If he knows BASIC he should know COBOL.

(d) The applicant should know BASIC.

Can you simplify the above conditions?

18. For what universe of discourse the proposition $\forall x(x \geq 5)$ is true?

19. By constructing a suitable universe of discourse, show that $\exists x(P(x) \Rightarrow Q(x))$ $\Leftrightarrow (\exists x P(x) \Rightarrow \exists x Q(x))$ is not valid.

20. Show that the following argument is valid:

All men are mortal.

Socrates is a man.

So Socrates is mortal.

21. Is the following sentence true? If philosophers are not money-minded and some money-minded persons are not clever, then there are some persons who are neither philosophers nor clever.

22. Test the validity of the following argument: No person except the uneducated are proud of their wealth. Some persons who are proud of their wealth do not help others. Therefore, some uneducated persons cannot help others.

Solutions (or Hints) to Selected Exercises

CHAPTER 1

1. (a) The set of all strings in $\{a, b, c\}^*$.
   (b) $A \cap B = \{b\}$. Hence $(A \cap B)^* = \{b^n \mid n \geq 0\}$.
   (c) The set of all strings in $\{a, b, c\}^*$ which are in $\{a, b\}^*$ or in $\{b, c\}^*$.
   (d) $A^* \cap B^* = \{b^n \mid n \geq 0\}$.
   (e) $A - B = \{a\}$. Hence $(A - B)^* = \{a^n \mid n \geq 0\}$.
   (f) $(B - A)^* = \{c^n \mid n \geq 0\}$.

2. (a) Yes.
   (b) Yes.
   (c) Yes. The identity element is Λ.
   (d) $\bigcirc$ is not commutative since $x \bigcirc y \neq y \bigcirc x$ when $x = ab$ and $y = ba$; in this case $x \bigcirc y = abba$ and $y \bigcirc x = baab$.

3. $\bigcirc$ is commutative and associative. $\varnothing$ is the identity element with respect to $\bigcirc$. $A \cup B = A \cup C$ does not imply that $B = C$. For example, take $A = \{a, b\}$, $B = \{b, c\}$ and $C = \{c\}$. Then $A \cup B = A \cup C = \{a, b, c\}$. Obviously, $B \neq C$.

4. (a) True. 1 is the identity element.
   (b) False. 0 does not have an inverse.
   (c) True. 0 is the identity element.
   (d) True. $\varnothing$ is the identity element. The inverse of A is A^c.

5. (c) Obviously, mRm. If mRn then $m - n = 3a$. So, $n - m = 3 (-a)$. Hence nRm. If mRn and nRp then $m - n = 3a$ and $n - p = 3b$. $m - p = 3 (a + b)$, i.e. mRp.

6. (a) R is not reflexive.
   (b) R is neither reflexive nor transitive.
   (c) R is not symmetric since $2R4$, whereas $4R'2$.
   (d) R is not reflexive since $1R'1$ ($1 + 1 \neq 10$).

7. An equivalance class is the set of all strings of the same length. There is an equivalance class corresponding to each non-negative number. For a non-negative number n, the corresponding equivalance class is the set of all strings of length n.

8. R is not an equivalence relation since it is not symmetric (For example, $abR\ aba$, whereas $abaR'\ ab$)

9. $R = \{(1, 2), (2, 3), (1, 4), (4, 2), (3, 4)\}$
   $R^2 = \{(1, 3), (2, 4), (1, 2), (4, 3), (3, 2)\}$
   $R^3 = \{(1, 4), (2, 2), (1, 3), (4, 4), (3, 3)\}$
   $R^4 = \{(1, 2), (2, 3), (1, 4), (4, 2), (3, 4)\} = R$

Hence

$R^+ = R \cup R^2 \cup R^3$
$R^* = R^+ \cup \{(1, 1)\}$

11. $R^+ = R^* = R$, Since $R^2 = R$ (an equivalence relation is transitive).

12. Suppose $f(x) = f(y)$. Then $ax = ay$. So, $x = y$. Therefore, f is one-one. f is not onto as any string with b as the first symbol cannot be written as $f(x)$ for any $x \in \{a, b\}^*$.

14. (a) Tree given in Fig. 1.9.

15. (a) Yes.
    (b) 4, 5, 6 and 8.
    (c) 1, 2, 3 and 7.
    (d) 3 (The longest path is $1 \to 3 \to 7 \to 8$).
    (e) $4 - 5 - 6 - 8$.
    (f) 2.
    (g) 6 and 7.

16. Form a graph G whose vertices are persons. There is an edge connecting A and B if A knows B. Apply Theorem 1.3 to graph G.

17. Proof is by induction on $|X|$. When $|X| = 1$, X is a singleton. Then $2^X = \{\varnothing, X\}$. There is basis for induction. Assume $|2^X| = 2^{|X|}$ when X has $n - 1$ elements. Let $Y = \{a_1, a_2, ..., a_n\}$.
    $Y = X \cup \{a_n\}$, where $X = \{a_1, a_2, ...\}$. Then X has $n - 1$ elements. As X has $n - 1$ elements, $|2^X| = 2^{|X|}$ by induction hypothesis.
    Take any subset Y_1 of Y. Either Y_1 is a subset of X or $Y_1 - \{a_n\}$ is a subset of X. So each subset of Y gives rise to two subsets of X. Thus $|2^Y| = 2\,|2^X|$. But $|2^X| = 2^{|X|}$. Hence $|2^Y| = 2^{|Y|}$. By induction the result is true for all sets X.

18. (a) When $n = 1$, $1^2 = \dfrac{1(1 + 1)\,(1 + 2)}{6} = 1$. Thus there is basis for induction.
    Assume the result for $n - 1$. Then

$$\sum_{k=1}^{n} k^2 = \sum_{k=1}^{n-1} k^2 + n^2$$

$$= \frac{(n - 1)\,(n - 1 + 1)\,(2n - 1)}{6} + n^2 \qquad \text{[by induction hypothesis]}$$

$$= \frac{n(n + 1)\,(2n + 1)}{6} \qquad \text{on simplification.}$$

Thus the result is true for n.

(c) When $n = 2$, $10^{2n} - 1 = 99$ which is divisible by 11. Thus there is basis for induction. Assume $10^{2(n-1)} - 1$ is divisible by 11. Then $10^{2n} - 1 = 10^2 10^{2(n-1)} - 1 = 10^2 [10^{2(n-1)} - 1] + 10^2 - 1$. As $10^{2(n-1)} - 1$ and $10^2 - 1$ are divisible by 11, $10^{2n} - 1$ is divisible by 11. Thus the result is true for n.

19. (b) $2^2 > 2$ [Basis for induction]. Assume $2^{n-1} > n - 1$ for $n > 2$. Then $2^n = 2 \cdot 2^{n-1} > 2(n-1)$, i.e., $2^n > n + n - 2 > n$ ($n > 2$). The result is true for n. By the Principle of Induction, the result is true for all $n > 1$.

20. (i) When $n = 1$, $F(2n + 1) = F(3) = F(1) + F(2) = F(0) + F(2)$. So,

$$F(2n + 1) = \sum_{k=0}^{1} F(2k).$$

Thus there is basis for induction. Assume

$$F(2n - 1) = \sum_{k=0}^{n-1} F(2k) \qquad \text{[by induction hypothesis]}$$

$$F(2n + 1) = F(2n - 1) + F(2n) \qquad \text{[by definition]}$$

By induction hypothesis,

$$F(2n + 1) = \sum_{k=0}^{n-1} F(2k) + F(2n) = \sum_{k=0}^{n} F(2k)$$

So the result is true for n.

21. In a simple graph any edge connects two distinct nodes. The number of ways of choosing two nodes out of n given nodes is $^nC_2 = \dfrac{n(n-1)}{2}$. So the maximum number of edges in a simple graph is $\dfrac{n(n-1)}{2}$.

22. We prove by induction on $|w|$. When $w = \Lambda$, we have $ab\Lambda = \Lambda ab$. Clearly, $|\Lambda| = 0$, which is even. Thus there is basis for induction. Assume the result for all w with $|w| < n$. Let w be of length n and $abw = wab$. As $abw = wab$, $w = abw_1$ for some w in $\{a, b\}^*$. So $ababw_1 = abw_1ab$ and hence $abw_1 = w_1ab$. By induction hypothesis $|w_1|$ is even. As $|w| = |w_1| + 2$, $|w|$ is also even. Hence by the Principle of Induction, the result is true for all w.

23. Let $P(n)$ be the 'open nth envelope'. As the person opens the first envelope $P(1)$ is true. Assume $P(n-1)$ is true. Then the person follows the instruction contained therein. So the nth envelope is opened, i.e., $P(n)$ is true. By induction, $P(n)$ is true for all n.

CHAPTER 2

1. 101101 and 000000 are accepted by M. 11111 is not accepted by M.

2. $\{q_0, q_1, q_4\}$. $\delta(q_0, 010) = \{q_0, q_3\}$ and so 010 is not accepted by M.

3. Both the strings are not accepted by M.

4. As $\delta(q_1, a) = \delta(q_1, a)$, R is reflexive. Obviously it is symmetric.

If q_1Rq_2 then $\delta(q_1, a) = \delta(q_2, a)$.

If q_2Rq_3 then $\delta(q_2, a) = \delta(q_3, a)$. Thus $\delta(q_1, a) = \delta(q_3, a)$, implying that q_1Rq_3. So R is an equivalence relation.

5. The state table of NDFA accepting $\{ab, ba\}$ is given in Table A2.1.

Table A2.1   State Table for Exercise 2.5

State/Σ	a	b
q_0	q_1	q_2
q_1		q_3
q_2	q_3	
(q_3)		

The state table of the corresponding DFA is given in Table A2.2.

Table A2.2   State Table of DFA for Exercise 2.5

State/Σ	a	b
$[q_0]$	$[q_1]$	$[q_2]$
$[q_1]$	$\varnothing$	$[q_3]$
$[q_2]$	$[q_3]$	$\varnothing$
$([q_3])$	$\varnothing$	$\varnothing$
$\varnothing$	$\varnothing$	$\varnothing$

6. The NDFA accepting the given set of strings is given in Fig. A2.1. The corresponding state table is given in Table A2.3.

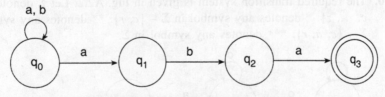

Fig. A2.1   NDFA for Exercise 2.6.

Table A2.3   State Table for Exercise 2.6

State/Σ	a	b
q_0	q_0, q_1	q_0
q_1		q_2
q_2	q_3	
q_3		

The DFA accepting the given set is given in Table A2.4.

Table A2.4   State Table of DFA for Exercise 2.6

State/Σ	a	b
$[q_0]$	$[q_0, q_1]$	$[q_0]$
$[q_0, q_1]$	$[q_0, q_1]$	$[q_0, q_2]$
$[q_0, q_2]$	$[q_0, q_1, q_3]$	$[q_0]$
$[q_0, q_1, q_3]$	$[q_0, q_1]$	$[q_0, q_2]$

7. The state table for the required DFA is given in Table A2.5.

Table A2.5   State Table for Exercise 2.7

States	0	1	2
$[q_0]$	$[q_1, q_4]$	$[q_4]$	$[q_2, q_3]$
$[q_4]$	$\varnothing$	$\varnothing$	$\varnothing$
$[q_1, q_4]$	$\varnothing$	$[q_4]$	$\varnothing$
$[q_2, q_3]$	$\varnothing$	$[q_4]$	$[q_2, q_3]$
$\varnothing$	$\varnothing$	$\varnothing$	$\varnothing$

9. The state table for the required DFA is given in Table A2.6.

Table A2.6   State Table for Exercise 2.9

States	0	1
$[q_1]$	$[q_2, q_3]$	$[q_1]$
$[q_2, q_3]$	$[q_1, q_2]$	$[q_1, q_2]$
$[q_1, q_2]$	$[q_1, q_2, q_3]$	$[q_1]$
$[q_1, q_2, q_3]$	$[q_1, q_2, q_3]$	$[q_1, q_2]$

10. The required transition system is given in Fig. A2.2. Let Σ denote $\{a, b, c, ..., z\}$. * denotes any symbol in $\Sigma - \{c, r\}$. ** denotes any symbol in $\Sigma - \{c, a, r\}$. *** denotes any symbol in Σ.

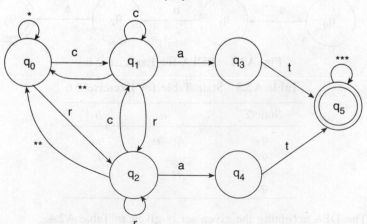

Fig A2.2   Transition system for Exercise 2.10.

11. The corresponding Mealy machine is given in Table A2.7.

Table A2.7   Mealy Machine of Exercise 2.11

| Present state | Next state | | | |
| | $a = 0$ | | $a = 1$ | |
	state	output	state	output
q_0	q_1	0	q_2	1
q_1	q_3	1	q_2	1
q_2	q_2	1	q_1	0
q_3	q_0	1	q_3	1

12. q_1 is associated with 1 and q_2 is associated with 0 and 1. Similarly, q_3 is associated with 0 and 1, whereas q_4 is associated with 1. The state table with new states q_1, q_{20}, q_{21}, q_{30}, q_{31} and q_4 is given in Table A2.8.

Table A2.8   State Table for Exercise 2.12

| Present state | Next state | | | |
| | $a = 0$ | | $a = 1$ | |
	state	output	state	output
q_1	q_1	0	q_{20}	0
q_{20}	q_4	1	q_4	1
q_{21}	q_4	1	q_4	1
q_{30}	q_{21}	1	q_{31}	1
q_{31}	q_{21}	1	q_{31}	1
q_4	q_{30}	0	q_1	1

The revised state table is given in Table A2.9.

Table A2.9   Revised State Table for Exercise 2.12

| Present state | Next state | | |
	$a = 0$	$a = 1$	output
→ q_0	q_1	q_{20}	0
q_1	q_1	q_{20}	1
q_{20}	q_4	q_4	0
q_{21}	q_4	q_4	1
q_{30}	q_{21}	q_{31}	0
q_{31}	q_{21}	q_{31}	1
q_4	q_{30}	q_1	1

13. The Mealy machine is given in Fig. A2.3.

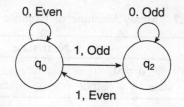

Fig. A2.3 Mealy machine of Exercise 2.13.

14. π_i's are given below:

$\pi_0 = \{\{q_6\}, \{q_0, q_1, q_2, q_3, q_4, q_5\}\}$

$\pi_1 = \{\{q_6\}, \{q_0, q_1, q_2, q_3, q_5\}, \{q_4\}\}$

$\pi_2 = \{\{q_6\}, \{q_4\}, \{q_0, q_1, q_3\}, \{q_2, q_5\}\}$

$\pi_3 = \{\{q_6\}, \{q_4\}, \{q_0\}, \{q_1\}, \{q_3\}, \{q_2, q_5\}\}$

$\pi_4 = \{\{q_6\}, \{q_4\}, \{q_0\}, \{q_1\}, \{q_3\}, \{q_2\}, \{q_5\}\}$

Here $\pi = Q$. The minimum state automaton is simply the given automaton.

CHAPTER 3

1. (a) $S \overset{*}{\Rightarrow} 0^n\, S1^n \overset{*}{\Rightarrow} 0^n\, 0^m\, A1^m1^n,\ n \geq 0,\ m \geq 1.$

$A \overset{*}{\Rightarrow} 1^k A \Rightarrow 1^{k+1},\ k \geq 0.$

$0^m1^n \in L(G)$ when $n > m \geq 1$. So $L(G) = \{0^m1^n: n > m \geq 1\}$

(b) $L(G) = \{0^m1^n \mid m \neq n \text{ and at least one of } m \text{ and } n \geq 1\}$. Clearly, $0^m \in L(G)$ and $1^n \in L(G)$, where $m, n \geq 1$.

For $m > n$, $S \overset{*}{\Rightarrow} 0^nS1^n \Rightarrow 0^n0A1^n \overset{*}{\Rightarrow} 0^n00^{m-n-1}\, 1^n = 0^m1^n$. Thus $0^m1^n \in L(G)$.

(c) $L(G) = \{0^n1^n0^n \mid n \geq 1\}$. The proof is similar to that of Example 3.10.

(d) $L(G) = \{0^n1^m0^m1^n \mid m, n \geq 1\}$.

For m,

$n \geq 1.\ S \overset{*}{\Rightarrow} 0^{n-1}\, S1^{n-1} \Rightarrow 0^{n-1}\, 0A11^{n-1} \Rightarrow 0^n1^{m-1}\, A0^{m-1}1^{n-1} \Rightarrow 0^n\, 1^m\, 0^m\, 1^n$

So,

$\{0^n\, 1^m\, 0^m\, 1^n \mid m, n \geq 1\} \subseteq L(G).$

It is easy to prove the other inclusion.

(e) $L(G) = \{x \in \{0, 1\}^+ \mid x \text{ does not contain two consecutive 0's}\}$

2. (a) $G = (\{S, A, B\}, \{0, 1\}, P, S)$, where P consists of $S \to 0B \mid 1A$, $A \to 0 \mid 0S \mid 1AA$, $B \to 1 \mid 1S \mid 0BB$.

Prove by induction on $|w|$, $w \in \Sigma^*$, that

   (i) $S \overset{*}{\Rightarrow} w$ if and only if w consists of equal number of 0's and 1's.

   (ii) $A \overset{*}{\Rightarrow} w$ if and only if w has one more 0 than it has 1's.

   (iii) $B \overset{*}{\Rightarrow} w$ if and only if w has one more 1 than it has 0's.

$A \Rightarrow 0$, $B \Rightarrow 1$ and S does not derive any terminal string of length one.

Thus there is basis for induction. Assume (i), (ii) and (iii) are true for strings of length $k - 1$. Let w be a string in Σ^* with $|w| = k$. Suppose $S \Rightarrow w$. The first step in this derivation is either $S \Rightarrow 0B$ or $S \Rightarrow 1A$. In the first case $w = 0w_1$, $B \overset{*}{\Rightarrow} w_1$ and $|w_1| = k - 1$. By induction hypothesis, w has one more 1 than it has 0's. Hence w has equal number of 0's and 1's. To prove the converse part, assume w has equal number of 0's and 1's and $|w| = k$. If w starts with 0, then $w = 0w_1$, where $|w_1| = k - 1$. w_1 has one more 1 than it has 0's. By induction hypothesis, $B \overset{*}{\Rightarrow} w_1$. Hence $S \Rightarrow 0B$ $\Rightarrow 0w_1 = w$. Thus (i) is proved for all strings w. The proofs for (ii) and (iii) are similar.

(b) The required grammar G has the following productions:

$$S \to 0S1, \ S \to 0A1, \ A \to 1A0, \ A \to 10.$$

Obviously, $L(G) \subseteq \{0^n 1^m 0^m 1^n \mid m, n \geq 1\}$. For getting any terminal string, the first production is $S \to 0S1$ or $S \to 0A1$, the last production is $A \to 10$. By applying $S \to 0S1$ ($n - 1$ times), $S \to 0A1$ (once) $A \to 1A0$ ($m - 1$ times), and $A \to 10$ (once) we get $0^n 1^m 0^m 1^n$. So, $\{0^n 1^m 0^m 1^n \mid m, n \geq 1\}$ $\subseteq L(G)$.

(c) The required productions are $S \to 0S11 \mid 011$.

(d) The required productions are $S \to 0A1 \mid 1B0$, $A \to 0A1 \mid \Lambda$, $B \to 1B0 \mid \Lambda$.

(e) Modify the constructions given in Example 3.7 to get the required grammar.

3. For the derivation of 001100, 001010 or 01010, the first production cannot be $S \to 0S1$. The other possible productions are $S \to 0A$ and $S \to 1B$. In these cases the resulting terminal strings are 0^n or 1^n. So none of the given strings are in the language generated by the grammar given in Exercise 1(b).

4. It is easy to see that any derivation should start with $S \Rightarrow 0AB \Rightarrow 0ASA$ $\Rightarrow 0A0ABA$ or $S \Rightarrow 0AB \Rightarrow 0A01 \Rightarrow 0S0B1$. If we apply $S \to 0AB$ we get A in the sentential form. If we try to eliminate A using $A0 \to S0B$ or $A1$ $\to SB1$, we get S in the sentential form. So one of the two variables, viz., A or S, can never be eliminated.

5. The language generated by the given grammar is $\{01^m 2^n 3 \mid m, n \geq 1\}$. This language can also be generated by a regular grammar (refer Chapter 4).

6. (a) False. Refer Remark 2 on Page 67.
   (b) True. If $L = \{w_1, w_2, \ldots, w_n\}$, then $G = (\{S\}, \Sigma, P, S)$, where P consists of $S \to w_1 \mid w_2 \mid \ldots \mid w_n$.
   (c) True. By Theorem 3.5 it is enough to show that $\{w\}$ is regular where $w \in \Sigma^*$. Let $w = a_1 a_2 \ldots a_n$. Then the grammar whose productions are $S \to a_1 A_1, A_1 \to a_2 A_2, \ldots A_{m-1} \to a_m$ generate $\{w\}$.

7. We prove (a) $S \Rightarrow A_1^n A_2^n A_4$ (b) $A_1^n A_2^n A_4 \overset{*}{\Rightarrow} a^{n^2} A_2^n A_4$ (c) $A_2^n A_1^n A_4 \Rightarrow$ a^{2n+1}.

We first prove (a). $S \Rightarrow A_3 A_4 \Rightarrow A_1 A_3 A_2 A_4 \overset{*}{\Rightarrow} A_1^{n-1} A_3 A_2^{n-1} A_4 \Rightarrow A_1^{n-1} A_1 A_2$
$A_2^{n-1} A_4$. (We are applying $A_3 \to A_1 A_3 A_2$ ($n-2$) times and $A_3 \to A_1 A_2$
once.) Hence (a). To prove (b) start with $A_1^n A_2^n A_4$. Then $A_1^{n-1} A_1 A_2 A_2^{n-1} A_4$
$\Rightarrow A_1^{n-1} a A_2 A_1 A_2^{n-1} A_4 \Rightarrow A_1^{n-2} a A_1 A_2 A_1 A_2^{n-1} A_4 \Rightarrow A_1^{n-2} a^2 A_2 A_1 A_1 A_2^{n-1} A_4$
$\Rightarrow A_1^{n-2} a^2 A_2 A_1 a A_2 A_1 A_2^{n-2} A_4 \overset{*}{\Rightarrow} A_1^{n-2} a^3 A_2 A_1 A_2 A_1 A_2^{n-2} A_4 \Rightarrow A_1^{n-2} a^3 A_2 a A_2$
$A_1 A_1 A_2^{n-2} A_4 \overset{*}{\Rightarrow} a^4 A_1^{n-2} A_2^2 A_1^2 A_2^{n-2} A_4$.

Proceeding in a similar way we get $A_1^n A_2^n A_4 \overset{*}{\Rightarrow} a^{n^2} A_2^n A_1^n A_4$. Hence (b).

Finally, $A_2^n A_1^n A_4 \Rightarrow A_2^n A_1^{n-1} A_4 a \overset{*}{\Rightarrow} A_2^n A_4 a^n \Rightarrow A_2^{n-1} A_5 a^{n+1} \overset{*}{\Rightarrow} A_5 a^{2n} \Rightarrow$
a^{2n+1}. (We apply $A_1 A_4 \to A_4 a$, $A_2 A_4 \Rightarrow A_5 a$, $A_2 A_5 \to A_5 a$ and finally $A_5 \to a$).

Using (a), (b) and (c), we get $S \Rightarrow a^{(n+1)^2}$.

8. The productions for (i) are $S \to aS|B$, $aS \to aa$, $B \to a$. For (ii) the
productions are $S \to AS|a$, $A \to a$. For (iii) the productions are $S \to aS|a$.

9. The required grammar $G = (\{S, S_1, A, B\}, \Sigma, P, S)$, where $\Sigma = \{0, 1, 2, \ldots,$
9$\}$ and P consists of

$S \to 0|2|4|6|8$, $S \to AS_1$, $A \to 1|2|\ldots|9$

$S_1 \to 0|2|4|6|8$, $S \to ABS_1$, $B \to 1|2|\ldots|9$

$S \to 0|2|4|6|8$ generate even integers with one digit.

$S \to AS_1$ and A-productions and S_1-productions generate all even numbers
with two digits. The remaining productions can be used to generate all
even integers with three digits.

10. (a) $G = (\{S, A, B\}, \{0, 1\}, P, S)$, where P consists of $S \to 0S1 \mid 0A \mid 1B$
$\mid 0 \mid 1$, $A \to 0A \mid 0$, $B \to 1B \mid 1$. Using $S \to 0S1$, $S \to 0$, $S \to 1$, we can
get $0^m 1^n$, where m and n differ by 1. To get more 0's (than 1's) in the string
we have to apply $A \to 0A \mid 0$, $S \to 0A$ repeatedly. To get more 1's, apply
$S \to 1B$, $B \to 1B \mid 1$ repeatedly.

(b) The required productions are $S \to aS_1$, $S_1 \to bS_1 c$, $S_1 \to bc$, $S \to aS_2 c$,
$S_2 \to aS_2 c$, $S_2 \to b$, $S \to S_3 c$, $S_3 \to aS_3 b$, $S_3 \to ab$. The first three productions
derive $a^m b c^m$. $S \to aS_2 c$ and the S_2-productions generate $a^m b c^m$. The remaining
productions generate $a^m b^m c$.

(c) The required productions are $S \to 0S1$, $S \to 01$, $S \to 0A1$, $A \to 1A$,
$A \to 1$.

(d) The required productions are $S \to aSc$, $S \to ac$, $S \to bc$, $S \to bS_1 c$, S_1
$\to bS_1 c$, $S_1 \to bc$. A typical string in the given language can be written in
the form $a^l b^m c^m c^l$ where $l, m \geq 0$. $S \to aSc$, $S \to bc$ generate $a^l c^l$ for $l \geq$
1. $S \to bS_1 c$, $S_1 \to bS_1 c$, $S_1 \to bc$ generate $b^m c^m$ for $m \geq 1$. For getting
$a^l b^m c^m c^l$, we have to apply $S \to aSc$ l times; $S \to bc$, $S \to bS_1 c$, $S_1 \to bS_1 c$
and $S_1 \to bc$ are to be applied. For $m = 1$, $S \to bc$ has to be applied. For
$m > 1$, we have to apply $S \to bS_1 c$, $S_1 \to bS_1 c$ and $S_1 \to bc$ repeatedly.

The terminal c is added whenever the terminal a or b is added in the course of the derivation. This takes care of the condition $1 + m = n$.

(e) Let G be a context-free grammar whose productions are $S \to S0S1S0S$, $S \to S0S0S1S$, $S \to S1S0S0S$, $S \to \Lambda$. It is easy to see that elements in $L(G)$ are in L. Let $w \in L$. We prove that $w \in L(G)$ by induction on $|w|$. Note that every string in L is of length $3n$, $n \geq 1$. When $|w| = 3$, w has to be one of 010, 001 or 100. These strings can be derived by applying $S \to S0S1S0S$, $S \to S0S0S1S$ and $S \to S1S0S0S$ and then $S \to \Lambda$. Thus there is basis for induction. Assume the result for all strings of length $3n - 3$. Let $w \in L$ and let $|w| = 3n$. w should contain one of 010, 001 or 100 as a substring. Call the substring w_1. Write $w = w_2w_1w_3$. Then $|w_2w_3| = 3n - 3$ and by induction hypothesis $S \overset{*}{\Rightarrow} w_2w_3$. Note that all the productions (except $S \to \Lambda$) yield a sentential form starting and ending with S and having the symbol S between every pair of terminals. Without loss of generality we can assume that the last step in the derivation $S \overset{*}{\Rightarrow} w_2w_3$ is of the form $w_2Sw_3 \Rightarrow w_2w_3$. So $S \overset{*}{\Rightarrow} w_2Sw_3$. But $w_1 \in L$ and so $S \overset{*}{\Rightarrow} w_1$. Thus $S \overset{*}{\Rightarrow} w_2w_1w_3$. In other words, $w \in L(G)$. By the Principle of Induction $L = L(G)$.

11. The required productions are
   (a) $S \to aS_1$, $S_1 \to aS$, $S \to aS_2$, $S_2 \to a$
   (b) $S \to aS$, $S \to bS$, $S \to a$
   (c) $S \to aS_1$, $S_1 \to aS_1$, $S_1 \to bS_1$, $S_1 \to a$, $S_1 \to b$
   (d) $S \to aS_1$, $S_1 \to aS_1$, $S_1 \to bS_2$, $S_2 \to bS_2$, $S_3 \to cS_3$, $S_3 \to c$
   (e) $S \to aS_1$, $S_1 \to bS$, $S \to aS_2$, $S_2 \to b$.

12. $\overset{*}{\Rightarrow}$ is not symmetric and so the relation is not an equivalence relation (Refer Note (ii), Page 55)

13. It is clear that $L(G_1) = \{a^nb^n \mid n \geq 1\}$. In G_2, $S \Rightarrow AC \Rightarrow ASB \overset{*}{\Rightarrow} A^{n-1}ISB^{n-1}$. Also, $S \Rightarrow AB \overset{*}{\Rightarrow} ab$. Hence $S \overset{*}{\Rightarrow} a^nb^n$ for all $n \geq 1$. This means $L(G_2) = \{a^nb^n \mid n \geq 1\} = L(G_1)$.

14. $L(G) = \emptyset$ for we get a variable on the application of each production and so no terminal string results.

15. The required productions are $S \to aS_1$, $S_1 \to bS_2$, $S_2 \to c$, $S \to bS_3$, $S_3 \to cS_4$, $S_4 \to a$, $S \to cS_5$, $S_5 \to aS_6$, $S_6 \to b$.

16. The required productions are $S \to S_1$, $S_1 \to abS_1$, $S_1 \to ab$, $S \to S_2$, $S_2 \to baS_2$, $S_2 \to ba$.

17. Let the given grammar be G_1. The production $A \to xB$ where $x = a_1a_2 \ldots a_n$ is replaced by $A \to a_1A_1$, $A_1 \to a_2A_2$, ..., $A_{n-1} \to a_nB$. The production $A \to y$, where $y = b_1b_2 \ldots b_m$ is replaced by $A \to b_1B_1$, $B_1 \to b_2B_2$, ..., $B_{m-1} \to b_m$. The grammar G_2 whose productions are the new productions is regular and equivalent to G_1.

CHAPTER 4

1. (a) **0 + 1 + 2**
   (b) **1(11)***
   (c) w in the given set has only one a which can occur anywhere in w. So $w = xay$, where x and y consist of some b's (or none). Hence the given set is represented by **b* ab***.
   (d) Here we have three cases: w contains no a, one a or two a's. Arguing as in (c), the required regular expression is

   b* + b* ab* + b* ab* ab*

   (e) **aa(aaa)***
   (f) **(aa)* + (aaa)* + aaaaa**
   (g) **a(a + b)* a**

2. (a) The strings of length atmost 4 in **(ab + a)*** are Λ, a, ab, aa, aab, aba, $abab$, a^3, $aaba$, $aaab$ and a^4. The strings in **aa + b** are aa and b. Concatenating (i) strings of length atmost 3 from the first set and aa and (ii) strings of length 4 and b, we get the required strings. They are aa, aaa, $abaa$, $aaaa$, $aabaa$, $abaaa$, a^5, $ababb$, $aabab$, $aaabb$, and $aaaab$.
   (c) The strings in **(ab + a) + (ab + a)²** are a, ab, aa, $abab$, aab and aba. The strings of length 5 or less in **(ab + a)³** are a^3, $abaa$, $aaab$, $ababa$. The strings of length 5 or less in **(ab + a)⁴** are a^4, a^3ab, aba^3. In **(ab + a)⁵**, a^5 is the only string of length 5 or less. The strings in **a*** are in **(ab + a)*** also. Hence the required strings are Λ, a, ab, a^2, $abab$, aab, aba, a^3, $abaa$, $aaab$, $ababa$, a^4, $aaaab$, $abaaa$, and a^5.

3. (a) The set of all strings starting with a and ending in ab.
   (b) The strings are either strings of a's followed by one b or strings of b's followed by one a.
   (c) The set of all strings of the form vw where a's occur in pairs in v and b's occur in pairs in w.

5. (a) $\varnothing$, (b) $(a + b)^*$, (c) The set of all strings over $\{a, b\}$ containing two successive a's or two successive b's ; (d) the set of all strings containing even number of a's and even number of b's.

6. We get the following equations:

   $q_0 = \Lambda,$

   $q_1 = q_0 1 + q_1 1 + q_3 1$

   $q_2 = q_1 0 + q_2 0 + q_3 0$

   $q_3 = q_2 1$

   Therefore,

   $$q_2 = q_1 0 + q_2 0 + q_2 10 = q_1 0 + q_2(0 + 10)$$

   Applying Theorem 4.1, we get

   $$q_2 = q_1 0(0 + 10)^*$$

Now

$$q_1 = 1 + q_11 + q_211 = 1 + q_11 + q_10(0 + 10)* \, 11$$
$$= 1 + q_1(1 + 0(0 + 10)* \, 11)$$

By Theorem 4.1, we get

$$q_1 = 1(1 + 0(0 + 10)* \, 11)*$$

$$q_3 = q_21 = 1(1 + 0 \, (0 + 10) \, 11) * 0(0 + 10)* \, 1$$

As q_3 is the only final state, the regular expression corresponding to the given diagram is $1(1 + 0(0 + 10) * 11) * 0 \, (0 + 10) * 1$.

7. The transition system equivalent to $(ab + a)*(aa + b)$ is given in Fig. A4.1.

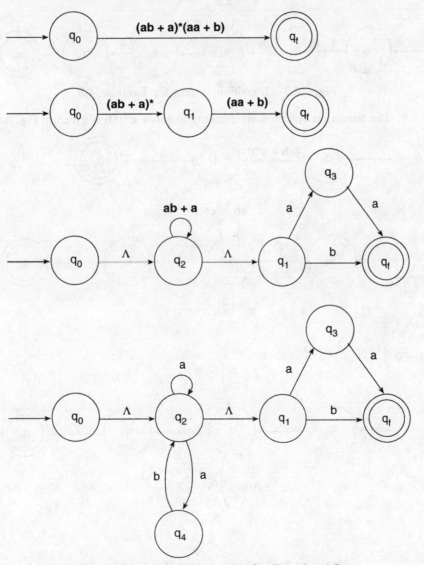

Fig. A4.1   Transition system for Exercise 4.7.

8. The transition system equivalent to **a(a + b)*ab** is given in Fig. A4.2.

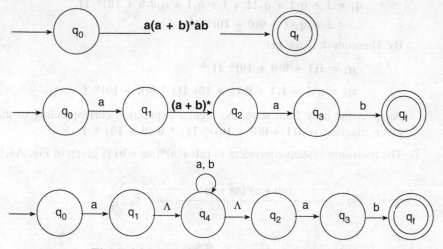

Fig. A4.2 Transition system for Exercise 4.8.

9. The transition system corresponding to **(ab + c*)*b** is given in Fig. A4.3.

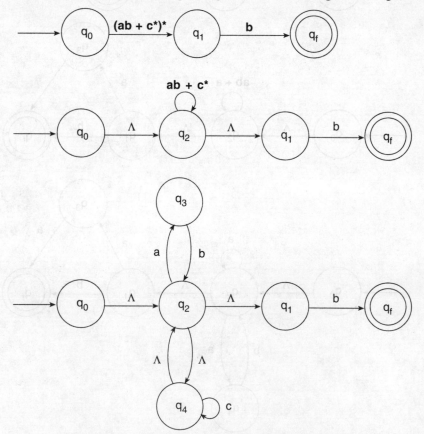

Fig. A4.3 Transition system for Exercise 4.9.

10. (a) The required regular expression is

$(1 + 01)$* + $(1 + 01)$ * $00(1 + 01)$ * + $(0 + 10)$ *+ $(0 + 10)$ * $11(0 + 10)$ *.
$(1 + 01)$ * represents the set of all strings containing no pair of 0's. $(1 + 01)$* 00 $(1 + 01)$* represents the set of all strings containing exactly one pair of 0's. The remaining two expressions correspond to a pair of 1's.

(c) Let w be in the given set L. If w has n a's then it is in a set represented by (b)*. If w has only one a then it is in a set represented by b* ab*. If w has more than one a write $w = w_1 a w_2$, where w does not contain any a. Then w_1 is in a set represented by $(b + abb)$*. So the given set is represented by the regular expression b* + $(b + abb)$ * ab*. (Note the regular set corresponding to b* is a subset of the set corresponding to $(b + abb)$*

(d) $(0 + 1)$* 000 $(0 + 1)$*

(e) $00(0 + 1)$*

(f) $1(0 + 1)$* 00.

12. The corresponding regular expression is $(0 + 1)$* $(010 + 0010)$. We can construct the transition system with Λ-moves. Eliminating Λ-moves we get the NDFA accepting the given set of strings. The NDFA is given in Fig. A4.4.

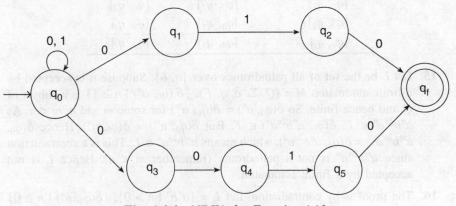

Fig. A4.4 NDFA for Exercise 4.12.

The equivalent DFA is given in Table A4.1.

Table A4.1 State Table of DFA for Exercise 4.12.

State/Σ	0	1
$[q_0]$	$[q_0, q_1, q_3]$	$[q_0]$
$[q_0, q_1, q_3]$	$[q_0, q_1, q_3, q_4]$	$[q_0, q_2]$
$[q_0, q_2]$	$[q_0, q_1, q_3, q_f]$	$[q_0]$
$[q_0, q_1, q_3, q_4]$	$[q_0, q_1, q_3, q_4]$	$[q_0, q_2, q_5]$
$[q_0, q_1, q_3, q_f]$	$[q_0, q_1, q_3, q_4]$	$[q_0, q_2]$
$[q_0, q_2, q_5]$	$[q_0, q_1, q_3, q_f]$	$[q_0]$

13. Similar to Exercise 2.10.

14. The state table for the NDFA accepting **(a+b)* abb** is given in Table A4.2.

Table A4.2   State Table for Exercise 4.14

State/Σ	a	b
q_0	q_0, q_1	q_0
q_1		q_2
q_2		q_f
q_f		

The corresponding DFA is given in Table A4.3.

Table A4.3   State Table of DFA for Exercise 4.14

State/Σ	a	b
$[q_0]$	$[q_0, q_1]$	$[q_0]$
$[q_0, q_1]$	$[q_0, q_1]$	$[q_0, q_2]$
$[q_0, q_2]$	$[q_0, q_1]$	$[q_0, q_f]$
$[q_0, q_f]$	$[q_0, q_1]$	$[q_0, q_f]$

15. Let L be the set of all palindromes over $\{a, b\}$. Suppose it is accepted by a finite automaton $M = (Q, \Sigma, \delta, q, F)$. $\{\delta(q_0, a^n) \mid n \geq 1\}$ is a subset of Q and hence finite. So $\delta(q_0, a^n) = \delta(q_0, a^m)$ for some m and n, $m < n$. As $a^n b^{2n} a^n \in L$, $\delta(q_0, a^n b^{2n} a^n) \in F$. But $\delta(q_0, a^m) = \delta(q_0, a^n)$. Hence $\delta(q_0, a^m b^{2n} a^n) = \delta(q_0, a^n b^{2n} a^n)$, which means $a^m b^{2n} a^n \in L$. This is a contradiction since $a^m b^{2n} a^n$ is not a palindrome (remember $m < n$). Hence L is not accepted by a finite automaton.

16. The proof is by contradiction. Let $L = \{a^n b^n \mid n > 0\}$. $\{\delta(q_0, a^n) \mid n \geq 0\}$ is a subset of Q and hence finite. So $\delta(q_0, a^n) = \delta(q_0, a^m)$ for some m and n, $m \neq n$. So $\delta(q_0, a^m b^n) = \delta(\delta(q_0, a^m), b^n) = \delta(\delta(q_0, a^n), b^n) = \delta(q_0, a^n b^n)$. As $a^n b^n \in L$, $\delta(q_0, a^n b^n)$ is a final state and so is $\delta(q_0, a^m b^n)$. This means $a^m b^n \in L$ with $m \neq n$, which is a contradiction. Hence L is not regular.

17. (a) Let $L = \{a^n b^{2n} \mid n > 0\}$. We prove L is not regular by contradiction. If L is regular, we can apply pumping lemma. Let n be the number of states. Let $w = a^n b^{2n}$. By pumping lemma, $w = xyz$ with $|xy| \leq n$, $|y| > 0$ and $xz \in L$. As $|xy| \leq n$, $xy = a^m$ and $y = a^l$ where $0 < l \leq n$. So $xz = a^{n-1} b^{2n} \in L$, a contradiction since $n - 1 \neq n$. Thus L is not regular.

(b) Let $L = \{a^n b^m \mid 0 < n < m\}$. We show that L is not regular. Let n be the number of states and $w = a^n b^m$, where $m > n$. As in (a), $y = a^l$, where $0 < l \leq n$. By pumping lemma $xy^k z \in L$ for $k \geq 0$. So $a^{n-1} a^{lk} b^m \in L$ for all $k \geq 0$. For sufficiently large k, $n - 1 + lk > m$. This is a contradiction. Hence L is not regular.

19. Let $M = (Q, \Sigma, \delta, q_0, F)$ be a DFA accepting a nonempty language. Then there exists $w = a_1a_2 \ldots a_p$ accepted by M. If $p < n$, the result is true. Suppose $p > n$. Let $\delta(q_0, a_1a_2 \ldots a_i) = q_i$ for $i = 1, 2, \ldots, p$. As $p > n$, the sequence of states $\{q_1, q_2, \ldots, q_p\}$ must have a pair of repeated states. Take the first pair (q_j, q_k) (Note $q_j = q_k$). Then $\delta(q_0, a_1a_2 \ldots, a_j) = q_j$, $\delta(q_j, a_{j+1} \ldots, a_k) = q_j$ and $\delta(q_j, a_{k+1} \ldots, a_p) \in F$. So $\delta(q_0, a_1a_2 \ldots a_ja_{k+1} \ldots a_p) = \delta(q_j, a_1a_2 \ldots, a_p) \in F$. Thus we have found a string in Σ^* whose length is less than p (and differs from $|w|$ by $k - j$). Repeating the process we get a string of length m, where $m < n$.

20. Let $M = (\{q_0, q_1, q_f\}, \{a, b\}, \delta, q_0, \{q_f\})$, where q_0 and q_1 correspond to S and A respectively.

   Then the NDFA accepting $L(G)$ is given in Table A4.4.

Table A4.4   Table for Exercise 4.20

State/Σ	a	b
q_0	q_0	q_1, q_f
q_1	q_1, q_f	q_0

21. The transitions are

$$\delta(q_1, a) = q_4, \quad \delta(q_2, b) = q_1$$
$$\delta(q_1, b) = q_2, \quad \delta(q_4, a) = q_1$$
$$\delta(q_2, a) = q_3$$
$$\delta(q_3, a) = q_2$$
$$\delta(q_3, b) = q_4$$
$$\delta(q_4, b) = q_3$$

Let A_1, A_2, A_3, A_4 correspond to q_1, q_2, q_3, q_4. The induced productions are $A_1 \to aA_4$, $A_1 \to bA_2$, $A_2 \to aA_3$, $A_3 \to aA_2$, $A_3 \to bA_4$, $A_4 \to bA_3$ (corresponding to the first six transitions) and $A_2 \to bA_1$, $A_2 \to b$, $A_4 \to aA_1$, $A_4 \to a$ (corresponding to the last two transitions). So $G = (\{A_1, A_2, A_3, A_4\}, \{a, b\}, P, A_1)$, where P consists of the induced productions given above.

22. The required productions are

$$S \to AS_1 \,|BS_1|\, \ldots \,|ZS_1,$$
$$S_1 \to AS_1 \,|BS_1|\, \ldots \,|ZS_1,$$
$$S_1 \to 0S_1 \,|1S_1|\ldots\, |9S_1$$
$$S_1 \to A \,|B|\, \ldots \,|Z \text{ and } S_1 \to 0|1| \ldots |9$$

24. The given grammar is equivalent to $G = (\{S, A, B\}, \{a, b\}, P, S)$, where P consists of $S \to aS|bS|aA$, $A \to bB$, $B \to a(B \to aC$ and $C \to \Lambda$ is replaced by $B \to a$). Let q_0, q_1 and q_2 correspond to S, A and B. q_f is the only final state. The transition system M accepting $L(G)$ is given as

$$M = (\{q_0, q_1, q_2, q_f\}, \{a, b\}, \delta, q_0, \{q_f\})$$

where q_0, q_1 and q_2 correspond to S, A and B and q_f is the (only) final state. $S \rightarrow aS$, $S \rightarrow bS$, $S \rightarrow aA$ and $A \rightarrow bB$ induce transitions from q_f to q_0 with labels b and a, from q_0 to q_1 with label a and from q_1 to q_2 with label b. $B \rightarrow a$ induces a transition from q_2 to q_f with label a. M is given in Fig. A4.5.

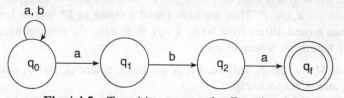

Fig A4.5 Transition system for Exercise 4.24.

The equivalent DFA is given in Table A4.5.

Table A4.5 State Table of DFA for Exercise 4.24

State/Σ	a	b
$[q_0]$	$[q_0, q_1]$	$[q_0]$
$[q_0, q_1]$	$[q_0, q_1]$	$[q_0, q_2]$
$[q_0, q_2]$	$[q_0, q_1, q_f]$	$[q_0]$
$[q_0, q_1, q_f]$	$[q_0, q_1]$	$[q_0, q_2]$

CHAPTER 5

1. The derivation tree is given in Fig. A5.1.

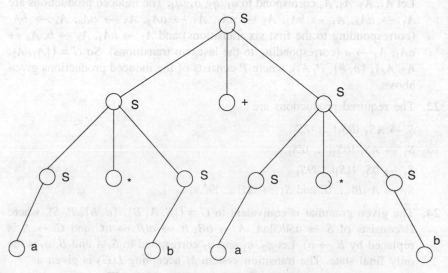

Fig. A5.1 Derivation tree for Exercise 5.1.

2. $S \rightarrow 0S0$, $S \rightarrow 1S1$ and $S \rightarrow A$ give the derivation $S \overset{*}{\Rightarrow} wAw$, where $w \in \{0, 1\}^+$. $A \rightarrow 2B3$ and $B \rightarrow 2B3$ give $A \overset{*}{\Rightarrow} 2^m B3^m$. Finally, $B \rightarrow 3$ gives $B \Rightarrow 3$. Hence $S \overset{*}{\Rightarrow} wAw \overset{*}{\Rightarrow} w2^m B3^m w \Rightarrow w2^m 3^{m+1} w$. Thus, $L(G) \subseteq \{w2^m 3^{m+1} w \mid w \in \{0, 1\}^+ \text{ and } m \geq 1\}$. The reverse inclusion can be proved similarly.

3. (a) X_1, X_3, X_5 (b) X_2, X_4 (c) As $X_1 = S$, $X_4 X_2$ and $X_2 X_4 X_4 X_2$ are sentential forms.

4. (i) $S \Rightarrow SbS \Rightarrow abS \Rightarrow abSbS \Rightarrow ababS \Rightarrow ababSbS \Rightarrow abababS \Rightarrow abababa.$

   (ii) $S \Rightarrow SbS \Rightarrow SbSbS \Rightarrow SbSbSbS \Rightarrow SbSbSba \Rightarrow SbSbaba \Rightarrow Sbababa \Rightarrow abababa$

   (iii) $S \Rightarrow SbS \Rightarrow abS \Rightarrow abSbS \Rightarrow abSbSbS \Rightarrow ababSbS \Rightarrow abababS \Rightarrow abababa.$

5. (i) $S \Rightarrow aB \Rightarrow aaBB \Rightarrow aaaBBB \Rightarrow aaabBB \Rightarrow aaabbB \Rightarrow aaabbaBB \Rightarrow aaabbabB \Rightarrow aaabbabbS \Rightarrow aaabbabbbA \Rightarrow aaabbabbba$

   (ii) $S \Rightarrow aB \Rightarrow aaBB \Rightarrow aaBbS \Rightarrow aaBbbA \Rightarrow aaBbba \Rightarrow aaaBBbba \Rightarrow aaabBbba \Rightarrow aaabbSbba \Rightarrow aaabbaBbba \Rightarrow aaabbabbba.$

6. $abab$ has two different derivations $S \Rightarrow abSb \Rightarrow abab$ (using $S \rightarrow abSb$ and $S \rightarrow a$) $S \Rightarrow aAb \Rightarrow abSb \Rightarrow abab$ (using $S \rightarrow aAb$, $A \rightarrow bS$ and $S \rightarrow a$).

7. ab has two different derivations.
   $S \Rightarrow ab$ (using $S \rightarrow ab$)
   $S \Rightarrow aB \Rightarrow ab$ (using $S \rightarrow aB$ and $B \rightarrow b$).

8. Consider $G = (\{S, A, B\}, \{a, b\}, P, S)$, where P consists of $S \rightarrow AB \mid ab$ and $B \rightarrow b$.

   Step 1: When we apply Theorem 5.4, we get
   $$W_1 = \{S\}, \qquad W_2 = \{S\} \cup \{A, B, a, b\} = W_3$$
   Hence $G_1 = G$.

   Step 2: When we apply Theorem 5.3, we obtain,
   $$W_1 = \{S, B\}, \qquad W_2 = \{S, B\} \cup \varnothing = W_3$$
   So $G_2 = (\{S, B\}, \{a, b\}, \{S \rightarrow ab, B \rightarrow b\}, S)$. Obviously, G_2 is not a reduced grammar since $B \rightarrow b$ does not appear in the course of derivation of any terminal string.

9. *Step 1:* Applying Theorem 5.3, we have
   $$W_1 = \{B\}, \quad W_2 = \{B\} \cup \{C, A\}, \quad W_3 = \{A, B, C\} \cup \{S\} = V_N$$
   Hence $G_1 = G$.

   Step 2: Applying Theorem 5.4, we obtain
   $$W_1 = \{S\}, \quad W_2 = \{S\} \cup \{A, a\}, \quad W_3 = \{S, A, a\} \cup \{B, b\}$$
   $$W_4 = \{S, A, B, a, b\} \cup \varnothing$$
   Hence $G_2 = (\{S, A, B\}, \{a, b\}, P, S)$, where P consists of $S \rightarrow aAa$, $A \rightarrow bBB$ and $B \rightarrow ab$.

10. The given grammar has no null productions. So we have to eliminate unit productions. This has already been done in Example 5.10. The resulting equivalent grammar is $G = (\{S, A, B, C, D, E\}, \{a, b\}, P, S)$, where P consists of $S \rightarrow AB$, $A \rightarrow a$, $B \rightarrow b \mid a$, $C \rightarrow a$, $D \rightarrow a$ and $E \rightarrow a$. Apply step 1 of Theorem 5.5. As every variable derives some terminal string, the resulting grammar is G itself.

    Now apply step 2 of Theorem 5.5. Then
    $W_1 = \{S\}$, $W_2 = \{S\} \cup \{A, B\} = \{S, A, B\}$, $W_3 = \{S, A, B\} \cup \{a, b\}$
    $= \{S, A, B, a, b\}$ and $W_4 = W_3$.
    Hence the reduced grammar is $G' = (\{S, A, B\}, \{a, b\}, P', S)$, where $P' = \{S \rightarrow AB, A \rightarrow a, B \rightarrow b, B \rightarrow a\}$.

11. We prove that by eliminating redundant symbols (using Theorem 5.3 and Theorem 5.4) and then unit productions, we may not get an equivalent grammar in the most simplified form. Consider the grammar G whose productions are $S \rightarrow AB$, $A \rightarrow a$, $B \rightarrow C$, $B \rightarrow b$, $C \rightarrow D$, $D \rightarrow E$ and $E \rightarrow a$.

    Step 1:   Using Theorem 5.3, we get

    $W_1 = \{A, B, E\}$, $W_2 = \{A, B, E\} \cup \{S, D\}$,

    $W_3 = \{S, A, B, D, E\} \cup \{C\} = V_N$.

    Hence $G_1 = G$.

    Step 2:   Using Theorem 5.4, we obtain

    $W_1 = \{S\}$, $W_2 = \{S\} \cup \{A, B\}$, $W_3 = \{S, A, B\} \cup \{a, c, b\}$,
    $W_4 = \{S, A, B, c, a, b\} \cup \{D\}$, $W_5 = \{S, A, B, C, D, a, b\} \cup \{E\} = V_N \cup \Sigma$.

    Hence $G_2 = G_1 = G$.

    Step 3:   We eliminate unit productions. We then have

    $W(S) = \{S\}$ $W(A) = \{A\}$, $W(E) = \{E\}$ $W_0(B) = \{B\}$,
    $W_1(B) = \{B\} \cup \{C\}$, $W_2(B) = \{B, C\} \cup \{D\}$,
    $W_3(B) = \{B, C, D, E\} = W(B)$, $W(C) = \{C, D, E\}$, $W(D) = \{D, E\}$.

    The productions in the new grammar G_3 are $S \rightarrow AB$, $A \rightarrow a$, $B \rightarrow b$, $B \rightarrow a$ and $E \rightarrow a$. G_3 contains the redundant symbol E. So G_3 is not the equivalent grammar in the most simplified form.

12. (a) As there are no null productions or unit productions, we can proceed to Step 2.

    Step 2:   Let $G_1 = (V'_N, \{0, 1\}, P_1, S)$, where P_1 and V'_N are constructed as follows:

    (i) $A \rightarrow 0$, $B \rightarrow 1$ are included in P_1.
    (ii) $S \rightarrow 1A$, $B \rightarrow 1S$ give rise to $S \rightarrow C_1A$, $B \rightarrow C_1S$ and $C_1 \rightarrow 1$.
    (iii) $S \rightarrow 0B$, $A \rightarrow 0S$ give rise to $S \rightarrow C_0B$, $A \rightarrow C_0S$ and $C_0 \rightarrow 0$.
    (iv) $A \rightarrow 1AA$, $B \rightarrow 0BB$ give rise to $A \rightarrow C_1AA$ and $B \rightarrow C_0BB$.
        $V'_N = \{S, A, B, C_0, C_1\}$.

Step 3: $G_2 = (V_N'', \{0, 1\}, P_2, S)$, where P_2 and V_N'' are constructed as follows:

(i) $A \to 0$, $B \to 1$, $S \to C_1A$, $B \to C_1S$, $C_1 \to 1$, $S \to C_0B$, $A \to C_0S$, $C_0 \to 0$ are included in P_2.

(ii) $A \to C_1AA$ and $B \to C_0BB$ are replaced by $A \to C_1D_1$, $D_1 \to AA$, $B \to C_0D_2$, $D_2 \to BB$.

Thus $G_2 = (\{S, A, B, C_0, C_1, D_1, D_2\}, \{0, 1\}, P_2, S)$ is in CNF and equivalent to the given grammar where P_2 consists of $S \to C_1A \,|C_0B$, $A \to 0 \,|C_0S|C_1D_1$, $B \to 1|C_1S|C_0D_2$, $C_1 \to 1$, $C_0 \to 0$, $D_1 \to AA$ and $D_2 \to BB$.

(b) *Step 2:* $G_1 = (V_N', \{a, b, c\}, P_1, S)$, where P_1 and V_N' are defined as follows:

(i) $S \to a$, $S \to b$ are included in P_1

(ii) $S \to cSS$ is replaced by $S \to CSS$, $C \to c$, $V_N' = \{S, C\}$

Step 3: $G_2 = (V_N'', \{a, b, c\}, P_2, S)$, where P_2 is defined as follows:

(i) $S \to a$, $S \to b$, $C \to c$ are included in P_2.

(ii) $S \to CSS$ is replaced by $S \to CD$ and $D \to SS$.

Thus the equivalent grammar in CNF is $G_2 = (\{S, C, D\}, \{a, b, c\}, P_2, S)$, where P_2 consists of $S \to a|b| \ CD$, $C \to c$, $D \to SS$.

13. Consider $G = (\{S\}, \{a, b, +, *\}, P, S)$, where P consists of $S \to S + S$, $S \to S * S$, $S \to a$, $S \to b$.

Step 2: $G_1 = (V_N', \{a, b, +, *\}, P_1, S)$, where P_1 is constructed as follows:

(i) $S \to a$, $S \to b$ are included in P_1.

(ii) $S \to S + S$ and $S \to S * S$ are replaced by $S \to SAS$, $S \to SBS$, $A \to +$, $B \to *$

$$V_N' = \{S, A, B\}$$

Step 3: $G_2 = (V_N'', \{a, b, +, *\}, P_2, S)$, where P_2 is constructed as follows:

(i) $S \to a$, $S \to b$, $A \to +$ and $B \to *$ are included in P_2.

(ii) $S \to SAS$ and $S \to SBS$ give rise to $S \to SA_1$, $A_1 \to AS$, $S \to SB_1$, $B_1 \to BS$.

The required grammar in CNF is

$$G_2 = (\{S, A, B, A_1, B_1\}, \{a, b, +, *\}, P_2, S)$$

where P_2 consists of

$$S \to a|b|SA_1|SB_1, \quad A \to +, \ B \to *, \quad A_1 \to AS \text{ and } B_1 \to BS$$

14. (a) Rename S as A_1. By remark following Theorem 5.9, it is enough to replace terminals by new variables to get an equivalent grammar G_1. G_1 is defined as

$$G_1 = (\{A_1, A_2, A_3\}, \{0, 1\}, P_1, A_1)$$

where P_1 consists of

$$A_1 \rightarrow A_1A_1 \mid A_2A_1A_3 \mid A_2A_3, A_2 \rightarrow 0 \text{ and } A_3 \rightarrow 1$$

This completes step 1.

Step 2: All productions of G_1 except $A_1 \rightarrow A_1A_1$ are in proper form. Applying Lemma 5.2 to $A_1 \rightarrow A_1A_1$, we get a new variable Z_1 and new productions $A_1 \rightarrow A_2A_1A_3Z_1 \mid A_2A_3Z_1$, $Z_1 \rightarrow A_1$, $Z_1 \rightarrow A_1Z_1$. The new grammar is

$$G_2 = (\{A_1, A_2, A_3, Z_1\}, \{a, b\}, P_2, A_1)$$

where P_2 consists of

$$A_1 \rightarrow A_2A_1A_3 \mid A_2A_3 \mid A_2A_1A_3Z_1 \mid A_2A_3Z_1$$

$$Z_1 \rightarrow A_1Z_1, Z_1 \rightarrow A_1, A_2 \rightarrow 0 \text{ and } A_3 \rightarrow 1$$

Step 3: As A_3-productions and A_2-productions are in proper form we have to modify only A_1-productions using Lemma 5.1. So the modified A_1-productions are

$$A_1 \rightarrow 0A_1A_3 \mid 0A_3 \mid 0A_1A_3Z_1 \mid 0A_3Z_1$$

Step 4: The productions $Z_1 \rightarrow A_1$ and $Z_1 \rightarrow A_1Z_1$ are modified using Lemma 5.1. They are

$$Z_1 \rightarrow 0A_1A_3 \mid 0A_3 \mid 0A_1A_3Z_1 \mid 0A_3Z_1$$
$$Z_1 \rightarrow 0A_1A_3Z_1 \mid 0A_3Z_1 \mid 0A_1A_3Z_1Z_1 \mid 0A_3Z_1Z_1$$

Thus the required equivalent grammar in GNF is
$G_3 = (\{A_1, A_2, A_3, Z_1\}, \{0, 1\}, P_3, A_1)$, where P_3 consists of

$$A_1 \rightarrow 0A_1A_3 \mid 0A_3 \mid 0A_1A_3Z_1 \mid 0A_3Z_1$$

$$A_2 \rightarrow 0, A_3 \rightarrow 1$$

$$Z_1 \rightarrow 0A_1A_3 \mid 0A_3 \mid 0A_1A_3Z_1 \mid 0A_3Z_1$$

$$Z_1 \rightarrow 0A_1A_3Z_1 \mid 0A_3Z_1 \mid 0A_1A_3Z_1Z_1 \mid 0A_3Z_1Z_1$$

(b) *Step 1:* Replace $B \rightarrow aSb$ by $B \rightarrow aSC$ and $C \rightarrow b$. Rename S, A, B and C by A_1, A_2, A_3 and A_4. The resulting grammar is

$$G_1 = (\{A_1, A_2, A_3, A_4\}, \{a, b\}, P_1, A_1)$$

where P_1 consists of $A_1 \rightarrow A_2A_3, A_2 \rightarrow A_3A_3$

$$A_2 \rightarrow A_3A_1A_3, A_2 \rightarrow b, A_3 \rightarrow aA_2A_4, A_3 \rightarrow a \text{ and } A_4 \rightarrow b.$$

Steps 2, 3 and 4: Step 2 construction is not necessary for G_1. The only A_4-production, $A_4 \rightarrow b$, is in proper form. So we go to step 4. The modified A_2-productions are

$$A_2 \rightarrow aA_2A_4A_3 \mid aA_3 \mid aA_2A_4A_1A_3 \mid aA_1A_3 \mid b.$$

The modified A_1-productions are

$$A_1 \rightarrow aA_2A_4A_3A_3 \mid aA_3A_3 \mid aA_2A_4A_1A_3A_3 \mid aA_1A_3A_3 \mid bA_3.$$

Step 5 is not necessary since there is no new variable in the form in Z_i. So an equivalent grammar in GNF is

$$G_2 = (\{A_1, A_2, A_3, A_4\}, \{a, b\}, P_2, A_1)$$

where P_2 consists of

$$A_1 \rightarrow aA_2A_4A_3A_3 \mid aA_3A_3 \mid aA_2A_4A_1A_3A_3 \mid aA_1A_3A_3 \mid bA_3$$

$$A_2 \rightarrow aA_2A_4A_3 \mid aA_3 \mid aA_2A_4A_1A_3 \mid aA_1A_3 \mid b$$

$$A_3 \rightarrow aA_2A_4 \mid a, \quad A_4 \rightarrow b$$

15. The grammar given in Exercise 5.7 has the following productions: $S \rightarrow aB$, $S \rightarrow ab$, $A \rightarrow aAB$, $A \rightarrow a$, $B \rightarrow ABb$ and $B \rightarrow b$. Of these $S \rightarrow aB$, $A \rightarrow aAB$, $A \rightarrow a$ and $B \rightarrow b$ are in the required form. So we replace the terminals which appear in the second and subsequent places of the RHS of $S \rightarrow ab$ and $B \rightarrow ABb$ by a new variable C and add a production $C \rightarrow b$. Renaming S, B, A and C as A_1, A_2, A_3 and A_4, the modified productions turn out to be $A_1 \rightarrow aA_2$, $A_1 \rightarrow aA_4$, $A_3 \rightarrow aA_3A_2$, $A_3 \rightarrow a$, $A_2 \rightarrow A_3A_2A_4$, $A_2 \rightarrow b$ and $A_4 \rightarrow b$.

This completes the first three steps.

Step 4: $A_2 \rightarrow A_3A_2A_4$ is replaced by $A_2 \rightarrow aA_3A_2A_2A_4 \mid aA_2A_4$. The other productions are in the proper form. The resulting grammar in GNF has the productions

$$A_1 \rightarrow aA_2 \mid aA_4, \quad A_2 \rightarrow aA_3A_2A_2A_4 \mid aA_2A_4 \mid b, \quad A_3 \rightarrow aA_3A_2 \mid a, \quad A_4 \rightarrow b.$$

The grammar in Exercise 10 has unit productions. Eliminating unit productions, we get an equivalent grammar G, where

$$G = (\{S, A, B, C, D, E\}, \{a, b\}, P, S)$$

where P consists of $S \rightarrow AB$, $A \rightarrow a$, $B \rightarrow a \mid b$, $C \rightarrow a$, $D \rightarrow a$ and $E \rightarrow a$. Rename S, A, B, C, D and E as A_1, A_2, A_3, A_4, A_5 and A_6.

Thus P consists of $A_1 \rightarrow A_2A_3$, $A_2 \rightarrow a$, $A_3 \rightarrow a \mid b$, $A_4 \rightarrow a$, $A_5 \rightarrow a$ and $A_6 \rightarrow a$.

We have to modify only $A_1 \rightarrow A_2A_3$ using Lemma 5.1.

Thus an equivalent grammar in GNF has the following productions:

$$A_1 \rightarrow aA_3, \quad A_2 \rightarrow a, \quad A_3 \rightarrow a|b, \quad A_4 \rightarrow a, \quad A_5 \rightarrow a \text{ and } A_6 \rightarrow a.$$

16. (a) The given language is generated by a grammar whose productions are $S \rightarrow aSa \mid bSb \mid c$.

Step 2:   (i) $S \rightarrow c$ is in P_1

(ii) $S \rightarrow aSa$ and $S \rightarrow bSb$ give rise to

$$S \rightarrow ASA, \quad S \rightarrow BSB, \quad A \rightarrow a, \quad B \rightarrow b \text{ in } P_1$$

Thus $G_1 = (\{S, A, B\}, \{a, b, c\}, P_1, S)$, where P_1 consists of $S \rightarrow ASA \mid BSB \mid c$, $A \rightarrow a$ and $B \rightarrow b$.

Step 3: The equivalent grammar G_2 in CNF is defined by
$G_2 = (\{S, A, B, A_1, B_1\}, \{a, b, c\}, P_2, S)$, where P_2 consists of

$$S \to AA_1, A_1 \to SA, S \to BB_1, B_1 \to SB, A \to a, B \to b, S \to c.$$

(b) The grammar generating the given set is having the productions $S \to bA|aB, A \to bAA|aS|a, B \to aBB|bS|b$.

Step 2: The productions obtained in this step are:
$S \to B_1A, B_1 \to b, S \to A_1B, A_1 \to a, A \to B_1AA, A \to A_1S, A \to a, B \to A_1BB, B \to B_1S, B \to b$.

Step 3: The equivalent grammar in CNF is given by
$G_2 = (V_N'', \{a, b\}, P_2, S)$, where P_2 consists of

(i) $S \to B_1A, B_1 \to b, S \to A_1B, A_1 \to a, A \to A_1S, A \to a, B \to B_1S, B \to b$
(ii) $A \to B_1C_1, C_1 \to AA, B \to A_1C_2, C_2 \to BB$ (corresponding to $A \to B_1AA$ and $B \to A_1BB$).

17. (a) The grammar generating the given language has the productions $S \to aSa, S \to bSb, S \to c$. The first two productions will be in GNF if the last symbols on RHS are variables. Hence $S \to aSa, S \to bSb$ can be replaced by $S \to aSA, A \to a, S \to bSB, B \to b$. Hence $G' = (\{S, A, B\}, \{a, b\}, P', S)$, where P' consists of $S \to aSA|bSB, S \to c, A \to a, B \to b$ is in GNF and is generating the given language.

(b) The given language is generated by

$G = (\{S, A, B\}, \{a, b\}, P, S)$, where P consists of

$S \to bA|aB, A \to bAA|aS| a, B \to aBB|bS|b$. This itself is in GNF.

(c) The given language is generated by a grammar whose productions are $S \to aAb, S \to aA, A \to aA, A \to a, S \to a, S \to bB, B \to b$ and $S \to b$. Of these productions we have to modify only one production viz., $S \to aSb$. This is done by replacing this production by $S \to aSB_1$, $B_1 \to b$. (*Note:* In this problem we can also replace $S \to aSb$ by $S \to aSB$ alone. $B \to b$ is already in the grammar and there are no other B-productions.)

(d) The given language is generated by a grammar whose productions are $S \to aSb, S \to cS, S \to c$. The equivalent grammar in GNF is

$$G = (\{S, B\}, \{a, b, c\}, P, S),$$

where P consists of $S \to aSB, B \to b, S \to cS, S \to c$.

18. (i) Let $w \in L(G)$ and $|w| = k$. In Chomsky normal form, each production yields one terminal or two variables but nothing else. For getting the terminals in w, we have to apply production of the form $A \to a$ (k times). The corresponding string of variables, which is of length k, can be obtained by $k - 1$ steps. (Each production $A \to BC$ increases the number of variables by one.) So the total number of steps is $2k - 1$. (The reader is advised to prove this result by induction on $|w|$.)

(ii) When G is in GNF, the number of steps in the derivation of w is k (k

$= |w|$). The number of terminals increases by 1 for each application of a production to a sentential form. Hence the number of steps in the derivation of w is k.

19. *Step 1:*   Let n be the natural number got by applying pumping lemma.

Step 2:   Let $z = a^{n^2}$. Write $z = uvwxy$ where $1 \leq |vx| \leq n$ (This is possible since $|vwx| \leq n$ by (ii) of pumping lemma). Let $|vx| = m$, $m \leq n$. By pumping lemma, uv^2wx^2y is in L. As $|uv^2wx^2y| > n^2$, $|uv^2wx^2y| = k^2$, where $k \geq n + 1$. But $|uv^2wx^2y| = n^2 + m < n^2 + 2n + 1$. So $|uv^2wx^2y|$ strictly lies between n^2 and $(n+1)^2$ which means $uv^2wx^2y \notin L$, a contradiction. Hence $\{a^{n^2} : n \geq 1\}$ is not context-free.

20. (a) Take $z = a^n b^n c^n$ in $L(G)$. Write $z = uvwxy$, where $1 \leq |vx| \leq n$. So vx cannot contain all the three symbols a, b and c. So uv^2wx^2y contain additional occurrences of two symbols (found in vx) and the number of occurrences of the third symbol remains the same. This means the number of occurrences of the three symbols in uv^2wx^2y are not the same and so $uv^2wx^2y \notin L$. This is a contradiction. Hence the language is not context-free.

(b) As usual, n is the integer obtained from pumping lemma. Let $z = a^n b^n c^{2n}$. Then $z = uvwxy$, where $1 \leq |vx| \leq n$. So vx cannot contain all the three symbols a, b and c. If vx contains only a's and b's then we can choose i such that uv^iwx^iy has more than $2n$ occurrences of a (or b) and exactly $2n$ occurrences of c. This means $uv^iwx^iy \notin L$, a contradiction. In other cases also we can get a contradiction by proper choice of i. Thus the given language is not context-free.

21. (a) Suppose $G = (V_N, \Sigma, P, S)$ is right-linear. A production of the form $A \to a_1a_2 \ldots a_mB$, $m \geq 2$ can be replaced by $A \to a_1A_1$, $A_1 \to a_2A_2 \ldots$, $A_{m-1} \to a_mB$. $A \to b_1b_2 \ldots b_m$, $m \geq 2$, can be replaced by $A \to b_1B_1$, $B_1 \to b_2B_2$, $\ldots B_{m-2} \to b_{m-1}B_{m-1}$, $B_{m-1} \to b_m$. The required equivalent regular grammar G' is defined by the new productions constructed above.

If $G = (V_N, \Sigma, P, S)$ is left-linear, then an equivalent right-linear grammar can be defined as $G_1 = (V'_N, \Sigma, P_1, S)$, where P_1 consists of

(i) $S \to w$ when $S \to w$ is in P and $w \in \Sigma^*$,
(ii) $S \to wA$ when $A \to w$ is in P and $w \in \Sigma^*$,
(iii) $A \to wB$ when $B \to Aw$ is in P and $w \in \Sigma^*$,
(iv) $A \to w$ when $S \to Aw$ is in P and $w \in \Sigma^*$.

Let $w \in L(G)$. If $S \Rightarrow w$ then $S \to w$ is in P. Therefore, $S \to w$ is in P_1 (by (i)).

Assume $S \Rightarrow A_1w_1 \Rightarrow A_2w_2w_1 \Rightarrow \ldots A_{m-1}w_{m-1} \ldots w_1 \Rightarrow w_mw_{m-1} \ldots w_1 = w$ is a derivation in G. Then the productions applied in the derivation are $S \to A_1w_1$, $A_1 \to A_2w_2$, $\ldots$, $A_{m-1} \to w_m$.

The induced productions in G_1 are

$$A_1 \to w_1, \quad A_2 \to w_2A_1, \quad A_3 \to w_3A_2, \quad \ldots, \quad S \to w_mA_{m-1}.$$

(by (ii), (iii) and (iv) in the construction of P_1).

Taking the productions in the reverse order we get a derivation of G_1 as follows:

$$S \Rightarrow w_m A_{m-1} \Rightarrow \cdots \Rightarrow w_m w_{m-1} \cdots w_3 A_2 \Rightarrow w_m \cdots w_2 A_1 \Rightarrow w_m \cdots w_1.$$

Thus $L(G) \subseteq L(G')$. The other inclusion can be proved in a similar way. So G is equivalent to a right-linear grammar G_1 which is equivalent to a regular grammar.

(b) Let $G = (\{S, A\}, \{a, b, c\}, P, S)$, where P consists of $S \to Sc|Ac, A \to aAb|ab$. G is linear (by the presence of $A \to aAb$).

$$L(G) = \{a^n b^n c^m \mid m, n \geq 1\}$$

Using pumping lemma we prove that $L(G)$ is not regular. Let n be the number of states in a finite automaton accepting $L(G)$.

Let $w = a^n b^n c^m$. By pumping lemma $w = xyz$, where $|xy| \leq n$ and $|y| > 0$. If $y = a^k$ then $xz = a^{n-k} b^n c^m$. This is not in $L(G)$. By pumping lemma, $xz \in L(G)$ a contradiction.

22. $L = L(G)$, where G is a regular grammar. For every variable A in G, $A \overset{*}{\Rightarrow} \alpha$ implies $\alpha = uB$, where $u \in \Sigma^*$ and $B \in V$. Thus G is nonself embedding. To prove the sufficiency part assume G is a nonself-embedding, context-free grammar. If G' is reduced, in Greibach normal form and equivalent to G, then G' is also nonself-embedding. (This can be proved). Let $|\Sigma| = n$ and m be the maximum of the lengths of right hand sides of productions in G'. Let α be any sentential form. By considering left-most derivations we can show that the number of variables in α is $\leq mn$. (Use the fact that G' is in GNF). Define

$$G_1 = (V'_N, \Sigma, P_1, S) \text{ where}$$

$$V'_N = \{[\alpha] \mid |\alpha| \leq mn \text{ and } \alpha \in V_N^+\}$$

$$S_1 = [S_1]$$

$$P_1 = \{[A\beta] \to b[\alpha\ \beta] \mid A \to b\alpha \text{ is in } P, \beta \in V'_N \text{ and } |\alpha\beta| \leq mn\}$$

G_1 is regular. It can be verified that $L(G_1) = L(G')$.

CHAPTER 6

1. $(q_0, aacaa, Z_0) \vdash (q_0, acaa, aZ_0) \vdash (q_0, caa, aaZ_0) \vdash (q_1, a, aaZ_0) \vdash$
    $(q_1, a, aZ_0) \vdash (q_1, \Lambda, Z_0) \vdash (q_f, \Lambda, Z_0).$
    (i)   Yes, the final ID is (q_f, Λ, Z_0).
    (ii) Yes, the final ID is (q_1, Λ, aZ_0).
    (iii) No, the pda halts at (q_1, ba, aZ_0).
    (iv) Yes, the final ID is $(q_1, \Lambda, abaZ_0)$.
    (v)   Yes the final ID is $(q_0, \Lambda, babaZ_0)$.

2. (i) (q_1, Λ, aZ_0).
    (ii) Halts at (q_1, b, Λ).

(iii) (q_0, Λ, a^5Z_0).
(iv) Does not move.
(v) Does not move.
(vi) Halts at (q_1, ab, Z_0).

3. (a) Example 6.9.
   (b) The required pda A is defined as follows:

   $A = (\{q_0, q_1, q_2\}, \{a, b\}, \{a, Z_0\}, \delta, q_0, Z_0, \varnothing)$. δ is defined by

   $\delta(q_0, a, Z_0) = \{(q_1, aZ_0)\}$, $\delta(q_1, a, a) = \{(q_1, aa)\}$
   $\delta(q_1, b, a) = \{(q_2, a)\}$, $\delta(q_2, b, a) = \{(q_1, \Lambda)\}$
   $\delta(q_1, \Lambda, Z_0) = \{(q_1, \Lambda)\}$.

   (c) $A = (\{q_0, q_1\}, \{a, b, c\}, \{Z_0, Z_1\}, \delta, q_0, Z_0, \varnothing)$

   δ is defined by
   $\delta(q_0, a, Z_0) = \{(q_0, Z_1Z_0)\}$, $\delta(q_0, a, Z_1) = \{(q_0, Z_1Z_1)\}$
   $\delta(q_0, b, Z_1) = \{(q_1, \Lambda)\}$, $\delta(q_1, b, Z_1) = \{(q_1, \Lambda)\}$
   $\delta(q_1, c, Z_0) = \{(q_1, Z_0)\}$, $\delta(q_1, \Lambda, Z_0) = \{(q_1, \Lambda)\}$

   Note that, on reading a, we add Z_1; on reading b we remove Z_1 and the state is changed. If the input is completely read and the stack symbol is Z_0, then it is removed by a Λ-move.

4. (a) Example 6.9 gives a pda accepting $\{a^n b^m a^n \mid m, n \geq 1\}$ by null store. Using Theorem 6.1, a pda B accepting the given language by final state is constructed.

   $B = (\{q_0, q_1, q_0', q_f\}, \{a, b\}, \{a, Z_0, Z_0'\}, \delta, q_0', Z_0', \{q_f\})$

   δ is defined by
   $\delta(q_0', \Lambda, Z_0') = \{(q_0, Z_0Z_0')\}$

   $\delta(q_0, \Lambda, Z_0') = \{(q_f, \Lambda)\} = \delta(q_0, \Lambda, Z_0')$

   $\delta(q_1, \Lambda, Z_0') = \{(q_f, \Lambda)\} = \delta(q_1, \Lambda, Z_0')$

   $\delta(q_0, a, Z_0) = \{(q_0, aZ_0)\}$, $\delta(q_0, a, a) = \{(q_0, aa)\}$
   $\delta(q_0, b, a) = \{(q_1, a)\}$, $\delta(q_1, b, a) = \{(q_1, a)\}$
   $\delta(q_1, a, a) = \{(q_f, \Lambda)\}$, $\delta(q_1, \Lambda, Z_0) = \{(q_1, \Lambda)\}$

5. (a) $G = (\{S, S_1, S_2\}, \{a, b\}, P, S)$ generates the given language, where P consists of $S \to S_1, S \to S_2, S_1 \to aS_1b, S_1 \to ab, S_2 \to aS_2bb, S_2 \to abb$. The pda accepting $L(G)$ by null store is

   $A = (\{q\}, \{a, b\}, \{S, S_1, S_2, a, b\}, \delta, q, S, \varnothing)$

   where δ is defined by the following rules:

   $\delta(q, \Lambda, S) = \{(q, S_1), (q, S_2)\}$
   $\delta(q, \Lambda, S_1) = \{(q, aS_1b), (q, ab)\}$
   $\delta(q, \Lambda, S_2) = \{(q, aS_2bb), (q, abb)\}$
   $\delta(q, a, a) = \delta(q, b, b) = \{(q, \Lambda)\}$

6. (i) $G = (\{S\}, \{a, b\}, P, S)$, where P consists of $S \to aSb, S \to aS, S \to a$, generates

$\{a^m b^n \mid n < m\}$. For $S \Rightarrow a^m Sb^m$, $m \geq 0$.

$S \Rightarrow a^n$, $n \geq 1$, and hence $S \Rightarrow a^m a^n b^m$, $m \geq 0, n \geq 1$.

So $L(G) \subseteq \{a^m b^n \mid n < m\}$. The other inclusion can be proved similarly.

(ii) The pda A accepting $L(G)$ by null store is given by

$$A = (\{q\}, \{a, b\}, \{S, a, b\}, \delta, q, S, \varnothing),$$

where δ is defined by the following rules:

$$\delta(q, \Lambda, S) = \{(q, aSb), (q, aS), (q, a)\}$$
$$\delta(q, a, a) = \delta(q, b, b) = \{(q, \Lambda)\}$$

(iii) Define $B = (Q', \Sigma, \Gamma', \delta_B, q_0', Z_0', F)$, where

$$Q' = \{q_0, q_0', q_f\}, \Gamma' = \{S, a, b, Z_0'\}$$
$$F = \{q_f\}. \text{ (We apply Theorem 6.1 to (ii)).}$$

δ_B is given by

$\delta_B (q_0', \Lambda, Z_0') = \{(q, Z_0 Z_0')\}$

$\delta_B (q, \Lambda, S) = \{(q, aSb), (q, aS), (q, a)\}$.

$\delta_B (q, a, a) = \{(q, \Lambda)\} = \delta_B (q, b, b)$

$\delta_B (q, \Lambda, Z_0') = \{(q_f, \Lambda)\}$

(Note $\delta_B (q, a, S) = \delta(q, a, s) = \varnothing)$ and $\delta_B (q, b, S) = \delta(q, b, S) = \varnothing$

7. (i) Define $G = (\{S\}, \{a, b\}, P, S)$, where P consists of

$$S \to SaSbSaS, S \to SaSaSbS, S \to SbSaSaS, S \to \Lambda$$

(refer Exercise 3.10 (e)). G is the required grammar. (ii) Apply Theorem 6.3. (iii) Apply Theorem 6.1 to the pda obtained in (ii).

8. Let $A = (\{q_0, q_1\}, \{a, b\}, \{Z_0, a, b\}, \delta, q_0, Z_0, \varnothing)$, where δ is given by

$\delta(q_0, a, Z_0) = \{(q_0, aZ_0)\}, \delta(q_0, b, Z_0) = \{(q_0, bZ_0)\}$

$\delta(q_0, a, b) = \{(q_0, ab)\}, \delta(q_0, b, a) = \{(q_0, ba)\}$

$\delta(q_0, a, a) = \{(q_0, aa), (q_1, \Lambda)\}$

$\delta(q_0, b, b) = \{(q_0, bb), (q_1, \Lambda)\}$

$\delta(q_0, \Lambda, Z_0) = \{(q_1, \Lambda)\}$

$\delta(q_1, a, a) = \{(q_1, \Lambda)\}, \delta(q_1, b, b) = \{(q_1, \Lambda)\}$

$\delta(q_1, \Lambda, Z_0) = \{(q_1, \Lambda)\}$

A makes a guess whether it has reached the centre of the string. A reaches the centre only when the input symbol and the topmost symbol on PDS are the same. This explains the definition of $\delta(q_0, a, a)$ and $\delta(q_0, b, b)$. A accepts the given set by null store.

9. Example 6.6 gives a pda A accepting the given set by empty store. The only problem is that it is not deterministic. (We have $\delta(q, a, Z_0) = \{(q, aZ_0)\}$ and $\delta(q, \Lambda, Z_0) = \{(q, \Lambda).\}$ So A is not deterministic (refer Definition 6.5). But the construction can be modified as follows:

$$A_1 = (\{q, q_1\}, \{a, b\}, \{Z_0, a, b\}, \delta, q, Z_0, \varnothing)$$

where δ is defined by the following rules:

$\delta(q, a, Z_0) = \{(q_1, aZ_0)\}, \quad \delta(q, b, Z_0) = \{(q_1, bZ_0)\}$
$\delta(q_1, a, a) = \{(q_1, aa)\}, \quad \delta(q_1, b, b) = \{(q_1, bb)\}$
$\delta(q_1, a, b) = \{(q_1, \Lambda)\}, \quad \delta(q_1, b, a) = \{(q_1, \Lambda)\}$
$\delta(q_1, \Lambda, Z_0) = \{(q_1, \Lambda)\}$

A_1 is deterministic and accepts the given set by empty store.

10. The S-productions are

$$S \to [q_0, Z_0, q_0] \mid [q_0, Z_0, q_1]$$
$$\delta(q_1, b, a) = \{(q_1, \Lambda)\}, \delta(q_1, \Lambda, Z_0) = \{(q_1, \Lambda)\}$$

and $\qquad \delta(q_0, b, a) = \{(q_1, \Lambda)\}$

Now these induce $[q_1, a, q_1] \to b$, $[q_1, Z_0, q_1] \to \Lambda$ and $[q_0, a, q_1] \to b$, respectively. $\delta(q_0, a, Z_0) = \{(q_0, aZ_0)\}$ induces

$[q_0, Z_0, q_0] \to a \; [q_0, a, q_0] \; [q_0, Z_0, q_0]$
$[q_0, Z_0, q_0] \to a \; [q_0, a, q_1] \; [q_1, Z_0, q_0]$
$[q_0, Z_0, q_1] \to a \; [q_0, a, q_0] \; [q_0, Z_0, q_1]$
$[q_0, Z_0, q_1] \to a \; [q_0, a, q_1] \; [q_1, Z_0, q_1]$

$\delta(q_0, a, a) = \{(q_0, aa)\}$ induces

$[q_0, a, q_0] \to a \; [q_0, a, q_0] \; [q_0, a, q_0]$
$[q_0, a, q_0] \to a \; [q_0, a, q_1] \; [q_1, a, q_0]$
$[q_0, a, q_1] \to a \; [q_0, a, q_0] \; [q_0, a, q_1]$
$[q_0, a, q_1] \to a \; [q_0, a, q_1] \; [q_1, a, q_1]$

13. Let $M = (Q, \Sigma, \delta, q_0, F)$ be a DFA accepting a given regular set. Define a pda A by $A = (Q, \Sigma, \{Z_0\}. \delta_1, q_0, Z_0, F)$. δ is given by the following rule:

$$\delta_1 (q, a, Z_0) = \{(q', Z_0)\} \text{ if } \delta(q, a) = q'$$

It is easy to see that $T(M) = T(A)$. Let $w \in T(M)$. Then $\delta(q_0, w) = q' \in F$. $\delta(q_0, w, Z_0) = \{(q', Z_0)\}$. So $w \in T(A)$, i.e., $T(M) \subseteq T(A)$. The proof that $T(A) \subseteq T(M)$ is similar.

15. If $\delta(q, a, z)$ contains $(q', Z_1 Z_2 \ldots Z_n)$, $n \geq 3$, we introduce new states q_1, $q_2, \ldots, q_{n-2}$. We define new transitions involving new states as follows:

(i) $(q_1, Z_{n-1} Z_n)$ is included in $\delta(q, a, Z)$

(ii) $\delta(q_i, \Lambda, Z_{n-i}) = \{(q_{i+1}, Z_{n-i-1} Z_{n-i})\}$ for $i = 1, 2, \ldots, n-3$

(iii) $\delta(q_{n-2}, \Lambda, Z_2) = \{(q', Z_1 Z_2)\}$

This construction is repeated for every transition given by $(q', \gamma) \in \delta(q, a, Z)$, $|\gamma| \geq 3$. Deleting such transitions and adding the new transitions induced by them we get a pda which never adds more than one symbol at a time.

CHAPTER 7

2. The set of quintuples representing the TM consists of q_1b1Lq_2, q_100Rq_1, $q_2\,bbRq_3$, q_200Lq_2, q_211Lq_2, q_30bRq_4, q_31bRq_5, q_4b0Rq_5, q_400Rq_4, q_411Rq_4, q_5b0Lq_2.

3. The computation for the first symbol 1 is $q_111b11 \vdash bq_2b11$. Afterwards it halts.

4. The computation sequence for the substring 12 of 1213 is

$$q_11213 \vdash bq_2213 \vdash bbq_313.$$

As $\delta(q_3, 1)$ is not defined, the TM halts. For 2133 and 312 the TM does not start.

6. Modify the construction given in Example 7.7.

8. We have the following steps for processing even-length palindromes:

(a) The Turing machine M scans the first symbol of the input tape (0 or 1), erases it and changes state (q_1 or q_2).

(b) M scans the remaining part without changing the tape symbol until it encounters b.

(c) The R/W head moves to the left. If the rightmost symbol tallies with the leftmost symbol (which can be erased but remembered), the rightmost symbol is erased. Otherwise M halts.

(d) The R/W head moves to the left until b is encountered.

Steps (a), (b), (c), (d) are repeated after changing the states suitably. The transition table is given in Table A7.1.

Table A7.1   Transition Table for Exercise 7.8

Present state	Input symbol		
	0	1	b
$\rightarrow$ q_0	bRq_1	bRq_2	bRq_7
q_1	$0Rq_1$	$1Rq_1$	bLq_3
q_2	$0Rq_1$	$1Rq_2$	bLq_4
q_3	bLq_5		
q_4		bLq_6	
q_5	$0Lq_5$	$1Lq_5$	bRq_0
q_6	$0Lq_6$	$1Lq_6$	bRq_0
q_7			

9. We have three states q_0, q_1, q_f. q_0 is the initial state which is used for remembering that even number of 1's are encountered so far. q_1 is used to remember that odd number of 1's are encountered so far. q_f is the final state. The transition table is given in Table A7.2.

Table A7.2   Transition Table for Exercise 7.9

Present state	0	1	b
$\rightarrow$ q_0	$0Rq_0$	$1Rq_1$	bRq_f
q_1	$0Rq_1$	$1Rq_0$	
$\widehat{q_f}$			

10. The construction given in Example 7.7 can be modified. As the number of occurrences of c is independent of that of a or b, after scanning the rightmost c, the R/W head can move to the left and erase c.

11. Assume that the input tape has $0^m 1 0^n$ where $m \dot{-} n$ is required. We have the following steps:
(a) The leftmost 0 is replaced by b and R/W head moves to the right.
(b The R/W head replaces the first 0 after 1 by 1 and moves to the left. On reaching the blank at the left end the cycle is repeated.
(c) Once the 0's to the left of 1's are exhausted, M replaces all 0's and 1's by b's. $a \dot{-} b$ is the number of 0's left over in the input tape and equal to 0.
(d) Once the 0's to the right of 1's are exhausted, n 0's have been changed to 1's and $n + 1$ of m 0's have been changed to b. M replaces 1's (there are $n + 1$ 1's) by one 0 and n b's. The number of 0's left over gives the values of $a \dot{-} b$. The transition table is given in Table A7.3.

Table A7.3   Transition Table for Exercise 7.11

Present state	Input symbol		
	0	1	b
$\rightarrow$ q_0	bRq_1	bRq_5	
q_1	$0Rq_1$	$1Rq_2$	
q_2	$1Lq_3$	$1Rq_2$	bLq_4
q_3	$0Lq_3$	$1Lq_3$	bRq_0
q_4	$0Lq_4$	bLq_4	$0Rq_6$
q_5	bRq_5	bRq_5	bRq_6
$\widehat{q_6}$			

12. Suppose the problem is solvable. Then there is an algorithm to decide whether a given terminal string w is in L. Let M be a TM. Then there is a grammar G such that $L(G)$ is the same as the set accepted by M (refer section 7.7.1). Then $w \in L(G)$ if and only if M halts on w. This means the halting problem of TM is solvable, which is a contradiction. Hence the recursiveness of a type 0 grammar is unsolvable.

14. By Example 7.12 there exists a Turing Machine M over $\{0, 1\}$ and a state q_m such that the problem of determining whether or not M will enter q_m is unsolvable. Define a new Turing machine M' which simulates M and have the additional transition given by $\delta(q_m, \Lambda) = (q_m, 1, R)$. Then M enters q_m when it starts with a given tape configuration if and only if M' prints 1 when it starts with a given tape configuration. Hence the given problem is unsolvable.

17. According to Church's thesis (section 7.9.1), we can construct a Turing Machine which can execute any given algorithm. Hence the given statement is false. (Of course, Church's thesis is not proved. But there is enough evidence to justify its acceptance.)

18. Let $\Sigma = \{a\}$, Let $x = (x_1, x_2, ..., x_n)$ and $y = (y_1, y_2, ..., y_n)$, where $x_i = a^{k_i}$, $i = 1, 2, ..., n$ and $y_j = a^{l_j}$, $j = 1, 2, ..., n$. Then $(x_1)^{l_1} (x_2)^{l_2} ... (x_n)^{l_n} = (y_1)^{k_1} (y_2)^{k_2} ... (y_n)^{k_n}$. Both are equal to $a^{\Sigma k_i l_i}$. Hence PCP is solvable when $|\Sigma| = 1$.

20. $x_1 = 01$, $y_1 = 011$, $x_2 = 1$, $y_2 = 10$, $x_3 = 1$, $y_3 = 1$. Hence $|x_i| < |y_i|$ for $i = 1, 2, 3$. So $x_{i_1} x_{i_2} ... x_{i_m} \neq y_{i_1} y_{i_2} ... y_{i_m}$ for no choice of i's. *Note:* $|x_{i_1} x_{i_2} ... x_{i_m}| < |y_{i_1} y_{i_2} ... y_{i_m}|$. Hence the PCP with the given lists has no solution.

21. $x_1 = 0$, $y_1 = 10$, $x_2 = 110$, $y_2 = 000$, $x_3 = 001$, $y_3 = 10$. Here no pair (x_1, y_1), (x_2, y_2) or (x_3, y_3) have common nonempty initial substring. So $x_{i_1} x_{i_2} ... x_{i_m} \neq y_{i_1} y_{i_2} ... y_{i_m}$ for no choice of i_j's. Hence the PCP with the given lists has no solution.

22. As $x_1 = y_1$, the PCP with the given lists has a solution.

23. In this problem, $x_1 = 1$, $x_2 = 10$, $x_3 = 1011$, $y_1 = 111$, $y_2 = 0$, $y_3 = 10$. Then $x_3 x_1 x_1 x_2 = y_3 y_1 y_1 y_2 = 101111110$. Hence the PCP with the given lists has a solution. Repeating the sequence 3, 1, 1, 2 we can get more solutions.

24. Both (a) and (b) are possible. One of them is possible by Church's thesis (find which one).

CHAPTER 8

1. For a sentential form such as $a^{n+1}b^n$, $A \rightarrow a$ is the production applied in the last step only when a is followed by ab. So $A \rightarrow a$ is a handle production if and only if the symbol to the right of a is scanned and found to be b. Similarly, $A \rightarrow aAb$ is a handle production if and only if the symbol to the right of aAb is b. Also, $S \rightarrow aAb$ is a handle production if and only if the

symbol to the right of *aAb* is Λ. Therefore, the grammar is LR(1), but not LR(0).

2. We can actually show that the given grammar is not LR(k) for any $k \geq 0$. Suppose it is LR(k) for some k. Consider the rightmost derivations of $01^{2k+1}2$ and $01^{2k+3}2$ given by:

$$S \underset{R}{\overset{*}{\Rightarrow}} 01^{k}A1^{k}2 \underset{R}{\Rightarrow} 01^{2k+1}2 = \alpha\beta w \tag{A8.1}$$

where $\alpha = 01^{k}$, $\beta = a$, $w = 1^{k}2$.

$$S \underset{R}{\overset{*}{\Rightarrow}} 01^{k+1}A1^{k+1}2 \underset{R}{\Rightarrow} 01^{2k+3}2 \Rightarrow \alpha'\beta'w' \tag{A8.2}$$

where $\alpha' = 01^{k+1}$, $\beta' = a$, $w' = 1^{k+1}2$. As the strings formed by first $2k+1$ symbols (note $|\alpha\beta| + k = 2k + 1$) of $\alpha\beta w$ and $\alpha'\beta'w'$ are the same, $\alpha = \alpha'$, i.e. $01^{k} = 01^{k+1}$, which is a contradiction. Thus the given grammar is not LR(k) for any k.

3. The given grammar is ambiguous and hence is not LR(k) for any k. For example, there are two derivation trees for *ab*.

4. As $a^{n}b^{n}c^{n}$ appears in both the sets, it admits two different derivation trees. So the set cannot be generated by an unambiguous grammar.

CHAPTER 9

1. (a) The function is defined for all natural numbers divisible by 3.
   (b) $x = 2$
   (c) $x \geq 2$
   (d) all natural numbers
   (e) all natural numbers

2. (a) $\chi_{\{0\}}(0) = 1$, $\chi_{\{0\}}(x+1) = \chi_{\{0\}}\text{sgn }(p(x))$.
   (b) $f(x+1) = x^2 + 2x + 1$.

   So $f(x + 1) = f(x) + S(S(Z(x))) * U_1^1(x) + S(Z(x))$.

   Hence f is obtained by recursion and addition of primitive recursive functions

   (c) $f(x, y) = y + (x \overset{.}{-} y)$

   (d) Define parity function $P_r(y)$ by

   $$P_r(0) = P_r(2) = \ldots = 0, \qquad P_r(1) = P_r(3) = \ldots = 1$$

   P_r is primitive recursive since $P_r(0) = 0$, $P_r(x+1) = \chi_{\{0\}}(U_2^2(x), P_r(x))$.
   Define f by $f(0) = 0$, $f(x+1) = f(x) + P_r(x)$.

   (e) $\text{sgn }(0) = Z(0)$, $\text{sgn }(x+1) = S(Z(U_2^2 (x, \text{sgn }(x))))$

   (f) $L(x, y) = \text{sgn }(x \overset{.}{-} y)$

   (g) $E(x, y) = \chi_{\{0\}} ((x \overset{.}{-} y) + (y \overset{.}{-} x)$

   All the functions (a)–(g) are obtained by applying composition and recursion to known primitive functions and hence primitive recursive functions.

3. $A(1, y) = A(1 + 0, y - 1 + 1) = A(0, A(1, y - 1))$ using (9.10) of Example 9.11. Using (9.8), we get

$$A(1, y) = 1 + A(1, y - 1).$$

Repeating the argument, we have

$A(1, y) = y - 1 + A(1, 1) = y + 2$ (By Example 9.12, $A(1, 1) = 3$).

This result is used in evaluating $A(3, 1)$.

$A(2, 3) = A(1+ 1, 2 + 1) = A(1, A(2, 2)) = A(1, 7)$ using Example 9.12.

Using $A(1, y) = y + 2$, we get $A(2, 3) = 2 + 7 = 9$. Then using (9.10),
$A(3, 1) = A(2 + 1, 0 + 1) = A(2, A(3, 0))$

By Example 9.12, $A(2, 1) = 5$. Also, $A(3, 0) = A(2, 1)$ by (9.9). Hence
$A(3, 1) = A(2, 5) = A(1+ 1, 4 + 1) = A(1, A(2, 4))$. Since $A(1, y) = y + 2$,
$A(3, 1) = 2 + A(2, 4)$. Applying (9.10), we have

$A(2, 4) = A(1, A(2, 3)) = 2 + A(2, 3) = 2 + 9 = 11$.

Hence,

$A(3, 1) = 2 + 11 = 13$,

$A(3, 2) = A(2, A(3, 1)) = A(2, 13) = A(1, A(2, 12)) = 2 + A(2, 12)$
$= 2 + A(1, A(1, 11)) = 2 + A(1, 13) = 2 + 2 + 13 = 17$.

To evaluate $A(3, 3)$, we prove $A(2, y + 1) = 2y + A(2, 1)$. Now

$A(2, y + 1) = A(1+ 1, y + 1) = A(1, A(2, y)) = 2 + A(2, y)$.

Repeating this argument, $A(2, y + 1) = 2y + A(2, 1)$. Now

$A(3, 3) = A(2 + 1, 2 + 1) = A(2, A(3, 2)) = A(2, 17) = 2(16) + A(2, 1)$
$= 32 + 5 = 37$.

4. (b) It is clear that $r(x, 0) = 0$. Also, $r(x, y)$ increases by 1 when y is increased by 1 and $r(x, y) = 0$ when $y = x$. Using these observations we see that $r(x, y + 1) = S(r (x, y)) * \text{sgn} (x \dotdiv S(r (x, y)))$. Hence $r(x, y)$ is defined by

$$r(x, 0) = 0$$

$$r(x, y + 1) = S(r(x, y)) * \text{sgn} (x \dotdiv S(r(x, y))).$$

5. $f(x)$ is the smallest value of y for which $(y + 1)^2 > x$. Therefore, $f(x) = \mu_y$ $(\chi_{\{0\}}((y + 1)^2 \dotdiv x))$, f is partial recursive since it is obtained from primitive recursive functions by application of minimisation.

8. The constant function $f(x) = 1$ is primitive recursive for $f(0) = 1$ and $f(x + 1) = U_2^2(x, f(x))$. Now χ_{A^c}, $\chi_{A \cap B}$ and $\chi_{A \cup B}$ are recursive for $\chi_{A^c} = 1 \dotdiv \chi_A$, $\chi_{A \cap B} = \chi_A * \chi_B$ and $\chi_{A \cup B} = \chi_A + \chi_B \dotdiv \chi_{A \cap B}$
(Addition and proper subtraction are primitive recursive functions and the given functions are obtained from recursive functions using composition.)

9. Let E denote the set of all even numbers. $\chi_E(0) = 0$, $\chi_E(n+1) = 1 \doteq \text{sgn}$ $(U_2^2(n, \chi_E(n)))$. The sign function and proper subtraction function are primitive recursive. Thus E is obtained from primitive recursive functions using recursion. Hence χ_E is primitive recursive and hence recursive. To prove the other part use Exercise 9.8.

11. Define f by $f(0) = k$, $f(n+1) = U_2^2(n, f(n))$. Hence f is primitive recursive.

12. $\chi_{\{a_1, a_2, \ldots, a_n\}} = \chi_{\{a_1\}} + \chi_{\{a_2\}} + \cdots + \chi_{\{a_n\}}$. As $\chi_{\{a_1\}}$ is primitive recursive. (Refer Exercise 2(a)) and sum of primitive recursive functions is primitive recursive, $\chi_{\{a_1, a_2, \ldots, a_n\}}$ is primitive recursive.

13. Represent x and y in tally notation. Using Example 7.6 we can compute concatenation of strings representing x and y which is precisely $x + y$ in tally notation.

14. Let M in the Post notation have $\{q_1, q_2, \ldots, q_n\}$ and $\{a_1, a_2, \ldots, a_m\}$ as Q and Σ respectively. Let $Q' = \{q_1, \ldots, q_n, q_{n+1}, \ldots, q_{2n}\}$, where $q_{n+1}, \ldots, q_{2n}$ are new states. Let a quadruple of the form $q_i a_j R q_k$ induce the quintuple $q_i a_j a_j R q_k$. Let a quadruple of the form $q_i a_j L q_k$ induce the quintuple $q_i a_j a_j L q_k$. Finally let $q_i a_j a_k q_l$ induce $q_i a_j a_k R q_{n+i}$. We, introduce quintuples $q_{n+i} a_t a_t L q_i$ for $i = 1, 2, \ldots, n$ and $t = 1, 2, 3, \ldots, m$. The required TM has Q' as the set of states and the set of quintuples represent δ.

15. $q_0 1111 x_1 by \overset{*}{\vdash} 1111 q_0 x_1 by \vdash 1111 q_1 x_1 by$. As b lies between x_1 and y, $Z(4) = 0$ (given by b).

16. In section 9.4.5 we obtained $q_0 1 x_1$ by $\overset{*}{\vdash} q_5 1 x_1 b1y$. Similarly, $q_0 111 x_1 by$ $\overset{*}{\vdash} q_5 111 x_1 b1y \vdash 1 q_0 11 x_1 b1y$. Proceeding further, $1 q_0 11 x_1 b1y \overset{*}{\vdash}$ $1 q_5 11 x_1 b11y \vdash 11 q_0 1 x_1 b11y \overset{*}{\vdash} 111 q_9 x_1 1111y$ (as in section 9.4.5). Hence $S(3) = 4$.

18. Represent the argument x in tally notation. $f(x) = S(S(x))$. Using the construction given in section 9.4.7, we can construct a TM which gives the value $S(S(x))$.

19. $f(x_1, x_2) = S(S(U_1^2(x_1, x_2)))$. Use the construction in Section 9.4.7.

20. Represent (x_1, x_2) by $1^{x_1} b1^{x_2}$. By taking the input as $\mathcal{S}1^{x_1} b1^{x_2}$ ($\mathcal{S}$ is representing the left-end) and suitably modifying the TM given in Example 7.6, we get the value of $x_1 + x_2$ to the right of $\mathcal{S}$.

CHAPTER 10

1. All the sentences except (g) are propositions.

2. Let L, E, and G denote $a < b$, $a = b$ and $a > b$. Then the sentence can be written as $(E \wedge \neg G \wedge \neg L) \veebar (G \wedge \neg E \wedge \neg L) \veebar (L \wedge \neg E \wedge \neg G)$.

3. (i) David gets a first class or he does not get a first class. Using the Truth Table given in Table A10.1, $\veebar$ is associative since the columns corresponding to $(P \veebar Q) \veebar R$ and $\bar{P} \veebar (Q \veebar R)$ coincide.

Table A10.1 Truth Table for Exercise 10.3

P	Q	R	$P \mathbin{\bar\vee} Q$	$Q \mathbin{\bar\vee} R$	$(P \mathbin{\bar\vee} Q) \mathbin{\bar\vee} R$	$P \mathbin{\bar\vee} (Q \mathbin{\bar\vee} R)$
T	T	T	F	F	T	T
T	T	F	F	T	F	F
T	F	T	T	T	F	F
T	F	F	T	F	T	T
F	T	T	T	F	F	F
F	T	F	T	T	T	T
F	F	T	F	T	T	T
F	F	F	F	T	F	F

The other properties can be proved similarly.

4. Using $\vee$ and $\neg$, all other connectives can be described. $P \wedge Q$ and $P \Rightarrow Q$ can be expressed as $\neg(\neg P \vee \neg Q)$ and $\neg P \vee Q$.

5. $\neg P = P \uparrow P$, $P \wedge Q = (P \uparrow Q) \mid (P \uparrow Q)$

   $P \vee Q = (P \uparrow P) \uparrow (Q \uparrow Q)$ (Verify these three equations using truth table).

6. $\neg P = P \downarrow P$, $P \vee Q = (P \downarrow Q)(P \downarrow Q)$, $P \wedge Q = (P \downarrow P) \mid (Q \downarrow Q)$

7. (a) **Table A10.2** Truth Table for Exercise 10.7

P	Q	R	$P \vee Q$	$P \vee R$	$R \vee Q$	$P \vee R \Rightarrow R \vee Q$	$P \vee Q \Rightarrow ((P \vee R) \Rightarrow (R \vee Q))$
T	T	T	T	T	T	T	T
T	T	F	T	T	T	T	T
T	F	T	T	T	T	T	T
T	F	F	T	T	F	F	F
F	T	T	T	T	T	T	T
F	T	F	T	F	T	T	T
F	F	T	F	T	T	T	T
F	F	F	F	F	F	T	T

8. (a) $\neg P \Rightarrow (\neg P \wedge Q) \equiv \neg(\neg P) \vee (\neg P \wedge Q)$ by I_{12}

   $\equiv P \vee (\neg P \wedge Q)$ by I_7

   $\equiv (P \vee \neg P) \wedge (P \vee Q)$ by I_4

   $\equiv \mathbf{T} \wedge (P \vee Q)$ by I_8

   $\equiv P \vee Q$ by I_9

   $\neg P \Rightarrow (\neg P \Rightarrow (\neg P \wedge Q)) \equiv \neg(\neg P) \vee (P \vee Q)$ by I_{12}

   $\equiv P \vee (P \vee Q)$ by I_7

   $\equiv P \vee Q$ by I_3 and I_1

9. We prove I_5 and I_6 using truth table.

Table A10.3   Truth Table for Exercise 10.9

P	Q	$P \wedge Q$	$\neg P$	$\neg Q$	$P \vee (P \wedge Q)$	$\neg(P \wedge Q)$	$\neg P \vee \neg Q$
T	T	T	F	F	T	F	F
T	F	F	F	T	T	T	T
F	T	F	T	F	F	T	T
F	F	F	T	T	F	T	T

$P \vee (P \wedge Q) \equiv P$ since the columns corresponding to P and $P \vee (P \wedge Q)$ are identical; $\neg(P \wedge Q) = \neg P \vee \neg Q$ is true since the columns corresponding to $\neg(P \wedge Q)$ and $\neg P \vee \neg Q$ are identical.

11. We construct the truth table for $(P \Rightarrow \neg P) \Rightarrow \neg P$.

Table A10.4   Truth Table for Exercise 10.11

P	$\neg P$	$P \Rightarrow \neg P$	$(P \Rightarrow \neg P) \Rightarrow \neg P$
T	F	F	T
F	T	T	T

As the column corresponding to $(P \Rightarrow \neg P) \Rightarrow \neg P$ has T for all combinations $(P \Rightarrow \neg P) \Rightarrow \neg P$ is a tautology.

12. $P \wedge (P \Rightarrow \neg Q) \equiv P \wedge (\neg P \vee \neg Q) \equiv (P \wedge \neg P) \vee (P \wedge \neg Q) \equiv \mathbf{F} \vee (P \wedge \neg Q)$
$= P \wedge \neg Q$

So $(P \wedge (P \Rightarrow \neg Q)) \vee (Q \Rightarrow \neg Q) \equiv (P \wedge \neg Q) \vee (\neg Q \vee \neg Q) \equiv (P \wedge \neg Q)$
$\vee \neg Q \equiv \neg Q$. Hence

$((P \wedge (P \Rightarrow \neg Q)) \vee (Q \Rightarrow \neg Q)) \Rightarrow \neg Q \equiv (\neg Q \Rightarrow \neg Q) \equiv \neg(\neg Q) \vee Q \vee$
$\neg Q \equiv Q \vee \neg Q \equiv \mathbf{T}$

13. $\alpha \equiv (Q \wedge \neg R \wedge \neg S) \vee (R \wedge S)$

$\equiv (Q \wedge \neg R \wedge \neg S) \vee (R \wedge S \wedge Q) \vee (R \wedge S \wedge \neg Q)$

$\equiv (Q \wedge \neg R \wedge \neg S) \vee (Q \wedge R \wedge S) \vee (\neg Q \wedge R \wedge S)$.

14. Let the literals be P, Q, R. Then

$\alpha \equiv 110 \vee 100 \vee 010 \vee 000$

$\equiv ((P \wedge Q \wedge \neg R) \vee (P \wedge \neg Q \wedge \neg R)) \vee (010 \vee 000)$

$\equiv (P \wedge \neg R) \vee (\neg P \wedge Q \wedge \neg R) \vee (\neg P \wedge \neg Q \wedge \neg R))$

$\equiv (P \wedge \neg R) \vee (\neg P \wedge \neg R)$

$\equiv \neg R$

15. (a) The given premises are: (i) $P \Rightarrow Q$, (ii) $R \Rightarrow \neg Q$. To derive $P \Rightarrow \neg R$, we assume (iii) P as an additional premise and deduce $\neg R$.

1. P Premise (iii)
2. $P \Rightarrow Q$ Premise (i)
3. Q RI_4
4. $\neg(\neg Q)$ I_7
5. $R \Rightarrow \neg Q$ Premise (ii)
6. $\neg R$ RI_5
7. $P \Rightarrow \neg R$ Lines 1 and 6

Hence the argument is valid.

(b) Valid

(c) Let the given premises be (i) P (ii) Q (iii) $\neg Q \Rightarrow R$ (iv) $Q \Rightarrow \neg R$. Then

1. Q Premise (ii)
2. $\neg R$ Premise (iv)

Hence the given argument is valid.

(d) Let the given premises be (i) S (ii) P (iii) $P \Rightarrow Q \wedge R$ (iv) $Q \vee S \Rightarrow T$

1. P Premise (ii)
2. $Q \wedge R$ Premise (iii)
3. Q RI_3
4. $Q \vee S$ RI_1
5. T Premise (iv)

Hence the argument is valid. Note that in (c) and (d) the conclusions are obtained without using some of the given premises.

16. We name the propositions in the following way:

R denotes "Ram is clever"
P denotes " Prem is well-behaved"
J denotes "Joe is good"
S denotes "Sam is bad"
L denotes "Lal is educated"

The given premises are (i) $R \Rightarrow P$ (ii) $J \Rightarrow S \wedge \neg P$ (iii) $L \Rightarrow J \vee R$. We have to derive $L \wedge \neg P \Rightarrow S$. Assume (iv) $L \wedge \neg P$ as an additional premise.

1. $L \wedge \neg P$ Premise (iv)
2. L RI_3
3. $\neg P$ RI_3
4. $J \vee R$ Premise (iii)
5. $R \Rightarrow P$ Premise (i)
6. $\neg R$ Line 3, Premise (i) and RI_5
7. J Line 5 and 4 and RI_6
8. $S \wedge \neg P$ Premise (ii)
9. S RI_3

Hence $L \wedge \neg P \Rightarrow S$.

17. The candidate should be a graduate and know BASIC, COBOL and FORTRAN.

18. $\{5, 6, 7, \ldots\}$.

19. Let the universe of discourse be the set of all complex numbers. Let $P(x)$ denote "x is a root of $t^2 + at + b = 0$". Let a and b be nonzero real numbers and $b \neq 1$. Let $P(x)$ denote "x is a root of $t^2 + at + b = 0$". Let $Q(x)$ denote "x is a root of $bt^2 + at + 1 = 0$". If x is a root of $t^2 + at + b = 0$ then $1/x$ is a root of $bt^2 + at + 1 = 0$. But x is a root of $t^2 + at + b = 0$ as well as $bt^2 + at + 1 = 0$ only when $x = \pm 1$. This is not possible since $b \neq 1$. So $\exists x(P(x) \Rightarrow Q(x)) \Leftrightarrow (\exists x P(x) \Rightarrow \exists x Q(x))$ is not valid.

20. Similar to Example 10.22.

21. Let the universe of discourse be the set of all persons. Let $P(x)$ denote "x is a philosopher". Let $Q(x)$ denote "x is not money-minded". Let $R(x)$ denote "x is not clever". Then the given sentence is

$$(\forall x(P(x) \Rightarrow Q(x))) \wedge (\exists x(\neg Q(x) \wedge R(x))) \Rightarrow (\exists x(\neg P(x) \wedge R(x)))$$

1. $\neg Q(c) \wedge R(c)$ RI_{14}
2. $\neg Q(c)$ RI_3
3. $\neg P(c)$ RI_5
4. $R(c)$ Line 1 and RI_3
5. $\neg Q(c) \wedge R(c)$ Lines 2 and 4

Hence the given sentence is true.

22. Similar to Exercise 10.21.

Further Reading

DAVIS, M.D. and WEYUKER, E.J., Computability, Complexity and Languages, Fundamentals of Theoretical Computer Science, Academic Press, New York, 1983.

DEO, N., Graph Theory with Applications to Engineering and Computer Science, Prentice-Hall of India, New Delhi, 1984.

GINSBURG, S., The Mathematical Theory of Context-Free Language, McGraw-Hill, New York, 1966.

GLORIOSO, R.M., Engineering Cybernetics, Prentice-Hall, Englewood Cliffs (New Jersey), 1975.

GRIES, D., The Science of Programming, Narosa Publishing House, New Delhi, 1981.

HARRISON, M.A., Introduction to Formal Language Theory, Addison-Wesley, Reading (Mass.), 1978.

HOPCROFT, J.E. and ULLMAN, J.D., Formal Languages and Their Relation to Automata, Addison-Wesley, Reading (Mass.), 1969.

HOPCROFT, J.E. and ULLMAN, J.D., Introduction to Automata Theory, Languages and Computation, Narosa Publishing House, New Delhi, 1987.

KAIN, R.Y., Automata Theory: Machines and Languages, McGraw-Hill, New York, 1972.

KOHAVI, ZVI, Switching and Finite Automata Theory, Tata McGraw-Hill, New Delhi, 1986.

KORFHAGE, R.R., Discrete Computational Structures, Academic Press, New York, 1984.

KRISHNAMURTHY, E.V., Introductory Theory of Computer Science, Affiliated East-West Press, New Delhi, 1984.

LEVY, L.S., Discrete Structures of Computer Science, Wiley Eastern, New Delhi, 1988.

MANDELSON, E., Introduction to Mathematical Logic, D. Van Nostrand, New York, 1964.

MANNA, Z., Mathematical Theory of Computation, McGraw-Hill Kogakusha, Tokyo, 1974.

MINSKY, M., Computation: Finite and Infinite Machines, Prentice-Hall, Englewood Cliffs (New Jersey), 1967.

NELSON, R.J., Introduction to Automata, Wiley, New York, 1968.

PREPARATA, F.P. and YEH, R.T., Introduction to Discrete Structures, Addison-Wesley, Reading (Mass.), 1973.

RANI SIROMONEY, Formal Languages and Automata, The Christian Literature Society, Madras, 1979.

REVESZ, G.E., Introduction to Formal Languages, McGraw-Hill, New York, 1986.

SAHNI, S., Concepts in Discrete Mathematics, Narosa Publishing House, New Delhi, 1987.

STANAT, D.F. and McALLISTER, D.F., Discrete Mathematics in Computer Science, Prentice-Hall, Englewood Cliffs (New Jersey), 1977.

TREMBLAY, J.P. and MANOHAR, R., Discrete Mathematical Structures with Applications to Computer Science, McGraw-Hill, New York, 1975.

ULLMAN, J.D., Fundamental Concepts of Programming Systems, Addison-Wesley, Reading (Mass.), 1976.

Index